Genreflecting

GENREFLECTING

A Guide to Reading Interests in Genre Fiction

Fourth Edition

Diana Tixier Herald

1995

Libraries Unlimited, Inc.
Englewood, Colorado

*To Rick, for his
constant support and encouragement.*

❄

Libraries Unlimited, Inc.
P.O. Box 6633
Englewood, CO 80155-6633
1-800-237-6124

Production Editor/Copy Editor: Jason Cook
Typesetting and Interior Design: Kay Minnis

Library of Congress Cataloging-in-Publication Data

Herald, Diana Tixier.
  Genreflecting : a guide to reading interests in genre fiction /
Diana Tixier Herald. -- 4th ed.
  xxvi, 367 p. 17x25 cm.
  Rev. ed. of: Genreflecting / Betty Rosenberg. 3rd ed. 1991.
  Includes bibliographical references and index.
  ISBN 1-56308-354-X
  1. American fiction--Stories, plots, etc. 2. Popular literature--
Stories, plots, etc. 3. English fiction--Stories, plots, etc.
4. Fiction genres--Bibliography. 5. Fiction--Bibliography.
6. Reading interests. I. Rosenberg, Betty. Genreflecting.
II. Title.
PS374.P63R67   1995
016.813009--dc20   95-7633
                                                      CIP

Contents

2—WESTERN (continued)

6—SCIENCE FICTION (*continued*)

Preface to the Fourth Edition

Rosenberg's First Law of Reading:
Never apologize for your reading tastes.

GENERAL REMARKS

The moment I opened the first edition of *Genreflecting* in a library school collection development class and saw Rosenberg's First Law of Reading, I was hooked. It actually took seriously the kind of reading I had done all my life. Rosenberg's opening paragraph echoed my sentiments exactly:

> This book is the fruit of a blissfully squandered reading life—
> except for the exigencies of a formal education, I read only what I
> enjoyed. Granted, I enjoyed, and enjoy, some extremely odd read-
> ing matter: these pleasures are impertinent to my also enjoying a
> considerable body of genre fiction.

One of the most pleasurable aspects of public library service is the satisfaction derived from knowing that users are happy with the titles one has recommended. Betty Rosenberg's first two editions of *Genreflecting* allowed me many of those successes. I not only used it when advising readers but also as a starting point when selecting titles for bibliographies and displays.

This fourth edition updates the earlier editions. Much of the general information has not changed from edition to edition. Betty Rosenberg's voice echoes through this edition; so much of what she originally wrote still stands, as she stated it, with no reason to alter her erudite observations. This edition does, however, take a different approach to the chapter formerly identified as "Thriller." That chapter has been divided here into two—"Crime" and "Adventure." Crime fiction has become so popular and diverse that it completely overruns the boundaries of a "thriller" classification. The "Fantasy" chapter has been expanded with several new subgenres.

Many new authors and titles, as well as subgenres, have been added throughout, and books no longer easily available in libraries have been deleted.

In response to reader requests, the index has been extensively enlarged, now including subjects and series characters, as well as authors and titles.

As an avid reader of many genres, I am often asked to recommend titles. Beginning in this edition, the final "Topic" of each chapter is a brief list of books I have greatly enjoyed—D's Picks. In no way do these lists endorse the included titles as being any better, or worse, than other genre titles. They are merely my personal favorites, and perhaps a starting place for the reader overwhelmed by the abundance of genre fiction.

Happy reading,

Diana Tixier Herald

Acknowledgments

I (and genre readers throughout the country) owe a huge debt of gratitude to the memory of Betty Rosenberg, who validated our love of purely fun reading matter and gave genre fiction the status and legitimacy it well deserves.

I wish to thank all the avid genre readers who have shared their favorites with me, including but not limited to Arlene Findlay, R. Preston Sheldon, and Nathan Herald. Special recognition goes to Desirée Sallee, Holly Koelling, Liz Campbell, and Lorna Peralta, the librarians who shared their knowledge of titles and authors: all are friends to genre readers. Sue Smith provided encouragement and sage advice.

Grateful acknowledgment is made for permission to reprint the following copyrighted material:

To Sue Grafton for *K Is for Killer*, © 1994 [p. 50].

To Heron Enterprises for Georgette Heyer's *The Quiet Gentleman*, © 1951 Georgette Heyer, copyright renewed 1979 by Richard George Rougier [p. 185].

To Delacorte Press/Seymour Lawrence for Kurt Vonnegut, Jr.'s *God Bless You, Mr. Rosewater*, © 1965 [p. 207].

Introduction

Reading is not a duty, and has consequently no business
to be made disagreeable.

—Augustine Birrell
"The Office of Literature" (1887)

GENERAL REMARKS

The reading of genre fiction is an escape into fantasizing. The reader identifies with the hero or heroine, vicariously, as if in a daydream, sharing adventures—physical, romantic, intellectual—quite beyond the grasp of reality but not beyond the imagination. The reader may then live in different countries, historical times, or even other worlds, entering into a society and meeting persons impossible to know or see in any other way. A fantasy world may be familiar, but it still provides "experiences" for the reader that are outside the realm of possibility or probability. The reader of fiction is interested in the lives of other people, identifying with the characters. In genre fiction, however, the characters are elemental heroes and heroines—heroic or romantic—images of the reader's fantasy self.

Readers who do not read fiction are often persistent readers of biography and autobiography, the most popular reading matter next to fiction. Here the reader chooses the type of person admired, one whose life provides a fantasy world, like fiction but with the substance of reality. Genre fiction readers are Walter Mittys, their rich fantasy lives coexisting cozily with humdrum daily living—the parallel worlds of fantasy are their natural habitat. They are not like poor Miniver Cheevy, who "loved the days of old" and "mourned Romance," knew he was "born too late," and sadly "kept on drinking." There is no despondency for the genre readers who know they are fantasizing and welcome fantasy's leavening of monotony within their lives. Each reader can choose desirable worlds and characters, the type of genre, with which they can identify. "Why certain fictional characters inhabit a reader's imagination can only be explained subjectively," states Jessica Mann in the book *Deadlier Than the Male* (London: David & Charles, 1981).

Genre fiction is for entertainment; its intent is to divert and amuse, to hold the mind in enjoyment. Reading for pleasure is carefree; purposeful reading to improve the mind is not within its province. Not for genre fiction is the evasion used by early writers for children: to edify *and* amuse, the amusement a tool to ensure edification. Like all sweeping generalizations, this one is, of course, in error. For instance, not all science fiction is edifying, but much is instructive. Still, it is read largely for entertainment.

Intellectuals are uneasy when confronted with genre fiction and popular taste. "The reading of detective novels," wrote Edmund Wilson, "is a kind of vice." He equated it with the drug habit—addictive, wasteful of time, and degrading to the intellect. He thus demonstrated the scorn for popular taste that is characteristic of those who take it upon themselves to judge the recreations of others (Mann, 1981). Literary critics and academics view literature with respect, often with awe. But genre fiction is not to be taken seriously, nor is it to be analyzed to death. It should be written about by those who enjoy it.

The academic world has taken upon itself the study of genre fiction. Courses in the western, the detective or the mystery story, science fiction, and fantasy abound at the secondary and college levels. Approaches to these courses vary. As literary history, the genre's roots are traced through writings of all times and types; as sociology, genre fiction reflects and interprets the society that nurtures it; as psychology, genre fiction may be used to analyze the nature of reading interests, to illuminate differences, and to study fiction as communication.

Such studies afford innocent pastimes for critics and scholars and provide considerable pleasant reading for certain fans of the several genres, fans who find a consuming interest in every aspect and detail concerning a particular genre. This in-depth delving is, in effect, a hobby. The common reader, contentedly patronizing the public library or buying paperbacks off the stands, continues to read in simple unawareness of the abundant scholarly and critical exegeses constantly appearing.

We have, therefore, the fan, who not only reads the genre but reads all about it; the "scholarly" reader, who not only reads genre fiction but *studies* it; and the common reader, who reads the genre simply for enjoyment. Fortunately, the scholarly critic may enjoy the genre as well as study it; the resulting commentaries are then graced by both wit and understanding. If enjoyment is lacking, however, the criticism often suffers from the kiss of dullness. Genre authors have resented the intrusion of academe, considering the scholars' attitudes snobbish and their comments condescending (e.g., all genre fiction should be taken out of the classroom and be put back in the street or gutter with the common reader where it belongs).

NATURE OF GENRE FICTION

Genre fiction is a patterned fiction. Each genre follows rules governing plot and characters—and abides by certain taboos—that are acknowledged by the authors and required by the publishers. This is not to say that a maverick author who flouts the rules cannot get published (this is, however, the exception). The pattern is usually established by one or more successful novels that become the prototypes imitated or emulated by later authors, any of whom may achieve the status of prototype by a single novel. Manuals for apprentice authors contain publishers' explicit formulas. Dean R. Koontz's *Writing Popular Fiction* (Writer's Digest, 1972, 1973, 1974) has chapters on science fiction and fantasy, suspense, mysteries, Gothic romance, and westerns; gives the formulas and rules for characters, plot, and techniques; and notes verboten ploys. Separate manuals for mystery, detective stories, romance, and science fiction are listed later in this guide with the secondary works on these genres.

The authors of genre fiction, with few exceptions, are notable for being prolific. They have to be to survive economically in so competitive a field of publishing. Also, genre readers are not only devoted to a genre, they are devoted to particular authors, expecting a new book from an author each year. Once this following is established, it ensures the success of every book the author writes, however unequal in quality. One book a year is considered "respectable"; too many written and published each year suggests a factory-like hack writer. To avoid this stereotype, many genre authors use pseudonyms, writing in the same genre under several pseudonyms or using a different pseudonym for each of several genres, the name being identified with a genre. For example, Victoria Holt writes historical romance, as do Jean Plaidy and Philippa Carr; all these names are pseudonyms for Eleanor Hibbert and appear on over 100 romances (the books under each pseudonym demonstrating different subgenres within the greater grouping of historical romance). The late Georges Simenon readily turned out one book a month, and Barbara Cartland continues to do so, being assured of their readership. The two have published several hundred titles under their own names with no diminution of respect.

John Creasey and Georges Simenon capitalized on an important characteristic of genre fiction: the popularity of series. Prolific Creasey dedicated each pseudonym to the adventures of a series character. The series appears in all types of genre fiction, providing a dual appeal to readership: the author and the series character. Readers become attached to the series books in their youth. Many of the indomitable series heroes, with their heroines as well, are found in Arthur Praeger's *Rascals at Large; or, The Clue in the Old Nostalgia* (Doubleday, 1971). In this guide can be found Tarzan, the Hardy Boys, Tom Swift, and many others, all evoking the absorption the author describes here:

> A few karmas ago, circumstance compelled me to raise a small daughter, without benefit of wife and mother, in the insecure atmosphere of a large hotel. Emily was ten, and because of my busy schedule, she had to spend a great deal of time alone, inventing her own amusement. One evening I observed her curled up in a ball on the sofa, shoes off, face unusually serious and preoccupied. Interrogated, she answered in a manner so vague, so ruminative, that if I had been a husband of ten years instead of a father I would have been certain she had taken a lover. She had discovered Nancy Drew.

The straight love story is the only genre that seemingly discourages the series: there is something so final in that closing clinch "And they lived happily ever after." Unless, of course, one is writing a family saga, where, given a sufficiency of offspring, there can be linked romances until the original heroine is a many times great-grandmother! The series detective dominates the detective-story genre, and the spy series character is also important in that genre.

The most amazing characteristic of much genre fiction is its immortality. It is obviously not classic literature, in the sense of the classic that is revered though seldom read, but examples from all periods of genre fiction continue to be read, with pleasure, by successive generations of readers. The style of writing in these genre "classics" may seem quaintly mannered, and the background and characters may seem part of a world long vanished. The patterned story still has the appeal that keeps the fan enchanted, whatever magic is inherent in the genre. Libraries, both public and academic, are now building historical collections of genre fiction, many based on the libraries of private collectors. (Several collections contain pulp magazines that, like the early paperbacks, will have to be replicated in some way before they disintegrate into dust.)

REVIEWS OF GENRE FICTION

The reader of genre fiction is more interested in being made aware that genre of the desired type exists than in finding extended critical appraisal. Satisfactory, then, is the usual reviewing allotted to genre fiction: annotation or inclusion in an omnibus review. The unsatisfactory aspect is that few reviewers can write that most demanding of reviews, an annotation providing story-line synopsis without revealing too much (but enough to ensure interest) and succinct critical appraisal, the latter preferably no more than a phrase or brief sentence. A 500-word review is child's play compared to framing 50 words or less of apt and decisive evaluation.

Betty Rosenberg felt that many annotations lacked the most necessary information: To what genre or subgenre does the book belong? It is not adequate to say "thriller" or "crime" or "suspense" or "adventure" or "romance"; to say "science fiction" when it is really "fantasy" is particularly misleading. The reader wants to know the specific type of a genre: police procedural, Victorian period romance, sword-and-sorcery, demonic possession, and the like. Jacket descriptions sometimes are no more accurate as to genre designation than the cover illustrations are accurate to the story.

Reviews of individual genres are generally found in their fanzines, and some of these are listed in this guide among the secondary works on each genre. The journals discussed in this section on reviews are those readily available to librarians and the common reader.

The "Forecasts" in *Publishers Weekly* provide annotations for genre fiction, both hardcover and paperback, in advance of publication date. There is necessarily selectivity in titles annotated, however, and westerns and paperback romance series get short shrift. Under fiction, there are separate groupings for mystery and suspense and science fiction, which includes fantasy and sometimes horror. Romance is usually found lurking among the general novels. Being aware that these annotations are for the use of booksellers to alert them to potential good sellers, the reader not in the trade should use them with discrimination. Still, the annotations are critical, for the reviewer does criticize a book's quality. *Publishers Weekly* also features genre fiction in articles called "Category Closeup."

The *Kirkus Reviews'* annotations are rarely accessible to the common reader. They are often quoted in publishers' advertisements. Public libraries and bookstores rely on these critical and often caustic evaluations. The reviewers in this source seem rarely to like science fiction and fantasy releases. This semimonthly loose-leaf service provides advance-of-publication coverage of a large amount of genre fiction, particularly in hardcover.

The New York Times Book Review often discusses genre fiction in reviews, grouping three or four titles by currently best-selling authors. The columns are "Crime by Marilyn Stasio," appearing usually twice a month, "Spies and Thrillers by Newgate Callendar," which turns up usually once a month, and "Science Fiction by Gerald Jonas, " published sporadically. The comments are critical, but obviously written by canny and devoted readers of these genres.

The professional journals for librarians provide good, though uneven, coverage for genre fiction. *Booklist* has annotations of fiction inclusive of all genres, both hardcover and paperback, and is the only journal that consistently annotates westerns. The annotations are brief and critical. *Library Journal*'s general fiction annotations include romance, historical romance, adventure, and an occasional western. The column on thrillers alternates with one on science fiction and fantasy, both providing brief, critical annotation. The column "Prepub Alert" frequently includes genre fiction and has been a good source for advance notice on technothrillers. No longer being published, *Wilson Library Bulletin* ran monthly columns, "Murder in Print," by Gail Pool (who succeeded Kathleen Maio), and "Science Fiction Multiverse," by Fred Lerner. The specialized journal *VOYA: Voice of Youth Advocates* is also useful, as young adults read genre fiction enthusiastically. *VOYA* reviews many adult titles that are of interest to teens, with critical reviews of both hardcover and paperback science fiction, fantasy, and horror, which are grouped together.

The most rewarding ways to keep aware of genre fiction are the simplest and the most fun: just read the advertisements in *Publishers Weekly*, particularly the seasonal announcement issues, and (if obtainable) those in the British *Bookseller*. The *Bookseller* seasonal announcement issues, in addition to a bulk of advertisements, contain sections of historical, adventure and crime, and science fiction genres; within each is a running text, grouped by publisher, describing forthcoming books. Most rewarding is to scan the publishers' catalogs, not the dull listing in the *Publishers' Trade List Annual*, but the illustrated and annotated publicity catalogs sent to bookstores and libraries. Those from the paperback houses are issued frequently, many monthly, and are treasure troves of news. Baker & Taylor and Ingram, two big jobbers, publish extremely useful resources for discerning new genre fiction. Baker & Taylor's *Hot Picks* and Ingram's *Paperback Advance* offer excellent coverage of genre paperbacks, both originals and reprints. Both feature annotations and photographs of the covers, grouping titles by rather specific genre classifications. Ingram's *Advance* annotates forthcoming hardcover and trade paperback titles; genre fiction is divided into the categories of espionage/thriller, fantasy, historical, horror, mystery/detective, science fiction, suspense/psychological, and western. *Book Alert*, also from Baker &

Taylor, annotates both hardcover and paperback, with the genre designation at the end of each annotation.

OVERVIEW OF THIS GUIDE

Organization

This guide originated with the syllabus for a class on reading interests taught by Betty Rosenberg in the graduate School of Library and Information Science at the University of California, Los Angeles. The manner in which the class was organized derived from an article she had read, written jointly by several recent library school graduates who became public librarians. They lamented that, during their years in college, they became unfamiliar with what the public library patron—the common reader—was reading. Nothing in library school had prepared them for understanding popular reading tastes, and they were dismayed on encountering their patrons.

Materials in this guide are organized to define each genre and its subgenres. As detailed in the table of contents, the authors in each genre are grouped either by types within the genre or by subgenres, generally followed by a discussion of topics, such as best-selling authors, anthologies, history and criticism, book clubs, and publishers. The inclusion of these topics varies according to the genre being discussed. This grouping by type is relevant to readers' tastes, which tend to be selective within particular genres. Indeed, many readers are specific about the types of books they will *not* read. A savvy bookstore clerk or library reader advisor would do well to discuss a reader's likes before suggesting new authors. New subgenres continue to emerge as one best-selling book spawns many imitators (e.g., prehistoric epics and technothrillers). The types of books included in this work are not exhaustive. Cross-references to related genres are provided in many genre and subgenre descriptions.

Selection of Authors

This guide is not a bibliography, nor is it a history of genres through historical sequences of listings by author. Authors listed are almost all prolific, popular, and important in the history of their genre; these authors contribute to a certain aspect of their genre, and usually their books are available either in hardcover or paperback editions. With few exceptions, books listed are hardcover editions or paperback reprints of hardcover editions; few are original paperback editions. Listed authors have been selected because they illustrate an aspect of their genre. Many additional authors could have been listed (though they would not necessarily have been *substituted* for those listed—each author's writing emphasizes a unique combination of the aspects of a particular genre).

Genre authors are notably prolific; thus, one criterion for inclusion in this guide is sheer quantity, not necessarily linked to quality. Prolific may be defined as producing between 20 and 100 titles. (Having published between

20 and 50 titles is not uncommon. Georges Simenon published over 200, and Barbara Cartland has written almost 300 books. *The Guinness Book of Records* once listed romance writer Ursula Bloom as the author with the greatest number of published books—420.)

Mere literary profusion, however, is not enough for an author to be included in this guide; the writer's books must be available. With few exceptions, the authors listed here have one or more works in print either in hardcover or paperback, older authors being available in reprint editions in both formats. The few prolific authors listed who have not remained in print are usually readily available in many libraries. For some prolific authors, only one or a few titles have survived the winnowing of time and are still reprinted (sometimes it only takes one title to ensure genre immortality). Vagaries of publishing and taste govern—often inexplicably—the in-print status of genre authors. Grace Livingston Hill wrote her first romance in 1882 and her 80th in 1947; they are still being reprinted regularly in paperback. Mary Roberts Rinehart, mistress of the "had-I-but-known" school, wrote her first mystery in 1908 and her last in 1953; many were on the best-seller lists and, after being reprinted in paperback from the 1940s through the 1960s, are now rarely found. The thrillers of Dorothy B. Hughes, paperback reprint best-sellers in the 1940s, vanished from the stands to be reprinted again with acclaim at the end of the 1970s. Publishers' reprint programs, both hardcover and paperback, may suddenly rejuvenate an author by reprinting one title or a substantial number of titles.

Although most genre authors are prolific, several of the most renowned secured their fame through only a few genre titles: Owen Wister with *The Virginian*, having only one other western, *Lin McLean*, among his works; Dorothy L. Sayers, Dashiell Hammett, and Raymond Chandler remain acknowledged classic detective authors with only 12, 5, and 7 titles (respectively) published in the genre; Margaret Mitchell's only book is *Gone with the Wind*.

Most of the authors listed in this guide are established: publishers are confident their books will sell, readers are impatient for each new title, and libraries stock them because of patron demand. I have been reluctant to list new authors whose first, and sometimes second, book indicated that "here is an important new author in the genre." There is always the chance that, with only one or two books, an author may become a recognized key author in the genre. However, the few new authors included are those I think will continue writing in the genre, usually with a series character. At least one book title is usually listed with these authors.

No attempt has been made to list the myriad authors, many writing under several pseudonyms, currently writing for the paperback romance series. Publishers of the romance series support a "stable" of authors, all writing to formulas, many producing a large volume of indistinguishable titles. For example, several Harlequin authors have published 50 or more titles, but their names are unknown except to the devoted readers of Harlequins. Harlequin has published over 50 genteel Janet Dailey romances, but she later became "America's Queen of Romance" with her lusty romances issued by Pocket Books. The romance genre is extremely volatile, with series starting and being discontinued rapidly. The subgenres within romance are in an exciting state of flux and, over continued years of publication, the names of key romance authors should become defined.

In this guide, authors are listed *as published*, without pseudonyms revealed. Thus, some prolific authors may be listed under one or more pseudonyms without reference to being a single identity. However, special note is made of the pseudonyms of certain authors (e.g., Max Brand and John Creasey: both authors write under a great many pseudonyms, but their reprinted works are usually issued under one currently best-known name).

Prolific authors are often indistinguishable in terms of quantity of books written, but their books are not necessarily of like type or quality. My own preferences naturally favored certain inclusions, and my lack of acquaintance with certain other authors may have caused their absence. To ameliorate this personal bias, some lists of "best" authors, compiled from various sources, have been included for the western, detective story, and science fiction. The secondary works listed for each genre often provide "best" reading lists.

Selection of Titles

It is not the intent of this guide to provide lists of titles for any particular author. When an author is listed without any titles, it may be assumed that most of the author's works fall into the category in which the author is found. That a title is listed does not indicate the author has not written other books of a similar type; the one noted may be of importance or popularity, perhaps the first work that established the author's name. Some authors are listed more than once, under different types of a genre or under different genres; a title is often given to distinguish that these authors write in more than one genre or subgenre. In a few instances, the title is given for a first (and, to date, only) book by an author when I considered it of special quality or interest.

Publication Dates

Genre fiction is timeless, if not immortal. The reader eager for a particular kind of fiction cares not when it was written or published. A pristine paperback may be an original genre novel in its first appearance or a reprint of a novel published 145 years ago. (There is seemingly a new edition of Charlotte Bronte's *Jane Eyre* [1847] issued every year.)

Were this a study in the history of reader tastes in genre fiction, the sequence of editions, dates, and formats would be essential. How long did the original edition and printings remain available? What were the periods when no edition was in print? Did some of the author's titles remain perennially popular while others were forgotten by all but literary historians? Did a particular genre fluctuate in popularity, causing an author's works to be kept available erratically? A chronological listing of a title in any genre would illustrate changes in style, akin to changing fashion, but not in basic genre patterns, nor in readers' tastes.

Original publication or reprint dates are usually not given in this guide because, first, it is not a history of genre fiction, and, second, the reader of genre fiction will read a genre title no matter the publication date. Occasionally, however, an original publication date is noted to emphasize the perennial nature of genre fiction. For one subgenre, spy/espionage, the original date of each prototype novel is given to illustrate the extended periods during which prototypes emerged in this genre, each prototype distinctively defining important and much-imitated aspects of that genre. Similar chronologies of prototype could be cited for other genres and subgenres—such a critical exercise, however desirable, is beyond the scope of this guide.

Annotations

The ideal guide would annotate each author to identify quality and individual genre characteristics so the reader might discover those authors whose styles are conformable to the reader's tastes. This assistance is provided in the guides and bibliographies listed for each genre. There is, alas, no single ideal guide to any of the genres. The annotations in this guide, except for romance, are used to distinguish prototype, classic, or perhaps exceptionally popular authors.

The extensive annotation for the romance genre is a deliberate (and perhaps desperate) stratagem. Almost all genre novels are, despite their patterned plot and characters, indistinguishable from the standard novel in narration and style. Some hover, uneasily, in status between genre novel and mainstream novel. Critics and reviewers, intrigued by an author's intelligence and stylistic artistry, will insist that this genre novel must be evaluated amongst the mainstream novels. Almost all genres are so considered. Many highly regarded novels follow the romance format; but if the author is considered to be a "serious writer," the novel is considered standard fiction rather than genre fiction. In recent years, the romance genre has become both more experimental and more mainstream as "fiction."

The romance genre is *sui generis*, a polite way of saying "peculiar." It seems that every reader of romance holds vehement opinions as to what is and what is not a romance novel. What one expert or reader considers a womanly romance another may cast as a mainstream novel.

Secondary Sources

The lists of bibliographies, histories and criticisms, guides, and background books are selective and only *suggest* the wealth of material available.

Publishers

Publishers listed in this guide are those regularly issuing genre fiction, either hardcover or paperback, original titles or reprints, in substantial numbers. Many publishers issue their genre fiction in distinctively labeled series, knowing that fans faithfully select by "brand" name. Series are listed and described, but these descriptions are subject to change as new types within the genre become popular or older types lapse in appeal.

Purpose and Use

This book is a guide for those who help readers identify genre authors and titles of desired types in both libraries and bookstores. Its secondary purpose is as a textbook for library school students, familiarizing them with the common reader interests in genre fiction that they will encounter in libraries, particularly in public libraries. The paragon advisor who is equally well read in all genres is an anomaly; however, anyone serving in a library or bookstore is presumed by the customers to know everything about all books. *Genreflecting* may help advisors who are not readers in genre fiction to become knowledgeable about this fiction.

As this guide's emphasis is on authors currently available, its users will need access to a retrospective bibliography for each genre, and such bibliographies are found listed in the sections for secondary works. The bibliographies, guides, histories, and criticisms listed describe a large proportion of the authors included in this guide; as has been noted, genre authors seem immortal, and many that are currently available and popular were first published in the early part of this century; a few were published in the prior century. The annotations for the secondary works indicate their provision of lists of "best" books and prizewinners in the genre; not all titles are in print, but all should be available in libraries. Lists of "best" or classic authors and titles are given for several genres and are meant to be illustrative, not exhaustive.

The author listings for several categories in this guide include the name of the series character or characters with whom the author is particularly identified. Indeed, so important is the series character to the reader that the books are commonly referred to by the series character's name (e.g., Sherlock Holmes, James Bond, Conan, Hornblower, Hopalong Cassidy, and many others). The readers' advisor must have a recognition of series characters; patrons may request books by series character rather than by author. Lists of series are included in some of the secondary works listed, and such lists are sometimes compiled in libraries as aids for reader advising. Series characters are dominant in detective fiction, and secondary works frequently include biographical lists of detectives or a name index. So alive are the detective characters to readers that several compilations of biographies of series detectives have appeared and are annotated among this guide's secondary works.

A cautionary note is necessary for the user of this guide. It should be used as an introduction in need of continual supplementation. New authors, new series, and new subgenres proliferate, although not all survive to assured popularity. Regular scanning of reviews, and of news of trade books, along with attention to the new secondary works on the genres, is essential. If you are constantly reading a particular genre, or several genres, you are one up.

The Common
1 Reader, Libraries,
and Publishing

What is not found in life—success, prestige, pleasure—is sought in reading material.

—Richard Baumberger
"Promoting the Reading Habit," *UNESCO Reports and Papers on Mass Communication* 72 (1975)

THE COMMON READER AND GENRE FICTION

Critics, and often librarians, look somewhat askance at the types of literature enjoyed wholeheartedly by the common reader. Some will, albeit shamefacedly, admit to indulging in a favorite genre in those late hours when the stress of life must be relieved. They take the literature of storytelling too seriously, forgetting the enjoyment they found, as children, in reading.

Impelled by omnivorous curiosity, ignoring selectivity, and innocent of critical taste, children read whatever it is that they enjoy. Isaac Bashevis Singer, in accepting the Nobel Prize for literature in 1978, explained why he began to write for children: "They still believe in God, the family, angels, devils, witches, interesting stories, not commentaries. . . . They don't expect their beloved author to redeem humanity." Asking only for a strong story line, lots of dialogue, and a happy ending with all loose ends tied, the child happily devours beloved "trash"[1]: the Wizard of Oz books, Tarzan, Nancy Drew, Tom Swift, and others of their ilk (rejected by many teachers and librarians as totally lacking in literary value). This golden age of leisure reading introduces children to almost all types of genre fiction.

Genre fiction no doubt developed out of that childhood capacity for innocent enjoyment. It has its roots in the time when books were unavailable and grandfathers told tales, or minstrels and bards sang songs around the fire. Literary history records that these narrations were full of miraculous adventures, wondrous beings, gods and goddesses, and fabulous beasts, with ordinary mortals as the heroes or the heroines who played out their

1

stories in a world full of magic and the supernatural. These tales provided an escape from the drab reality of everyday life into worlds of adventure, mystery, and romance—wars, sea voyages, quests in search of excitement and treasure. And so the stage was set for the common reader, who retained an avidity for action-filled narratives, chase plots, and gory, revenge-filled tales. For a time, ballads and chapbooks catered to the tastes of the common reader by providing a gallery of picaresque heroes in highwaymen, pirates, and outlaws. The ballads lamented the cruel fates of star-crossed lovers; necromancy and ghosts were commonplace in many types of stories and dramas. Through the centuries, the forms of popular fiction varied, but the subject matter remained the same. It wasn't until the nineteenth century, however, that genre fiction was really able to take root.

A new and large reading public emerged in the nineteenth century, as a result of increased urbanization and industrialization, accompanied by broadening education and literacy. New technology provided fast and cheap means of printing. Some of the earliest mass-produced books were the "yellowback thrillers"—lurid accounts of adventure, mystery, crime, and detection—sold at the railroad station stands in nineteenth-century England. And it was at the railway stations in Europe that the first paperback line for the common reader, the Tauchnitz Editions,[2] was marketed. The "dime novel" and pulp magazines followed. By the 1940s, the common reader could choose from a variety of genre fiction as the paperback lines proliferated.

A history of popular reading tastes is beyond the scope of this book, but the following books provide essential background.

Atlick, Richard. *The English Common Reader: A Social History of the Mass Reading Public, 1800–1900*. University of Chicago Press, 1970.

Bonn, Thomas L. *Undercover: An Illustrated History of American Mass Market Paperbacks*. Penguin, 1982.

Goldstone, Tony, ed. and comp. *The Pulps: Fifty Years of American Popular Culture*. Chelsea, 1970.

Goulart, Ron. *Cheap Thrills: An Informal History of the Pulp Magazines*. Arlington House, 1972.

Griest, Guinevere L. *Mudie's Circulating Library and the Victorian Novel*. Indiana University Press, 1970.[3]

Johannsen, Albert. *The House of Beadle and Adams and the Dime and Nickel Novels*. University of Oklahoma Press, 1950–1962. 2 vols.

Neuberg, Victor E. *The Batsford Companion to Popular Literature*. London: Batsford, 1982.

O'Brien, Geoffrey. *Hardboiled America: The Lurid Years of Paperbacks*. Van Nostrand Reinhold, 1981.

Schreuders, Piet. *Paperbacks U.S.A.: A Graphic History, 1939–1959*. Translated from the Dutch by Josh Pachter. Blue Dolphin Enterprises, 1981.

The best studies of the common reader can currently be found within the broad field of popular culture. A scanning of the *Journal of Popular Culture* (published by the Popular Press) shows articles on the common reader's genre interests as a component of the popular arts (called mass culture). These studies of what constitutes popular entertainment cover all media—theater, music, motion pictures, radio, television, comic strips—in addition to books, the circus, and sports.[4] Viewed in this perspective, the common reader's interests in genre fiction correspond to the nonreader's devotion to radio and television soap operas, television series in several genres, and motion pictures in which the genres from western to horror have always been standard productions.[5] To fully understand the nature of the common reader's interests, one must see these interests in relation to the popular culture of society as a whole. A delightful introduction is provided by Russel Nye's *The Unembarrassed Muse: The Popular Arts in America* (Dial, 1970), covering the arts, very broadly defined, and reading interests from colonial times to the present. Among the chapters in *The Unembarrassed Muse* are "The Dime Novel Tradition," "Novels in the Marketplace" (a discussion of best-sellers and popular tastes), "Murders and Detection," "The Future Is History: Science Fiction," and "Sixshooter Country." A more specialized approach to the popular arts is found in J. G. Catwelti's *Adventure, Mystery, and Romance: Formula Stories as Art and Popular Culture* (University of Chicago Press, 1976). Anthologies on the popular arts provide a synthesis of the broad purview in the *Journal of Popular Culture*, an example being *Mass Culture: The Popular Arts in America* (Free Press, 1957), edited by Bernard Rosenberg and David M. White. The *Handbook of American Popular Literature* (Greenwood, 1988), edited by M. Thomas Inge, is an attempt to define with academic precision 15 fields of study in popular literature. The *Handbook* contains chapters on (among others) detective and mystery novels, science fiction, westerns, fantasy novels, Gothics, best-sellers, and comic books.

A discussion of the common reader and popular reading tastes would not be complete without mention of best-sellers. The controversies that have raged—and that continue to arouse critics—on the perniciousness versus the innocuousness of popular reading tastes tend to center around best-sellers, many of which fall into several genre categories. Romance novels were the target of acrimonious debate in 1981. "These books are trash, antifeminist and pornographic," charged Ann Douglas, a professor of English, in a televised debate with romance novelist Janet Dailey. When *Publishers Weekly* ran a parody short story in a special section on romance in November 1981, an indignant author wrote: "The story was not only insulting to me as a writer, but to the ladies who buy and read my books! The message was plain: you consider romance writers morons, and the ladies who enjoy the books simpletons." Intellectuals become uneasy when confronted with popular taste. It seems that few have the assurance to recognize simply that to "judge this part [readers of light fiction] of the book reading world by the highest standards of literary criticism is an error, to despise it for its simplicity is arrogance."[6]

The persistence of this disturbance over the common reader's preference for best-sellers and light literature is tellingly shown in the books of two British critics, writing 50 years apart. Q. D. Leavis in *Fiction and the Reading*

Public (London: Chatto, 1932), uses two approaches in her analysis of the reading tastes of the 1930s: a questionnaire to 50 authors of best-sellers and a historical survey of publishing and reading tastes in England. She concludes that "the public has acquired the reading habit while somehow failing to exercise any critical intelligence about its reading." Her book, still in print, is frequently quoted and states the disdain that classic intellectuals have for popular reading, which they consider false in values, misleading in interpretation of society, and meretricious as literature. John Sutherland, in *Bestsellers: Popular Fiction of the 1970s* (London: Routledge, 1981), discusses in detail, and as types, most of the best-sellers of the decade. His conclusions are as negative as Leavis's, but he insists that best-sellers have had an important role in the histories of British and American publishing and culture: "They are anodynes. They soothe. No one could guide their lives by the codes, awareness and information which bestsellers furnish. But they clearly make lives more livable for millions of British and American consumers. . . . These pre-eminently successful novels provide much in the way of thrills and excitement, but nothing in the way of serious intellectual, moral or social disturbance of received stupidity."

Critics and librarians might find it helpful to peruse best-seller lists as they appear weekly and to read analyses of the popular books in *80 Years of Best Sellers, 1895–1975*, by Alice Payne Hackett and James Henry Burke (Bowker, 1977). The running commentary in the Hackett and Burke volume indicates popularity of types of books while reflecting changes in society's attitudes and mores. That the complete 1895–1975 list now appears in three forms (hardcover titles, paperback titles, and a combined list of both formats) reflects dramatically the effect the paperback revolution has had on both sales figures and the types of books appearing on the lists. Paperback titles have, of recent years, displaced the long-standing hardcover leaders, replacing total sales in the thousands with sales in the millions. Many of these new leaders are genre fiction titles.

All types of genre fiction appeared on the best-seller lists from the beginning, and their history will be found in two now old but still informative and interesting books: James Hart's *The Popular Book: A History of America's Literary Taste* (Oxford University Press, 1950) and F. L. Mott's *Golden Multitudes: The Story of Best Sellers in the United States* (Macmillan, 1947).

Two recent collections of essays on individual best-sellers highlight that genre titles are memorable and long-lived. It is interesting that a genre title, P. C. Wren's *Beau Geste*, is the only title mentioned in both collections. The first collection, Geoffrey Bocca's *Best Seller: A Nostalgic Celebration of the Less-Than-Great Books You Have Always Been Afraid to Admit You Loved* (London: Wyndham, 1981), has essays on 15 books. The genre titles in addition to Wren's are H. Rider Haggard's *King Solomon's Mines*, Kathleen Winsor's *Forever Amber*, E. Phillips Oppenheim's *The Great Impersonation*, Ouida's *Under Two Flags*, Edgar Rice Burroughs's *Tarzan of the Apes*, Elinor Glyn's *Three Weeks*, E. C. Bentley's *Trent's Last Case*, George Barr McCutcheon's *Graustark*, R. C. Sherriff's *The Hopkins Manuscript*, Owen Wister's *The Virginian*, and Baroness Orczy's *The Scarlet Pimpernel*. The second collection of essays, Claude Cockburn's *Bestseller: The Books That Everyone Reads, 1900–1939* (London: Sidgwick, 1972), also discusses 15 books, and, though some possibly fall into the romance genre, his obvious genre choices, in addition to the Wren title, are Erskine Childers' *The Riddle of the Sands*, Jeffery Farnol's *The Broad Highway*, and E. M. Hull's *The Sheik*.

LIBRARIES AND GENRE FICTION

As might be expected, the controversy over genre fiction also rages within library circles. Disdain for the tastes of the common reader is apparent in some librarians. One of Betty Rosenberg's students, interning in a public library branch, checked out a western to read for her class on genre fiction, and the branch librarian said disdainfully, "Of course, you know westerns are trash!" Fortunately, there are some public librarians who read and enjoy such "trash." Unfortunately, the public library has always been defensive about stocking popular fiction; its educational and informational services are lauded, but there has too often been a suggestion that providing readers with entertaining books was pandering. Not all libraries are so blessed as is the Little Rock (Arkansas) Public Library: a local trust company set up a trust fund so that the librarian could, in clear conscience, buy "not-so-good" books—defined as westerns, detective stories, science fiction, romances, and the like. A former British librarian writing in "Of 'Luv's and Lights' " (K. F. Kister in *Wilson Library Bulletin*, January 1967) cites disparaging remarks about such fiction; for example, it "subverts the public's perspective of society." (Nothing changes: In 1877 in the United States, a librarian, William Kite, wanted to exclude all fiction from public libraries because, he maintained, novels gave persons in "lowly but honest" occupations "false ideas about life." In 1966, *Library Journal* headlined a news note: "Oz Comes to D.C. Libraries after 66 Years." Fond aunts still steadily gave the Oz books as gifts during the banned period. In 1929, *Tarzan* was removed from the Los Angeles Public library because "Tarzan was allegedly living in sin with Jane.")

Librarians are also castigated for providing books of poor literary quality. There is pressure on them to be concerned with improving patrons' tastes. The professional library journals worry about this sporadically, the problem becoming complicated with implications of censorship. Librarians *do* get upset. In 1960, *Library Journal* ran an article criticizing the selection of books for the *Fiction Catalog*, which is used by librarians to identify authors and titles deemed necessary for a public library's permanent stock of fiction. The article (Dorthy Broderick, "Libraries and Literature," August 15, 1960, 2709–12) was so controversial that the editor solicited initial comment to accompany it and later published a group of comments and letters to the editor of an irate nature (Dorothy Broderick, "Libraries and Literature," October 15, 1960, 2713–17). One passage gives the tenor of the article: "We know that librarians read mysteries. We know this because ten percent of the total entries in the 1950 edition [*Fiction Catalog*] are mysteries. Does anyone actually believe that these approximately 340 mysteries are worth the space they take up? It has been my experience that the most useful mystery is the newest one and once read it can be forgotten. Obviously one would retain a few of the 'classics' in the field and this would mean the entries in the *Catalog* would be truly selective." Other types of genre fiction were also to be ruthlessly weeded out, allowing for an increase in the number of worthwhile fiction titles. Among the comments from Margaret E. Cooley, the books editor of *Library Journal*, "I see little virtue in stocking a library with books that will *not* be read simply because the librarian has a fixed idea of what her borrowers *should* read." A library school professor, Howard W. Winger, objected to some of the deletions: "I don't want to be accused of defending *all* the trivial books in libraries—just those I liked!"

An academic librarian, Ellsworth Mason, entered the fray, stating flatly: "The function of libraries is to get people reading and to keep them coming back" ("The Sobering Seventies: Prospects for Change," *Library Journal*, 1 October 1972). Citing his own youthful devouring of pulp magazines and Hopalong Cassidy before writing a doctoral thesis on James Joyce, he queries, "Who in the world can tell at what age, or by what book, anyone is going to get an interest in anything under the sun?" The thinking of librarians disturbed him: "There is a deprecation of reading for pleasure, and much pride in the great increase in serious books in their collections for serious readers."

"Trash in the Library" is the forthright title of an article written by a branch librarian in New York's Queensborough Public Library, Rudolph Bold (*Library Journal*, 15 May 1980). He spoke out against the elitist librarians who would not stock Harlequin romances, though conceding, "It's the human heart, not the mind, that Harlequins touch." Firmly on the side of the common reader, he concluded, "It is questionable practice to limit any public library's collection to material of a certain quality if a large percentage of the community does not find what it wishes to read in that collection." *Library Journal* received a lively spate of letters supporting his thesis but objecting to his tone of "humanistic tolerance," considered contemptuous of the genre readers.

The puritan ethic maintains that all books must be useful. The hedonist holds that the justification of any book lies in its capacity to entertain. The poor librarian who wants to satisfy all the library's patrons may wish a plague on both philosophies, not having, indeed, sufficient finances to quiet either. What now bothers librarians is economics, not ethics—how to stretch increasingly inadequate budgets to cover both the useful and the entertaining. To the comment "Let 'em buy paperbacks," the conscientious public librarian replies that the library should supply what the patrons want, knowing, sadly, that economics will frustrate desire.

Dissension among public librarians is by no means quiescent. Richard Hoggart, reviewing in *TLS* (30 December 1977) three books on the public library in Great Britain, noted something said by foes of the nineteenth-century Public Libraries Act: "[T]he public libraries would be in the main ways of providing cheap fiction at public expense . . . [and] to establish them would encourage laziness among the working class (especially through the reading of cheap fiction)." The apologists for the public libraries buying cheap fiction would not call such fiction improving nor valuable but insisted that libraries must be catholic in their buying: "Librarians must therefore cater for people's 'recreational' needs. They should not be highbrow, snooty, elitist in their attitudes to popular fiction. A further turn of the screw resurrects the old and highly dubious 'ascending ever upwards' model, by which readers are assumed to move naturally from virtually pulp-fiction to George Eliot." Hoggart's conclusion is against "cheap fiction": "Librarians do not have to be what is fashionably called 'narrowly moralistic'; but they cannot escape the need to make judgments of quality. Their first duty is still to the idea of 'self-improvement,' with that phrase very imaginatively interpreted. To do less is a form of false democracy, which the whole history of the library service itself should call into question." When Hoggart addressed the Centenary Conference of the United Kingdom Library Association on the "Uses of Literacy," he stated bluntly, "The public's self-improvement, not its recreation, is the librarian's first concern." *Wilson Library Bulletin* (February 1978) reported: "The conferees were aghast at this 'imposition of middle-class values' and the moral superiority involved in 'censoring' the meretricious."

The problems facing public librarians in selecting popular fiction should neither be laughed at nor ignored. Edifying for librarians to read to gain a commonsense perspective are the two meticulous surveys of the selection of fiction for public libraries in the United States by Esther Jane Carrier: *Fiction in Public Libraries 1876–1900* (Scarecrow Press, 1965) and *Fiction in Public Libraries 1900–1950* (Libraries Unlimited, 1985). The author lets the record speak eloquently, quoting contemporary works extensively. Seemingly, there is no philosophy, prejudice, or solution (from restrictive censorship to the toleration of "trash") that has not been exhaustively discussed. (Librarians do need to ponder the justification of public libraries. They might read Robert A. Heinlein's *Job: A Comedy of Justice* [Ballantine Books, 1984], in which a character finds a serious deficiency in Heaven: "It lacks a public library.")

Assuming the attainment of that Elysium in which education and recreation coexist tranquilly, the librarian still faces problems, both in maintaining a satisfactory stock of genre fiction and in displaying it to assure optimum use by patrons. That a goodly part of genre fiction is now in original edition in paperback, or available for replacement largely in paperback reprint, complicates the problem.[7]

The common practice for display in public libraries is to segregate genre fiction, grouping it by type on labeled shelves. (Bookstores also tend to group genre fiction, particularly paperbacks.) Genres usually labeled are westerns, mysteries, and thrillers; and science fiction (in both hardcover and paperback). Paperback romances are also separately shelved. Some libraries attach color-coded labels to the books, color-code the catalog cards, or maintain card files by subject or type of genre. Many libraries dislike labeling and segregation, as some patrons will look only at labeled shelves, while others never use them. Books, then, that might be of interest to both types of patrons will never be seen by them. Few libraries can afford, or find it manageable, to have copies on both the genre shelves and within the general fiction collection. An additional hazard is that it is often tricky to label a novel within the correct genre. Shelving all fiction, including genre, in one alphabetical arrangement makes it difficult for the fan to find desired genre titles without knowing the author. Labeling by genre *and* interfiling within the general fiction collection is disliked by the genre fan, who wants the easy access of a separate shelving, and may offend the fiction reader who objects to labeling as denigratory.

No solution will please everyone. David R. Slavitt, writing in *American Libraries* (November 1973), takes a realistic view of what is published versus readers' tastes in his article "Trash: Most Novels Are Trash. Most Books Are Trash. But There Is a Delight in Trash Heaps." However, in responding to a letter in the January 1974 issue, he said that segregating genre fiction on library shelves "represents a judgment on the books—and not a flattering one." Pyke Johnson, Jr., a publisher, had an illuminating stay at the Orange (New Jersey) Public Library, observing how a public library functions. The story appeared in *Publishers Weekly* (28 March 1977) under the heading "What Publishers Should Know about the Public Library . . . A Book Editor's Firsthand Report." The librarian wanted the publishers to do the labeling: "He would like to see categories printed on the spine. And at Orange he has solved the problem for himself by having small stickers reading 'A Man's Book,' 'Gothic,' a 'Regency' placed on the spines of appropriate titles."

Unless genre fiction in paperback is cataloged, with or without binding, expediency leads to displaying the books in a somewhat haphazard and uncontrolled manner. The stock proves transitory, and no basic collection is formed. That a good basic collection is desirable is determined by the library's degree of commitment to serving the genre fiction reader, a reader who discovers an author and wants *all* the author's titles, or a reader of omnivorous tastes who seeks everything ever published in the genre. Original titles in the paperback romance series may end in chaos; some public libraries, serving a heavy demand, arrange each series by publisher's number.

Selection of genre fiction for public libraries is fairly uncritical. One public librarian in England reported buying titles "by the yard" from a dealer who specialized in review copies; expending 8 percent of his book fund for these books, the librarian provided over 20 percent of the books on the shelves. The number of genre titles in hardcover published each year is not beyond the means of most libraries. Paperback genre titles are becoming an increasing part of the collections. A survey reported in *Publishers Weekly* (9 October 1981) said up to 30 percent of public library budgets were spent on paperbacks. A public library reported an experimental purchase of 800 new paperback titles, finding that none of the titles had been previously available in the library. Libraries have found that circulation increases with the paperback stock (readers evidently like the small size and light weight) and that, on a per-title basis, paperbacks have higher circulation than hardcovers. Librarians also complained about the quality of hardcover books, which has deteriorated so much over the years that some paperbacks are now as durable as hardcover. Thus, paperbacks often give libraries more use per dollar. These relatively inexpensive paperbacks, then, are purchased with minimal selectivity, processed with minimal records, and shelved with little order; if they wear out or become lost, there is little, if any, lamentation.

There is still another problem: which, if any, of these paperbacks should be bound, cataloged, and made part of the permanent stock? Some of the titles are, after all, original works, however awkward the format may be for libraries. Replacement copies, if the library wishes to maintain a good collection, are often available only in paperback. The publishing trend toward trade-format paperbacks (i.e., large-format) for some mass-market paperbacks is helpful. Also, many genre titles are being reprinted in hardcover large-print editions.

Reader Advisory Service

Putting people together with the books they want to read is the purpose of a reader advisory service. Knowing the literature, knowing the reader, and facilitating the meeting of the two is the key to being an effective reader advisor.

Reader advisory service is one of the most interesting and demanding functions of a library; it draws on a librarian's background of reading and on an awareness of current publishing. *Library Journal* (15 November 1977) published "Day-One Basics for MLS" (Master of Library Science): of the 36 basics, two pertained to reader advising—"to utilize knowledge of books and authors in order to assist and advise patrons in selection of appropriate reading material in a variety of genres and subject areas," and "to write clear, concise reviews and abstracts of library materials in order to provide guidance in their use."

To provide guidance in genre fiction, librarians should (ideally) be readers of the genres. Few libraries will have a staff completely composed of genre-fiction addicts; however, querying the staff will probably turn up more genre readers than might be expected. No one person, however, could become an avid reader of all genres. Therefore, the fan asking for assistance in selecting books in a genre too often knows more than the librarian being queried. As library users have a touching faith in the omniscience of librarians—for it is common knowledge that they have read everything!—subterfuge is necessary.

A well-armed reader advisor keeps at hand an arsenal of resources, including bibliographies and book lists, in the form of bookmarks, broadsides, or pamphlets, as provided by many libraries. A helpful method, particularly for librarians who follow a reading plan, is to maintain a list of all titles read. Some librarians prefer to keep the list on index cards in a file, others use a database, and some prefer to keep a chronological list in their day planners. A short annotation and indication of genre and type not only makes the list extremely useful for reader advisory service but also sharpens the librarian's writing skills.

Reading plans, looked on with disfavor by some, are simply a way of mapping out in advance a plan to sample various genres. Several years ago, in libraries with a dedication to reader advisory services (which had substantially more staff than libraries have now), initiate reader advisors were assigned a variety of novels that they were to read to become conversant in the different genres. An example of such a reading plan would be to read one book from each of the genres and go back through the genres again, this time reading a book by a different author in each genre. Some reading plans were very specific; for example, to read a novel by Dorothy Sayers, followed by a novel by Zane Grey, one by Isaac Asimov, and one by Grace Livingston Hill. A second pass in such a specific plan might call for novels by Raymond Chandler, Max Brand, Robert Silverberg, and Danielle Steel. The effect of this was to ensure that the reader advisors became familiar with a diversity of authors within each genre.

The most frequent query from patrons (in bookstores as well as in libraries): "Do you have any more books *like* . . . ?" Although the object of book lists is to group books by type or subject, the end is not really to group books by "likes," for "likes" are a matter of taste and appeal, and such groupings can be made only by readers who are discriminating fans. What qualities of plot, character, and style are appealing in the novels of any one author? Will these same qualities be found in books by another author? Are certain treatments of character or action (e.g., explicit sex, gory violence) present in the works of one and not in those of another? The criteria for defining "likes" is more complex than a simple "both authors write in the same genre."

Joyce G. Saricks and Nancy Brown have written a wonderful short book, *Readers' Advisory Service in the Public Library* (American Library Association, 1989). It is a must-read for anyone striving to perform reader advisory service with any degree of excellence. In it the authors detail ways to determine the appeal of a book so that similar books can be found. Discovering "likes" comes only from reading the books themselves, not from reading a reference book about genres. Just because two books are similar by virtue of belonging to the same genre does not mean that they have similar appeal.

In her brief chapter "Advising the Reader" in *Happily Ever After: A Guide to Reading Interests in Romance Fiction* (Libraries Unlimited, 1987), Kristin Ramsdell gives some excellent ideas for reader advising in general. She also notes that not all readers in need of assistance will ask for it—hence the need for passive reader advisory.

Passive reader advisory includes shelving genre fiction separately, providing book lists and displays, and labeling spines. All these things, though not a substitute for an interview with a good reader advisor, help readers to find books in the genres they like.

In large collections, separate shelving, in addition to access to genre collections, also helps avoid information overload.[8] Sharon L. Baker, who has written on information overload and fiction classification, has suggested that physically separating genre books from the general collection helps users of large collections select books without becoming overwhelmed. In addition to giving browsers a smaller and less intimidating set of books to choose from, it allows them to select from particular genres of interest. Spine labeling by genre is another widely used method.

Nothing is so gratefully received by the library user as an interested common-reader librarian. Readers love to talk about their reading. A patron desires in a librarian an advisor who can enthusiastically exclaim, "But haven't you read . . . ?" Publishers have long known that the popularity of books is determined by word of mouth. By listening to each patron's interests, a librarian will become better able to offer personalized advice. No one likes to be told what to read, but most will engage with interest in a discussion about the enjoyment of reading a certain book. The librarian "is a missionary. He wants to communicate to others the enormous pleasure he has had from personal discovery."[9]

PUBLISHING GENRE FICTION

Publishing is a gamble as well as an art; this becomes trenchantly apparent when scanning successive issues of *Publishers Weekly*. Book buyers' tastes are akin to the vagaries of fashion in their scurry after the current fad, and the publishers, particularly those of paperback lines, provide accordingly. The amazing proliferation of romance series by paperback publishers (and one by a hardcover publisher) in 1981 emphasized this well-established genre but also diversified the types of romances available, including several new series on teenage love. A similar pattern is evident in the action/adventure subgenre. For example, though its audience type is traditionally male, two series of action/adventure for women were announced in 1986.

Genre fiction and best-sellers remain a solid core for paperback publishers. A delightful parody of mass-market paperback genre fiction was published in 1981 by Jove: No Frills Books. With starkly white covers and simple labels (western, science fiction, romance, or mystery), each volume is marketed as a type. Neither an author nor a title is listed, and each consists of 60 pages. "After you've read one," maintains the Jove blurb, "you won't mind the others." However, several trends in publishing have emerged that will undoubtedly change the patterns for genre fiction publishing in both paperback and hardcover.

There has been a notable increase in hardcover publication of genres, particularly of period romance, fantasy, and science fiction. Original publication of genre books in hardcover has been traditional in Great Britain, with extensive paperback reprinting. In the United States, there has been more original publication of genre titles in paperback. All of the paperback houses, except Zebra, are now publishing in hardcover as well as paperback. Susan Petersen, president of Ballantine Books, suggests one reason for this: "Paperback book publishers have been known to publish a hardcover edition simply to get reviews. . . . The librarians believe what they read in the paper" (*Publishers Weekly*, 29 March 1985). In reviewing science fiction and fantasy titles, the reviewers at *Kirkus Reviews* often note when a book will be an author's first hardcover publication (by a formerly all-paperback house) to indicate that the author has achieved greater status.

Another reason that these paperback houses are expanding into hardcover publishing is that hardcover publishers themselves are now doing a great deal of paperback reprinting of their backlists, decreasing the amount of material available to the paperback houses. Also notable has been the large amount of paperback reprinting in trade format by the hardcover houses. A small amount of simultaneous publication in hardcover and paperback formats is evident, a recent example being Academy Chicago's Women Science Fiction Writers series. The paperback publishers have found a market for certain very popular romance authors whose works are issued in both mass and trade formats, notably Janet Dailey, Kathleen Woodiwiss, and Louis L'Amour, an author of westerns. Recommended reading for background on the changing publishing field is *Paperback Talk* by Roy Walters (Academy Chicago, 1985), a compilation drawn from his long-time column in *The New York Times Book Review*.

Genre titles dominate fiction publishing in both hardcover and paperback, as a scanning of any weekly-review medium will make obvious. The number of reviews in the standard media is largest for thrillers (mystery, detective, spy), followed by science fiction, fantasy, horror, and romance. For romance, with its bulk of original paperbacks, usually only hardcover editions are reviewed (mainly period romance and romantic suspense).

At least half of the titles on the weekly best-seller lists (hardcover and paperback) are genre titles. It is obvious that prolific and popular authors appear regularly; anything they publish, regardless of its quality, will sell. (Nigel Cross writes: "Librarians are only too familiar with readers who ask for another title by the same author—it is part of the conservatism of the reading public" [*TLS*, September 17, 1985].) This popularity of an author (often because of a series character) has given impetus to a type of book, often of questionable quality, that continues the adventures of a series character after the popular author's death. Examples are works involving Sir Arthur Conan Doyle's Sherlock Holmes, Ian Fleming's James Bond, Rex Stout's Nero Wolfe, Robert E. Howard's Conan, and characters from Jane Austen's novels. (Claudia Rosett, in the *Wall Street Journal*, lamented: "Once upon a time, the great characters of fiction were allowed to live happily every after.")

Publishers and librarians would do well to ponder the reports of Great Britain's Public Lending Right program. That romance and thriller (mystery, detective, spy) authors (e.g., Evelyn Anthony, Catherine Cookson, Dick Francis, Victoria Holt, Alistair McLean, and Wilbur Smith) were the most popular was not a surprise. That the authors were not necessarily those on best-seller lists and that the books of these authors had been published from five to forty years previously was a revelation. The immortality of authors, which is the continued reading of their works, is obviously dependent on the availability of books in libraries or on books being in-print (as John Creasey mordantly commented in *Books and Bookmen* [February 1960]: "If novelists aren't read, they're dead; and the dead neither sow nor reap oats."). Continued availability in libraries requires that the titles be in hardcover (either originally or as a paperback capable of being bound) or forever in-print. Librarians and readers of genre fiction are vitally concerned, then, not only with the initial form of genre publication but with its reprint publication.

Mass-market paperback reprinting, the fate of most genre fiction, is the least satisfactory. It does, however, keep authors alive and may bring some back from the grave. Noting which authors are reprinted, it seems a truism that the more prolific an author, the more he or she is apt to survive. A reprinting in trade paperback format is essentially as satisfactory as a hardcover reprinting. Examples of such satisfactory editions are the handsome Dover and Virago Press trade reprints. For the library market, the large-print editions, in which most genres appear, are excellent. Also appropriate for the library market are the extensive series that encompass several genres, such as those by Severn House, Gregg Press, and Garland. Many genre titles are now being "reprinted" in an audio format in both abridged and unabridged forms. The joy of audio genre fiction is that the "reader" may hear the story while at the same time driving or accomplishing other tasks. The selector must beware, though, as the quality of both the narration and the production vary greatly. Librarians, as major purchasers of all types of reprints, should lobby publishers to produce needed titles in any format.

The supply of new genre fiction titles is augmented by "created" books—frowned on by the critics but selling merrily to the common readers. The most prominent "creator" was the late Lyle Kenyon Engel, who formed Book Creations, Inc. in 1973: "When better books are built, Book Creations, Inc. will build them!" To date, this firm has "built" 375 books in scores of series for a number of publishers, and the firm claims that 120 million copies of these titles are currently in print, with translations into 16 languages. Each year, the firm constructs 20 to 30 books. (For the firm's most famous historical saga, the eight-volume Kent Family Chronicles, the sales figure was 35 million copies.) The firm's operating pattern is simple: one of Engel's successors thinks up the plot and engages a writer, the staff does the editing, and the profits are split 50/50 with the author.

Mention should be made of the popularity of specialist bookstores devoted to types of genre fiction, for they attest to the sufficient number of fans eager to buy the books to satisfy their passion. Many of these started in the 1970s and have prospered: Murder Ink and The Mysterious Bookshop, in New York; Scene of the Crime, in Los Angeles, specializing in the thriller; Dark They Were and Golden Eyed, in London; A Change of Hobbit and Fantasy Castle, in Los Angeles, specializing in science fiction and fantasy. Many other stores could be noted, for both new and antiquarian books; advertisements may be found in fanzines for the particular genres.

WOMEN AND GENRE FICTION

Women have always written genre fiction, and women have always been featured in genre fiction, but the 1980s saw a tremendous surge in the popularity of the woman's role. By the end of the decade, thrillers featuring women as private investigators or amateur investigators were appearing weekly. Who by now has not heard of V. I. Warshawski or Kinsey Milhone? Women also gained recognition in science fiction and fantasy, no longer having to resort to male pseudonyms or to using only their initials. It became more acceptable in those genres for authors to have first names like Margaret, Sherri, or Pamela.

Female characters from series are listed in Bernard A. Drew's *Heroines* (Garland, 1990). Containing 1,199 entries in the main section, it covers female characters from all genres as well as from series of books for juveniles.

L'ENVOI

Should this introductory chapter seem portentous, remember that genre reading is for entertainment. Dorothy L. Sayers said it best (with an assist from Hamlet) in her "Author's Note" to *Gaudy Night*: "The novelist's only native country is Cloud-Cuckooland, where they do but jest, poison in jest: no offense in the world."

NOTES

1.   Arthur Praeger's *Rascals at Large* (Doubleday, 1971) delightfully dissects this beloved "trash" and provides story synopses and abundant quotations for those benighted adults whose childhood was bereft of such reading.

2.   The final defeat of Napoleon allowed the English to travel on the continent again, and travel they did in large numbers, especially the increasingly large and prosperous middle class who went on tours with travel agent Thomas Cook. The Tauchnitz Editions, published in Germany, were begun in 1837 and provided these tourists with the works of popular English and American authors.

3.   From the 1840s to the 1890s in England, the commercial circulating libraries largely determined the nature of the English novel. They catered to popular tastes at the higher economic levels—the history of the dominant one is found in this book.

4.   The scope of what constitutes popular culture is, of course, much more extensive than the media noted here and includes many aspects of folklore, hobbies, and, indeed, any activity in which the mass of people in a society participate.

5.   In the following chapters, there is a section for several genres that lists books on the genre in film. *The Movies,* by Richard Griffith and Arthur Mayo (Revised edition, Simon & Schuster, 1970), lavishly illustrated, covers the history through the sixties, and all the genres are represented.

6.   Peter H. Mann, *Books: Buyers and Borrowers* (London: Deutsch, 1971), page 174. In the chapter "Light Fiction and the Romantic Novel," Dr. Mann, a British sociologist, synthesizes history and social attitudes as a background to readers' tastes. His article in *Journal of Popular Culture* (Summer 1981), "The Romantic Novel and Its Readers," reports on a survey made for the British romance publisher Mills and Boon and contrasts the publishing pattern (serious novels in less than 5,000 copies and light novels in printings up to the millions) and readership of serious fiction and mass-culture novels (light, popular, and read wholly for pleasure). Women reading light fiction wanted romances first, then historical novels; men preferred thrillers and mysteries, followed by war and adventure stories. Mann concludes that readers of light fiction want escape and relaxation in a story that conforms to their mores and values. "Real life is often incredibly boring" to these readers, just as is the realistic novel. Additional pertinent books are: *Books and Reading* by Peter H. Mann and Jacqueline L. Burgoyn (London: Deutsch, 1969) and *From Author to Reader: A Social Study of Books* by Peter H. Mann (London: Routledge, 1982).

7. One solution was reported in *Publishers Weekly* (September 13, 1979) in "The Selling of the Library: Baltimore County System Challenges Assumptions About Library's Role," by Kenneth C. Davis. Mini-libraries, blending bookstore and library atmosphere, were established in shopping centers. They stocked genre fiction (80 percent in paperback, mostly romance) and best-sellers, and had a policy of stocking "what people want, not what librarians think they should read." Circulation jumped, and the library benefited as paperbacks allowed many more circulations per dollar expended. Overall (in the mini- and the standard libraries), the system claimed 92 percent satisfaction in supplying books requested.

8. Sharon L. Baker, "Overload, Browers and Selection," *Library and Information Science Research* (October–December, 1986); "Fiction Classification Schemes: The Principles Behind Them and Their Success," *RQ* (Winter 1987; "Will Fiction Classification Schemes Increase Use?" *RQ* (Spring 1988).

9. Frank M. Gardner, "To Fill the Empty Mind," *Library Journal* (2 October, 1964).

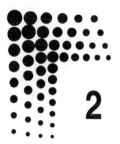

2 Western

In Westerns you were permitted to kiss your horse but never your girl.

—Gary Cooper
"Well, It Was This Way,"
Saturday Evening Post (17 March 1958)

The East is settled, it is orderly, it is governed by women's ideas. This is still a man's country. Make no mistake about that.

—Ernest Haycox
Free Grass (1957)

THEMES AND TYPES

The western is essentially an adventure novel, but it is too large and too diverse to be subsumed into the adventure genre. Although action and adventure usually dominate the plot, they are secondary to the setting. A compound of pulp and paperback westerns and the motion picture and television "horse operas" have tended to limit this genre to only a few plot stereotypes. However, plots are not confined to revolving around the cowboy of the 1865–1890 ranchlands. Story lines derive from the entire westward movement in North America, beginning in the early nineteenth century and continued into the twentieth century to the Far West of the United States.

The western is defined by an attitude toward life—the "complete life mode," which is not dependent on the historical limits of the West in the United States. For example, *Wilderness Trek* is Zane Grey's story of a cattle drive in Australia. *The Overlanders*, a classic Australian motion picture, is the heroic saga of ranchers undertaking a cattle drive in Australia during World War II because they fear an invasion; the trek lasts months and takes the ranchers through deserts and over mountains more daunting than those of the American West (this western lacks only the Indians).

The appeal of this genre is worldwide, based in a dream of freedom in a world of unspoiled nature, a world independent of the trammels of restraining society. The hero dominates the western: competent, self-reliant, and self-sufficient, whether in conflict with nature, with man, or with himself.

16

This most enduring of genres appeals to readers of all cultures, even those far removed geographically from the West of the United States, even those to whom its history and life modes are alien. For example, there was a Wild West in Asia in the nineteenth century. Not content with translations of U.S. westerns, the Germans (Karl May in the nineteenth century), Scandinavians, and Britons write their own. Why this universal appeal?

The simplest reason may be that it is just a good story, strong on adventure and thrilling action, having readily defined characters, supplying a satisfying resolution of conflicts in terms of simple blacks and whites (good and evil, right and wrong—the black and white stetson hats of hero and villain), and even supplying a minor plot of romance. Add to this the characters and setting of the West. For example, the motion picture *Star Wars*, which has been labeled a horse opera in space; its saloon scene is immediately recognized as the classic western movie saloon. The Japanese motion picture *The Seven Samurai* appealed to fans of the western (not just because of the horses) and was later adapted by Hollywood as an American western.

Basic to the appeal is the lure of the frontier, offering an escape from towns, schools, churches, and women in a freedom that cannot exist in communities of organized society. The western frontier showed the "savage" Indian living in adventurous freedom as a beckoning symbol. Allied is a nostalgia for a simpler way of life and simpler values—modern life is too complex, too technological, too oppressive toward conformity. The history of the westward-moving frontier is *the* great adventure story in U.S. history. The liveliest field of book collection in the world is probably Western Americana. The Westerners Corrals—organizations of collectors, writers, and historians both academic and amateur—exist in many countries, and individual Corrals flourish in cities from west to east in the United States. Whether interest in this history spurs reading of the western novel for many readers is open to question, but the fact that the reader of westerns absorbs a good deal of history is not. The shoot-em-up standard western is long in action but is lacking or negligible in history. Frequently, even the locale and time are undefined. What is capitalized on is the background of wild, open country and an often legendary way of life. Serious writers of westerns know both the country and the history—Zane Grey, however melodramatic, describes a West that old-timers could identify by specific place and time. Both types of westerns continue to be published.

The historical novel of the West, contrasted invidiously with the western, has (until recently) always been published as a hardcover book. The early 1990s brought an upsurge in the publishing of historical novels of the West in both trade and mass-market paperbacks. Historical novels of the West are usually longer than genre westerns. That many westerns are also historical novels of the West is obvious, but the denigratory label (or the original publication in paperback format) may deter the fan of Western Americana from reading westerns. Librarians and booksellers should be aware that the fan of the western might be interested in Western Americana (note the popularity of the several Time-Life volumes on the Indians, cowboys, and gunfighters), and that the reader of Western Americana might also enjoy the many westerns with strong historical background. That the genre western and the historical novel of the West may be differentiated by quality of writing is not a problem to be discussed here. Literary quality within the western varies as widely as it does within examples of the standard novel. Many westerns do suffer from stereotyped plots and characters, stiff or overly romantic dialogue (witness Zane Grey's, which is often embarrassing to read), misuse of dialect, and other defects. Each reader of westerns will develop personal standards of evaluation.

The popular stereotype of a genre is unfortunately too often accepted as the definition of the genre. The stereotypic western can be recognized on the first page: A lone rider is crossing a valley or desert and a shot knocks off his hat or hits a rock, startling his horse, and a range war begins. There is so much variety in themes in the western that the stereotype can be easily ignored. The following groupings by theme and type of western are not exhaustive nor do they include all authors who have used the themes. Also, as in any genre, many novels have multiple themes. The order of the groupings reflects both history and theme.

Mountain Men

The trappers of the early nineteenth century often lived with Indians and either married or were "adopted" into the tribes. They became the prototype loners who escaped society's restrictions and lived a free life. James Fenimore Cooper's Natty Bumppo of *The Leatherstocking Tales* (*The Pioneers, The Last of the Mohicans, The Prairie, The Pathfinder, The Deerslayer*) is the natural man free of a corrupting society and the prototype for the mountain man in the western. He frequently appears as a guide for the wagon trains. Guthrie's trilogy, among the following books, provides the prototype.

Fergusson, Harvey. *Wolf Song*.

Fisher, Vardis. *Mountain Man*.
    Source for the motion picture *Jeremiah Johnson*.

Guthrie, A. B. *The Big Sky. The Way West. These Thousand Hills*.

Johnston, Terry C. *Border Lords. One-Eyed Dream*.

Wagons West
and Early Settlement

Wagon trains took settlers to the prairie country, the Rocky Mountains, and the Pacific Northwest, and miners to the Dakotas and California. This type of western may present the greatest diversity of characters, including women. There is scope for varied adventures—the hazards of terrain and natural disasters as well as conflicts with Indians and other settlers. At the end of the journey is the homesteading. Most of the aspects of this type of western appear in the following books, with Hough's being the early prototype.

Gulick, Bill. *They Came to a Valley.*

Haycox, Ernest. *The Earthbreakers. The Adventurers.*

Hough, Emerson. *The Covered Wagon.*

Mead, Robert Douglas. *Heartland.*

Taylor, Robert Lewis. *The Travels of Jaimie McPheeters.*
     Pulitzer Prize winner; a long, picaresque adventure.

Texas and Mexico

The settling of Texas and the war with Mexico are topics for many westerns. The following are a few books on the special character of the border country and the battles with Mexico.

Brown, Sam. *The Long Season.*

Kelton, Elmer. *After the Bugles.*

Lea, Tom. *The Brave Bulls. The Wonderful Country.*

LeMay, Alan. *The Unforgiven.*

Land Rush

The opening of Oklahoma's Indian Territory to settlers appears in many westerns, but it dominates Edna Ferber's *Cimarron,* which is also a classic motion picture.

Mormons

The Mormons are the focus of many westerns, with their heroic journey to Zion (Utah) being a popular theme and their group being distrusted and hated by the Gentiles being a common plot. The following books provide the basic story.

Bailey, Paul. *For Time and All Eternity.*
     One of the few novels written from the Mormon point of view.

Card, Orson Scott. *A Woman of Destiny.*
     Also published as *Saints.*

Grey, Zane. *Riders of the Purple Sage.*

Wells, Marian. *The Wedding Dress.*

Wormser, Richard. *Battalion of Saints.*
     The Mormon Battalion marching to the war with Mexico.

Merchants, Mule Trains, Stage Lines

Before the settlers arrived in the West, there were trading posts, largely for the fur trade and the military. With the coming of ranchers, farmers, and miners, the economy needed merchants and means of transportation. The following books show how vital trade and transportation were in building the West.

Culp, John H. *Whistle in the Wind*.
> The Comanchero traders in the Spanish Southwest. Trade along the Santa Fe Trail was active in the nineteenth century.

Giles, Janice Holt. *Six-Horse Hitch*.
> In effect, a dramatic and long history of the stagecoach lines in the West and the Pony Express.

Haycox, Ernest. *Canyon Passage*.
> Mule-train freight line in the Pacific Northwest.

Reese, John. *Sure Shot Shapiro*.
> A Jewish traveling salesman in California's Mohave Desert.

Railroads

The building of the railroads is usually treated in the western in terms of the troubles encountered in the brawling construction camp towns, with Indians, robber gangs, and the like, and there is often a troubleshooter hero or railroad detective. (That Buffalo Bill was a hunter supplying meat to the crews is an aspect for a good story.) The following prototype books are full of adventurous action centering on the building of the railroad. That the railroad changed the character of the Far West is shown in many westerns, with the depot a vital center of any town.

Grey, Zane. *U. P. Trail*.

Haycox, Ernest. *Trouble Shooter*.

Spearman, Frank. *Whispering Smith*.

Mining

The mining towns were undoubtedly the toughest in the West, whether in the Dakotas, Rocky Mountain country, Arizona Territory, or California. The characters were equally tough, with claim jumping, lynchings, robbery of stage-coach shipments, and political and labor troubles to keep them busy. The following books include a ghost town setting in the picaresque *Dead Warrior*.

Ballard, Todhunter. *Gold in California.*

Cushman, Dan. *Silver Mountain.*

L'Amour, Louis. *The Empty Land.*

Myers, John Myers. *Dead Warrior.*

Lost Mines

Among the most romantic legends of the Southwest are those of lost Indian and Mexican mines of fabulous treasure. The following novels about fictional mines are remarkably realistic.

Henry, Will. *MacKenna's Gold.*

Nye, Nelson. *A Lost Mine Named Salvation.*

Shirreffs, Gordon D. *Southwest Drifter. The Manhunter.*

The Army in the West

The Indian wars and the campaigns to control the tribes provide the background for an exceedingly large number of westerns. The cavalry-and-Indian story is usually told from the cavalry side. (The Indian version can be found in "The Indian," below.) Officers and scouts are the heroes. Here is the classic description of the life for men and horses—"Forty miles a day on beans and hay." Stories both realistic and romantic are among the following novels.

Brown, Dee. *Action at Beecher Island. The Girl from Fort Wicked.*

Haycox, Ernest. *Border Trumpet. Bugles in the Afternoon.*

Olsen, Theodore V. *Arrow in the Sun.*

Short, Luke. *Ambush.*

Straight, Michael. *Carrington.*

The Indian

The story as told by the Indian is usually a distressing one. It provides a telling contrast to the attitudes toward the Native American common in many westerns. Most of the novels are rich in detail on customs and legends. The story of "adopted" white men, noted previously in the mountain men books, and the story of the mixed-race character appear here and in the novels listed under "Precontact Indians" (see p. 22). (See also "The Indian Today," p. 35.) Several of the following novels are narrated by an Indian character. Many explore the troubled relations between Indians and Anglos.

Arnold, Elliott. *Blood Brother*.
  Source of the motion picture *Broken Arrow*.

Blake, Michael. *Dances with Wolves*.

Capps, Benjamin. *The White Man's Road*.

Carter, Forrest. *Cry Geronimo*.
  Also called *Watch for Me on the Mountain*.

Comfort, Will L. *Apache*.

Conley, Robert. *Nickajack. Mountain Windsong: A Novel of the Trail of Tears*.

Cooke, John Byrne. *Between the Worlds*.

Crawford, Max. *Lords of the Plain*.

Fast, Howard. *The Last Frontier*.

Fisher, Clay. *Nino*.

Henry, Will. *From Where the Sun Now Stands*.

Johnson, Dorothy M. *The Hanging Tree and Other Stories. Indian Country*.

Jones, Douglas C. *Gone the Dreams and Dancing*.

La Farge, Oliver. *Laughing Boy*.

L'Amour, Louis. *Hondo*.

Lutz, Giles A. *The Magnificent Failure*.

Oliver, Chad. *The Wolf Is My Brother*.

Patten, Lewis B. *Bones of the Buffalo*.

Smith, C. W. *Buffalo Nickel*.

Stratham, Frances Patton. *Trail of Tears*.

Vernam, Glenn R. *Indian Hater*.

Welch, James. *Fools Crow*.

Precontact Indians

Although not strictly westerns, these novels deal with Native Americans in the times prior to contact with Europeans. The following books have appeal to readers of westerns featuring Indians.

Bruchac, Joseph. *Dawn Land*.

Conley, Robert J. *The Dark Way. The Way of the Priests*.

Indian Captivities

Popular since colonial times, captivity stories, factual and fictional, provide a narrative that is both sad and romantic. Captured as children or as adults, the captives may be rescued or may remain with the tribe to marry and become, in effect, Indians. If rescued, the women, who may have married into the tribe and borne children, may be unwilling to leave their Indian families. The following novels concern both the captivity story and the search for the captives.

Baker, Will. *Track of the Giant.*

Berger, Thomas. *Little Big Man.*

Blake, Michael. *Dances with Wolves.*

Capps, Benjamin. *A Woman of the People.*

Culp, John H. *Whistle in the Wind.*

Johnson, Dorothy M. *Indian Country.*
Source of the motion picture *A Man Called Horse.*

Jones, Douglas C. *Season of Yellow Leaf.*

LeMay, Alan. *The Searchers. The Unforgiven.*

Buffalo Runners

The buffalo "runners" (hunters) left a sad litter of whitening bones, destroyed the economy of the Plains Indians, and reduced buffalo herds of millions to almost extinction. Though many westerns have a few scenes of buffalo hunting, Fred Grove's *The Buffalo Runners* and *Buffalo Spring* are totally concerned with the topic.

Cattle Kingdoms

Cattle ranching, large- and small-scale, dominates the story of many westerns, with varying amounts of attention paid to ranching as such. The immense spreads provide the background for wealthy and powerful families. Ranching, of course, dominates the story of the cowboy, with its most dramatic aspect being the cattle drive (see "Cattle Drive," p. 25). The following three books illustrate the immensity of ranching operations.

Fergusson, Harvey. *Grant of Kingdom.*

Guthrie, A. B. *These Thousand Hills.*

Richter, Conrad. *The Sea of Grass.*

The Hired Man on Horseback

The cowboy is *the* great folk hero of the West. He appears in legendary guise in too many westerns. He appears as a "working cowboy" in too few. The nonfiction books on the cowboy (see "The Cowboy" in the "Topics" section of this chapter, pp. 46-48) treat both legend and reality. For example, although many cowboys may have been illiterate, many became inveterate readers in their lonely lives. That they were inveterate smokers abetted their literacy. (See the long passage, pp. 63–65, in Eugene Manlove Rhodes's novel *Bransford in Arcadia* on the 303 books the cowboys obtained through the yellow coupons in each Bill Durham pouch!) The early prototype novels listed here are by Adams and Wister; the most recent is by Decker.

Adams, Andy. *The Log of a Cowboy.*

Borland, Hal. *The Seventh Winter.*

Brown, Sam. *The Big Lonely.*

Decker, William. *To Be a Man.*

James, Will. *Sand.*

Mulford, Clarence E. *Hopalong Cassidy.*

Schaefer, Jack. *Monte Walsh.*

Wister, Owen. *The Virginian.*

Black Cowboy

From the early westerns and the majority of popular westerns, the reader would never know that black cowboys existed. *The Negro Cowboy* by Philip Durham and Everett L. Jones gives their history. Several recent westerns have a black cowboy as the hero. (The reader must wait for the Mexican or Native American cowboy to receive similar fictional status.) The following novels are realistic portrayals.

Everett, Wade. *Top Hand.*

Garfield, Brian. *Tripwire.*

Henry, Will. *One More River to Cross.*

Range War

The troubles in the typical popular western frequently stem from range wars—conflict over water rights or with encroaching nesters, the marauding rustler gangs, barbed wire, and the demise of the free range. Many books have as a plot device the hired gunman brought in to start or stop trouble.

The following novels merely suggest the great number of westerns with this theme.

Clarke, Richard. *The Homesteaders*.

Grey, Zane. *To the Last Man*.

Haycox, Ernest. *Free Grass*.

Hoffman, Lee. *West of Cheyenne*.

Vories, Eugene. *The Man from Colorado. Saddle a Whirlwind*.

Sheepmen

The sheepmen were always resented by cattlemen as spoilers of the range. Grey's novel deals with the historic Graham-Twekesbury feud, still a sore subject in the Tonto Basin area of Arizona. Readers of the western would enjoy *Sweet Promised Land* by Robert Laxalt, the moving story (with a novel's structure) of his father, a Basque sheepherder in Nevada, that captures the loneliness and danger of a sheepherder's life. Grey's novel is the early prototype for the range war.

Doig, Ivan. *Dancing at the Rascal Fair*.

Grey, Zane. *To the Last Man*.

Cattle Drive

The drive to rail's head is the epic saga of the western. Hazards of nature and stampedes were compounded by problems with rustlers and Indians. The following books cover many aspects of the topic, including ingenious instances in Australia and Siberia.

Adams, Andy. *The Log of a Cowboy*.
   The classic story, first published in 1903.

Barry, Jane. *A Shadow of Eagles*.

Capps, Benjamin. *The Trail to Ogallala*.

Flynn, Robert. *North to Yesterday*.

Grey, Zane. *Trail Driver. Wilderness Trek*.
   The second story takes place in Australia.

McMurtry, Larry. *Lonesome Dove*.
   Pulitzer Prize, 1986.

Bad Men and Good

The flawed hero is a popular figure in westerns. In the rough frontier world, a good man found it hard to remain good, at least if he wanted to stay alive. Whether treated as a romantic or as a realistic figure, the hero in this type of western is always a dramatic one, and, as in the following books, not always a stereotyped one.

Brand, Max. *Destry Rides Again*.
    Not like the classic motion picture that took the title.

Burnett, W. R. *Bitter Ground*.

Carter, Forrest. *Gone to Texas*.
    Source of the motion picture *The Outlaw Josey Wales*. *Vengeance Trail of Josey Wales*.

Doctorow, E. L. *Welcome to Hard Times*.

Fackler, Elizabeth. *Blood Kin. Backtrail*.

Grey, Zane. *Lone Star Ranger*.

Hall, Oakley. *The Coming of the Kid*.

Haycox, Ernest. "Stage to Lordsburg."
    The classic short-story western, source for *the* classic motion picture *Stagecoach*. To be found in Haycox's *By Rope and Lead* and in the anthology by Durham and Jones, *The Western Story*, listed later.

Henry, Will. *Death of a Legend*.

Rhodes, Eugene Manlove. *Pasó por Aquí*.

Swarthout, Glendon. *The Shootist*.

Law and Lawmen

The West was wide and lonesome, and lawmen were few. "An honest man is all the law you could find" (*The Virginian*). The western is full of men taking law into their own hands out of necessity—lynch law, the "kangaroo" courts of the mining towns, the shoot-out at sunset. The U.S. marshal in the territories was a powerful figure, as were the Texas Rangers. ("Only one Ranger?" "There's only one war, ain't there?") Oklahoma's Indian Territory was a haunt of outlaws, and the name Robber's Roost appeared throughout the West in isolated areas. Commonly asserted in the western: "There is no law West of the Pecos." The following novels show the law in action in an often lawless society.

Ballard, Todhunter. *The Sheriff of Tombstone*.

Burnett, W. R. *Bitter Ground*.

Clark, Walter Van Tilburg. *The Ox-Bow Incident.*

Conquest, Ned. *The Gun and Glory of Granite Hendley.*

Hall, Oakley. *The Warlock.*

Haycox, Ernest. *Trail Town.*

Leonard, Elmore. *Valdez Is Coming.*

Locke, Charles O. *The Hell Bent Kid.*

Poole, Richard. *Gun Vote at Valdoro.*

Portis, Charles. *True Grit.*

Town Marshal

The frontier town—cattle, mining, or railroad—was a troublesome place, its saloons full of gamblers and dance-hall girls. There was always a footloose stranger wandering through (as though the more stable residents couldn't cause enough trouble). The man with the star was the bulwark against anarchy and possibly the most romantic figure in western legend. In many westerns, the marshal is the secondary figure, but in the following books, he is the dominant character.

Adams, Clifton. *The Hottest Fourth of July in the History of Hangtree County.*

Bennett, Dwight. *Legend in the Dust.*

Burnett, W. R. *Bitter Ground.*

Everett, Wade. *Shotgun Marshal.*

Haycox, Ernest. *Trail Town.*

Leonard, Elmore. *Valdez Is Coming.*
    Mexican town constable.

Patten, Lewis B. *Death of a Gunfighter. No God in Saquaro.*

Boy into Man

The frontier was demanding country, and the boys had to prove competence at an early age. Most of the western's heroes are young, but in these books, they range from children to teenagers.

Bass, Milton. *Jory.*

Blevins, Winifred. *The Misadventures of Silk and Shakespeare.*

Hoffman, Lee. *The Valdez Horses.*

Knibbs, H. H. *The Ridin' Kid from Powder River.*

L'Amour, Louis. *Chancy. Down the Long Hills.*

Leighton, Lee. *Killer Guns.*

McMurtry, Larry. *Horseman Pass By.*
Source of the motion picture *Hud.*

Matthews, Greg. *The Further Adventures of Huckleberry Finn.*

Santee, Ross. *Cowboy.*

Stark, Cruce. *Chasing Uncle Charley.*

Wagoner, David. *Where Is My Wandering Boy Tonight?*

Mysterious Rider

Jack Schaefer describes him: "The man with the gun using it to right wrongs, in a sense the American version of a knight on horseback." Frequently, he is the hero with a shady past who rides out as lonely as he came in. He is a highly romantic figure, often a secondary character in westerns. In Schaefer's *Shane*, he became the legendary prototype.

The Singular Woman

The heroine in the western, less important than the horse, is rarely *the* leading character. However, the few dominant heroines are varied and notable. Note should be made of the heroines in Ernest Haycox's westerns, who are strong and liberated, as interesting as the heroes. There is a current trend in the western toward a more significant role for the woman. There has also been an increase in the number and quality of romance subplots in westerns; some are included in the following list of books that combine both the romantic and the realistic.

Banis, V. J. *San Antone.*

Bickham, Jack M. *The War on Charity Ross. Target: Charity Ross.*

Bittner, Roseanne. *Outlaw Hearts.*

Bonner, Cindy. *Lily. Looking After Lily.*

Cooke, John Byrne. *The Snowblind Moon.*

Frazee, Steve. *A Gun for Bragg's Woman.*

Kent, Simon. *Charlie Gallagher, My Love.*
First published 1961; the Signet reprint, 1976, is under the name Max Catto.

Locke, Charles O. *Amelia Rankin.*

Long, Elaine. *Jenny's Mountain.*
Contemporary.

Marvine, Dee. *Last Chance.*

Olsen, Theodore V. *Arrow in the Sun.*

Overholser, Wayne D. *The Cattle Queen.*

Portis, Charles. *True Grit.*

Richter, Conrad. *Tacey Cromwell.*

Stratham, Frances Patton. *Trail of Tears*
Features a Cherokee school teacher.

Webster, Jan. *Muckle Annie.*

Romance

There is romance, or *a* romance, in most westerns, often subordinate to the adventure interest but occasionally providing an important love story. One of this author's students, in a report on westerns, noted: "Westerns are no different than any other romance—except that the heroine is a man who carries guns and rides a horse!" A few are unabashedly romances, particularly the original paperback romances (a few are included in the following list).

Aldrich, Bess Streeter. *Spring Came on Forever.*

Brown, Sandra. *Sunset Embrace. Another Dawn.*

Busbee, Shirlee. *The Tiger Lily.*

Carroll, Shana. *Paxton Pride.*

Dailey, Janet. Calder series: *This Calder Sky. This Calder Range. Stands a Calder Man. Calder Born, Calder Bred. The Pride of Hannah Wade.*

Durham, Marilyn. *The Man Who Loved Cat Dancing.*

Grey, Zane. *The Light of Western Stars.*

Hagan, Patricia. *The Savage Heart.*

Walsh, M. M. B. *Dolly Purdo.*

Williams, Jeanne. *The Valiant Women.*

Doctor and Preacher

The hero in most westerns, even the unheroic hero of parody, falls into easily recognized types (e.g., cowboy, soldier, miner, lawman), making the doctor and the preacher unusual. The following two books are such satisfactory westerns that one wishes for more such nontypical heroes.

Everett, Wade. *Bullets for the Doctor.*

Reese, John. *My Brother John. Jesus on Horseback.*

Wild-Horse Hunt

The horse is important in the western (although, in fact, the canny rider swore by the smart and surefooted mule) and often proves one of the most interesting characters. It is the wild horse, symbolic of freedom and innocence, that provides the romantic story. Although a subsidiary theme in many westerns, in the following books the wild-horse hunt dominates.

Grey, Zane. *Forlorn River.*

O'Rourke, Frank. *The Last Ride.*

Picaresque

The rogue hero is a staple in adventure fiction. He usually has some saving graces, and he often reforms, at least partially. Frequently, an antihero or unheroic character is still cunning and competent—he survives and, sometimes, even wins out. His adventures are frequently comic, and he will often be found as the hero in the westerns in "Comedy and Parody," (see p. 31). The heroes in the following westerns are eccentric and often of quite a different pattern than the typical western hero.

Berger, Thomas. *Little Big Man.*

Culp, John H. *The Bright Feathers.*

Foreman, L. L. *Spanish Grant.*

McCague, James. *The Fortune Road.*

McCaig, Robert. *The Shadow Maker.*

Nye, Nelson. *Trail of Lost Skulls.*

O'Rourke, Frank. *The Swift Runner.*

Shelley, John, and David Shelley. *Hell-for-Leather Jones. The Relentless Rider.*

Shrake, Edwin. *Blessed McGill.*

Taylor, Robert Lewis. *Two Roads to Guadalupe.*

The West Unromanticized

The dark side of the western experience is being portrayed more often, somewhat in the picaresque tradition, but with raunchy, harshly realistic incidents not for the squeamish. Many older westerns contain both violence and horror, but the following recent westerns portend a new trend.

Dexter, Pete. *Deadwood*.

Matthews, Greg. *Heart of the Country*.

McCarthy, Cormac. *Blood Meridian*.

Swarthout, Glendon. *The Homesman*.

Comedy and Parody

Folk humor and vernacular humor are common in the western, both in characters and language. The western as a comic novel, where an author has fun with the standard patterns of the genre and often inverts its values, sometimes becomes true parody. The reader is advised to know the themes of the standard western before taking on the parodies. The following books parody all periods of the western story.

Adams, Clifton. *Shorty*.

Bickham, Jack. *The Apple Dumpling Gang*.

Brand, Max. *The Gentle Desperado*.

Condon, Richard. *A Talent for Loving: Or, The Great Cowboy Race*.

Evans, Max. *The Rounders*.

Greenberg, Alvin. *The Invention of the West*.

Gulick, Bill. *The Hallelujah Train. Liveliest Town in the West*.

LeMay, Alan. *Useless Cowboy*.
　　The perfect parody. The motion picture based on it, *Along Came Jones*, is a classic.

Markson, David. *The Ballad of Dingus Magee*.
　　For the sophisticated reader of westerns, being vulgar and bawdy.

Matthews, Jack. *Sassafras*.

McNab, Tom. *The Fast Men*.

Myers, John Myers. *Dead Warrior*.

Nye, Nelson. *Wolf Trap*.

O'Rourke, Frank. *The Bride Stealer*.

Pronzini, Bill. *The Last Days of Horse-Shy Halloran.*

Purdum, Herbert R. *A Hero for Henry.*

Reese, John. *Horses, Honor and Women. Singalce. Sure Shot Shapiro.*

Rhodes, Eugene Manlove

Ross, Ann B. *The Pilgrimage.*

Shelley, John. *Hell-for-Leather Jones.*

Turner, William O. *Destination Doubtful.*

Celebrity Western

The characters of the celebrity western have recognizable names from the history of the American West. All contain some historical facts mixed in with the fiction.

Aggeler, Geoff. *Confessions of Johnny Ringo.*

Camp, Deborah. *Belle Star: A Novel of the Old West.*

Cooke, John Byrne. *South of the Border.*
Butch Cassidy and Charlie Siringo, 1919 movie set.

Garfield, Brian. *Manifest Destiny.*
Teddy Roosevelt in the Badlands.

Irving, Clifford. *Tom Mix and Pancho Villa.*

McMurtry, Larry. *Anything for Billy.*
Billy the Kid.

McMurtry, Larry. *Buffalo Girls.*
Calamity Jane.

Swarthout, Glendon. *The Old Colts.*
Bat Masterson and Wyatt Earp, now old, get together in 1916.

Series

The popularity of the series character in the western has boomed with original paperback publishing. There are several of these series originally in hardcover (e.g., Bower, Foreman, McCarthy, Mulford). Many of the heroes are lawmen and are often in the picaresque tradition. (For other series, see " 'Adult' Western," p. 37.) The following listing is by series character or series label.

Benteen, John.	Neal Fargo.
Bower, B. M.	Chip of the Flying U.
Braun, Matthew.	Luke Starback, range detective.
Christian, Frederick H.	Justice.
Clinton, Jeff.	Wildcat O'Shea.
Cody, Al.	Montana Abbott.
Estleman, Loren D.	Page Murdoch, U.S. Marshal.
Foreman, L. L.	Rogue Bishop and Don Ricardo de Risa.
Gilman, George.	Edge. Adam Steele.
James, William M.	Cuchillo Oro. Apache.
Knott, Will C.	Wolf Caulder.
L'Amour, Louis.	The Sacketts.
Longtree, Warren T.	Ruff Justice.
McCarthy, Gary.	Derby Buckingham. A New York writer of Wild West yarns goes West and is a marvelous tough-guy hero.
McCoy, Marshal.	Larry and Streak. Nevada Jim.
McCurtin, Peter.	Carmody.
Martin, Larry Jay.	El Lazo.
Mitchum, Hank.	Stagecoach series. Background for action is a stagecoach run; 39 titles by 1990.
Mulford, Clarence E.	Hopalong Cassidy.
Newton, D. B.	Jim Bannister.
Overholser, Stephen.	Molly Owens, woman detective agency operative.

Saga Series

Several historical series have appeared as paperback originals following the success of The Kent Family Chronicles. (These are akin to the family chronicles or sagas noted later in chapter 5, "Romance.") Several of these series are the creation of packager Lyle Engel: for example, The Kent Family Chronicles, Wagons West, A Saga of the Southwest, and The Colonization of America. Because of the popularity of saga series, some are now published in hardcover.

Coldsmith, Don. The Spanish Bit Saga (Bantam).

The Colonization of America series (Bantam).

Cooke, John Byrne. The Snowblind Moon (Tor).

Jakes, John. The Kent Family Chronicles (Jove).
Originally called the American Bicentennial series.

James, Leigh Franklin. Saga of the Southwest series (Bantam).

L'Amour, Louis. Sackett family series (Hardcover series).

McCord, John S. The Baynes Clan (Doubleday).

The Making of America series (Dell).
The publisher labeled these eight volumes "romantic historical novels." Here the contents scope is briefly described in a listing of titles: Lou Cameron, *The Wilderness Seekers*, Kentucky in the late 1700s; Aaron Fletcher, *The Mountain Breed*, the mountain men in the early 1800s; Jeanne Sommers, *The Conestoga People*, westward migration in the mid-1800s; John Tombs, *The Forty Niners*; Paula Moore, *Hearts Divided*, the Civil War in the West; Jeanne Sommers, *The Builders*, the Union-Pacific railroad; Elizabeth Zachery, *The Land Rushers*, the Oklahoma land rush; Georgia Grange, *The Wild and the Wayward*, the last days of the Wild West.

Porter, Donald Clayton. Taming of the West series (Bantam).
White Indian series (an "eastern" western, Indians in colonial times).

Ross, Dana Fuller. Wagons West series (Bantam).

The West Still Lives—The Modern Scene

The western with a twentieth-century setting attests that the special mode of life distinctive in the western, particularly in ranching and with the cowboy and horse still dominant, continues in the wide-open Far West. Many regional novelists could be included here (e.g., Wallace Stegner, Walter Van Tilburg Clark, Conrad Richter, Frank Waters, Barbara Kingsolver). The vitality of the western and its appeal as a genre emerge strongly in the following books with modern settings.

Abbey, Edward. *The Brave Cowboy. Fire on the Mountain. The Monkey Wrench Gang. Hayduke Lives!*
The Brave Cowboy is the basis of the film *Lonely Are the Brave*.

Bradford, Richard. *Red Sky at Morning. So Far from Heaven.*

Brown, J. P. S. *Jim Kane. The Outfit: A Cowboy's Primer.*

Davis, H. L. *Winds of Morning.*

Day, Robert. *The Last Cattle Drive.*

Doig, Ivan. *Ride with Me, Mariah Montana.*

Evans, Max. *The Hi Lo Country. The One-Eyed Sky. The Rounders.*

Lutz, Giles A. *Wild Runs the River.*

McMurtry, Larry. *Horseman Pass By. Leaving Cheyenne.*

Miller, Arthur. *The Misfits.*

Schott, Max. *Ben. Murphy's Romance.*

Williams, Philip Lee. *All the Western Stars.*

The Indian Today

The story of the Native American in the West after the wars, on the reservation or dispersed within the West, is still of a people belonging to a distinctive and cherished culture. There is conflict with Anglo society and its government as well as with the more subtle and psychological distresses of adapting to or adjusting within an essentially incompatible culture. Folklore and poetry are found in several of the following books.

Borland, Hal. *When the Legends Die.*

Dorris, Michael. *A Yellow Raft in Blue Water.*

Eastlake, William. *The Bronc People. Portrait of an Artist with 26 Horses. Go in Beauty.*

Grey, Zane. *The Vanishing American.*

Heifetz, Harold. *Jeremiah Thunder.*

Herbert, Frank. *Soul Catcher.*

Hillerman, Tony. *Coyote Waits. Talking God. Skinwalkers.*
    Detective stories featuring Navajo tribal police (also listed in Chapter 3, "Crime").

Huffaker, Clair. *Nobody Loves a Drunken Indian.*

King, Thomas. *Medicine River.*

Momaday, N. Scott. *House Made of Dawn.*

Eccentric Variations

The combining of the western with other genres has not been tried too often, but the following novels combine one or more genres.

GOTHIC WESTERN

MacDonald, Elizabeth. *The House at Grey Eagle.*

Rowan, Deirdre. *Shadow of the Volcano. Time of the Burning Mask.*

Winston, Daoma. *The Golden Valley.*

SWEET-AND-SAVAGE WESTERN

Matthews, Patricia. *Love, Forever More.*

Sakol, Jeannie. *Flora Sweet.*

DETECTIVE STORY WESTERN

Braun, Matt. *Bloodstorm.*

Guthrie, A. B., Jr. *Wild Pitch. The Genuine Article. No Second Wind. Playing Catch-Up. Murder in the Cotswolds.*
Sheriff Charleston and deputy Jason Beard series. Present-day Montana background.

Meredith, Doris. *The Sheriff and the Branding Iron Murders.*

Wren, M. K. *Oh, Bury Me Not.*
Private investigator, 1970s Oregon ranch.

FANTASY WESTERN

L'Amour, Louis. *The Haunted Mesa.*
Anasazi and a breach in the universe opening parallel worlds to each other.

SCIENCE FICTION/DETECTIVE WESTERN

Foster, Alan Dean. *Cyber Way.*
Detective thriller featuring a tribal policeman cooperating with a Florida detective, set on a southwestern reservation in the next century.

BRITISH WESTERN

This is also called the "coyote in the sky" western because of the ludicrous error made by John Creasey, a prolific thriller writer who also wrote a few westerns under pseudonyms: meaning to note the vultures circling in the sky, he carelessly called them coyotes. There are several prolific British writers of westerns, but few of their books appear in the United States.

Edson, J. T. Floating Outfit series.
Reprinted in paperback by Berkley Books, 55 titles to date.

Pike, Charles R. Jubal Cade series.
Chelsea House published 13 titles in 1981.

"Adult" Western

These are "hot" paperback originals, strong on sexual adventures by the tough series heroes. Playboy Press started this type in 1975 with the Jake Logan series, and the imitators quickly followed. Playboy started a second series in 1979, the J. D. Hardin series. Some critics consider them to be simply pornography, although the pornography is sometimes leavened by comedy. Several books in each series are published yearly and seem to be kept in supply by reprintings. The authors of most are "house names"—several authors writing to fit the house's prescribed guidelines. Adult westerns may be considered the male adventure-fantasy counterpart to the female sweet-and-savage romance. A Jove editor commented: "This is escapist stuff. Adult westerns serve the same purpose as romances do for women. It's heroic fantasy, and it's fun." The tone of the following books distinguishes these series from those listed in the previous "Saga Series" section (see pp. 33-34).

Ellis, Wesley. Lone Star series.
"Jessie Starbuck—shooting like a man, loving like a woman, driven to avenge her father's murder . . . Ki—the martial arts master sworn to protect her and the Starbuck empire. . . . Together they rode for vengeance and conquered the West as no other man and woman ever had!"

Evans, Tabor. Longarm series, featuring Deputy U.S. Marshal Long.
"Longarm is a lot more than sagebrush and shoot-'em-up. It's the Wild West with emphasis on the Wild! Beautiful Women, Barroom Brawling, Bits of Fascinating History, Lots of Humor, and—Plenty of Sex! All the elements that appeal to men and women—Alike!"—Publisher's advertisement.

Hardin, J. D. Series featuring Pinkerton agents Doc and Raider.
" 'The most exciting writer since Louis L'Amour.' Jake Logan." From the cover of several titles. Jake Logan is a house name, as is J. D. Hardin.

Logan, Jake. Series featuring John Slocum.
"A little sadism, a little sex popularly blended and set in a West never known by the likes of Grey or Brand."

Sharpe, Jon. The Trailsman series, featuring Sky Fargo.
"We try not to overdo the sex stuff, but it is a factor to reckon with. Our audience is much younger and includes fans of adventure and spy series, so violence and sex are necessary ingredients."—NAL editor.

Inspirational Western

The Christian publishing houses are also coming out with westerns. The stories feature characters who come through their problems with help of a spiritual nature. Crossway Books publishes some, as does Council Press, a Mormon publishing house.

Bly, Stephen. *Last Hanging at Paradise Meadow.* Stuart Brannon series.

Nelson, Lee. Storm Testament series.

TOPICS

Classic Authors: Early

Most of the classic authors remain in print, largely in paperback. (See "Reprint Publishers," p. 49.) Many of the following authors are listed as examples in the previous subject groupings. The following authors have endured, either with one or a few titles, or, as with Brand and Grey, with all their titles.

Adams, Andy.
His *The Log of a Cowboy* (1903) is the classic and authentic story of a trail drive from the Mexican border to Montana.

Brand, Max.
Pseudonym of Frederick Faust. Used 13 (or more) pseudonyms and wrote 215 westerns, publishing the first in 1919. His three top sellers (over two million copies) are *Destry Rides Again, Fightin' Fool, Singing Guns.* Twenty-seven of his novels were made into motion pictures. (He also wrote the Dr. Kildare series for MGM.) A great many of his titles are currently in paperback, with all of the pseudonyms now appearing as Max Brand.

Easton, Robert. *Max Brand: The Big "Westerner."* University of Oklahoma Press, 1970.

Burroughs, Edgar Rice.
Better known for his Tarzan series and science fiction adventures. Two of his westerns were reprinted in the Gregg Press Western Fiction series: *The War Chief* and *Apache Devil* (both serialized in 1927 and 1928 before publication in book form).

Grey, Zane.
From 1903 to his death in 1939 he wrote 89 books, including nonfiction. Westerns have been issued since 1939 "from the estate of Zane Grey," by Harpers, but the earlier titles are the classic ones. He

appeared on the best-seller list in 1915, *The Lone Star Ranger*, and again each year from 1917 to 1924. Over 40 novels became motion pictures.

Gruber, Frank. *Zane Grey, a Biography*. World, 1970.

Harte, Bret.
Immortalized the miners, gamblers, and good-hearted fancy ladies of the West of the 1860s in "The Luck of Roaring Camp" and "The Outcasts of Poker Flat."

Hough, Emerson.
The Covered Wagon (1922) set a pattern for the Oregon Trail western.

Knibbs, H. H.
The Ridin' Kid from Powder River (1919) is a classic boy-into-man western.

Mulford, Clarence E.
Hopalong Cassidy (1910) became immortal in a long series on the Bar-20 Ranch, appearing in novel, motion picture, and television.

Raine, William MacLeod.
He wrote about 85 westerns, his first published in 1908, and they are still being reprinted in paperback.

Rhodes, Eugene Manlove.
"The Hired Man on Horseback" whose romantic western heroes, frequently at odds with the law, were, as his first book affirmed, *Good Men and True* (1910). Most remember for *Pasó por Aquí* (1926), with its tag line, " 'We are all decent people.' " His typical humor is evoked by the compiler, W. H. Hutchinson of *The Rhodes Reader: Stories of Virgins, Villains and Varmints* (University of Oklahoma Press, 1957).

Twain, Mark.
Twain brought welcome humor to the western scene in "The Celebrated Jumping Frog of Calaveras County" (1867) and *Roughing It* (1872).

White, Stewart Edward.
A prolific writer on the western scene, White is chiefly remembered for *Arizona Nights* (1904), stories of the range, and a trilogy (1913–1915) gathered as *The Story of California*.

Wister, Owen.
The Virginian, on the best-seller list in 1902 and 1903 and never out of print, set the pattern for the popular cowboy western in hero, heroine (the schoolmarm), rustlers, shoot-out at sundown, and other incidents. It gave the genre its classic line: "When you call me that, *smile!*"

Classic Authors: Recent

This list of classic authors could be extended as certain authors are reprinted more fully or as new authors become established. Most of them are, or were, prolific and write westerns with a variety of themes.

Burnett, W. R.

Capps, Benjamin

Garfield, Brian

Gulick, Bill

Guthrie, A. B.
Big Sky is one of the top-selling westerns.

Haycox, Ernest
Rawhide Range and *Bugles in the Afternoon* are among the top-selling westerns. Haycox is important as a touchstone in the criticism of the western: his writings, in style and characterization, set standards for the genre that have influenced others writing in the genre.

Henry, Will
Also publishes as Clay Fisher.

Johnson, Dorothy M.

Kelton, Elmer

L'Amour, Louis
When L'Amour died in 1988, sales of 101 books, almost all westerns, were nearing the 200 million mark. Forty-five of his novels were made into movies or television shows. "The Homer of the oaters."—*Time.*

LeMay, Alan

Olsen, T. V.

O'Rourke, Frank

Patten, Lewis B.
About 80 titles.

Schaefer, Jack
Shane is one of the top-selling westerns and became a classic motion picture.

Short, Luke
In some 57 novels, he covered most of the themes in the genre.

"Best Westerns"

Polls to determine the best westerns are idiosyncratic. A list of *The Roundup* (monthly journal of the Western Writers of America) in 1956 included A. B. Guthrie's *The Big Sky* and *The Way West*; Ernest Haycox's *Bugles in the Afternoon*; Owen Wister's *The Virginian*; Andy Adams's *The Log of a Cowboy*; Walter Van Tilburg Clark's *The Ox-Bow Incident*; and Conrad Richter's *The Sea of Grass*. A similar list in 1969 duplicated only *The Log of a Cowboy*; the others were Will Henry's *From Where the Sun Now Stands*; Benjamin Capps's *The Trail to Ogallala*; Tom Lea's *The Wonderful Country*; Oakley Hall's *Warlock*; Milton Lott's *Back Track*; Alan LeMay's *The Searchers*; Frederick Manfred's *Conquering Horse*; and Max Evans's *The Rounders*.

A list of the 10 best westerns in the London *Daily Telegraph* in 1976 is notable in that all were made into motion pictures: Zane Grey's *Riders of the Purple Sage*; Walter Van Tilburg Clark's *The Ox-Bow Incident*; A. B. Guthrie's *The Big Sky*; W. R. Burnett's *Adobe Walls*; Ernest Haycox's *Man in the Saddle*; Luke Short's *Ride the Man Down*; Alan LeMay's *The Searchers*; Jack Schaefer's *Shane*; Dorothy M. Johnson's "The Man Who Shot Liberty Valance"; Max Brand's *Destry Rides Again*.

The following winners of awards from the Cowboy Hall of Fame and the Spur award from the Western Writers of America (some are not listed elsewhere) should be noted: Leigh Brackett, Matthew Braun, Will C. Browne, Leslie Ernenwein, L. P. Holmes, Noel M. Loomis, Giles A. Lutz (over 50 titles), Stephen Overholser, Wayne D. Overholser (about 70 titles), and Glendon Swarthout.

Writers in this genre tend to be prolific: Tom Curry (125); J. T. Edson (British author, over 100); Cliff Farrell (about 30); Ray Hogan (about 90); Louis Masterman (the pseudonym of Norwegian author Kjell Hallbing; over 100 westerns some of which have been translated and published in England); Nelson Nye (about 90); T. V. Olsen (over 30); Frank C. Robertson (116); Gordon D. Shirreffs (about 70); Tom West (over 50). But Peter Field, with a seemingly unending number, is the name of a publishing house.

New authors emerge regularly, and as they continue to turn out new titles steadily, they become the familiar names as candidates for the best of genre lists (e.g., Kelly P. Gast and Frank Roderus, each now turning out about one book a year).

Anthologies

Into the 1940s, authors of westerns wrote steadily for the pulp magazines that published both short stories and serials. They also had a ready market in many of the slick magazines, notably *The Saturday Evening Post*. These magazines were a rich source for anthology stories. The following partial list of these late and lamented pulp magazines in this genre makes obvious the popularity of the genre.

Ace-High Magazine: Real Western Stories

Big-Book Western

Cowboy Stories

Dime Western Magazine

Double Action Western

Famous Western

Pioneer Western

Ranch Romances

Rangeland Romances

Real Western Romances

Star Western

Texas Rangers

West

Western Story Magazine

Wild West Stories

Wild West Weekly

Since 1953 the Western Writers of America has edited an annual anthology, each on a theme of the western story. All stories are by members, and each volume is a good introduction to the writers in the genre. A few of the anthology titles reveal the use of themes: *Badman and Good; The Fall Roundup; Holsters and Heroes; Branded West; The Wild Horse Roundup; Wild Streets; Trails of Adventure; Rawhide Men; They Opened the West; Iron Men and Silver Stars; Hoof Trails and Wagon Tracks; Rivers to Cross.* Most of the following anthologies are several years old, but their stories are ageless.

Collier, Ned, ed. *Great Stories of the West.* Doubleday, 1971.

Durham, Philip, and Everett L. Jones, eds. *The Western Story: Fact, Fiction, and Myth.* Harcourt, 1975.
    The fiction section has stories by Bret Harte, Jack London, Owen Wister, Stephen Crane, Clarence Mulford, Zane Grey, Vardis Fisher, Ernest Haycox, Max Brand, John M. Cunningham, Clay Fisher, Luke Short, Allan Bosworth, Thomas Thompson, Donald Hamilton, and Walter Van Tilburg Clark.

Knight, Damon, ed. *Westerns of the 40's: Classics from the Great Pulps.* Bobbs-Merrill, 1977.

Lenniger, August, ed. *Western Writers of America: Silver Anniversary Anthology.* Ace, 1977.

Maule, Harry E. *Pocket Book of Western Stories*. Pocket Books, 1945.
Reprinted as *Great Tales of the American West*. Modern Library, 1945.

Muller, Marcia, and Bill Pronzini, eds. *She Won the West: An Anthology of Western and Frontier Stories by Women*. Morrow, 1985.
Fourteen stories, including authors B. M. Bower, Gertrude Atherton, Willa Cather, Mary Austin, Eleanor Gates, Dorothy M. Johnson, Mari Sandoz, Ann Ahlswede, Carla Kelly, Jeanne Williams.

Piekarski, Vicki, ed. *Westward the Women: An Anthology of Western Stories by Women*. Doubleday, 1984.

Pronzini, Bill, and Martin H. Greenberg, eds. *The Arbor House Treasury of Great Western Stories*. Arbor House, 1982.
Early greats: Mark Twain, Bret Harte, Stephen Crane, Gertrude Atherton, O. Henry, Owen Wister, Jack London, Stewart Edward White, Eugene Manlove Rhodes, Zane Grey, B. M. Bower, Clarence E. Mulford, Emerson Hough, William MacLeod Raine, Rex Beach, Max Brand. Later greats: Luke Short, Ernest Haycox, Louis L'Amour, A. B. Guthrie, Jr., Dorothy M. Johnson, Jack Schaefer, John Jakes, Elmore Leonard, William R. Cox, Steve Frazee, Brian Garfield, Evan Hunter, Marcia Muller, Wayne D. Overholser, Stephen Overholser, Clay Fisher.

Pronzini, Bill, and Martin H. Greenberg, eds. *Best of the West: Stories That Inspired Classic Western Films*. New American Library, 1986.

Pronzini, Bill, and Martin H. Greenberg, eds. *Christmas Out West*. Doubleday, 1990.

Pronzini, Bill, and Martin H. Greenberg, eds. *The Western Hall of Fame: An Anthology of Classic Western Stories Selected by the Western Writers of America*. Morrow, 1984.
The 17 stories do warrant the "Hall of Fame" label. Includes Haycox's "Stage to Lordsburg," and two classic novellas, Schaefer's *Stubby Pringle's Christmas* and Rhodes's *Pasó por Aquí*.

The Saturday Evening Post Reader of Western Stories. Doubleday, 1960.

Schaefer, Jack, ed. *Out West: An Anthology of Stories*. Houghton, 1955.

Short, Luke, ed. *Cattle, Guns and Men*. Bantam, 1955.

Targ, William, ed. *Western Story Omnibus*. World, 1945.
Reprinted by Penguin as *Great Western Stories*.

Taylor, J. G., ed. *Great Short Stories of the West*. Ballantine, 1971. 2 vols.

Tuska, Jon, ed. *The American West in Fiction*. Mentor/NAL, 1982.
An interpretive grouping of authors: "The East Goes West" (Mark Twain, Bret Harte, Stephen Crane, Frederic Remington, Owen Wister); "Where West Was West" (Dorothy M. Johnson, Willa Cather, John G. Neihardt, Eugene Manlove Rhodes, Ernest Haycox); "The

West of the Storytellers" (Zane Grey, Max Brand, Louis L'Amour, James Warner Bellah, Luke Short); "The West in Revision" (Elmer Kelton, Will Henry, Benjamin Capps, Walter Van Tilburg Clark, Max Evans). There are bibliographies of suggested further reading, including fiction in three groupings: "Formulary Westerns" (18 authors), "Romantic Historical Reconstructions" (16 authors), "Historical Reconstruction" (18 authors).

Ward, Don, ed. *Pioneers West*. Dell, 1966.

Wollheim, D. A., ed. *A Quintet of Sixes*. Ace, 1969.

Bibliographies and Encyclopedias

The following are the first reference books of various types of westerns within the genre (which indicates how much remains to be done).

Erisman, Fred, and Richard W. Etulain, eds. *Fifty Western Writers*. Greenwood, 1982.
Essays by several people on both writers of westerns and writers on the American West. Western authors include Zane Grey and Louis L'Amour.

Tuska, Jon, and Vicki Piekarski, eds. *Encyclopedia of Frontier and Western Fiction*. McGraw-Hill, 1983.
Over 300 authors are discussed. Includes the following general entries: "Historical Personalities"; "House Names"; "Native Americans"; "Pulp and Slick Western Stories"; "Women on the Frontier." Films based on an author's titles are noted. The prefatory essays by the editors define the genre.

Twentieth Century Western Writers. Edited by James Vinson and D. L. Kirkpatrick. Preface by C. L. Sonnichsen. London: Macmillan, 1982.
Brief biography, bibliography, and critical essay for 310 authors.

History and Criticism

Discussion of the western genre novel sometimes encompasses the regional novel of the West as well. While the two types may merge, the regional novel has a quite different plot structure and its authors rarely also write the western genre novel. The following books deal with the western as a genre; the books by Folsom and Milton extend their treatment to the regional novel.

Durham, Philip, and Everett L. Jones, eds. *The Western Story: Fact, Fiction, and Myth*. Harcourt, 1975.
Designed as a textbook. Classes on the western are now offered at the high school and college levels. This is an anthology with critical introductions.

Etulain, Richard W. "The Western." In Inge, M. Thomas, ed. *Handbook of American Popular Culture.* 1978. Vol. 1, pp. 355–76.

Etulain, Richard W., and Michael T. Marsden, eds. *The Popular Western.*
This anthology includes essays on B. M. Bower, Zane Grey, Clay Fisher/Will Henry, Luke Short, Jack Schaefer, and general critical essays.

Folsom, J. K. *The American Western Novel.* College and University Press, 1966.
Begins with James Fenimore Cooper; the discussion is critical but selective of authors.

Gruber, Frank. "The Basic Western Novel Plots." In *Writer's Year Book*, 1955: 49–53, 160.

Milton, John R. *The Novel of the American West.* University of Nebraska Press, 1980.
The first chapter is on "The Popular or Formula Western," and the author then discusses those novels on the West that are "a higher form of literature, not a genre."

Sonnichsen, C. L. *From Hopalong to Hud: Thoughts on Western Fiction.* Texas A&M University Press, 1978.
The author's collected essays on the West of fact and "The West That Wasn't" include essays on the unheroic hero, sex, and violence in the western, fictional treatment of the Indian, and the influence of motion picture interpretations.

Tuska, Jon. "The Westerner Returns." *West Coast Review of Books* 4 (#6, 1978), pp. 73–79.
A discussion of Sonnichsen's *From Hopalong to Hud* and the Gregg Press Western Fiction series (listed under "Reprint Publishers," p. 49) is a critical evaluation of the western genre.

Background on the West

Books on the American West in all its aspects are myriad. Many are specialized (e.g., on the history of barbed wire in the West). University presses in the western states, particularly the University of Oklahoma Press, publish Western Americana regularly. Both university and commercial press publications are often full of illustrations. The few in the following list are intended to suggest the diversity offered.

Adams, Ramon F. *Western Words: A Dictionary of the American West.* New Edition, Revised and Enlarged. University of Oklahoma Press, 1968.
The definitions reveal the way of life with humor and anecdotes. "Wish book. A cowboy's term for a mail order catalog." "Montgomery Ward woman sent west on approval. A homely woman."

Bergon, Frank, and Zeese Papnikolas, eds. *Looking Far West: The Search for the American West in History, Myth, and Literature*. NAL, 1978.
An imaginatively selected anthology, with sections on the mountain man, "The Wild West," and western films suggesting its diversity.

Brown, Dee. *The Gentle Tamers: Women of the Old West*. University of Nebraska Press, 1968.
First edition, 1958. They came as settlers, army wives, shady ladies, schoolmarms, mail order brides and were always in short supply. There is lively quotation from journals and letters.

Horan, James D. *The Authentic Wild West*. Crown, 1976–1980. 3 vols.
The volumes are subtitled: *The Gunfighters, The Outlaws, The Lawmen*.

Myers, John Myers. *Print in a Wild Land*. Doubleday, 1967.
They were hungry for news, and the tramp printers were seemingly always on hand in cow town or mining town. Bret Harte and Mark Twain wrote for the frontier newspapers. The editors, notably eccentric and often drunken, enliven the history. There are many selections, hilarious and poetical, from the multitude of newspapers.

Redford, Robert. *The Outlaw Trail: A Journey Through Time*. Grossett, 1978.
The author, friends, and photographers rode the old trails—here is adventure accompanied by superb color photographs.

Steckmesser, K. L. *The Western Hero in History and Legend*. University of Oklahoma Press, 1965.
Four types are discussed: "The Mountain Man: Kit Carson"; "The Outlaw: Billy the Kid"; "The Gunfighter: Wild Bill Hickok"; "The Soldier: George Armstrong Custer."

The Cowboy

The great American folk hero—his image in fact, myth, picture, music, and motion picture provides the matter of an awesome bibliography. Many of the following books contain reference to the cowboy as represented in the western genre novel.

Branch, Douglas. *The Cowboy and His Interpreters*. Cooper Square, 1961.
First published in 1926 and still possibly the most interesting analysis of fact, legend, and the novel. Illustrated by Will James, Joe de Yong, and Charles M. Russell.

Dary, David. *Cowboy Culture: A Saga of Five Centuries*. Knopf, 1981.
From Spanish times to the present, the cattle, the people, and the ranches are described in great detail. All aspects of the life and the forces of history that shaped the cowboy world receive illuminating attention. Illustrated with photographs and line drawings.

Frantz, Joe B., and Julian Ernest Choate, Jr. *The American Cowboy: The Myth and Reality*. University of Oklahoma Press, 1955.
Illustrated with photographs by Erwin E. Smith from the Library of Congress collection. Footnotes and bibliography.

Harris, Charles W., and Buck Rainey, eds. *The Cowboy: Six-Shooters, Songs, and Sex*. University of Oklahoma Press, 1976.
A lively and irreverent anthology with illustrations to match. A few of the essay titles give the flavor: "The 'Reel' Cowboy," "The Pistol Packin' Cowboy," "The Cowboy's Bawdy Music."

Hudson, Wilson M., and Allen Maxwell, eds. *The Sunny Slopes of Long Ago*. Southern Methodist University Press, 1966.
Texas Folklore Society Publication Number 33. Includes: "Cowboy Lingo," by J. A. Lomax; "The Cowboy: His Cause and Cure," by E. M. Rhodes; "The Cowboy's Code," by Paul Patterson; "The American Cowboy," by Andy Adams; "The Cowboy Enters the Movies," by M. C. Boatright.

Life on the Texas Range. Photographs by Erwin E. Smith. Text by J. Evetts Haley. University of Texas Press, 1952.
Photographs of ranch life and the working cowboy at the turn of the century that tell the whole story with artistry.

McCracken, Harold. *The American Cowboy*. Doubleday, 1973.
Art illustrations and photographs illustrate the history of the cowboy and the cattle country from Spanish times.

Meigs, John, ed. *The Cowboy in American Prints*. Sage Books, Swallow Press, 1972.
Seventy-five full page plates, 39 illustrations within the introduction, and 13 on the endpapers give a glowing interpretation of the cowboy by nineteenth- and twentieth-century artists.

The Old West: The Cowboys. By the editors of Time-Life Books. With Text by William H. Forbis. Time-Life Books, 1973.
Extensively illustrated with drawings, maps, and photographs. The text is excellent.

Rosa, Joseph G. *Guns of the American West*. Crown, 1985.

Rounds, Glen. *The Cowboy Trade*. Holiday House, 1972.
Delightfully illustrated by the author to show the cowboy at work. For children, but why deny adults the pleasure of a charming and informative text—"Western story magazines of all kinds were popular in the bunkhouses. The cowboys on paper led vastly more exciting lives than the readers, and such disagreeable subjects as barbed wire stretching and pigpen repairing were seldom mentioned."

Savage, William W., Jr. *The Cowboy Hero: His Image in American History and Culture.* University of Oklahoma Press, 1979.

The image is pervasive, drawn not from the working cowboy but from the folk hero embodied in the rodeo performer or the star of horse opera in motion pictures and television series. The hero emerges in works of art, comic strips, or cigarette advertising. His garb becomes transmogrified into bizarre fashions.

Savage, William W., Jr., ed. *Cowboy Life: Reconstructing an American Myth.* University of Oklahoma Press, 1975.

This anthology of contemporary accounts of cowboy life from the 1870s to the turn of the century is fascinating in its variety. The 43 photographs and the narratives are from the Western History Collections of the University of Oklahoma Library.

Taylor, Lonn, and Ingrid Maar. *The American Cowboy.* American Folklife Center, Library of Congress, 1983.

This colorfully illustrated catalogue of a traveling exhibit is a delight. There are three sections: "The Real Live Cowboy"; "The Cowboy Hero" (including the hero in fiction, on the stage, in music and motion picture, and as a rodeo performer); "Meanwhile, Back at the Ranch."

Western Writers of America

The Western Writers of America has a membership of writers of western fact and westerns. It publishes (since 1953) a monthly journal, *The Roundup*, which includes book reviews and is available for subscription by libraries. At its annual convention, "Spur" awards are given in several categories, and the Golden Saddleman Award is given for an "outstanding contribution to the history and legend of the West." The Western Writers of America has a book club, which is managed by Doubleday.

Publishers

Two publishers regularly issue westerns in hardcover: Doubleday (Double D Westerns) and Walker. These are largely the standard type of genre western, and Walker also imports many written by British authors. An occasional western or historical novel of the West appears from other houses. As all of the major paperback houses are now also publishing in hardcover, more westerns are appearing in both formats, including reprintings of titles originally issued in paperback. Almost all the paperback houses issue some westerns, both originals and reprints, with several issuing original series of both standard and adult westerns. Zebra issues a line of western romances in paperback, the Leather and Lace series, described in *Heart Line* as a "Marriage between historical romance and adult westerns. . . . Adventures encountered by the bold beautiful women who conquered the untamed men of the Old Frontier." Zane Grey and Max Brand continue to be available in both hardcover (Harper and Dodd) and paperback (Pocket Books).

Reprint Publishers

A great number of paperback westerns are reprints, and all the large-print houses are now bringing out several western reprints each year. Although some are in hardcover, many large-print westerns are trade paperbacks. Aeonian Press, Walter J. Black, and Gregg Press have issued reprints of a limited number of titles. Linsford and several other large-print houses regularly issue reprints.

D's Western Picks

Blake, Michael. *Dances with Wolves*. Ballantine, 1988.

Bonner, Cindy. *Lily*. Algonquin Books of Chapel Hill, 1992.

Carter, Forrest. *Gone to Texas*. Delacorte Press, 1973.

Vories, Eugene. *The Man from Colorado*. Thomas Bouregy, 1960.

Welch, James. *Fools Crow*. Viking, 1986.

3 Crime

The statutory definition of homicide is the "unlawful killing of one human being by another." Sometimes the phrase
"with malice" is employed, the concept serving to distinguish murder from the numerous other occasions in which
people deprive each other of life—wars and executions
coming foremost to mind. "Malice" in the law doesn't
necessarily convey hatred or even ill will but refers instead
to a conscious desire to inflict serious injury or cause
death. In the main, criminal homicide is an intimate, personal affair insofar as most homicide victims are killed by
close relatives, friends, or acquaintances. Reason enough
to keep your distance, if you're asking me.

—Sue Grafton
"K" Is for Killer (1994)

THEMES AND TYPES

The novels involving crime fall into several of many popular subgenres
that could be grouped as thrillers. Crime novels include detective stories,
mysteries, crime capers, and courtroom dramas. The driving force in these
novels is a crime of some sort, most commonly murder, but theft, assault, and
confidence games are also popular. Spy and espionage novels, though considered by some (citizens of the "targeted" country) to be crime novels,
revolve more around the adventure aspects of their plots and are thus treated
in chapter 4, "Adventure."

The murder mystery, or detective novel, has long been a staple in the
book world. It makes up the largest of genre collections in most public
libraries. A rising star in the crime genre is the legal thriller, typified by the
best-selling novels of John Grisham.

Crime fiction, like any fiction, essentially begins "Once upon a time . . .";
the reader is enticed to read on, filled with curiosity or a tingling suspense
to find out what happens next.

Detective Story and Detectives

The mystery tale involving detection to solve a problem through analysis of clues—physical evidence and the characteristics of persons—has been ever present in popular literature. What emerged as new in the nineteenth century was the formal detective. Historians of this genre speculate on the significance of the formation of France's Sûreté and England's Scotland Yard (and the earlier Bow Street Runners) as a necessary background for the development of the detective as a credible figure in literature. The writings on the detective story provide a lively literature on its origins and development, and only one aspect needs to be noted here: the genre was naturalized in France, England, and the United States, the countries where strongly organized police forces emerged in the nineteenth century. These three countries are still the source of most of the detective novels now being published and translated for readers throughout the world.

Individual fans may prefer a type or types of detective stories, but fans unite in devotion to the particular detective as a personality. Thus, the detective, whose cases are continued through a series of short stories or novels, never lacks a readership. Often, a series may be referred to not by the author's name but by the detective's. The fan reads them all, ignoring, but not oblivious of, the quality of any single work. (It thus behooves a reader advisor, starting out a neophyte reader on some particular author, to know the particular *work* that should be read first to ensure that the reader becomes properly enchanted with the starring detective.)

The types of detectives are diverse by occupation, and almost all have some defining eccentricity. Police detectives are the most numerous, appearing in what are labeled "police procedurals" or "romans policier." Though detectives from the large city forces are most common—Scotland Yard, the Sûreté, New York or Los Angeles police departments—there are many from the county CID (Criminal Investigation Department) as well as the village constable in England, or the state police, sheriff, and small-town police chiefs and detectives in the United States. Equal in popularity as detectives are the private investigators, who operate alone or work out of large agencies. Insurance investigators often function as private investigators. Private detectives fall into roughly two types: the straightforward sleuth (much like a police detective) and the hard-boiled private eye. The third type of detective is the amateur, characterized by an inveterate nosiness, who may be of either sex and of any occupation. (More information will be provided on these types as examples are listed.)

The pattern in detective stories is determined by a series of events expected by the reader—an incident or catastrophe, preferably murder, demanding the attention of the police and perhaps private or amateur detectives as well; the process of detection; the denouement. The manner in which the pattern is developed is limited only by the imagination of the author, but the detective must be the dominant character. The variation in type of detective and background of the plot often determines the readership.

In tone, the detective story varies dramatically, from comic and polite social comedy to harsh realism and horror. Traditionally, a romance has been frowned upon for the detective but is allowed as a minor theme for secondary characters. A few of the series detectives marry or are married, a matter of small interest in most cases to the readers. However, the sexual affairs, particularly of many private eyes, have provided a colorful part of the characterization of some detectives, and there is increasing sexual explicitness, with sensationalism, in many private eye novels. The reader has a wide variation of tones to choose from, ranging from the ladylike gentility of Agatha Christie to the savage crudeness of Mickey Spillane.

Some fans read only British detective stories, others only American. Some prefer police procedurals and may read those from any country; some want their private detectives to be hard-boiled private eyes. There are those who delight in the amateur detective, and those who dote on the genteel social comedy of the English country-house murder. Some devotees eclectically try them all, but they usually end up with favored authors, types of detectives, or backgrounds. The groupings given here suggest the identification needed in reviews and by reader advisors, with a special section for readers who desire a particular background.

The critics ingeniously analyze why the detective story is so popular. Is it simply the fascination of a mystery or puzzle, enticing the reader to match wits with the detective? For the many readers who do not attempt logically to follow the clues, the appeal may be simply in the mounting suspense before all is finally made clear. Does the story satisfy a desire to find in a disorderly world a pattern of rationality that brings order out of chaos? Is there a vicarious solution to original sin: There but for the grace of God go I?

Note must be made of the recurrent and bluntly definite statement that the detective story is dead, worn out, all its variations and plots tiresomely repetitious. Its patterned artificiality is unrealistic and readers now want the more credible crime story or story of psychological suspense deriving from characters of real life. Neither the crime story nor the psychological-suspense novel substitutes for the detective story. (Both, incidentally, are more related to the standard novel, particularly to the sensational and sexy best-seller type than to the genre detective story.) Crime and psychological-suspense stories frequently concern the mentally marred or psychologically deranged. The detective story may concern such defective characters, but its great attraction for many readers is that the perpetrator of the crime is a normal being (even as you and I!) who succumbs to one of the deadly sins through a flaw of character and not of mind. The police procedural is likely to deal with characters of the sick mind but is apt to be a bore if this is the only type of criminal involved in the plot.

The detective story continues to be written, published, and read because of the readers' fascination with the personality of the detective. Age does not alter the detective's appeal, and several have been around for over half a century: Hercule Poirot (1920), Lord Peter Wimsey (1923), Sam Spade (1930), Jules Maigret (1931), Nero Wolfe (1934), John Appleby (1936), and Philip Marlowe (1939). Sherlock Holmes is alive after more than 100 years (1887). They are all very much in print in hardcover and paperback, being discovered by succeeding generations of readers. When the devotee of the detective cannot find new detective stories with the type of detective the reader demands, the reader's recourse is clear—back to rereading the old favorites (which may be done periodically, anyway). The detective, the more eccentric the better, has become a folk hero.

There have been changes in the 1990s. The pendulum has swung away from police detectives and toward private investigators. It seems that every week a new detective debuts. Romance is now finding its way into the lives of the detectives, and, though generally thwarted, their need for love and companionship is manifesting itself.

More and more female sleuths have appeared in all subgenres of crime detective novels. Previously, women sleuths were most often amateurs. Now they are seen regularly as police detectives, as private investigators in their own one-woman operations, or even as medical examiners.

In genre series, the detective novel is now the rule (with, of course, some exceptions) rather than just the very common. New mysteries frequently identify the sleuth on the cover, even if it is his or her first appearance. Another trend is the publication in hardcover of later titles in series that were started in paperback.

POLICE DETECTIVES

Police procedurals are a large component in the bibliography of the detective novel. (The French term *romans policier* appears frequently in works on the detective story.) The detective of the story usually belongs to an actual named police department, although all personnel are fictional. Scotland Yard, the Sûreté, and the police departments of New York, Los Angeles, and San Francisco are the most common. However, many writers in England use the local police in areas outside London, inventing a rural town or using one of the larger cities, such as Oxford. Authors in the United States gain a distinctively regional tone by using cities or small towns other than New York, Los Angeles, or San Francisco. British and American writers also use countries other than Great Britain or the United States to provide an exotic setting. As the following listing by country indicates, there are fewer police procedurals from foreign countries (at least those that are available in translation) than there are from Great Britain and the United States.

The detective in the police procedural must function within the rules of the police department; he or she lacks the freedom of the private detective. Although the pattern may vary because of the personality of the detective, most police detectives work as part of a team (as opposed to the private detective, who is often a loner). Two plot patterns are common. One uses a single murder (or several linked murders) or mystery for the basic plot. The other, in effect, uses the police blotter: every case followed up by the police station staff is observed in varying degrees, although one case is the key focus of detection, and, often, the other cases are ingeniously linked to the main crime.

As a type, the police detective may seem circumscribed in character by the very nature of police procedures. Nevertheless, writers of police procedurals have been able to create detectives with interesting, often eccentric, personalities so that the readers eagerly follow their cases in book after book. The police detective may be an educated gentleman or a street-wise tough, or fall into a wide range of variations in between. Regional, class, and ethnic backgrounds allow for intriguing diversity in the types of detectives. A welcome addition to the ranks of fictional police detectives has been women; several are noted in the following list.

The following authors are listed by the country to which the police detective belongs. Great Britain is further subdivided; there are several series about the Bow Street Runners, the early-nineteenth-century precursors of Scotland Yard; and Scotland Yard detectives are grouped separately from those in the rest of Great Britain. Under the United States heading, the grouping is by state (note that crime thrives in California and New York).

Australia
Cleary, Jon (Detective Sergeant Scobie Malone)

McNab, Claire (Detective Inspector Carol Ashton, lesbian)

Upfield, Arthur (Inspector Napoleon "Bony" Bonaparte, half-aborigine)

Brabt (Fictional European state)
Rathbone, Julian (Commissioner Jan Argand)

Brazil
Fish, Robert L. (Captain José da Silva)

Canada
Craig, Alisa (Madoc Rhys, Royal Canadian Mounted Police)

Gough, Laurence (Detectives Jack Willows and Claire Parker, Vancouver)

Reeves, John (Inspector Andrew Coggin and Sergeant Fred Stemp, Toronto)

Sale, Medora (Detective Inspector John Sanders, Toronto)

Wood, Ted (Reid Bennett, Murphy's Harbor, Ontario)

Wright, Eric (Charlie Salter, Toronto)

Wright, L. R. (Staff Sergeant Karl Aberg, Royal Canadian Mounted Police, British Columbia)

Young, Scott (Inspector Matteesie, Royal Canadian Mounted Police)

China
Van Gulik, Robert (Judge Dee, seventh century)

Czechoslovakia
Skvorecky, Josef (Lieutenant Boruvka)

Denmark
Nielsen, Torben (Superintendent Archer)

Orum, Poul (Detective Inspector Jonas Morck, Copenhagen)

Finland

Joensuu, Matti (Detective Timo Harjunpaa, SUOPO)

France

Audemars, Pierre (Inspector Pinaud, Sûreté)

Freeling, Nicolas (Henri Castang)

Grayson, Richard (Inspector Gautier, Sûreté)

Hebden, Mark (Inspector Evariste Clovis Désiré Pel, Burgundy)

Jacquemard, Yves, and Jean-Michel Sénécal (Superintendent Dullac)

McConnor, Vincent (Francois Vidocq, founder of Sûreté, nineteenth century)

Simenon, Georges (Inspector Maigret)

Simpson, Howard R. (Inspector Roger Bastide)

Germany

Gerson, Jack (Inspector Ernst Lohman)

Kirst, Hans Hellmut (Anton Keller, CID, Munich)

Great Britain—Bow Street Runners

Falkirk, Richard (Edmund Blackstone)

Foxall, Raymond (Harry Adkins)

Jeffreys, J. G. (Jeremy Sturrock)

SeBastian, Margaret (Ned Denning)

Great Britain—Scotland Yard

Allen, Michael (Detective Chief Superintendent Ben Spence)

Ashe, Gordon (Patrick Dawlish, freelance before joins the Yard)

Barnard, Robert (Superintendent Percy Trethowan and Superintendent Sutcliffe)

Butler, Gwendoline (Inspector Coffin)

Clark, Douglas (Superintendent Masters and Inspector Green)

Crisp, N. J. (Detective Inspector Kenyon)

Crofts, Freeman Wills (Inspector Joseph French)

Crombie, Deborah (Superintendent Duncan Kincaid and Sergeant Gemma James)

Deighton, Len (Detective Inspector Douglas Archer, SS-GB)

Dickinson, Peter (Inspector James Pibble)

Gardner, John (Detective Inspector Derek Torry)

Garve, Andrew (Chief Inspector Charles Grant)

Grimes, Martha (Detective Superintendent Richard Jury and amateur Melrose Plant)

Hare, Cyril (Inspector Mallett)

Harrison, Ray (Sergeant Bragg and James Morton, London City Police, 1890s)

Heyer, Georgette (Chief Inspectors Hannasyde and Hemingway)

Hill, Peter (Chief Superintendent Robert Staunton and Detective Inspector Leo Wyndsor)

Hilton, John Buxton (Inspector Kenworthy)

Hunter, Alan (Chief Superintendent George Gently)

Inchbald, Peter (Francis Corti, Art and Antiques Squad)

Innes, Michael (Inspector, later Sir John Appleby, and also in retirement)

James, P. D. (Commander Adam Dalgliesh)

Jones, Elwyn (Detective Chief Superintendent Barlow)

Kenyon, Michael (Inspector Henry Peckover)

Lemarchand, Elizabeth (Detective Inspector Tom Pollard and Inspector Gregory Toye)

Lewis, Roy (Inspector Crow)

Lovesey, Peter (Sergeant Cribb and Constable Thackeray, nineteenth century)

Marric, J. J. (Commander George Gideon)

Marsh, Ngaio (Inspector Roderick Alleyn)

Martin, Ian Kennedy (Inspector Jack Regan)

MacKenzie, Donald (Detective Inspector Raven, retired)

Moyes, Patricia (Chief Superintendent Henry Tibbett and his wife Emmy)

Ormerod, Roger (Detective Harry Kyle)

Perry, Anne (Inspector Pitt, nineteenth century)

Selwyn, Francis (Sergeant Verity, nineteenth century)

Smith, D. W. (Harry Fathers)

Stubbs, Jean (Inspector Lintott, nineteenth century)

Symons, Julian (Inspector Bland)

Tey, Josephine (Inspector Alan Grant)

Wainwright, John (Chief Inspector Lennox)

Winslow, Pauline (Superintendent Merle Capricorn and Inspector Copper)

Parodies of Scotland Yard
Giles, Kenneth (Inspector Harry James and Sergeant Honeybody)

Porter, Joyce (Inspector Dover)

Great Britain—Other Than Scotland Yard
Aird, Catherine (Inspector Sloan)

Anderson, J. R. L. (Chief Constable Pier Deventer)

Ashford, Jeffrey (Detective Inspector Don Kerry)

Atkins, Meg Elizabeth (Chief Inspector Henry Beaumont)

Barnard, Robert (Chief Inspector Meredith, Superintendent Ian Dundy)

Beaton, M. C. (Constable Hamish MacBeth, Scotland)

Burley, W. J. (Chief Superintendent Wycliffe)

Cork, Barry (Angus Straun)

Dexter, Colin (Chief Inspector Morse, Oxford)

Eccles, Marjorie (Inspector Mayo)

Evans, Geraldine (Detective Inspector Rafferty and Sergeant Llewellyn)

Fraser, Anthea (Chief Inspector David Webb)

Geddes, Paul (Ludovic Fender)

George, Elizabeth (Inspector Thomas Lynley)

Gilbert, Michael (Chief Superintendent Charlie Knott)

Graham, Caroline (Chief Inspector Tom Barnaby)

Granger, Ann (Chief Inspector Markby and former Foreign Service Officer Meredith Mitchell)

Greenwood, Jack (Inspector Mosley and Sergeant Beamish, Lancashire)

Hart, Roy (Inspector Roper)

Haymon, S. T. (Detective Inspector Benjamin Jurnet)

Hill, Reginald (Superintendent Dalziel and Sergeant Pascoe)

Hilton, John Buxton (Inspector Pickford, Detective Brunt, and Sergeant Nadin, Derbyshire, nineteenth century)

James, Bill (Chief Superintendent Colin Harpur)

King, Pauline (Detective Inspector Evan Morgan)

Knox, Bill (Colin Thane and Phil Moss, Glasgow; Webb Carrick, Fishery Protection Service)

McGowan, Jill (Detective Chief Inspector Lloyd and Sergeant Judy Hall)

McIlvanney, William (Detective Inspector Laidlaw, Glasgow)

Melville, Jennie (Sergeant Charmain Daniels)

Murray, Stephen (Alec Stainton)

Penn, John (Detective Superintendent George Thorne and Sergeant Abbott, the Cotswolds)

Peters, Ellis (Detective Inspector George Felse)

Radley, Sheila (Chief Inspector Douglas Quantrill, Suffolk)

Rankin, Ian (Inspector John Rebus, Edinburgh)

Rendell, Ruth (Chief Inspector Wexford and Inspector Borden)

Robinson, Peter (Chief Inspector Alan Banks)

Ross, Jonathan (Detective Superintendent George Rogers)

Ruell, Patrick (Detective Inspector Dog Cicero)

Scott, Jack S. (Detective Sergeant Rosher, Detective Chief Inspector Peter Parsons, and Sergeant Wammo Wimbrush)

Simpson, Dorothy (Inspector Thanet, Kent)

Stacey, Susannah (Superintendent Bone)

Thomson, June (Detective Inspector Finch: in U.S. editions, Detective Inspector Rudd)

Turnbull, Peter (Police Constable Phil Hamilton, Detective Roy Sussock)

Watson, Colin (Inspector Purbright and Miss Teatime)

Webster, Noah (Jonathan Gaunt, Treasury agent; Andrew Laird)

Whitehead, Barbara (Police Inspectors Dave Smart and Bob Southwell, York)

Hong Kong

Konkel, K. G. E. (*The Glorious East Wind*)

Marshall, William (Chief Harry Pfeiffer)

Sela, Owen (Chief Inspector Chan)

India

Keating, Henry R. F. (Inspector Ghote, Bombay)

Ireland

Brady, John (Inspector Matt Minogue)

Gill, Bartholomew (Chief Inspector Peter McGarr, Dublin)

Kenyon, Michael (Detective Superintendent O'Malloy)

Israel

Gur, Batya (Detective Michael Ohayon, Jerusalem)

Klinger, Henry (Captain Shomri Shomar)

Rosenberg, Robert (Avram Cohen, head of the Jerusalem District Criminal Investigations Department)

Italy

Dibdin, Michael (Aurelio Zen)

Fruttero, Carlo, and Franco Lucentini (Inspector De Palma, Turin)

Holme, Timothy (Achille Peroni, Venice)

Leon, Donna (Commissarrio Guido Brunetti, Venice)

Nabb, Magdalen (Marshal Guarnaccia, Florence)

Quinn, Simon (Francis Xavier Killy, Inquisitor series, investigator for the Vatican)

Williams, Timothy (Commissario Trotti)

Japan

Melville, James (Superintendent Otani, Tokyo)

Van de Wetering, Janwillem (Inspector Saito, Kyoto)

Luong (Fictional Southeast Asian Kingdom)
Alexander, Gary (Superintendent Bamsan Kiet)

Mexico

Blanc, Suzanne (Inspector Menendes, Indian, *The Green Stone*)

Netherlands

Baantjer, Albert (*Dekok and the Dead Harlequin. Murder in Amsterdam*)

Freeling, Nicolas (Inspector Van der Valk)

Van de Wetering, Janwillem (Detective Grijpstra and Detective Sergeant de Grier)

New Zealand

Mantell, Laurie (Chief Inspector Peacock and Detective Steven Arrow)

Norway

Barnard, Robert (Inspector Fagermo, *Death in a Cold Climate*)

South Africa

McClure, James (Lieutenant Tromp Kramer, Afrikaner and Detective Sergeant Zondi, Bantu)

Spain

Jeffries, Roderic (Inspector Enrique Alverez, Majorca)

Serafin, David (Superintendent Louis Bernal, Madrid)

Sweden

Blom, K. Arne (*The Moment of Truth, The Limits of Pain*)

Hogstrand, Olle (Chief Inspector Lars Kollin)

Hubert, Tord (*Trap*)

Sjöwall, Maj, and Per Wahlöö (Martin Beck)

Switzerland

Campbell, R. Wright (Inspector Yves Faucon)

United States

Alabama
Cook, Thomas H. (Ben Wellman)

Arizona
Garfield, Brian (Sam Watchman, Navajo, Arizona Highway Patrol)

Hillerman, Tony (Lieutenant Joe Leaphorn and Jim Chee, Navajo Tribal Police)

Arkansas
Hess, Joan (Chief Arly Hanks)

California
Ball, John (Virgil Tibbs, black, Pasadena)

Bass, Milton (Benjamin Friedman, San Diego)

Boucher, Anthony (Lieutenant Jackson, Los Angeles)

Campbell, Robert (Eddie Heath, Wilbur Monk, Los Angeles)

Connelly, Michael (Detective Harry Bosch, Los Angeles)

Crowe, John (Sheriff Beckett, Buena Costa)

Cunningham, E. V. (Masao Masuto, Nisei, Beverly Hills)

Davis, Robert (Harry Edwards, Los Angeles)

Dunlap, Susan (Detective Jill Smith, Berkeley)

Dunne, John Gregory (Tom Spellacy, Los Angeles, *True Confessions*)

Egan, Lesley (Detective Varallo, Glendale)

Ellroy, James (Sergeant Lloyd Hopkins, Los Angeles)

Gillis, Jackson (Jonas Duncan, Los Angeles, retired)

Harris, Alfred (Baroni, Southern California)

Kellerman, Faye (Peter and Rina Lazarus, Los Angeles)

Lantique, John (San Francisco)

La Pierre, Janet (Vince Guttierez)

Lewis, Lange (Detective Tucker, Los Angeles, *The Birthday Murder*)

Linington, Elizabeth (Sergeant Maddox, Hollywood)

Ludwig, Jerry (Detective Sergeant Edward Brenner, Los Angeles)

Montecino, Marcel (Los Angeles)

Oster, Jerry (Lieutenant Sam Branch and Jeff Derry)

Petievich, Gerald (Charles Carr and Jack Kelly, U.S. Treasury Agents, Los Angeles)

Pike, Robert L. (Lieutenant Jim Reardon, San Francisco)

Pronzini, Bill (John Quincannon, Federal Secret Service, San Francisco, 1890s)

Ray, Robert (Newport Beach)

Shannon, Dell (Lieutenant Luis Mendoza and Delia Reardon, Los Angeles)

Wallace, Marilyn (Sergeant Carlo Cruz and Jay Goldstein, Oakland)

Wambaugh, Joseph (Los Angeles Police Department)

Westbrook, Robert (Nicky Rachmaninoff, Beverly Hills)

Weston, Carolyn (Detective Casey Kellog and Sergeant Al Krug, Santa Monica)

Wilcox, Collin (Lieutenant Hastings, San Francisco)

Colorado
Burns, Rex (Gabriel Wager, Chicano, Denver)

Paulsen, Gary (Ed Tincker, Denver)

Connecticut
Forrest, Richard (Detective Tommy Lark)

Skedgell, Marian (Lieutenant Dave Littlejohn, State Trooper)

Waugh, Hillary (Police Chief Fred Fellows)

Florida
King, Rufus (Stuff Driscoll)

Leonard, Elmore (Lieutenant Vincent Mora, Miami)

Willeford, Charles (Sergeant Hoke Moseley, Miami)

Georgia
Cook, Thomas H. (Clemons, Atlanta)

Hawaii
Biggers, Earl Derr (Inspector Charlie Chan, Honolulu)

Indiana
Lewin, Michael Z. (Lieutenant Leroy Powder, Indianapolis)

Illinois
Bland, Eleanor Taylor (Marti MacAlister and Vik Jessenovik, Lincoln Prairie)

Blank, Martin (John Lamp, Chicago)

Campbell, Robert (Jimmy Flannery, sewer inspector)

Cormay, Michael (Kruger, Chicago)

Di Pego, Gerald (Chicago)

Kaminsky, Stuart M. (Sergeant Abe Lieberman, Chicago)

Pulver, Mary Monica (Sergeant Peter Brichter)

Kansas
Weir, Charlene (Police Chief Susan Wren, Hampstead)

Louisiana (all have New Orleans locales or connections)
Burke, James Lee (Dave Robicheaux)

Colbert, James (Skinny)

Corrington, John William (Rat Trapp)

Smith, Julie (Skip Langdon)

Massachusetts
Burke, Alan Dennis (Assistant District Attorney Jack Meehan, Boston)

Dunham, Dick (Sergeant Joe Knight, Boston)

Langton, Jane (Homer Kelly, retired detective)

McDonald, Gregory (Inspector Francis Xavier Flynn, Boston)

Rennert, Maggie (Detective Lieutenant Guy Silvestri, Buxford)

Michigan
Jackson, Jon A. (Sergeant Mulheisen, Detroit)

Minnesota
Hinkemeyer, Michael T. (Sheriff Emil Whippletree)

McInerny, Ralph (Sheriff Oscar Ewbank)

Montana
Guthrie, A. B. (Sheriff Chick Charleston and Jason Beard)

Hugo, Dick (*Death and the Good Life*)

New Jersey
Kent, Bill (Louis Monroe, Atlantic City)

New Mexico
Hillerman, Tony (Lieutenant Joe Leaphorn and Jim Chee, Navajo Tribal
   Police)

Stern, Richard Martin (Lieutenant Johnny Ortiz, Apache)

New York (New York City unless otherwise noted)
Arrighi, Mel (Detective Romano)

Bagby, George (Inspector Schmidt)

Baxt, George (Pharoah Love, African-American; Detective Van Larsen)

Boyle, Thomas (De Sales)

Caspary, Vera (Mark McPherson, *Laura*)

Caunitz, William J. (Gallegher)

Charyn, Jerome (Isaac Sidel)

Chastain, Thomas (Deputy Chief Inspector Max Kauffman)

Cunningham, E. V. (Lieutenant Harry Golding and his wife Fran)

Delman, David (Lieutenant Jacob Horowitz, Nassau County)

Early, Jack (Police Chief Waldo Halleck, Long Island)

Heffernan, William (Stanislaus Polk)

Hentoff, Nat (Detective Noah Green)

Himes, Chester (Coffin Ed Johnson and Grave Digger Jones, Harlem)

Horansky, Ruby (Nikki Trakos, Brooklyn)

Jahn, Michael (Donovan)

Katz, William (Detective Leonard Anthony Karlov)

Leuci, Bob (Detective Alexander Simon)

Lieberman, Herbert (Lieutenant Frank Mooney)

Lockridge, Richard (Captain Heinrich, State Police; Lieutenant Nathan Shapiro)

McBain, Ed (Steve Carella, 87th Precinct)

Minahan, John ("Little John" Rawlings)

Newman, Christopher (Lieutenant Joe Dante)

O'Donnell, Lillian (Norah Mulcahany; Detective Ed Stiebeck and Mici Anhalt)

Paul, Barbara (Detective Marian Larch and Lieutenant Murtaugh)

Reilly, Helen (Inspector McKee)

Rifkin, Shepard (Detective Damian McQuaid)

Sanders, Lawrence (Edward X. Delaney, retired Chief of Detectives)

Uhnak, Dorothy (Detective Christie Opara and Detective Miranda Torres)

Waugh, Hillary (Detective Fred Sessions)

North Carolina
Malone, Michael (Chief Cudbarth Mangum)

Ohio
Leeke, Jim

Pyle, A. M. (Cesar Frank, Cincinnati)

Oklahoma
Cooper, Susan Rogers (Milt Kovack)

Hager, Jean (Chief Mitch Bushyhead)

Pennsylvania
Constantine, K. C. (Chief of Police Mario Balzic, Rocksburg)

Texas
Cooley, Marilyn, and James Edward Gunn (Tony McIver, Houston)

Crider, Bill (Sheriff Don Rhodes)

Lindsey, David L. (Stuart Haydon, Houston)

Martin, Lee (Policewoman Deb Ralston, Fort Worth)

Wingate, Anne (Mark Shigata, Bayport)

Utah
Levitt, J. R. (Jason Coulter, Salt Lake City)

Vermont
Koenig, Joseph

Mayor, Archer (Lieutenant Joe Gunther, Brattleboro)

Washington
Beck, K. K. (Seattle)

Emerson, Earl (Mac Fontana, fire chief)

West Virginia
Douglas, John (Detective Edward Harter, Shawnee)

U. S. S. R.

Hill, Reginald (Inspector Lev Chislenko, Moscow)

Kaminsky, Stuart (Inspector Rostnikov, Moscow)

Litvinov, Ivy (*His Master's Voice*, Moscow, first published 1930, revised 1973)

Smith, Martin Cruz (Chief Homicide Investigator Arkady Renko)

West Indies

York, Andrew (Colonel James Munroe Tallant, black police commissioner, Caribbean island)

Yugoslavia

Wright, Campbell R. (*Honor*)

PRIVATE DETECTIVES

The official private detective is one of two types—the employee of a large agency or a lone operator (sometimes duos; sometimes women). Dashiell Hammett created two immortal prototypes: the Continental Op, simply identified for his agency and never named, and Sam Spade, a detective who strikes out on his own after his partner is killed in *The Maltese Falcon*. Sam Spade is also the prototype for the hard-boiled private eye, a type often short on morals but long on integrity. Although not officially labeled private detectives, other investigators function as such because of the demands of their occupations—insurance investigators, reporters, psychiatrists, public relations men, and bankers (lawyers and doctors also qualify and are grouped separately in later sections). Except for the insurance investigators, these job-related detectives could be considered amateur detectives. The distinction is not vital to most readers—what they want is an investigator who acts like a private detective. Readers who prefer the inquisitive amateur detective may like some of those in the following list, at least those non-official private investigators that act more like amateurs than private detectives.

Argentina
Borges, Jorge Luis (Don Isidro Parodi, *Six Problems of Don Isidro Parodi*)

Australia
Corris, Peter (Cliff Hardy)

Day, Marele (Claudia Valentine)

Canada
Engel, Howard (Benny Cooperman)

Ritchie, Simon (J. K. G. Jantarro, one-armed)

France
Demouzon, Alain (Robert Flecheux)

Great Britain
Bush, Christopher (Ludovic Travers, insurance investigator)

Butler, Ragan (Captain Nash, eighteenth century)

Christie, Agatha (Tuppence and Tommy Beresford; Hercule Poirot)

Cody, Liza (Anna Lee, London)

Creasey, John (Emmanuel Cellini, psychiatrist)

Doyle, Sir Arthur Conan (Sherlock Holmes)

Fredman, Mike (Willie Halliday, vegetarian and Buddhist)

Geddes, Paul (Ludovic Fender)

James, P. D. (Cordelia Gray, *An Unsuitable Job for a Woman*)

Kavanagh, Dan (Duffy)

Kirk, Michael (Andrew Laird, insurance investigator)

Milne, John (Jimmy Jenner, London)

Tripp, Miles (John Sampson and Shandy)

Wentworth, Patricia (Miss Maude Silver)

Whalley, Peter (Harry Somers)

Yuill, P. B. (James Hazell)

Mexico
Alexander, Gary (Louis Balam, Mayan Indian)

Taibo, Paco Ignacio, II (Hector Belascoaran Shayne)

United States

Alaska
Stabenow, Dana (Kate Shugak, former District Attorney)

California
Alverson, Charles (Joe Goodey, San Francisco)

Babula, William (Jeremiah St. John)

Boucher, Anthony (Fergus O'Breen, Los Angeles)

Byrd, Max (Mike Haller, San Francisco)

Campbell, Robert (Whistler)

Chandler, Raymond (Philip Marlowe, Los Angeles)
  Chandler, like Hammett, wrote only a few novels (seven, the first in 1939) and short stories, but these established his detective, Philip Marlowe, as a standard aspired to by later writers. Marlowe is the loner, white knight, tough private eye whose personality dominates the novels. Chandler is notable for his image-laden style and for the portrayal, cherished by Angelenos, of Los Angeles and its environs in the thirties. (Chandler's critical essays on detective fiction are listed in the section on criticism.) Marlowe is a private investigator who will not die. He was resurrected in 1989 in *Poodle Springs*, a book Chandler started and Robert B. Parker completed. *Perchance to Dream*, written by Parker, is a sequel to *The Big Sleep*.

Crais, Robert (Elvis Cole)

Cutler, Stan (Rayford Goodman)

Dawson, Janet (Jeri Howard, Oakland)

Dunlap, Susan (Kiernan O'Shaugnessy, Hollywood)

Gault, William (Brock Callahan, former guard, Los Angeles Rams)

Gores, Joe (Neal Fargo; Daniel Kearny Associates, skip-tracing agency)

Grafton, Sue (Kinsey Millhone)

Greenleaf, Stephen (John Marshall Tanner, San Francisco)

Hammett, Dashiell (The Continental Op; Sam Spade; Nick Charles)
  Five novels (the first in 1930) and over 70 short stories made Hammett the great name for the American hard-boiled private eye tradition. (A personal opinion: the Continental Op is *the* master creation in the U.S. hard-boiled detective story.) Fans have organized a three-mile Dashiell Hammett Walking Tour in San Francisco. The members of another group, Continental Detective Agency, hold an annual caper, members garbed in twenties-style clothing.

Hansen, Joseph (David Brandstetter, insurance investigator, homosexual)

Israel, Peter (B. F. Cage, Los Angeles)

Kaminsky, Stuart (Toby Peters, Los Angeles)

Kennealy, Jerry (Nick Polo)

Larson, Charles (Blixon, television executive, Los Angeles)

Lochte, Dick (Leo G. Bloodworth, Los Angeles)

Lupoff, Richard A. (insurance investigator Hobart Lindsey and Marvia Plum, police officer)

Lyons, Arthur (Jacob Asch, Los Angeles)

Macdonald, Ross (Lew Archer, Santa Barbara)

Maxwell, A. E. (Fiddler)

Mosley, Walter (Easy Rawlins, Los Angeles)

Muller, Marcia (Sharon McCone, San Francisco)

Pierce, David M. (Vic Daniel, San Fernando Valley)

Platt, Kin (Max Roper, Los Angeles)

Prather, Richard S. (Shell Scott, Los Angeles)

Pronzini, Bill (Nameless detective, San Francisco)

Ray, Robert J. (Matt Murdock)

Roberts, Les (Saxon)

Sadler, Mark (Paul Shaw, Los Angeles)

Sangster, Jimmy (James Reed)

Simon, Roger L. (Moses Wine, Los Angeles)

Singer, Shelley (Jake Samson and Rosie)

Upton, Robert (Amos McGuffin, Los Angeles)

Wager, Walter (Alison Gordon, Los Angeles)

Walker, Walter (Hector Gronig, San Francisco)

Washburn, L. J. (Lucas Hallam)

Colorado
Allegretto, Michael (Jake Lomax)

Burns, Rex (Devlin Kirk)

Downing, Warwick (Joe Reddman, Cheyenne, Denver)

District of Colombia
Grady, James (John Rankin)

Law, Janice (Anna Peters)

Pelecanos, George P. (Nick Stefanos)

Schutz, Benjamin B. (Leo Haggerty)

Sucher, Dorothy (Victor Newman)

Florida
Halleran, Tucker (Cam Maccardle)

Lutz, John (Fred Carver, physically handicapped)

MacDonald, John D. (Travis McGee)

Illinois
Brown, Fredric (Ed and Am Hunter, Chicago)

Dewey, Thomas B. (Mac, Chicago)

McConnell, Frank (Harry Garnish)

Paretsky, Sara (V. I. Warshawski)

Raleigh, Michael (Paul Whelan, Chicago)

Spencer, Ross H. (Kirby; Willow; Luke Lassiter; Chance Purdue)

Indiana
Lewin, Michael Z. (Albert Samson, Indianapolis)

Louisiana
Donaldson, D. J. (Dr. Kit Franklin, criminal psychologist, and Chief
    Medical Examiner Andy Broussard)

Shuman, M. K. (Micah Dunn, one-armed)

Wiltz, Chris (Neal Rafferty)

Massachusetts
Barnes, Linda (Carlotta Carlyle; Michael Spraggue, Boston)

Coxe, George Harmon (Jack Fenner, Boston; Ken Murdock, photographer)

David, Daniel (Alex Rasmussen, Lowell)

Doolittle, Jerome (Tom Bethany)

Kiker, Douglas (Mac McFarland)

Parker, Robert B. (Spenser, Boston)

Rosen, Richard (Blissberg)

Ross, Philip (James Marley)

Michigan
Bunn, Thomas (Jack Bodine)

Estleman, Loren D. (Ralph Poteet; Amos Walker, Detroit)

Leonard, Elmore (Frank Ryan, process server, Detroit)

Werry, Richard (J. D. Mulroy and Ahmad Dakar, African American)

Missouri
Lutz, John (Alo Nudger, St. Louis)

Montana
Crumley, James (Sughrue and Milo Milodragovitch)

Prowell, Sandra West (Phoebe Siegel)

Nebraska
Reynolds, William J. (Nebraska)

New Jersey
Gallison, Kate (Nick Magaracz, Trenton)

New Mexico
Brewer, Steve (Bubba Mabry)

Zollinger, Norman (Jack Lautrec)

New York
Beinhart, Larry (Tony Cassella)

Berger, Thomas (Russel Wren)

Block, Lawrence (Matthew Scudder)

Box, Edgar (Peter Cutler Sargent III, public relations). Reprints of the Box
   novels now reveal the author's real name, Gore Vidal.

Burke, J. F. (Sam Kelly, house detective, African American)

Chesbro, George C. (Dr. Robert "Mongo" Frederickson, Ph.D., little
   person)

Coe, Tucker (Mitch Tobin, museum night guard)

Coffey, Brian (Harris, clairvoyant)

Cohen, Stephen Paul (Eddie Margolis)

Collins, Michael (Dan Fortune, one-armed)

Cook, Thomas H. (Frank Clemons)

Daly, Elizabeth (Henry Gamadge, rare book investigator)

DeAndrea, William (Matt Cobb, television troubleshooter)

Dobyns, Stephen (Charles Bradshaw, Saratoga)

Friedman, Kinky (Kinky Friedman)

Geller, Michael (Reznick)

Hall, Parnell (Stanley Hastings)

Jeffers, H. Paul (Harry MacNeil)

Kaplan, Arthur (Charity Bay)

Kaye, Marvin (Hilary Quayle, public relations)

Livingston, Jack (Joe Binney, deaf)

Lundy, Mike (Raven)

Mason, Clifford (Joe Cinquez, African American, Harlem)

Pentecost, Hugh (Julian Quist, public relations)

Randisi, Robert J. (Miles Jacoby)

Resnicow, Herbert (Norma and Alexander Gold)

Rosten, Leo (Sidney "Silky" Pincus)

Schorr, Mark (Red Diamond)

Scoppettone, Sandra (Lauren Laurano)

Smith, J. C. S. (Quentin Jacoby)

Solomita, Stephen (Stanley Moodrow)

Spillane, Mickey (Mike Hammer)

Stout, Rex (Nero Wolfe and Archie Goodwin)

Tidyman, Ernest (John Shaft, African American)

Vachss, Andrew (Burke)

Ohio
Roberts, Les (Milan Jacovich)

Valin, Jonathan (Harry Stoner, Cincinnati)

Oklahoma
Knickmeyer, Steve (Steve Cranmer, Oklahoma City)

Oregon
Wren, M. K. (Conan Flagg)

South Dakota
Adams, Harold (Carl Wilcox)

Texas
Abshire, Richard (Jack Kyle)

Mathis, Edward (Dan Roman, Dallas)

Utah
Irvine, R. R. (Moroni Traveler)

Virginia
Hornig, Doug (Loren Swift, Charlottesville)

Washington
Beck, K. K. (Jane da Silva, Seattle)

Emerson, Earl W. (Thomas Black, Seattle)

Hoyt, Richard (John Denson, Seattle)

EX-COP

Former police officers now working as private investigators is a subgenre that offers the best of both major types of sleuths. The investigator has an autonomy and independence that is not possible within the confines of an official law enforcement agency while, at the same time, he or she can believably display a knowledge and use of police procedures. Some of the following sleuths are also listed in the section on police detectives (see pp. 53-65), as they played the role of police detectives in their earlier books.

Abshire, Richard (Jack Kyle)

Barnes, Linda (Carlotta Carlyle)

Block, Lawrence (Matthew Scudder)

Burke, James Lee (Dave Robicheaux)

Cook, Bruce (Chico Cervantes)

Craig, Philip R. (Jeff Jackson)

Daniel, David (Alex Rasmussen)

Dobyns, Stephen (Charlie Bradshaw)

Geller, Michael (Slots Resnick)

Gillis, Jackson (Jonas Duncan)

Haddam, Jane (Gregor Demarkian)

Love, William F. (Davey Goldman)

Lutz, John (Fred Carver, physically handicapped)

Margolis, Seth Jacob (Joe Di Gregorio)

Pendleton, Don (Joe Copp)

Raleigh, Michael (Paul Whelan)

Solomita, Stephen (Stanley Moodrow)

Wambaugh, Joseph (Winnie Farlowe)

Wesley, Valerie Wilson (Tamara Hayle)

West, Charles (movie stuntman, former Australian Detective Superintendent)

Whittingham, Richard (Joe Morrison)

COMEDY AND PARODY

Humorous Private Eye
The ranks of witty, sardonic, and comic private eyes could be extended at great length. In the following books, crime or murder is treated lightly.

Fair, A. A. (Donald Lam and Bertha Cool)

Page, Marco (Joel Glass)

Rice, Craig (Jake Malone, lawyer)

Parody
Because of the eccentric personal characteristics that make the individual detective memorable, and because of the subgenre's formula conventions, the detective is easily parodied. (For parodies of Sherlock Holmes and Lord Peter Wimsey, see pp. 89-90 of "Immortal Investigations.") Some fictional detectives are so eccentric as to become unintentional parodies of the type. The following examples are intentional. (See also the section on parody under detective story criticism.)

Berger, Thomas. *Who Is Teddy Villanova?*

Brautigan, Richard. *Dreaming of Babylon.*

Spencer, Ross H. (Chance Purdue)
The epigraphs are inspired lunacy.

AMATEUR DETECTIVES

Amateur detectives appear in every walk of life. The amateur detective may simply be nosy, becoming inquisitively involved in mysteries natural to the amateur's ordinary life. Others are in somewhat unusual occupations. Most have their share of eccentricities. Unlike either the police or private investigators, they have no official responsibilities. Indeed, they are often an annoyance to the police. Their means of investigation are limited, though they often work cooperatively with the police. Women are often portrayed as amateur detectives, with the curious spinster being a stereotype (additional examples are found in the later section on women detectives, p. 84).

Retirees with extra time on their hands are an emerging subgenre of the amateur detective. In the following list of amateur detectives, occupations are noted. After the following list are lists by various groupings (e.g., senior citizens, doctor, lawyer, rogue, or thief).

Allbert, Susan Wittig (China Bayles, herb shop proprietor)

Allen, Rene (Elizabeth Elliot, clerk of a Quaker Meeting)

Asimov, Isaac (Henry, a waiter; Black Widowers series)

Barthelme, Peter (Beaumont, advertising)

Borland, John C. (Donald McCarry, stockbroker)

Breen, Jon L. (Jack Brogan, racetrack announcer, California)

Brett, Simon (Charles Paris, actor)

Delving, Michael (Dave Cannon and Bob Eddison, antiquarian dealers)

Dominic, R. B. (Ben Stafford, congressman)

Fennelly, Tony (Matt Sinclair, antiques dealer)

Ferrars, E. X. (Andrew Basnett, retired professor)

Foley, Rae (Hiram Potter, New York society figure)

Gash, Jonathan (Lovejoy, antiques dealer)

Gollin, James (Alan French, musician)

Hadley, Joan (Theo Bloomer, botanist)

Hammond, Gerald (Keith Calder, gunsmith, Scotland)

Holt, Samuel (Sam Holt, actor)

Kellerman, Jonathan (Alex Delaware, psychologist)

Lacey, Sarah (Leah Hunter, tax inspector)

Lathen, Emma (John Putnam Thatcher, banker)

Leasor, James (Dr. Jason Love, insurance investigator)

Leather, Edwin (Rupert Conway, art dealer)

Linscott, Gillian (Birdie Linnett)

Livingston, Nancy (G. D. H. Pringle and Mavis Bignell)

Malcolm, John (Tim Simpson, art investment advisor)

McCormick, Clair (John Wirtz, "headhunter")

McCrumb, Sharyn (Elizabeth MacPherson, anthropologist)

Moore, Barbara (Gordon Christy, veterinarian, New Mexico)

Morison, B. J. (Elizabeth Lamb, child)

Murray, William ("Shifty" Lou Anderson, gambler-magician, Los Angeles racetrack)

Orenstein, Frank (Ev Franklin, advertising)

Pentecost, Hugh (Pierre Chambrun, hotel manager)

Pickard, Nancy (Jenny Cain, administrator)

Pulver, Mary Monica (Kori Brichter, heiress)

Rowe, Jennifer (Verity Birdwood, Australian T. V. researcher)

Sprinkle, Patricia (Sheila Travis)

Sherwood, John (Celia Grant, botanist)

Sublett, Jesse (Martin Fender, R & B bass player)

Taylor, Phoebe Atwood (Asey Mayo, New Englander)

West, Charles (movie stuntman, former Australian Detective Superintendent)

Williams, David (Mark Treasure, banker)

Senior Citizen Sleuths

Active, inquisitive retired folks with time on their hands turn to solving crime. The prototype is of course Agatha Christie's Miss Jane Marple.

Babson, Marian (Trixie Dolan and Evangaline Sinclair, aging movie stars)

Barth, Richard (Margaret Binton, retired)

Comfort, B. (Tish McWinny, septuagenarian, Vermont)

Ferrars, E. X. (Andrew Basnett, retired professor)

Gray, Gallagher (T. S. Hubbert, retired Wall Street executive, and his octogenarian Aunt Lil)

Mancini, Anthony (Minnie Santangelo, elderly resident of New York's Little Italy)

Sawyer, Corinne Holt (Angela Benbow and Caledonia Wingate, widowed residents of a San Diego retirement home)

Doctor

The doctor is a natural amateur (as is the nurse) who is often involved with a suspicious or unnatural death. (Hospital backgrounds are often used effectively. A classic is Christianna Brand's Inspector Cockrill novel, *Green for Danger*. P. D. James also has used the background effectively in her Commander Dalgliesh series.) Psychologists, psychiatrists, and pathologists are included. In the following list (all are series), the doctor (or nurse) is the actual sleuth.

Bell, Josephine (Dr. David Wintringham)

Boyer, Rick (Doc Adams, oral surgeon)

Cornwell, Patricia D. (Kay Scarpetta, Chief Medical Examiner, Virginia)

Eberhart, Mignon Good (Nurse Sarah Keate)

Kellerman, Jonathan (Alex Delaware, psychologist)

Kittredge, Mary (Edwina Crusoe, R.N.)

McCloy, Helen (Dr. Basil Willing, forensic psychiatrist)

Rinehart, Mary Roberts (Nurse Adams, *Miss Pinkerton*)

White, Stephen Walsh (Dr. Alan Gregory, psychologist, Colorado)

Wyllie, John (Dr. Quarshie, black West African physician)

Zimmerman, Bruce (Quinn Parker, phobia therapist)

Lawyer
Lawyers might qualify more as private investigators than amateurs, as they seek to extricate clients from jeopardy. This type of detective story often features scenes of courtroom interrogation in which all is revealed, often dramatically. In some of the following books, the reader is treated to considerable analysis of the law, which is sometimes a bit confusing when the focus is on British jurisprudence. Jon Breen's bibliography *Novel Verdicts: A Guide to Courtroom Fiction* supplies this background information.

The legal thriller has achieved great prominence in the 1990s. Scott Turow, John Grisham, and Steve Martini all made it to the best-seller lists with their crime novels that feature lawyers. However, the legal thriller's emphasis is not necessarily on detection but rather on a crafty attorney's abilities to extricate him- or herself or others from danger. The legal thriller is covered later in this chapter (see p. 110).

Great Britain

Caudwell, Sarah (Professor Hilary Tamar, Oxford don and his inimitable Lincoln's Inn lawyer friends, including two delightful women lawyers, Julia Larwood and Selena Jardine)

Cecil, Henry
   The detection and mystery in this British author's novels are urban social comedy concerning both lawyers and judges. *Daughters in Law* features women lawyers.

Giroux, E. X. (Robert Forsythe)

Meek, M. R. D. (Lennox Kemp)

Mortimer, John (Horace Rumpole of the Bailey)

Underwood, Michael (Rose Epton, London)

Woods, Sara (Anthony Maitland)

United States

Deverell, William (Oliver Gulliver, *Platinum Blues*)

Egan, Lesley (Jesse Falkenstein, Los Angeles)

Gardner, Erle Stanley
> Over 80 novels (the first in 1933) celebrate Perry Mason with his aides, Paul Drake and Della Street. Gardner has written more than 100 volumes.

Fugate, Francis L., and Roberta B. Fugate
> *Secrets of the World's Best-Selling Writer: The Storytelling Techniques of Erle Stanley Gardner*. Morrow, 1980.

Hughes, Dorothy B.
> *Erle Stanley Gardner: The Case of the Real Perry Mason*.

Hailey, J. P. (Steve Winslow)

Hall, Parnell (Stanley Hastings, ambulance chaser)

Hensley, Joe L. (Don Robak)

Maron, Margaret (Deborah Knott, North Carolina)

Kruger, Paul (Phil Kramer, Colorado)

Lewis, Roy (Eric Ward, solicitor)

McBain, Ed (Matthew Hope, Florida)

McInerny, Ralph (Andrew Broom, Indiana)

Murphy, Haughton (Reuben Frost)

Nielsen, Helen (Simon Drake, Los Angeles)

Pairo, Preston (Dallas Henry, Ocean City, Maryland)

Phillips, Edward (Chadwick, homosexual)

Smith, Julie (Rebecca Schwartz, San Francisco)

Stockley, Grif (Gideon Page, Arkansas)

Tapply, William G. (Brady Coyne, Boston)

Yarbro, Chelsea Quinn (Charles Spotted Moon, Ojibwa, San Francisco)

Rogue or Thief

The tradition of rogue or thief as detective is so well established in detective novels that it nearly negates the status of amateur detectives. However, this is a convenient niche for listing the following books. Some private investigators skirt the fringes of roguery. The rogues in the following novels are all cheerfully amoral.

Block, Lawrence
Bernard Rhodenbarr is a burglar who runs a bookstore on the side. One of his adventures, *The Burglar Who Liked to Quote Kipling*, will intrigue those who like bibliography and rare books mixed with murder.

Bonfiglioli, Kyril (Honorable Charles Mortdecai, rogue)

Charteris, Leslie (Simon Templar, "The Saint," Robin Hood type)

Creasey, John (The honorable Richard Rollison, "The Toff," gentleman burglar, "The poor man's Lord Peter Wimsey")

Hoch, Edward D. (Nick Velvet, thief)

Hornung, E. W.
The exploits of Raffles, gentleman cracksman, have been continued by Barry Perowne.

Morton, Anthony
Reprints reveal the authorship by John Creasey, who used this pseudonym for the cases of John Mannering, "The Baron," jewel thief turned detective.

Parrish, Frank (Don Mallett, poacher, British)

Shaw, Simon (Philip Gletcher, actor and murderer)

Ecclesiastical
The souls of sinners are one of the responsibilities of the clergy, who often are concerned with proving innocence as well as with finding guilt. As the listing demonstrates, the practice of detection is open to all religious groups.

Chesterton, G. K. (Father Brown, Roman Catholic, British)

Eco, Umberto (Brother William of Baskerville, fourteenth century, *The Name of the Rose*)

Greeley, Andrew (Father Blackie Ryan)

Holmes, H. H. (Sister Mary Ursula, Order of the Sisters of Martha of Bethany, Los Angeles. Also reprinted under the better known pseudonym Anthony Boucher.)

Kemelman, Harry (Rabbi David Small, New England)

Kienzle, William X. (Father Bob Koesler, Roman Catholic, Detroit)

Love, William F. (Bishop Ragan)

McInerny, Ralph (Father Dowling, Roman Catholic, Chicago area)

O'Marie, Sister Carol Anne (Sister Mary Helen)

Peters, Ellis (Brother Cadfael, Benedictine monastery, Shrewsbury, twelfth century)

Quill, Monica (Sister Mary Teresa Dempster)

Smith, Charles (Reverend C. P. Randolph, Episcopal Church, Chicago)

Sullivan, Winona (Sister Cecile, licensed private investigator and nun)

English Aristocrat
That everyone loves a lord is a questionable truism, but many readers of detective stories are intrigued by the aristocrat as amateur detective. This detective is similar to the gentleman detective, whether as police or amateur: Ngaio Marsh's Inspector Roderick Alleyn, Michael Innes's Sir John Appleby, S. S. Van Dine's Philo Vance, and Frederic Dannay's Ellery Queen are a few examples. Members of the British aristocracy appear regularly in the British thriller, often as the corpse, and they are natural characters in the popular English "country-house mystery" (see p. 94). The following are notable aristocrat detectives.

Allingham, Margery (Albert Campion)

Dickinson, Peter (King of England, *King and Joker*)

George, Elizabeth (Inspector Thomas Linley, Eighth Earl of Asherton)

Ross, Kate (Julian Kestrel)

Sayers, Dorothy L. (Lord Peter Wimsey)

Academic
The section "College and University" (see p. 97) lists novels that have academic backgrounds, but the professors therein are not necessarily the detectives. The professors in the following novels use their scholarly training for crime detection, and not always on the campus. Eccentricity—that obvious characteristic of academics—is present in most.

Arnold, Margot (Penny Spring and Sir Toby Glendower)

Bruce, Leo (Carolus Deane, schoolteacher, London)

Clinton-Baddeley, V. C. (Dr. Davie, Cambridge don)

Cory, Desmond (Professor John Dobie)

Crispin, Edmund (Dr. Gervase Fen, Cambridge don)

Cross, Amanda (Dr. Kate Fansler, professor of English)

Dean, S. F. X. (Professor Neal Kelly)

Elkins, Aaron (Dr. Gideon Oliver, anthropologist)

Haynes, Conrad (Professor Bishop)

Kelly, Nora (Gillian Adams, professor of history)

Kemelman, Harry (Professor Nicky Welt)

Levi, Peter (Ben Johnson)

MacLeod, Charlotte (Professor Peter Shandy, New England)

Reeves, Robert (Professor Thomas Theron)

Smith, Joan (Loretta Lawson, London University lecturer)

Stinson, Jim (Stoney Wilson, film instructor)

Truman, Margaret (Mac Smith, law professor)

Journalists

The investigative reporter may also be considered a private detective (without license) and is often listed as a detective type in critical works on the genre. Books by the following authors illustrate this type.

Babson, Marian (Doug Perkins)

Beechcroft, William (Forrest)

Burke, Jan (Irene Kelly)

D'Amato, Barbara (Cat Marsala)

Gorman, Ed (Tobin)

Kiker, Douglas (Mac McFarland)

Lupica, Mike (Peter Finley, television newsman)

Phillips, Mike (Sampson Dean, African American)

Porter, Anna (Judith Hayes, reporter)

Riggs, John R. (Garth Ryland, newspaper editor and owner)

Robinson, Kevin (Stick Foster, wheelchair-bound reporter)

Shuman, M. K. (Pete Brady, Louisiana)

Stout, David (Will Schafer, newspaper editor)

Warmbold, Jean (Sarah Calloway)

Wilcox, Collin (Stephen Drake, crime reporter)

Wilcox, Stephen F. (T. S. W. Sheridan, freelance reporter)

Biblio-Mysteries

The world of books is a popular setting for thrillers. In the following books, the amateur sleuths are somehow involved in the world of books, whether as writers, illustrators, publishers, or booksellers.

Dunning, John (*Booked to Die*)

Goodrum, Charles (Edward George, Crighton Jones, and Steve Carson)

Hart, Carolyn G. (Annie Laurance and Max Darling, bookstore owner)

Heald, Tim (Simon Bognor, publisher)

Jordan, Jennifer (Mr. and Mrs. Barry Vaughan, writers)

Knight, Kathryn Lasky (Calista Jacobs, illustrator)

Papazoglou, Orania (Patience McKenna, writer)

Peters, Elizabeth (Jacqueline Kirby, romance writer)

Philbrick, W. R. (Jack Hawkins, wheelchair-bound mystery writer)

Richardson, Robert (Augustus Maltravers)

Shankman, Sarah (Samantha Adams, writer)

Sinclair, Murray (Ben Crandel, writer)

Husband-and-Wife Teams

The Dr. Watson figure is commonplace in detective fiction, and there are many variations on the amateur of either sex acting as a companion of a police detective. A combination of considerable charm is the married pair of sleuths. The increase in recent years of the importance of relationships in the lives of sleuths is evidenced by the increased number of paired significant others appearing on the following list.

Allen, Steve (Steve Allen and Jayne Meadows, *The Murder Game*)

Ames, Delano (Jane and Dogobert Brown)

Dank, Gloria (Bernard and Snooky Woodruff)

Ferrars, E. X. (Virginia and Felix Freer. They are divorced but still a pair of sleuths.)

Goulart, Ron (H. J. Mavity and her ex-husband, Ben Spanner)

Hammett, Dashiell (Nick and Nora Charles, *The Thin Man*)

Hammond, Gerald (Inspector Ian Fellows and wife Deborah)

Kellerman, Faye (Orthodox Jewish housewife Rina Lazarus and her husband LAPD Detective Sergeant Peter Decker)

Lockridge, Frances, and Richard Lockridge (Pam and Jerry North)

MacGregor, T. J. (Quin St. James and Mike McCleary)

Sandstrom, Eve K. (Sheriff Sam and wife Nicky Titus, Oklahoma)

Sayers, Dorothy L. (Lord Peter and Harriet, *Busman's Honeymoon*)

Truman, Margaret (Mac Smith and Annabel Reed)

Wilhelm, Kate (Charlie Meiklejohn and Constance Leidl)

Human-and-Animal Teams

Americans have a great affection and fascination with the pets in their lives. Several authors write about human sleuths or animal sleuths working together with the other species. The most famous team is probably that of

Qwilleran and his cats KoKo and YumYum in the series written by Lilian Jackson Braun.

Adamson, Lydia. Alice Nestleton cat mysteries—7 titles.

Braun, Lilian Jackson. The Cat Who series—17 titles as of 1994 (featuring Qwilleran, a human journalist, and KoKo and YumYum of the Siamese persuasion).

Brown, Rita Mae. (Mary Minor "Harry" Haristeen, postmistress, and feline Mrs. Murphy, with occasional assistance from canine Tee Tucker.)

Conant, Susan J. The Dog Lover's series (featuring Holly Winter and Alaskan malamutes Rowdy and Kimi). *Ruffly Speaking.*

Douglas, Carole Nelson. *Catnapped. Pussyfoot. Cat on a Blue Monday.* (Los Vegas publicist Miss Temple Barr and Midnight Louie, a studly big black cat.)

DETECTIVE BACKGROUNDS

Who a detective is—her or his gender, race, ethnicity, and sexual orientation—plays a major role in how that detective relates to the crime to be solved, as well as to the world in general. A variety of backgrounds bring a wealth of diversity to the detective novel, adding fascinating insights to the unfolding of the characters within.

Gay and Lesbian

Mysteries featuring lesbian characters are a staple of the lesbian publishing trade. Naiad Press and Cleis Press frequently publish lesbian mysteries. Often, the stories contain sex and romance along with the mystery. Many are published in trade paperback; however, mysteries featuring gay men are more often produced in hardcover by major publishers. Alyson does publish gay mysteries, but gay detectives are just as likely to be published by major houses. Joseph Hansen's Dave Brandstetter novels have been published by Viking and Mysterious Press, while Michael Nava's mysteries have been published by HarperCollins.

Nancy Clue and the Case of the Not-So-Nice Nurse by Mabel Maney is a delightful parody of both long-standing series read and loved by children (e.g., Nancy Drew, Cherry Ames) and lesbian mystery novels.

Allen, Kate (Alison Kane, *Tell Me What You Like*)

Baker, Nikki (Virginia Kelly)

Hansen, Joseph (David Brandstetter, insurance investigator)

Hart, Ellen (Jane Lawless, restaurateur)

Knight, Phyllis (Lil Ritchie, private investigator)

Maiman, Jaye (Robin Miller)

McNab, Claire (Detective Inspector Carol Ashton)

Myers, John L. (David Harriman, *Holy Family*)

Nava, Michael (Henry Rios, lawyer)

Phillips, Edward (Chadwick)

Scoppettone, Sandra (Lauren Laurano)

Welch, Pat (Helen Black)

African American Sleuths

Frankie Y. Bailey takes a historical and scholarly look at black characters in *Out of the Woodpile: Black Characters in Crime and Detective Fiction*. The author includes a directory of black characters in crime and detective fiction, film, and television. The book lists exotic settings and backgrounds and includes historical crime novels. There is an annotated sampling of detective cases and, most importantly (to readers of this guide), a list of black detectives in fiction.

The following list of books is just a small sampling of detective novels featuring African American sleuths.

Ball, John D. (Virgil Tibbs)

Baxt, George (Pharoah Love)

Bland, Eleanor Taylor (Marti MacAlister, homicide detective)

Burke, J. F. (Sam Kelly, house detective)

Hill, Reginald (Sixsmith, lathe operator turned private detective)

Komo, Dolores (Clio Browne)

Mosley, Walter (Easy Rawlins, private investigator)

Neely, Barbara (Blanche, a cleaning woman, *Blanche on the Lam*)

Hispanic Sleuths

Unfortunately, there is not yet a book like Bailey's *Out of the Woodpile* for either Hispanic or Native American crime and detective fiction.

Cook, Bruce (Chico Cervantes, private investigator)

Ramos, Manuel (Luis Montez, lawyer)

Taibo, Paco Ignacio (Hector Belascoaran Shayne)

Native American Sleuths

Hager, Jean (Mitch Bushyhead, police chief; Molly Bearpaw, Native American League)

Hillerman, Tony (Jim Chee and Joe Leaphorn, Navajo Tribal Police)

Stern, Richard Martin (Lieutenant Johnny Ortiz, Apache)

Yarbro, Chelsea Quinn (Charles Spotted Moon, Ojibwa, San Francisco)

Women Detectives

The species deadlier than the male appears in all types of detective stories. In her nineteenth-century origins in the genre, the woman detective tended to lean heavily on intuition. In more modern examples, while often remaining womanly, she uses her wits as ably as the male detective. For many fans there is still identification with the stereotyped, sometimes memorable, spinster sleuth, neatly characterized by the vicar in Agatha Christie's first Miss Marple case, *Murder at the Vicarage* (1930): "There is no detective in England equal to a spinster lady of uncertain age with plenty of time on her hands."

Women detectives have steadily been gaining ground in the past few years: V. I. Warshawski had her own eponymous film; Arly Hanks has recently been seen on television. Much of the growth of women in the genre can be attributed to Sisters in Crime, an organization that promotes and provides support to women who write crime fiction. For comment on women detectives, see *The Lady Investigates* by Craig and Cadogan, in the history section (see p. 119) and *Murderess Ink*, compiled by Dilys Winn, in the criticism section (see p. 120).

It would be impossible to list all female sleuths appearing in crime fiction, so the following list serves to provide a sampling of the great variety of women solving crimes in novels. Several of the listings in this category are repeated from other sections.

Barnes, Linda (Carlotta Carlyle, private investigator)

Ballard, Mignon Franklin (Eliza Figg)

Barth, Richard (Margaret Binton, retired)

Berry, Carole (Bonnie Underhill, amateur)

Bland, Eleanor Taylor (Marti Macalister, black homicide detective)

Brennan, Carol (Liz Wareham, public relations)

Brett, Simon (Mrs. Melita Pargeter, amateur)

Brown, Rita Mae (Mary Minor "Harry" Haristeen, postmistress)

Burke, Jan (Irene Kelly, newspaper reporter)

Carlson, P. M. (Maggie Ryan, statistician)

Carvic, Heron (Miss Seaton, British spinster)

Christie, Agatha (Miss Jane Marple, spinster)

Coker, Carolyn (Andrea Perkins, art restorer)

Cornwell, Patricia D. (Kay Scarpetta, medical examiner)

Cross, Amanda (Kate Fansler, professor, New York)

D'Amato, Barbara (Cat Marsala, freelance journalist)

Davis, Dorothy Salisbury (Julie Hayes, amateur)

Drummond, John Keith (Matilda Worthing, retired)

Dunlap, Susan (Detective Jill Smith, police; Vejay Haskell, meter reader)

Femling, Jean (Martha "Moz" Brant, insurance adjuster)

Fraser, Antonia (Jemima Shore, television reporter)

Grace, C. L. (Kathryn Swinbrooke, medieval physician)

Grafton, Sue (Kinsey Millhone, private investigator)

Grant-Adamson, Lesley (Morgan, reporter)

Hager, Jean (Molly Bearpaw, investigator for the Native American Advocacy League)

Hess, Joan (Arly Hanks, small town chief of police; Claire Malloy, amateur)

Holt, Hazel (Sheila Mallory, writer)

Hornsby, Wendy (Maggie MacGowen, investigative filmmaker)

Jance, J. A. (Joanna Brady, widow of a sheriff's deputy)

Johnston, Jane (Evers, reporter)

Keating, H. R. F. (Mrs. Craggs, charlady, England)

Kelly, Susan (Liz Connors, amateur)

Kijewski, Karen (Kat Colorado, private investigator)

Kittredge, Mary (Charlotte Kent, writer; Edwina Crusoe, RN)

Knight, Kathryn Lasky (Calista Jacobs, illustrator)

Martin, Lee (Deb Ralston, Fort Worth Police Department)

McCrumb, Sharyn (Elizabeth MacPherson, anthropologist)

MacLeod, Charlotte (Sarah Kelling, amateur)

McQuillan, Karin (Jazz Jasper, safari guide and animal activist)

Melville, Jennie (Detective Sergeant Charmian Daniels, British)

Mitchell, Gladys (Dame Beatrice Bradley, psychiatrist)

Moffat, Gwen (Miss Melinda Pink, mountain climber and justice of the peace)

Morice, Anne (Tessa Chrichton, actress)

Muller, Marcia (Sharon McCone, private eye; Elena Oliverez, art curator)

O'Brien, Meg (Jessica James, investigative reporter)

O'Connell, Catherine (Karen Levinson, homicide detective)

O'Donnell, Lillian (Detective Norah Mulcahaney, New York Police Department)

Oliver, Anthony (Liz Thomas, widow)

Oliver, Maria-Antonia (Lonia Gulu, Catalan private investigator)

Osborn, David (Margaret Barlow, "50-something" photo-journalist)

Palmer, Stuart (Hildegarde Withers, spinster)

Papazoglou, Orania (Patience McKenna, writer)

Paretsky, Sara (V. I. Warshawski, private investigator)

Peters, Elizabeth (Amelia Peabody, archaeologist; Jacqueline Kirby, librarian)

Pickard, Nancy (Jenny Cain, administrator)

Porter, Anna (Judith Hayes, reporter)

Porter, Joyce (The Honorable Constance Morrison-Burke, busybody)

Roberts, Gillian (Amanda Pepper, English teacher)

Roosevelt, Elliott (Eleanor Roosevelt)

Scherf, Margaret (Dr. Grace Severance, retired pathologist)

Shankman, Sarah (Samantha Adams, crime reporter)

Shannon, Dell (Delia Reardon, Los Angeles Police Department)

Sherwood, John (Celia Grant, botanist)

Slovo, Gillian (Kat Baeler, private investigator)

Smith, Joan (Loretta Lawson, London University lecturer)

Smith, Julie (Skip Langdon, New Orleans homicide detective)

Smith, Julie (Rebecca Schwartz, lawyer)
Interestingly enough, there are two Julie Smiths. Their novels are quite different from each other but both feature strong, engrossingly interesting women detectives.

Stabenow, Dana (Kate Shugak, former district attorney)

Taylor, Elizabeth Atwood (Maggie Elliott, private investigator)

Trocheck, Kathy Hogan (Callahan Garrity, cleaning lady, formerly a cop)

Van Gieson, Judith (Neil Hamel, private investigator)

Wager, Walter (Alison Gordon, private investigator)

Warner, Mignon (Mrs. Edwina Charles, clairvoyant)

Watson, Clarissa (Persis Willum, art curator)

Weir, Charlene (Susan Wren, police chief)

Wings, Mary (Emma Victor, feminist)

White, Gloria (Ronnie Ventura, private investigator)

Wolzien, Valerie (Susan Henshaw, homemaker)

By way of a footnote to the women detectives, there have been a fair number of women writers of detective fiction who have featured a hapless young heroine narrator who reiterates (too often) a variation of "had I but known." In the better versions the heroine is quite tough, but she still murmurs the refrain. This heroine became the stereotype of the Gothic romance and frequently appears in the romantic-suspense novel. The "had I but known" detective novel (also known as the "Fluttering Spinsters" School of Detection) is not a series novel. The heroine narrator is involved in the detecting, but there is usually a formal detective. Also, the heroine ends up safely married. Mary Roberts Rinehart is the queen of this school, notably in *The Album* (1933; her first book was in 1908). Mignon Good Eberhart wrote many indistinguishable detectives in this style. Mary Collins (*Dead Center*, 1942), and Lenore Offord (*Skeleton Key*, 1943), each wrote several of good quality. The masterpiece of the school is Mabel Seeley's *The Listening House* (1938).

IMMORTAL INVESTIGATORS

Among the immortals would be Dashiell Hammett's detectives and Chandler's Philip Marlowe, both noted previously. Here, then, are detectives who have become beings in their own right through the devotion of readers.

Christie, Agatha (Hercule Poirot, Miss Jane Marple)
"The first lady of crime" has published 83 titles, including original collections of short stories. (Over 40 of her titles have been reprinted in large-print editions.) Her dapper detective Hercule Poirot, who said that one must "employ the little grey cells," appeared in her first novel (*The Mysterious Affair at Styles*, 1920) and in 34 other novels, plus in some short stories. Miss Jane Marple, inquisitive village spinster, who insisted that "human nature is much the same in a village as anywhere else, only one has opportunities and leisure for seeing it at closer quarters," appeared in Christie's 11th novel (*Murder at the Vicarage*, 1930) and in 11 other novels, and in 20 short stories (collected as *Miss Marple: The Complete Short Stories* [Dodd, 1985]). A biography has been amusingly and lovingly constructed by Anne Hart from Christie's novels and short stories: *The Life and Times of Miss Jane Marple* (Dodd, 1985). A comedy detective couple, Tommy and Tuppence, appeared in her second novel (*The Secret Adversary*, 1922) and in three other novels, plus in short stories, but never rivaled the popularity of Poirot and Marple. In 1926, Christie successfully broke a sacred detective story law by having her narrator murdered in *The Murder of Roger Ackroyd*. Her *Autobiography* (London: Collins, 1977) reveals the lady and the writer. The following are a few books from a growing bibliography.

Barnard, Robert. *A Talent to Deceive: An Appreciation of Agatha Christie.* Dodd, 1980.
Barnard, a detective novelist, is both very critical and very appreciative. There is an extensive Christie bibliography. One appendix is a delightfully and critically annotated list of over 80 of her titles.

Fitzgibbon, Russell H. *The Agatha Christie Companion.* Popular Press, 1980.
Describes her detectives, and has several bibliographies and an index of characters.

Gill, Gillian. *Agatha Christie: The Woman and Her Mysteries.* Free Press, 1990.

Jacquemard, Yves, and Jean-Michel Sénécal. *The Eleventh Little Indian.* This detective novel featuring Superintendent Hector Parescot, Sûreté, is a spoof tribute to Christie and her *Ten Little Indians.*

Keating, H. R. F., ed. *Agatha Christie: First Lady of Crime.* Holt, 1977.
Thirteen essays by her peers, with delightful illustrations. Among the contributors: Julian Symons, Edmund Crispin, Michael Gilbert, Emma Lathen, Colin Watson, Celia Fremlin, Dorothy B. Hughes, Christiana Brand.

Morgan, Janet. *Agatha Christie: A Biography.* Knopf, 1984.

Riley, Rick, and Pam McAllister, eds. *The Bedside, Bathtub, & Armchair Companion to Agatha Christie.* Introduction by Julian Symons. Ungar, 1979.
This lavishly illustrated miscellany does have plot summaries. A comparison of these bland summaries with Barnard's (above) critical annotations is edifying.

Toye, Randall, comp. *The Agatha Christie Who's Who.* Holt, 1980.
All the characters, including the minor, are identified.

Doyle, Sir Arthur Conan (Sherlock Holmes and Dr. John Watson)
Four novels (*The Hound of the Baskervilles,* 1902; *The Sign of Four,* 1890; *A Study in Scarlet,* 1887; *The Valley of Fear,* 1915) and 56 short stories, some of novella length, comprise the canon of "sacred" writings presented with elaborate notes and period illustrations in the two-volume *The Annotated Sherlock Holmes,* edited by William S. Baring-Gould (Crown, 1967). A host of devout followers have continued the canon in novel and in short story.

Derleth, August. *The Solar Pons Omnibus.* Arkham House, 1982. 2 vols.
Contains the eight titles of Solar Pons's adventures.

Douglas, Carole Nelson. *Goodnight Irene.*

Fish, Robert L. *The Incredible Sherlock Holmes. The Memoirs of Sherlock Holmes.* (A Bagel Street Dozen)

Gardner, John. *The Return of Moriarity.*

Hanna, Edward B. *The Whitechapel Horrors.*

Irvine, R. R.
Short stories about Niles Brundage, actor of Sherlock Holmes roles.

King, Laurie R. *The Beekeeper's Apprentice, or, On the Segregation of the Queen.*

Siciliano, Sam. *The Angel of the Opera.*

Symons, Julian. *The Three-Pipe Problem.*
Novel about an actor of Holmes roles.

Watson, John H. *The Seven-Per-Cent Solution, Being a Reprint from the Reminiscences of John H. Watson, M.D., as edited by Nicholas Meyer.* With this 1974 pastiche, Nicholas Meyer (who did two more) incited a flood of imitators. These novels portray Sherlock Holmes either in his own period or (as, of course, he still lives!) in modern times. Many of these are of indifferent quality.

Writings about Sherlock Holmes are more voluminous than the canon. An association of admirers, the Baker Street Irregulars, publishes the *Baker Street Journal* and hosts events honoring Holmes. A novel by Anthony Boucher, *The Case of the Baker Street Irregulars*, has several of the Irregulars involved in and trying to solve a murder in Los Angeles.

Blackboard, Bill. *Sherlock Holmes in America.* Foreword by Dean Dickensheet. Abrams, 1981.

Bullard, Scott R., and Michael Leo Collins. *Who's Who in Sherlock Holmes.* Taplinger, 1980.

De Waal, Ronald. *The World Bibliography of Sherlock Holmes and Dr. Watson.* New York Graphic Society, 1973.

De Waal, Ronald. *The International Sherlock Holmes.* Archon/Shoe String Press, 1980. Supplement.

Haining, Peter, ed. *The Sherlock Holmes Scrapbook.* Potter, 1974.

Harrison, Michael. *In the Footsteps of Sherlock Holmes.* London: Cassell, 1958.

Harrison, Michael. *The London of Sherlock Holmes.* London: David & Charles, 1972.

McQueen, Ian. *Sherlock Holmes Detected: The Problems of the Long Stories.* Drake, 1974.

Rosenberg, Sam. *Naked Is the Best Disguise: The Death and Resurrection of Sherlock Holmes.* Bobbs-Merrill, 1974.

Tracey, Jack, ed. *Sherlock Holmes: The Published Apocrypha.* Houghton, 1980.

Sayers, Dorothy L. (Lord Peter Wimsey; Montague Egg)
Twelve novels (all but one featuring Lord Peter; the first in 1923) and 45 short stories (22 featuring Lord Peter) ensure Lord Peter's immortality. The short stories are to be found in *Lord Peter*, compiled by James Sandoe (Harper, 1972; however, the paperback Avon edition of the same date contains an additional story). This volume also contains an essay by Carolyn Heilbrun, "Sayers, Lord Peter and God," and a wicked parody by E. C. Bentley, "Greedy Night." Lord Peter is the urbane aristocrat as amateur detective. Sayers's other detective, appearing in 11 short stories, is Montague Egg, a traveling salesman of wine and a delightful character. The many recent books on Sayers deal also with her religious writings, plays, and translation of Dante. In 1993, the 100-year anniversary of her birth, Walker and Company published *Dorothy L. Sayers: The Centenary Celebration*, edited by Alzina Stone Dale.

Brabazon, James. *Dorothy L. Sayers: The Life of a Courageous Woman.* With a preface by Anthony Fleming and a foreword by P. D. James. London: Gollancz, 1981.
The "authorized" (by her son) biography, published early (Sayers stipulated no biography until 50 years after her death) puts into limbo the disgraceful book by Hitchman (in the following list). Brabazon knew Sayers, had access to all her papers, and was given complete editorial freedom. In style, wit, intelligence, and spirit, he matches his subject to perfection.

Brunsdale, Mitzi. *Dorothy L. Sayers: Solving the Mystery of Wickedness.* St. Martin's Press, 1990.

Durkin, Mary Brian. *Dorothy L. Sayers.* Twayne, 1980.
About half the volume is criticism on the detective writings.

Gaillard, Dawson. *Dorothy L. Sayers.* Ungar, 1981.
This critical appraisal of the detective works adds a distinctly feminist viewpoint.

Hannay, Margaret P., ed. *As Her Whimsey Took Her: Critical Essays on the Work of Dorothy L. Sayers.* Kent State University Press, 1979.
Five of the fifteen essays in this collection are on Sayers as a detective story writer.

Hitchman, Janet. *Such a Strange Lady: A Biography of Dorothy L. Sayers.* Harper, 1975.
This is a *very* strange book; the author has neither taste nor grace.

Hone, Ralph E. *Dorothy L. Sayers: A Literary Biography.* Kent State University Press, 1979.
The life and all the works are intertwined.

Kenney, Catherine McGehee. *The Remarkable Case of Dorothy L. Sayers.* Kent State University Press, 1990.

Scott-Giles, C. W. *The Wimsey Family: A Fragmentary History Compiled from Correspondence with Dorothy L. Sayers.* London: Gollancz, 1977.
The author, Fitzalen Pursuivant of Arms Extraordinary, has supplied heraldic drawings. Both Scott-Giles and Sayers obviously enjoyed this fanciful creation.

Stout, Rex (Nero Wolfe and Archie Goodwin)
Nero Wolfe's bulk is not matched by the number of published books about his detective genius: 46 titles (the first in 1934, of these 12 are collections of novellas). He never leaves his house willingly—legmen and witnesses bring him the information and *he* thinks. He loves food, orchids, language, and his privacy. Archie, his assistant, is of the hard-boiled detective mold. In *Gambit*, Archie informs a prospective client, who has been told that Wolfe is indignantly burning a copy of Webster's Third: "Once he burned up a cookbook because it said to remove the hide from a ham end before putting it in the pot with lima beans. Which he loves most, food or words, is a tossup." Nero Wolfe has an enthusiastic following: the Wolfe Pack (700 members) held its third annual Black Orchid Banquet in 1980; there is a *Rex Stout Newsletter* (appearing in *The Armchair Detective*) and a Nero Wolfe Award for Mystery Fiction. The following are some of the many imitations and continuations of the great man's adventures.

Baring-Gould, William S. *Nero Wolfe of West Thirty-Fifth Street: The Life and Times of America's Largest Private Detective.* Viking, 1969.
Goldsborough, Robert. Seven Nero Wolfe and Archie Goodwin capers.

Harrison, Chip. *The Topless Tulip Caper.* Gold Medal, 1975.
The author is now revealed as Lawrence Block. The detectives are Leo Haig as Wolfe and Chip Harrison as Archie.

McAleer, John L. *Rex Stout, a Biography.* Little, Brown, 1977.

Stout, Rex. *The Nero Wolfe Cook Book.* Viking, 1973.
This is a delicious introduction to the novels. Eating well is more important than detection, and the meals in the novels are meticulously described. Here are the recipes along with the passages from the novels in which Wolfe and Archie, and sometimes guests, dined.

DETECTIVE STORY SETTINGS AND SUBJECTS

Just as many readers of detective fiction prefer a type of detective, others seek those stories with a particular background of country, social order, activity, organization, or profession. Three bibliographies (by Barzun and Taylor, Hagen, and Hubin) provide some subject indexing. Happily, several guides have been published.

Barzun, Jacques, and Wendell Hertig Taylor. *A Catalogue of Crime*. Harper & Row, 1971.

Breen, Jon. *Novel Verdicts: A Guide to Courtroom Fiction*. Scarecrow, 1984.

Hagen, Ordean A. *Who Done It?* Bowker, 1969.

Hubin, Allen J. *Crime Fiction*. Garland, 1994.

Kramer, John E., Jr., and John E. Kramer, III. *College Mystery Novels: An Annotated Bibliography, Including a Guide to Professional Series-Character Sleuths*. Garland, 1983.

Menendez, Albert J. *Mistletoe Malice: The Life and Times of the Christmas Murder Mystery*. Holly Tree Press, 1982.

Menendez, Albert J. *The Subject Is Murder: A Selective Guide to Mystery Fiction*. Garland, 1986.

Rosenberg, Betty. *The Letter Killeth*. (Three Bibliographic Essays for Bibliomaniacs.) Kenneth Karmiole, 1982.

The 25 chapter headings in *The Subject Is Murder* indicate the variety of the 3,812 titles listed (unfortunately without annotation): "Advertising"; "Archaeology"; "The Art World"; "Circuses and Carnivals"; "Department Stores"; "Gardening"; "The Groves of Academe"; "Murder on the High Seas"; "Holy Terror: Ecclesiastical Murder"; "Hotels and Inns"; "Literary People"; "The Mike and the Tube: Radio/TV"; "Mistletoe Malice: The Christmas Mystery"; "Musical Murder"; "Politics and Murder"; "Murder Goes to Press"; "Quiet Please: Bookshops, Libraries and Murder"; "Murder Rides the Rails"; "Scalpel Please: Medical Murder"; "Sports"; "The Supernatural"; "The Theatre World"; "Tinseltown: Hollywood and Films"; "Weddings and Honeymoons"; and "Who Am I?: Amnesia and Murder."

Still needed are guides to titles having (among others) the following backgrounds: banking and business, food and cooking, villages and seaside resorts, country houses, and animals (birds, cats, dogs). (A fan group, Mystery Readers of America, in Berkeley, California, publishes a journal that always contains comment and bibliographies on settings. For example, volume 2, no. 2, June/July 1986, is almost completely devoted to "Murder in Transit"— railways and travel as settings. It also has a page on "Cat Mysteries.")

The possibilities are miscellaneous and intriguing: butlers, occult detectives, Victorian and Edwardian settings, chess, rogues, mysteries about detective fiction (e.g., *The Undetective* by Bruce Graeme). History buffs would enjoy Robert Player's *Oh! Where Are Bloody Mary's Earrings?*, and two books on Richard III, Elizabeth Peters's *The Murders of Richard III* and Josephine Tey's *The Daughter of Time*. The British Parliament is the background for *Who Goes Hang?* by Stanley Hyland, in which the detectives are committee members. (Incidentally, this is an extreme example of changes made when a British mystery is published in the United States—about 100 pages of text were deleted, including all the passages describing library and historical research that would be of fascinating interest to librarians.) For Jane Austen devotees, there is T. H. White's *Darkness at Pemberley*—a twentieth-century Elizabeth Darcy at the Pemberley of *Pride and Prejudice*. Dr. Johnson and, of course, Boswell are the detectives in Lillian De La Torre's period detective stories. Two recent novels by Robert Barnard, *Death of a Mystery Writer* and *Death of a Literary Widow*, indicate the substantial list to be made on the literary life in detective fiction. For those interested in Greek philosophy, there is Margaret Doody's *Aristotle Detective*.

An interesting list could be made of authors not associated with the subgenre who wrote detective stories: C. P. Snow, whose first published novel was a detective story, *Death Under Sail*, as was his last, *A Coat of Varnish*; Kingsley Amis with *The Riverside Villas Murder*; Charles Dickens, whose unfinished *The Mystery of Edwin Drood* has tempted several authors to write a conclusion and has even spawned a multiple-ending Broadway play.

The following are several of the available anthologies that deal with settings and subjects. A few examples of subject groupings are included after the following list to show the reader-advising potential of analysis by type. The groupings "Libraries and Librarians," "Book Trade and Publishing," and "College and University" will be of particular interest to librarians.

Godfrey, Thomas, ed. *Murder for Christmas*. Illustrations by Gahan Wilson. The Mysterious Press, 1982.

Hillerman, Tony, ed. *The Mysterious West*. HarperCollins, 1994.

Muller, Marcia, and Bill Pronzini, eds. *Chapter and Hearse: Suspense Stories About the World of Books*. Morrow, 1985.
Contains Lawrence G. Blochman's classic novella, *Murder Walks in Marble Halls*, set in the New York Public Library.

Muller, Marcia, and Bill Pronzini, eds. *Dark Lessons: Crime and Detection on Campus*. Macmillan, 1985. (Midnight Library, vol. 3)
Campus setting is from kindergarten to university.

Muller, Marcia, and Bill Pronzini, eds. *Kill or Cure: Suspense Stories About the World of Medicine*. Macmillan, 1985. (Midnight Library, vol. 4)

Muller, Marcia, and Bill Pronzini, eds. *The Wickedest Show on Earth: A Carnival of Circus Suspense*. Morrow, 1985.

Pronzini, Bill, and Marcia Muller, eds. *The Deadly Arts*. Arbor House, 1985.
Twenty-three tales with backgrounds in "the lively arts," from photography to vaudeville.

Waugh, Carol-Lynn Rossel, Martin Harry Greenberg, and Isaac Asimov, eds. *Show Business Is Murder*. Avon, 1983.

Locked Room

This plot device is used intriguingly by too many authors to list. The following two books serve as useful introductions.

Carr, John Dickson
Carr wrote several of these. In *The Three Coffins* (British title: *The Hollow Man*), his detective, Dr. Gideon Fell, gives a neat discourse on the problem of the locked room.

Santesson, Hans Stefan, ed. *The Locked Room Reader: Stories of Impossible Crimes and Escapes*. Random, 1968.
Sixteen stories, including "The Locked Room" by Carr.

English Country-House
Aird, Catherine. *The State Home Murders.*

Anderson, James. *The Affair of the Blood-Stained Egg Cosy.*

Barnard, Robert. *Corpse in a Gilded Cage.*

Heyer, Georgette. *Envious Casca. No Wind of Blame. The Unfinished Clue.*

Innes, Michael. *Hamlet, Revenge!*

Peters, Elizabeth. *The Murders of Richard III.*

Sports
Anderson, Douglas. *First and Ten.* (Santa Arkwright, player)

Elkins, Charlotte, and Aaron Elkins. *A Weekend Slice.* (women's golf)

Enger, L. L. (Gun Pedersen, baseball)

Francis, Dick (jockey, trainer, and others connected with British horse racing)

Geller, Michael. *Major League Murder.* (Slots Resnick, baseball)

Gordon, Alison (Kate Henry, baseball writer)

Hammond, Gerald (Captain Jack Cunningham, hunting)

Katz, Michael J. *Murder Off the Glass. Last Dance in Redondo Beach. The Big Freeze.* (Andy Sussman, sportscaster)

Leavitt, Alan J. *Shame the Devil.* (horse racing)

Llewellyn, Sam. *Blood Orange.* (boat racing)

Maxes, Anna. *Dead to Rights.* (women's college softball)

Miles, Keith. *Bullet Hole. Double Eagle.* (professional golf)

Nighbert, David F. *Squeezeplay. Strikezone.* (baseball)

Seaver, Tom, and Herb Resnicow. *Beanball.* (Marc Burr, sports reporter)

Soos, Troy. *Murder at Fenway Park.* (baseball, 1912)

Strip Joints

The environs of ecydiasts have appeared with great frequency in the last few years. Somehow, the denizens of these dens of inequity make interesting witnesses and victims of crime.

Douglas, Carole Nelson. *Pussyfoot.*

Fennelly, Tony. *The Hippie in the Wall.*

Gilpin, T. G. *The Death of a Fantasy Life.*

Hiaasen, Carl. *Strip Tease.*

Ritz, David. *Take It Off, Take It All Off.*

Cookery

The detective dines well, and attention to food is notable in the following selection of mysteries in which food and cooking are very important.

Babson, Marian. *Death Warmed Over.*

Barnes, Linda. *Cities of the Dead.*

Bond, Michael. *Monsieur Pamplemousse. Monsieur Pamplemousse and the Secret Mission. Monsieur Pamplemousse Aloft.*
And his dog, Pommes Frites.

Davidson, Diane Mott. *Catering to Nobody. Dying for Chocolate. The Cereal Murders. The Last Suppers.*

Gray, Nicholas Stuart. *Killer's Cookbook.*

Halliday, Fred. *Murder in the Kitchen.*

Heald, Tim. *Just Desserts.*

Laurence, Janet. *Recipe for Death,* fourth in the Darina Lisle Culinary Mysteries.

Lyons, Nan, and Ivan Lyons. *Someone Is Killing the Great Chefs of Europe. Someone Is Killing the Great Chefs of America.*

Myers, Tamar. *Too Many Crooks Spoil the Broth: A Pennsylvania Dutch Mystery with Recipes.*

Page, Katherine Hall. *The Body in the Basement.*

Pickard, Nancy. *27 Ingredient Chili con Carne Murders.*

Rich, Virginia. *The Cooking School Murders. The Baked Bean Supper Murders. The Nantucket Diet Murders.*

Roudybush, Alexandra. *A Gastronomic Murder.*

Simmel, Johannes Mario. *It Can't Always Be Caviar.*

Stout, Rex. *Too Many Cooks.*

Libraries and Librarians

Blackstock, Charity. *Dewey Death.*

Bosse, Malcolm. *The Man Who Loved Zoos.*

Dolson, Hildegarde. *Please Omit Funeral.*

Goodrum, Charles A. *Dewey Decimated.*

Harriss, Will. *The Bay Psalm Book Murder.*

Holding, James
> Hal Johnson, a library sleuth for overdue books, appeared in several short stories in *Ellery Queen's Mystery Magazine.*

Johnson, W. Bolingbroke. *The Widening Stain.*

Langton, Jane. *The Transcendental Murder.*

Peters, Elizabeth. *The Seventh Sinner. The Murders of Richard III.*

Valin, Jonathan. *Final Notice.*

Book Trade and Publishing

Allingham, Margery. *Flowers for the Judge.*

Asimov, Isaac. *Murder at the ABA.*

Blackburn, John. *Blue Octavo.* (U.S. title: *Bound to Kill*)

Blake, Nicholas. *End of Chapter.*

Carter, Robert A. *Casual Slaughters.*

Clarke, Anna. *The Lady in Black.*
> Chapman & Hall are the publishers; the reader is George Meredith.

Delving, Michael. *Smiling the Boy Fell Dead.*

Farmer, Bernard J. *Death of a Bookseller.*

Hallahan, William H. *The Ross Forgery.*

Hamilton, Henriette. *The Two Hundred Ghost.*

Hodgkin, M. R. *Dead Indeed.*

Kaewert, Julie Wallin. *Unsolicited.*

Lewis, Roy. Series about Matthew Coll (English book dealer).

Monteilhet, Herbert. *Murder at the Frankfurt Book Fair.*

Moore, Doris Langley. *My Caravaggio Style.*

Morley, Christopher. *The Haunted Bookshop.*

Page, Marco. *Fast Company.*

Porter, Anna. *Hidden Agenda.*

Reno, Marie R. *Final Proof.*

Rhode, John, and Carter Dickson. *Fatal Descent.*

Sims, George. *The Terrible Door.*

Stern, Richard Martin. *Manuscript for Murder.*

Symons, Julian. *The Narrowing Circle.*

College and University

Bernard, Robert. *Deadly Meeting.*

Blake, Nicholas. *The Morning After Death.*

Boucher, Anthony. *The Case of the Seven of Calvary.*

Bradberry, James. *The Seventh Sacrament.*

Clinton-Baddeley, V. C. *My Foe Outstretched Beneath the Tree.*

Cole, G. D. H., and Margaret Cole. *Off with Her Head.*

Constantine, K. C. *The Blank Page.*

Dillon, Ellis. *Death in the Quadrangle.*

Eustis, Helen. *The Horizontal Man.*

Fiske, Dorsey. *Academic Murder.*

Graham, John Alexander. *The Involvement of Arnold Wechsler.*

Hodgkin, M. R. *Student Body.*

Innes, Michael. *Death at the President's Lodging. Old Hall, New Hall.*

Johnson, W. Bolingbroke. *The Widening Stain.*

Levin, Ira. *Juliet Dies Twice.*

MacKay, Amanda. *Death Is Academic.*

Masterman, J. C. *An Oxford Tragedy.*

Mitchell, Gladys. *Fault in the Structure. Spotted Hemlock.*

Rees, Dilwyn. *The Cambridge Murders.*

Rennert, Maggie. *Circle of Death.*

Robinson, Robert. *Landscape with Dead Dons.*

Sayers, Dorothy L. *Gaudy Night.*

Vulliamy, C. E. *Don Among the Dead Men.*

Genre Writer's Conventions

The Papazoglou and Peters books in the following list take place at romance writers conventions and contain some very amusing criticism, with lovely quotations, of the romance genre. The McCrumb title, available only in paperback, is about a science fiction convention and has become somewhat of a cult classic. Jessica Fletcher is a fictional author from television's *Murder She Wrote*.

Barnard, Robert. *The Cherry Blossom Corpse (Death in Purple Prose)*.

Fletcher, Jessica, and Donald Bain. *Gin and Daggers*.

McCrumb, Sharyn. *Bimbos of the Death Sun*.

Papazoglou, Orania. *Sweet, Savage Love*.

Peters, Elizabeth. *Die for Love*.

Taylor, L. A. *A Murder Waiting to Happen*.

Historical Mysteries

Mystery and detective novels are essentially timeless—readers accept the period backgrounds. Some readers seek out the nineteenth-century sources of the detective story in Edgar Allan Poe, Wilkie Collins, Sheridan LeFanu, and others before the creation of Sherlock Holmes. However, an increasing number of novels are currently being written that are placed in the nineteenth century or earlier, or that hark back to the earlier decades of this century. History fans might find the backgrounds as interesting as the plots. Following are a couple of anthologies of nineteenth-century stories and some books of the historical types being issued now. A recent addition to collections of historical mysteries is *Once Upon a Crime: Historical Mysteries from Ellery Queen's Mystery Magazine*, edited by Janet Hutchings.

Cassidy, Bruce, ed. *The Roots of Detection: The Art of Deduction Before Sherlock Holmes*. Ungar, 1983.

Greene, Graham, and Hugh Greene, eds. *Victorian Villainies: The Great Tontine, The Rome Express, In the Fog, The Beetle*. Viking, 1985.

Ackroyd, Peter. *Hawksmoor*.
Some supernatural aspects as a twentieth-century Scotland Yard case is linked to the seventeenth century.

Alexander, Lawrence. *The Big Stick. Speak Softly*. (Teddy Roosevelt as Police Commissioner)

Baxt, George. *The Dorothy Parker Murder Case. The Alfred Hitchcock Murder Case*.

Borowitz, Albert. *The Jack the Ripper Walking Tour Murder*.

Burns, Ron. *Enslaved. The Mysterious Death of Meriwether Lewis*. (Harrison Hull)

Clynes, Michael. *The White Rose Murders*. (Sir Richard Shattot, sixteenth-century Britain)

Carr, Caleb. *The Alienist*. (Teddy Roosevelt on the New York Police Force)

Collins, Max Allen. *The Million-Dollar Wound*. (Private eye Nate Heller in Chicago of the 1940s)

Cooney, Eleanor and Daniel Altieri. *Deception: A Novel of Murder and Madness in T'ang China.*

De La Torre, Lillian. *The Exploits of Dr. Sam Johnson, Detector.*

Doherty, P. C. (Hugh Corbett, clerk and spy in the court of Edward II)

Doody, Margaret. *Aristotle Detective.*

Douglas, Carole Nelson. *Goodnight Irene. Irene's Last Waltz.* (Victorian)

Farnol, Jeffery (Jasper Shrig, Bow Street Runner, appeared in 10 novels by this author of Regency romances; the best known is *The Amateur Gentleman*)

Grace, C. L. (Kathryn Swinbrooke, medieval physician)

Harrison, Ray. *Deathwatch. Harvest of Death.* (Sergeant Bragg and Constable Morton, 1890s London City Police)

Heller, Keith. *Man's Illegal Life. Man's Storm.* (George Man, London parish watchman, eighteenth century)

Hervey, Evelyn. *The Governess.* (London, 1870s)

Hilton, John Buxton (Inspector Pickford, Detective Brunt, and Sergeant Nadin, Derbyshire, nineteenth century)

Kaminsky, Stuart M. (Toby Peters, private eye, Hollywood, in the 1940s, in a series in which actual motion picture stars are characters—e.g., John Wayne, Charlie Chaplin)

Linscott, Gillian. *Hanging on the Wire. Sister Beneath the Sheet.* (Nell Bray, English suffragette)

Lovesey, Peter (Sergeant Cribb and Constable Thackeray, London, nineteenth century; Prince Albert, *Bertie and the Seven Bodies. Bertie and the Tinman*)

McConnor, Vincent (François Vidocq, founder of the Sûreté, Paris, nineteenth century)

Maher, Mary. *The Devil's Card.* (Nineteenth-century Chicago)

Meyers, Maan. *The Dutchman.* (Seventeenth century)

Oates, Joyce Carol. *Mysteries of Winterthurn.* (Xavier Kilgarvan, detective, United States, late nineteenth and early twentieth centuries)

Palmer, William J. *The Detective and Mr. Dickens. The Highwayman and Mr. Dickens.* (Inspector William Field with Charles Dickens and Wilkie Collins)

Perry, Anne (Inspector Thomas Pitt and wife Charlotte, London, nineteenth century; William Monk, amnesiac Victorian police detective to private investigator)

Pullman, Philip. *The Ruby in the Smoke. A Shadow in the North. The Tiger in the Well.* (A young adult series enjoyed by adults)

Pronzini, Bill (John Quincannon, Federal Secret Service agent, San Francisco, 1890s)

Ross, Kate. *Cut to the Quick.* (Julian Kestrel)

Sarfoe, Steven. *Roman Blood.* (Gordanius the finder, ancient Rome)

Sedley, Kate (Roger the Chapman, fifteenth-century peddler cum-amateur detective)

Selwyn, Francis (Sergeant Verity, London, nineteenth century)

Stubbs, Jean (Inspector Lintott, Scotland Yard, nineteenth century) *Dear Laura* is a gem.

Mystery-Suspense, Psychological-Suspense

Those genre novels that publishers often label "A Novel of Suspense" fall into an amorphous catchall. What they have in common is abundant suspense. Some mystery-suspense novels may seem to differ little from the detective novel; there is a crime and its investigation. However, the formal detection, by police or by private investigator, is secondary. The narration is not by the detective but by a character disturbingly involved in the mystery or by a potential victim. The author and the reader are concerned with the background of the mystery, along with the emotions and personal and private relationships of the characters. Suspense heightens as the narrator becomes more and more dangerously involved, distrusts feelings of trust or love, or comes close to disaster. It may be that the detection is wholly the function of the involved narrator. Occasionally, the narrator is a detached observer or one in love with the central character in the mystery.

Psychological-suspense novels somewhat follow the same pattern. They may, however, center on the background or buildup of the crime. Usually, there is some aspect of psychological abnormality as a causal factor. The narrator may be warped, and the plot develops as the narrator's compulsion leads to the crime. Occasionally, there may be suggestions of the supernatural.

Both these types of suspense novels may seem indistinguishable from certain types to be described later. The psychological-suspense novel merges into the crime novel—in the first, the compulsions to crime are psychological; in the second, the crime is cold-bloodedly planned, however psychopathic the schemer. Mystery-suspense novels are often full of romance and seemingly akin to the novel of romantic-suspense—in the first, the mystery is the important story line; in the second, the romance dominates, with the Gothic romance, which incorporates elements of horror and the supernatural, being the extreme example.

What differentiates these thriller novels is largely the intent of the author. Genre authors are quite canny about the type of reader they want to entice. Atmosphere and background, style of narration, and the manner of characterization vary in each genre. Sometimes, however, the variations are so diluted as to be almost imperceptible. This frequently occurs among authors who write in more than one genre, but who are usually more successfull in one particular genre.

A thriller author, who can vary writing style to suit different subgenres and appeal to different readers, will frequently further differentiate by using a pseudonym distinctive to each subgenre. The reader, then, does not have the same expectation from each pseudonym, and the author can, in effect, become a different author for each. Indeed, the reader may be unaware of reading the same author in different guises. (A good example is Erle Stanley Gardner writing as A. A. Fair.) When the author uses the same name for more than one genre, the author's own distinctive style is usually a constant, allowing for the pattern characteristic of each genre.

Novels that can be categorized as mystery-suspense are issued in great quantity and are very diverse in character. Genre authors may write one or two of this type only, and authors not usually considered genre authors occasionally write a mystery-suspense. Therefore, the following authors were selected to display the variety of types available in this subgenre. The first listing includes authors prolific in this type, so several titles are listed. The books listed for Carpenter, Collins, and Eustis are considered classics of mystery-suspense.

For a brief sampling of the subgenre, try selections from *The Deadliest Games: Tales of Psychological Suspense from Ellery Queen's Mystery Magazine*, edited by Janet Hutchings.

Abrahams, Peter. *Hard Rain*.

Armstrong, Charlotte. *A Dram of Poison. The Turret Room. The Unsuspected*.

Babson, Marian. *Bejeweled Death. Cruise of a Death Time. Death Swap. Death Warmed Up. A Fool for Murder. The Lord Mayor of Death. Murder, Murder Little Star. A Trail of Ashes*.

Banks, Oliver. *The Rembrandt Panel*.

Beck, K. K. *Death in a Deck Chair*.

Berckman, Evelyn. *The Fourth Man on the Rope. The Victorian Album*.

Blackstock, Charity. *The Foggy, Foggy Dew. I Met Murder on the Way*.

Borgenicht, Miriam. *Fall from Grace. False Colors. True or False*.

Brandon, Jay. *Tripwire*.

Cairns, Alison. *New Year Resolution.*

Carpenter, Margaret. *Experiment Perilous.*

Clark, Mary Higgins. *The Cradle Will Fall. A Cry in the Night. A Stranger Is Watching. While My Pretty One Sleeps.*

Clarke, Anna. *The Lady in Black. Soon She Must Die.*

Collins, Wilkie. *The Woman in White.*

Crane, Caroline. *Wife Found Slain.*

Curtiss, Ursula. *Dog in the Manger. The House on Plymouth Street* (short stories). *The Poisoned Orchard.*

Deaver, Jeffery Wilds. *The Lesson of Her Death.*

Ellin, Stanley. *The Specialty of the House and Other Stories. The Valentine Estate. Very Old Money.*

Eustis, Helen. *The Horizontal Man.*

Fitzgerald, Penelope. *The Golden Child.*

Fremlin, Celia. *The Hours Before Dawn. The Jealous One. A Lovely Day to Die and Other Stories.*

Gilbert, Anna. *Miss Bede Is Staying.*

Gill, B. M. *Death Drop.*

Gloag, Julian. *Blood for Blood. Sleeping Dogs Lie.*

Graham, Winston. *Marnie. The Walking Stick.*

Guest, Judith, and Rebecca Hill. *Killing Time in St. Cloud.*

Harrison, Kathryn. *Exposure.*

Highsmith, Patricia. *Slowly, Slowly in the Wind* (short stories). *Strangers on a Train.*

Japrisot, Sebastien. *The Lady in the Car with Glasses and a Gun. One Deadly Summer.*

Kenney, Susan. *Garden of Malice.*

McGinley, Patrick. *Bogmail.*

Millar, Margaret. *Beast in View. Beyond This Point Are Monsters.*

Rendell, Ruth. *A Judgment in Stone. The Killing Doll. Make Death Love Me. Master of the Moor. The New Girl Friend and Other Stories. The Tree of Hands.*

Russell, Martin. *A Domestic Affair.*

Scholefield, Alan. *Night Child.*

PSYCHOPATHIC KILLERS

A psychopathic killer pursuing (usually) a woman is as common a plot element in this subgenre as are serial killers. Madness and murder appear in other genres, and some examples are included in chapter 8, "Horror" (e.g., Robert Bloch's *Psycho*).

Abercrombie, Barbara. *Run for Your Life.*

Bayer, William. *Wallflower.*

Cohen, Anthea. *Angel Without Mercy. Angel of Vengeance. Angel of Death.* A curious aspect of this series is that it features a nurse murderer, and one critic questioned the limited appeal of the murderer-as-heroine concept.

Cook, Thomas. *Mortal Memory.*

Cornwell, Patricia D. *Postmortem. Bodies of Evidence. All That Remains. The Body Farm.*

Crider, Bill. *Blood Marks.*

Fielding, Joy. *The Deep End. Kiss Mommy Goodbye.*

Fremlin, Celia. *The Parasite Person.*

Heckler, Jonellen. *Circumstances Unknown.*

Henderson, M. R. *By Reason Of. If I Should Die.*

Hunter, Jessie Prichard. *Blood Music.*

Johnston, Jane. *Pray for Ricky Foster.*

Kaminsky, Stuart. *Exercise in Terror.*

King, Tabitha. *The Trap.*

Lindsey, David L. *Mercy.*

Wiltse, David. *The Edge of Sleep.*

HOSPITAL SETTING

The hospital setting, with its doctor and nurse protagonists, appears in both the romance and horror genres, and categorization into a particular genre is dependent on the intent of the author.

Frede, Richard. *The Interns. The Nurses.*

Fried, John J., and John G. West. *Trauma.*

Marion, Robert. *Born Too Soon.*

Ravin, Neil. *Seven North.*

Scherer, Priscilla. *Half Life*.

Schneider, Joyce Anne. *Stryker's Children*.

DETECTION WRITERS

The following list is of occasional authors of mystery-suspense who are known principally for works of detection.

Barnard, Robert. *Death of a Perfect Mother. Out of the Blackout*.

Bell, Josephine. *Treachery in Type*.

Brett, Simon. *A Shock to the System. Dead Romantic*.

Butler, Gwendoline. *Sarsen Place*.

Candy, Edward. *Bones of Contention*.

Canning, Victor. *The Kingsford Mark*.

Craig, Alisa. *The Terrible Tide*.

Davis, Dorothy Salisbury. *A Death in the Life*.

Dickinson, Peter. *Death of a Unicorn. Hindsight. The Last House-Party*.

Eberhart, Mignon Good. *Casa Madrone. Next of Kin. The Patient in Cabin C. A Fighting Chance*.

Ferrars, E. X. *Experiment with Death. Something Wicked*.

Gosling, Paula. *Fair Game. Solo Blues*.

Hansen, Joseph. *Steps Going Down*.

Hughes, Dorothy B. *The So Blue Marble*.

James, P. D. *Innocent Blood*.

McCloy, Helen. *The Further Side of Fear*.

McDonald, Gregory. *Safekeeping. Who Took Toby Rinaldo?*

McMullen, Mary. *But Nellie Was So Nice. Death by Bequest. A Grave Without Flowers*.

Price, Anthony. *The '44 Vintage*.

Symons, Julian. *The Blackheath Poisonings. A Criminal Comedy. The Man Who Lost His Wife. The Name of Annabel Lee*.

Wainwright, John. *The Forest*.

Yorke, Margaret. *Find Me a Villain. Intimate Kill. The Smooth Face of Evil*.

ROMANCE WRITERS

Whether to label Mary Stewart's novels as mystery-suspense or romantic-suspense is a tossup. Her novels have been reviewed by reviewers of mystery and detective stories (Anthony Boucher asked, "Is anybody writing better adventure-suspense-romance than Miss Stewart?"). Stewart and Elizabeth Peters are listed in both sections for the same books; they are read equally by fans of both. The novels of the other romance writers tend to be simpler to label—all belonging in romantic-suspense and some also qualifying as mystery-suspense. Occasionally, an exceptional title by a romantic writer appears that is clearly a superior mystery-suspense (e.g., Barbara Paul's *The Renewable Virgin*).

Aikin, Joan. *Foul Matter.*

Cannell, Dorothy. *Down the Garden Path.*

Holland, Isabelle. *A Death at St. Anselm's.*

Kaye, M. M. *Death in Berlin.*

Lofts, Norah. *The Claw. Lady Living Alone.*

Macdonald, Malcolm. *Tessa D'Arblay.*

Michaels, Barbara. *Someone in the House. The Wizard's Daughter.*

Paul, Barbara. *The Renewable Virgin. Your Eyelids Are Growing Heavy.*

Peters, Elizabeth. *The Camelot Caper.*

Stewart, Mary. *My Brother Michael.*

Whitney, Phyllis. *Hunter's Green.*

Crime/Caper

The label "crime" is used quite generally in publishing and reviewing to encompass all thrillers. In this book it is used for the novel that centers on the perpetrator of a crime, whether a professional criminal or an amateur (the ordinary person who is pushed to the limits of endurance in a situation and then decides a criminal act is the only solution). Between the two extremes lies a plethora of rogues of both sexes, all degrees of education, and varying social classes, all sharing the trait of cunning, whether they are stupid or highly intelligent. Among the private eyes are found a number of rogues, but their criminous acts are usually for a good cause—the epithet for them is amoral rather than criminal. The day of the master criminal is past, although Sax Rohmer's Dr. Fu Manchu stories are finding some new fans. *Ellery Queen's Crookbook* celebrates the genre. These crime novels vary from harshly realistic to picaresque or comic. Many of the following authors write other types of thrillers; the titles noted are examples from their novels that distinctly involve a caper.

UNDERWORLD

A few authors write with harsh realism of the underworld of crime (Burnett, Greene, and Higgins are in the following list, but one might include Dashiell Hammett). Other authors treat the underworld and its criminals with realism but combine criminals and amoral rogues to allow for a character with whom the reader can sympathize.

Barnao, Jack. *Locke Step.*

Bayer, William. *Blind Side.*

Browne, Gerald. *Hot Siberian. 19 Purchase Street. 11 Harrowhouse. Green Ice. Stone 588.*

Burnett, W. R. *Little Caesar. The Asphalt Jungle.*

Chafets, Ze'ev. *Inherit the Mob.*

Chase, James Hadley. *No Orchids for Miss Blandish.*

Condon, Richard. *Prizzi's Honor. Prizzi's Family. Prizzi's Glory.*

Diehl, William. *Thai Horse.*

Doctorow, E. L. *Billy Bathgate.*

Dunet, Sarah. *Snowstorms in a Hot Climate.*

Estleman, Loren D. *Kill Zone. Roses Are Dead.*

Freemantle, Brian. *The Choice of Eddie Franks.*

Greene, Graham. *Brighton Rock. This Gun for Hire.*

Higgins, George V. *The Friends of Eddie Coyle.*

Izzi, Eugene. *Invasions. Prime Roll. King of the Hustlers. The Booster.*

Kakonis, Tom. *Michigan Roll.*

Katzenbach, John. *Day of Reckoning.*

Leonard, Elmore. *Stick. Cat Chase. Split Images. Glitz. Swag. The Switch.*

Puzo, Mario. *The Godfather. The Sicilian.*

Reardon, James. *Hard Time Tommy Sloane.*

Thomas, Ross. *Chinaman's Chance.*

Vachss, Andrew. *Strega.*

Woods, Stuart. *L. A. Times.*

ROGUE

The cheerfully amoral rogue is, with a few exceptions, a likable character who, though in contravention of the law, doesn't seem *too* serious to the reader. Many of them appear in series. In the following list are indifferent thieves, con men, and shady rogues who pull off their deals with a blithe disregard of law and, usually, morality. The first listing is a miscellany of capers; it is followed by several groupings of patterned types of capers.

Archer, Jeffrey. *Not a Penny More, Not a Penny Less.*
    A classic tale of the biter bit.

Buckman, Peter. *The Rothschild Conversion.*
    Period piece in the 1850s.

Butterworth, Michael. *X Marks the Spot.*
    Stealing Marx's bones.

Cain, James M. *The Postman Always Rings Twice.*
    Somber insurance swindle.

Canning, Victor. *Fall from Grace.*

Cecil, Henry. *Much in Evidence. The Painswick Line.*
    Many of his law court comedies are also comic capers.

Crichton, Michael. *The Great Train Robbery.*

Delacorta. *Diva. Nan. Luna. Lola.*

Drummond, Ivor. Series about a trio of roguish crime-busters: Lady Jennifer, Colley, and Count Sandro.

Fleming H. F. *The Day They Kidnapped Queen Victoria.*

Furst, Alan. *Your Day in the Barrel. The Paris Drop.*
    Feature Robert Levin.

Gilbert, Michael. *End-Game. The Long Voyage Home.*
    International business scams.

Godey, John. *The Taking of Pelham One Two Three.*
    Hijacking a New York subway train.

Hallahan, William H. *The Ross Forgery.*

Hill, Reginald. *A Very Good Hater: A Tale of Revenge.*

Hull, Richard. *The Murder of My Aunt.*
    A classic.

Lehman, Ernest. *The French Atlantic Affair.*

MacKenzie, Donald. John Raven series.
    An ex-Scotland Yard detective involved in all types of capers.

Petievich, Gerald. *To Die in Beverly Hills.*

Roudybush, Alexandra. *A Gastronomic Murder*.
Jewel theft *and* food.

Taylor, Andrew. *Caroline Minuscule*.
Jewel theft.

Wainwright, John. *Clouds of Guilt*.

Burglars

Block, Lawrence. *Burglars Can't Be Choosers. The Burglar in the Closet. The Burglar Who Liked to Quote Kipling. The Burglar Who Painted Like Mondrian. The Burglar Who Studied Spinoza*.
Feature Bernard Rhodenbarr.

Dodge, David. *To Catch a Thief*.

Gores, Joe. *Come Morning*.

Hoch, Edward D. *The Thefts of Nick Velvet*.

Hornung, E. W. *The Complete Short Stories of Raffles—The Amateur Cracksman*.
Series continued by Perowne (see entry in this list).

Leblanc, Maurice. *The Extraordinary Adventures of Arséne Lupin, Gentleman-Burglar*.

Perowne, Barry. *Raffles Revisited: Some New Adventures of a Famous Gentleman Crook. Raffles of the Albany*.

Royce, Kenneth. *The Crypto Man. Spider Underground. The Masterpiece Affair*.
Spider Scott, reformed cat burglar.

Stark, Richard. *Butcher's Moon. Deadly Edge*.
Pseudonym of Donald E. Westlake. The Parker series had a long run as original paperbacks before appearing in hardcover.

Art

Many art scam titles appear in mystery/detection.

Bonfiglioli, Kyril. *Don't Point That Thing at Me* (U.S. edition, *Mortdecai's Endgame*). *After You with the Pistol*.
Features the Honorable Charlie Mortdecai.

Butterworth, Michael. *A Virgin on the Rocks*.

Canning, Victor. *Vanishing Point*.

Delahaye, Michael. *The Sale of Lot 236*.

Follett, Ken. *The Modigliani Scandal*.

Goldman, James. *The Man from Greek and Roman*.

Harris, MacDonald. *The Treasure of Sainte Foy*.

Page, Martin. *The Man Who Stole the Mona Lisa* (British edition, *Set a Thief*).

Westheimer, David. *The Olmec Head.*

Smuggling

Ellin, Stanley. *The Luxembourg Run.*

Fish, Robert L. *Kek Huuygens, Smuggler. The Wager. Whirligig. The Tricks of the Trade.*
All are about Kek Huuygens.

Hallahan, William H. *Foxcatcher.*

Amoral Rogue and Hit Man

Highsmith, Patricia. *The Talented Mr. Ripley. Ripley Under Ground. Ripley's Game. The Boy Who Followed Ripley.*

Perry, Thomas. *The Butcher's Boy. Metzger's Dog. Big Fish.*

Smith, Evelyn. *Miss Melville Rides a Tiger. Miss Melville Returns. Miss Melville Regrets. Miss Melville's Revenge.*

Van de Wetering, Janwillem. *The Butterfly Hunter.*

Elderly Rogues

Carson, Robert. *The Golden Years Caper.*
Band of elderly in Long Beach, California, who find "The wages of sin are bankable."

Fish, Robert L. *The Murder League. Rub-A-Dub-Dub. A Gross Carriage of Justice.*
Three retired writers of mystery novels.

Women

Their capers are various.

Andress, Lesley. *Caper.*

Bailey, Hilary. *Hannie Richards, or The Intrepid Adventures of a Restless Wife.*

Cornelisen, Ann. *Any Four Women Could Rob the Bank of Italy.*

Garfield, Brian. *Necessity.*

Sheldon, Sidney. *If Tomorrow Comes.*

COMIC CAPER

Among the authors previously listed are several who use humor either broadly or sardonically. A determinedly comic treatment is used by the following authors, making felicitous the union of comedy and crime without the defects of farce. (See Frank Norman's private detective novels for his lovely depiction of cockney crooks.)

Butterworth, Michael. *The Man in the Sopwith Camel. The Man Who Broke the Bank at Monte Carlo.*

Childress, Mark. *Crazy in Alabama.*

Follett, Ken. *Paper Money.*

Hiaasen, Carl. *Double Whammy. Tourist Season. Skin Tight. Native Tongue. Strip Tease.*

Hunter, Evan. *Every Little Crook and Nanny.*

Lyons, Nan, and Ivan Lyons. *Someone Is Killing the Great Chefs of Europe. Champagne Blues.*

Westlake, Donald E. *Good Behavior. God Save the Mark. High Adventure. Why Me.*
And many, many more, many featuring John Dortmunder, burglar, all greeted with cheers by his many fans.

Legal Thriller

The legal thriller is playing big to movie houses and best-seller lists. This type features as the hero a lawyer who has gotten into a fix and needs to extricate him- or herself through clever use of a superior intellect. There actually is variety within this subgenre, from the earnest young attorney who finds out that he is unwittingly representing organized crime to the attorney wrongly accused of murder who is duped by those close to him. The hero can be a young legal student, who as an intellectual exercise, tries to solve murders but then, because of her theories, ends up as the target of the killers. In this type, the focus is not on the solving of a mystery but rather on the thrill of the chase, usually from the point of view of the one being chased!

Two of the top ten bestsellers for 1993, (according to *Publishers Weekly*) were legal thrillers; *The Client* by John Grisham, with over 2 million copies shipped, placing it in second place for the year; and *Pleading Guilty* by Scott Turow, in the eighth position with 710,000 copies shipped from the publisher.

Grisham, John. *A Time to Kill. The Firm. The Pelican Brief. The Client. The Chamber.*

Lescroart, John T. *The 13th Juror. Hard Evidence* (Dismas Hardy, defense attorney).

Martini, Steve. *Compelling Evidence. Prime Witness. Undue Influence.*

Rosenberg, Nancy Taylor. *First Offense. Mitigating Circumstances. Interest Of Justice.*

Stern, Mark. *Inadmissible.*

Tanenbaum, Robert K. *No Lesser Plea. Depraved Indifference. Immoral Certainty. Reversible Error. Material Witness.*

Turow, Scott. *Presumed Innocent. Burden of Proof. Pleading Guilty.*

Warfield, Gallatin. *Silent Son. State v. Justice.*

TOPICS

Biography of Fictional Detectives

The detective as a fictional character is given a biographical write-up in some studies on the detective story with a blandly literal tone, as though the detectives were actual living beings. Some books with biographical listings are noted later, but following are three works on, simply, the detectives themselves.

Pate, Janet. *The Book of Sleuths*. Contemporary Books, 1977.
    The lives of 40 detectives (including a few from comic strips, motion pictures, and television) are presented with emphasis on their careers. Bibliography and filmography are added with illustrations from the films. Among the detectives are: C. Auguste Dupin, Nick Carter, Sherlock Holmes, Father Brown, Bulldog Drummond, Hercule Poirot, Peter Wimsey, Charlie Chan, Philo Vance, Ellery Queen, Miss Marple, Sam Spade, The Saint, Nick Charles, Inspector Maigret, Perry Mason, Nero Wolfe, Philip Marlowe, Mike Hammer, Commander Gideon, and Piet Van der Valk.

Penzler, Otto, ed. *The Great Detectives*. Little, Brown, 1978.
    Twenty-six detectives are described by their creators: Roderick Alleyn (Ngaio Marsh); John Appleby (Michael Innes); Lew Archer (Ross Macdonald); Father Bredder (Leonard Holton); Flash Casey (George Harmon Coxe); Pierre Chambrun (Hugh Pentecost); Inspector Cockrill (Christianna Brand); Captain José Da Silva (Robert L. Fish); Nancy Drew (Carolyn Keene); the 87th Precinct (Ed McBain); Fred Fellows (Hillary Waugh); Inspector Ghote (H. R. F. Keating); Matt Helm (Donald Hamilton); Duncan Maclain (Baynard H. Kendrick); Mark McPherson (Vera Caspary); Lieutenant Luis Mendoza (Dell Shannon); Mr. and Mrs. North (Richard Lockridge); Patrick Petrella (Michael Gilbert); Superintendent Pibble (Peter Dickinson); Quiller (Adam Hall); Inspector Schmidt (George Bagby); The Shadow (Maxwell Grant); Michael Shayne (Brett Halliday); Virgil Tibbs (John Ball); Dick Tracy (Chester Gould); Inspector Van der Valk (Nicolas Freeling).

Penzler, Otto. *The Private Lives of Private Eyes, Spies, Crimefighters, & Other Good Guys*. Grossett, 1977.
    Twenty-five lives are illustrated from books and motion pictures, with bibliography and filmography for each: Lew Archer, Modesty Blaise, James Bond, Father Brown, Nick Carter, Charlie Chan, Nick and Nora Charles, Bulldog Drummond, C. Auguste Dupin, Mike Hammer, Sherlock Holmes, Jules Maigret, Philip Marlowe, Miss Jane Marple, Perry Mason, Mr. Moto, Hercule Poirot, Ellery Queen, The Shadow, John Shaft, Sam Spade, Dr. Thorndyke, Philo Vance, Lord Peter Wimsey, Nero Wolfe.

Best-Selling Authors

In 1990, four authors had titles that sold in excess of 100,000 copies for the year: Joseph Wambaugh (*The Golden Orange*), Tony Hillerman (*Coyote Waits*), P. D. James (*Devices and Desires*), and Robert B. Parker (*Stardust*). In 1975, the leading authors, in order of most sales (to that date), were: Mickey Spillane, Erle Stanley Gardner, Robert Traver, Joseph Wambaugh, and John D. MacDonald. Ten years earlier, Joseph Wambaugh did not appear and MacDonald was 11th in order. Following Spillane, Gardner, and Traver were: Ellery Queen, Agatha Christie, Richard S. Prather, A. A. Fair (Erle Stanley Gardner's pseudonym), Dashiell Hammett, Raymond Chandler, Earl Derr Biggers, Leslie Charteris, and Marco Page.

What type of detective has the greatest appeal? Wambaugh's Los Angeles policemen are realistic. Hillerman's detectives are Native Americans in a setting unfamiliar to most readers. Spillane's private eye is notorious for sex and sadism. Ellery Queen, the investigator, is a sophisticated gentleman. Christie's Poirot and Miss Marple are genteel figures suitable to social comedy. Bigger's Charlie Chan is unique. Charteris's The Saint is a rogue and a gentleman. The readers, then, take their popular choice.

In sheer volume of titles, which collectively have a large sale, John Creasey's books belong among the best-sellers. Creasey used some 28 pseudonyms to produce about 650 titles, largely mystery, detective, and spy stories, and some westerns (under three pseudonyms). He averaged about 12 titles per year. Reprints now appear with the pseudonymous works revealing the Creasey authorship. The Toff series was written under Creasey. His best-known pseudonyms are Kyle Hunt (psychiatrist Emmanuel Cellini series); Anthony Morton (The Baron John Mannering series); J. J. Marric (Commander Gideon of Scotland Yard series); Gordon Ashe (Pat Dawlish of Scotland Yard series); and Jeremy York (Superintendent Folly of Scotland Yard series).

Anthologies

Almost all of the early and current writers of detective stories have used the short story, and the following anthologies provide a satisfactory introduction for choosing those authors whose style in the subgenre is pleasing to individual reader's tastes. Many of the anthologies also include other types of thrillers: spy, psychological-suspense, crime, and the like. The following listing is selective. Included are several annual series.

Barzun, Jacques, ed. *The Delights of Detection*. Criterion, 1961.
> The anthology is delightful, beginning with Barzun's essay, "Detection and the Literary Art, " and followed by 17 stories written by Ernest Bramah, G. K. Chesterton, Kenneth Livingston, Dorothy L. Sayers, E. C. Bentley, H. C. Bailey, R. Austin Freeman, Harry Kemelman, Daniel Pattiward, John D. MacDonald, Edmund Crispin, Bayard Wendell, Michael Gilbert, Rex Stout, P. C. de Beaumarchais, William Leggett, Alexandre Dumas.

Best Detective Stories of the Year. 1945–1981.
Includes list of award winners and bibliography of nonfiction for the year. Title change: See *The Year's Best Mystery and Suspense Stories.*

Crime Writers Association Annual.
Sampling of titles: *Butcher's Dozen; A Pride of Felons; Crime Writers' Choice; Choice of Weapons; Some Like Them Dead; Planned Departures. John Creasey's Crime Collection. 1st Culprit. 2nd Culprit.*

Deadly Allies: Private Eye Writers of America/ Sisters in Crime Collaborative Anthology. Doubleday, 1992.

Deadly Allies II. Doubleday, 1994.

Greenberg, Martin H., and Bill Pronzini, eds. *Police Procedurals.* Academy Chicago, 1985. (Academy Mystery Novellas, vol. 2).

Greene, Hugh, ed. *The Further Rivals of Sherlock Holmes.* Pantheon, 1973.

Greene, Hugh, ed. *The Rivals of Sherlock Holmes: Early Detective Stories.* Pantheon, 1970.

Haycraft, Howard, and John Beecroft, eds. *A Treasury of Great Mysteries.* Simon & Schuster, 1957. 2 vols.
Includes four novels: Agatha Christie, *Murder in the Calais Coach;* Eric Ambler, *Journey into Fear;* Raymond Chandler, *The Big Sleep;* Daphne Du Maurier, *Rebecca;* and stories by Erle Stanley Gardner, Edgar Wallace, Georges Simenon, Patrick Quentin, Mary Roberts Rinehart, John Dickson Carr, Ellery Queen, Margery Allingham, William Irish, Dorothy L. Sayers, Leslie Charteris, Ngaio Marsh, Rex Stout, Stuart Palmer and Craig Rice, Carter Dickson.

Hitchcock, Alfred. *Alfred Hitchcock's Tales to Keep You Spellbound,* vol. 1. Dial, 1977.
From *Alfred Hitchcock's Mystery Magazine.*

Hubin, Allen J., ed. *Best of the Best Detective Stories.* Dutton, 1971.

Kittredge, William, and Steven M. Krauzen, eds. *The Great American Detective.* NAL, 1978.
The detectives: Nick Carter, Race Williams, Sam Spade, The Shadow, Philip Marlowe, Ellery Queen, Dan Turner, Susan Dare, Jerry Wheeler, Hildegard Withers, Nero Wolfe, Perry Mason, Michael Shayne, Lew Archer, Mack Bolan, the Executioner.

Manson, Cynthia, ed. *Death on the Verandah: Mystery stories of the South from Ellery Queen's Mystery Magazine and Alfred Hitchcock's Mystery Magazine.* Carroll & Graf, 1994.

McCullough, David Willis, ed. *Great Detectives: A Century of the Best Mysteries from England and America.* Pantheon, 1984.

Mystery Writers of America Annual.
Sampling of titles: *Crime Across the Sea; Sleuths and Consequences; With Malice Toward All; Crime Without Murder; Murder Most Foul; Dear Dead Days; Mirror Mirror, Fatal Mirror; Every Crime in the Book; When Last Seen.* (The 33rd edition, *The Edgar Winners* [1980], presents 23 stories, winners of the Edgar Award for the Best Mystery Short Story of the Year, 1947–1978. In 1990, *New Edgar Winners* was published.)

Pronzini, Bill, ed. *The Arbor House Treasury of Detective and Mystery Stories from the Great Pulps.* Arbor House, 1983.

Pronzini, Bill, and Martin H. Greenberg, eds. *The Ethnic Detectives.* Dodd, 1985.
Represented are Chinese, Jewish, American Indian, French, Czech, African American, Hispanic, and Tahitian.

Pronzini, Bill, Barry N. Malzberg, and Martin H. Greenberg, comps. *The Arbor House Treasury of Mystery and Suspense.* With an introduction by John D. MacDonald. Arbor House, 1981.
Among 41 authors are 12 usually not considered genre authors and a few science fiction authors.

Queen, Ellery, ed. *Ellery Queen's.* Too many different titles to list here but a great source of crime anthologies. This annual started in 1945 and was published for over 30 years.

Randisi, Robert J., ed. *The Eyes Have It.* Mysterious Press, 1985.
The first Private Eye Writers of America anthology. Other titles are: *Mean Streets; An Eye for Justice; Justice for Hire.*

Sayers, Dorothy L., ed. *Great Short Stories of Detection, Mystery and Horror.* Series one to three. London: Gollancz, 1929–1934.
Also published as *Omnibus of Crime.*

Sullivan, Eleanor, and Karen A. Prince, eds. *Ellery Queen's Memorable Characters.* Doubleday/Dial, 1984.
Stories from *Ellery Queen's Mystery Magazine.*

Winter's Crimes. Macmillan, 1969– .
A British annual.

The Year's Best Mystery and Suspense Stories. 1982– .
Supersedes *Best Detective Stories of the Year.* Continues sections: "The Yearbook of the Mystery and Suspense Story" and adds a list of the best novels of the year.

The Year's 25 Finest Crime and Mystery Stories. Edited by the staff of *Mystery Scene.* Carroll & Graf, 1993. annual.
The overview of the previous year's highlights and mystery news is great fun.

HARD-BOILED DETECTIVES

The hard-boiled detective had his first glory in the pulp magazines in the United States in the 1920s. Many of the authors of note in the history of the detective story in the United States first appeared in the pulp magazines. They wrote largely of the underworld of crime in which their tough detectives held their own. Although a few British authors created hard-boiled detectives, the following anthologies present stories by the originators of the type.

Goulart, Ron, ed. *The Hardboiled Dicks: An Anthology and Study of Pulp Detective Fiction*. Sherbourne, 1965.

Nolan, William F., ed. *The Black Mask Boys: Masters in the Hard-Boiled School of Detective Fiction*. Morrow, 1984.

Ruhm, Herbert, ed. *The Hard-Boiled Detective: Stories from Black Mask Magazine, 1920–1952*. Vintage Books, 1977.
There is an introduction by the editor to stories by Carroll John Daly, Dashiell Hammett, Norbert Davis, Frederick Nebel, Raymond Chandler, Lester Dent, Erle Stanley Gardner, George Harmon Coxe, Merle Constiner, William Brandon, Curt Hamlin, Paul W. Fairman, and Bruno Fischer.

Shaw, Joseph T., ed. *The Hard-Boiled Omnibus: Early Stories from Black Mask*. Simon & Schuster, 1946.
There is an introduction by Shaw, editor of *Black Mask*. The authors included: Lester Dent, Reuben Jennings Shaw, Raoul Whitfield, Raymond Chandler, Dashiell Hammett, Norbert Davis, Paul Cain, Thomas Walsh, Ed Lybeck, Roger Torrey, and Theodore Tinsley.

WOMEN DETECTIVES

Women appeared as fictional detectives as early as 1861. The following anthologies show the varieties in types of women detectives and that their modern role has changed dramatically.

Greenberg, Martin H., and Bill Pronzini, eds. *Women Sleuths*. Academy Chicago, 1985. (Academy Mystery Novellas, vol. 1).

Manley, Seon, and Gogo Lewis, comps. *Grande Dames of Detection: Two Centuries of Sleuthing Stories by the Gentle Sex*. Lothrop, 1973.
Among the authors are Baroness Orczy, Carolyn Wells, Agatha Christie, Dorothy L. Sayers, and Margery Allingham.

Manson, Cynthia, ed. *Women of Mystery*. Berkley Books, 1993.
Stories by the big names of the nineties, Mary Higgins Clark, Ruth Rendell, Antonia Fraser, Joan Hess, and many more.

Queen, Ellery, ed. *The Female of the Species*. Little, Brown, 1943.
This early short-story anthology includes women both as detectives and criminals.

Slung, Michele B., ed. *Crime on Her Mind: Fifteen Stories of Female Sleuths from the Victoria Era to the Forties*. Pantheon, 1975.
The introduction presents a critical history, and an appendix lists the lady detectives in chronological order from 1861 to 1973, with annotations.

Wallace, Marilyn, ed. *Sisters in Crime* annual anthology started in 1989.

DETECTIVES AND SCIENCE FICTION

In chapter 6, "Science Fiction," there is a section on the detective in space (see p. 231), a neat combination of genres. The following three anthologies indicate that this conjunction of the genres is not new.

Asimov, Isaac, Martin H. Greenberg, and Charles Waugh, eds. *Thirteen Crimes of Science Fiction*. Doubleday, 1979.

De Ford, Miriam Allen, ed. *Space, Time and Crime*. Paperback Library, 1964.

Santesson, Hans Stefan, ed. *Crime Prevention in the 30th Century*. Walker, 1970.

PLAYS

Agatha Christie and Dorothy L. Sayers, among others, have written plays of detection. Christie's *The Mousetrap* is London's longest-running play. Dorothy L. Sayers first wrote *Busman's Honeymoon* as a play, which had a successful run and was later made into a motion picture. Mary Roberts Rinehart's *The Bat* was also a stage success. Many of the plays of mystery and detection in the following anthologies were made into motion pictures. (See also "Film," p. 128.)

Cartmell, Van H., and Bennett Cerf, eds. *Famous Plays of Crime and Detection*. Blakiston, 1946.

Richards, Stanley, ed. *Best Mystery and Suspense Plays of the Modern Theatre*. Dodd, 1971.

Richards, Stanley, ed. *Ten Classic Mystery and Suspense Plays of the Modern Theatre*. Dodd, 1973.

Bibliographies

The following bibliographies vary in coverage. Some are of the authors in the genre, some include material on allied genres, some are of secondary works, and several embrace a number of aspects.

Albert, Walter. *Detective and Mystery Fiction: An International Bibliography of Secondary Sources*. Brownstone Books, 1985.
An exhaustive and indispensable bibliography, critically annotated. In four sections: bibliographies, dictionaries, encyclopedias, and

checklists; general reference works; dime novels, juvenile series, and pulps; authors. Over 5,000 citations, of which over 3,000 are in the author section. Excludes Sherlockiana.

Barnes, Melvin. *Best Detective Fiction: A Guide from Godwin to the Present.* London: Bingley, 1975.
Critical and highly selective, with surprising omissions (e.g., P. D. James).

Barzun, Jacques, and Wendell Hertig Taylor. *A Catalogue of Crime.* Harper, 1971.
Selective, idiosyncratic, and delightful for the personal annotations by two devoted academic fans who sometimes disagree in opinion, this is a bibliography to read for its critical flavor and bite. The scope encompasses ghost stories and true crime. There are sections on the short story and play, critical works on the genre, and all aspects of Sherlock Holmes. The bibliography is currently being continued in *The Armchair Detective.*

Breen, Jon L. *What About Murder? A Guide to Books About Mystery and Detective Fiction.* Scarecrow Press, 1981. Supplemented in 1993 with *What About Murder? 1981–1991.*
Two-hundred and thirty-nine books are listed and critically annotated. There are seven sections: General Histories, Reference Books, Special Subjects, Collected Essays and Reviews, Technical Manuals, Coffee-Table Books, Works on Individual Authors. The annotations are extensive and reveal Breen's wide reading and obvious enjoyment of the genre. Indispensable for serious fans.

Cox, J. Randolph. *Masters of Mystery and Detective Fiction.* Salem Press, 1989.
An annotated bibliography of 74 mystery authors including biographical information.

Hagen, Ordean A. *Who Done It? A Guide to Detective, Mystery and Suspense Fiction.* Bowker, 1969.
Now replaced by Hubin (see entry below) but still of interest for the subject and background sections, the bibliography of secondary material, and the like.

Hubin, Allen J. *Crime Fiction: A Comprehensive Bibliography, 1749–1990.* Garland, 1994.
The most comprehensive bibliography of crime fiction in its expanded third edition. Noted are series detectives and pseudonyms. There are two indices: title and series characters. In this edition are several new features: for each author are code-noted citations to eight reference books; a series character chronology; and an extensive "Settings Index" (50 pages), largely geographical but including academic, church, future, hospital, ships, theater, and trains.

Johnson, Timothy W., and Julia Johnson, eds. *Crime Fiction Criticism: An Annotated Bibliography.* Garland, 1981.

The annotations are concise and critical. "General Works," 350 items, includes reference works, monographs, dissertations, and articles and portions of books. There are 1,480 items on over 250 individual authors.

Melvin, David Skene, and Anne Skene Melvin, comps. *Crime, Detective, Espionage, Mystery and Thriller Fiction & Film: A Comprehensive Bibliography of Critical Writing Through 1979.* Greenwood Press, 1980.

An alphabetical listing without annotation. Omitted is "Holmesiana," for which the compilers refer the user to De Wall's bibliography, and the following genres: macabre, fantasy, ghosts, supernatural, Gothic, science fiction.

Nichols, Victoria, and Susan Thompson. *Silk Stalkings: When Women Write of Murder.* Black Lizard Books, 1988.

"A survey of series characters created by women authors in crime and mystery fiction." Characters are grouped by setting and extensive quotations provide a feel for the flavor of the subject stories. Appendices include a series character chronology placing characters in time with others of the same era from 1867 to 1987, a pseudonym to "autonym" section, and a section that links series characters to their authors.

Olderr, Steven. *Mystery Index: Subjects, Settings and Sleuths of 10,000 Titles.* American Library Association, 1987.

Books that have a good possibility of being in a public library collection are indexed by title, subject and setting, and characters.

Oleksiw, Susan. *A Reader's Guide to the Classic British Mystery.* G. K. Hall, 1988.

Covering more than 1,440 mystery novels and 121 authors, access is provided by indices to characters' occupations, time periods, and settings.

Twentieth-Century Crime and Mystery Writers. 2d ed. Edited by John M. Reilly. St. Martin's, 1985.

Some 600 writers are given bibliographical and critical coverage. Works listed include nongenre titles. The critical essays vary greatly in length and quality and are signed. Occasionally the author has also supplied a brief personal essay. The appendix adds 9 nineteenth-century writers and 16 foreign writers. About 100 new writers have been added to the second edition and about an equal number have been dropped.

History

There is now a voluminous body of history and criticism on the detective subgenre. Many titles include material on the mystery, crime, spy, and horror stories as well. Although *Genreflecting* makes a distinction between history and criticism (see p. 120), this categorization reflects each book's formal organization—both provide history *with* criticism. Despite the many works of history and criticism on the detective story, the definitive history is still to be written. The following works, excepting Haycraft's, are too specialized and idiosyncratic to be definitive.

Benvenuti, Stefano, and Gianni Rizzoni. *The Whodunit: An Informal History of Detective Fiction.* Translated by Anthony Eyre. With "A Report on the Current Scene" by Edward D. Hoch. London: Macmillan, 1981.
Delightfully written and illustrated. The Italian authors are appreciative and critical readers. There is a chapter on "The French Connection."

Craig, Patricia, and Mary Cadogan. *The Lady Investigates: Women Detectives and Spies in Fiction.* London: Gollancz, 1980. New York: St. Martin's Press, 1981.
The history starts with Mrs. Paschal in *The Revelations of a Lady Detective* (1861) and describes the variety of women detectives to date, with stringent criticism of their quality as detectives. The chapter "Spouses, Secretaries and Sparring Partners" acknowledges the women whose role was secondary to the male detectives'. "A Sweet Girl Sleuth: The Teenage Detective in America" discusses the tribe of Nancy Drew's ("You're a regular detective, Nancy!"). Many lovely quotations.

Haining, Peter. *Mystery! An Illustrated History of Crime and Detective Fiction.* Souvenir Press, 1977. New York: Stein and Day, 1981.
The history is sketchy but the illustrations are voluminous and imaginative.

Haycraft, Howard. *Murder for Pleasure: The Life and Times of the Detective Story.* Appleton, 1941.
Still the basic history despite its date. It includes a list of "Cornerstones," 1841–1938, and a guide to characters, "Who's Who in Detection."

LaCour, Tage, and Harold Mogensen. *The Murder Book: An Illustrated History of the Detective Story.* Herder, 1974.
This is translated from the Danish and contains interesting European references. The history is presented topically. The illustrations are varied and wonderful.

Murch, A. E. *The Development of the Detective Novel.* London: Owen, 1958.
Useful for the early history.

Ousby, Ian. *Bloodhounds of Heaven: The Detective in English Fiction from Godwin to Doyle*. Harvard, 1976.
Main coverage is on William Godwin, Vidocq, Dickens, Collins, and Conan Doyle.

Quayle, Eric. *The Collector's Book of Detective Fiction*. Photographs by Gabriel Monro. London: Studio Vista, 1972.
A history for the collector of the genre, with numerous illustrations, many in color, of bindings and illustrations of early classics.

Routley, Erik. *The Puritan Pleasures of the Detective Story*. London: Gollancz, 1972.
Emphasis is on the British story.

Scott, Sutherland. *Blood in Their Ink: The March of the Modern Mystery Story*. London: Stanley Paul, 1953.
His interest is largely in the detective story.

Siegel, Jeff. *The American Detective: An Illustrated History*. Dallas: Taylor, 1993.

Stewart, R. F. *. . . And Always a Detective: Chapters on the History of Detective Fiction*. London: David & Charles, 1980.
Not a standard history but a fascinating discussion of the origins of the sensational thriller in the nineteenth century and the development of the image of the detective. This is for the knowledgeable fan.

Symons, Julian. *Bloody Murder: From the Detective Story to the Crime Novel: A History*. Viking, 1985.
First published in 1972 (the U.S. edition with title *Mortal Consequences*). In this edition the author brings the history up-to-date and assesses as still valid his conclusion that the classic detective story is played out and the more realistic, psychological, sociological crime novel is in ascendance.

Thomson, H. Douglas. *Masters of Mystery: A Study of the Detective Story*. With a new introduction by E. F. Bleiler. Dover, 1978.
First published by Collins of London in 1931. Still cited often for its criticism of the early authors.

Criticism

The section of bibliographies (see p. 116) provides a guide to the voluminous critical material on the detection and mystery subgenres, including works on individual authors. The following selection from this voluminous literature is indicative of the many of the types of criticism available.

Allen, Dick, and David Chacko, eds. *Detective Fiction: Crime and Compromise*. Harcourt, 1974.
This is an anthology of stories, with a section on criticism, meant to be used as a textbook. There are questions, suggested topics, and a

reading list for students. The scope is extended to include writers not generally considered detective authors.

Baker, Robert A., and Michael T. Nietzel. *Private Eyes: One Hundred and One Knights: A Survey of American Detective Fiction, 1922–1984.* Popular Press, 1985.
An appendix, "Jousters and Contenders," briefly discusses many more private eyes.

Baker, Jane S., ed. *And Then There Were Nine . . . More Women of Mystery.* Popular Press, 1985.
Anthology of essays on: Daphne du Maurier, Margery Allingham, Anne Morice, Dorothy Uhnak, Lillian O'Donnell, Craig Rice, E. X. Ferrars, Patricia Highsmith, Shirley Jackson.

Ball, John, ed. *The Mystery Story.* University of California Publisher's, 1976.
Noted writers here comment on aspects of the subgenre: amateur, women, ethnic, police, and private detectives; locked rooms; spies, "Gothic Mysteries"; series characters; "The Great Crooks"; use of pseudonyms. There is also an annotated subject bibliography.

Bargainnier, Earl F., ed. *10 Women of Mystery.* Popular Press, 1981.
Anthology of critical essays on: Dorothy L. Sayers, Josephine Tey, Ngaio Marsh, P. D. James, Ruth Rendell, Anna Katharine Green, Mary Roberts Rinehart, Margaret Millar, Emma Lathen, Amanda Cross. Also a list of authors who might be included were 10 not the limit.

Bargainnier, Earl F., ed. *Twelve Englishmen of Mystery.* Popular Press, 1984.
Essays on Wilkie Collins, A. E. W. Mason, G. K. Chesterton, H. C. Bailey, Anthony Berkeley Cox, Nicholas Blake, Michael Gilbert, Julian Symons, Dick Francis, Edmund Crispin, H. R. F. Keating, and Simon Brett.

Chandler, Raymond. *Raymond Chandler Speaking.* London: Hamilton, 1962.

Chandler, Raymond. *The Simple Art of Murder.* Norton, 1968.
The first title contains letters, many pungently critical, on a variety of subjects relating to his writings and the detective story. The second is a collection of his short stories and includes the title essay, a classic statement much anthologized.

Dove, George N. *The Police Procedural.* Popular Press, 1982.
After chapters defining the procedural, there are chapters on woman, black, Jewish, and Hispanic detectives, followed by critical essays on John Creasey, Maurice Procter, Hillary Waugh, Ed McBain, Bill Knox, Nicolas Freeling, Maj Sjöwall and Per Wahlöö, Collin Wilcox and James McClure.

Eames, Hugh. *Sleuths Inc. Studies of Problem Solvers: Doyle, Simenon, Hammett, Ambler, Chandler.* Lippincott, 1978.

Freeman, Lucy, ed. *The Murder Mystique: Crime Writers on Their Art*. Ungar, 1982.
Eleven essays: five on the genre, six on techniques.

Geherin, David. *The American Private Eye: The Images in Fiction*. Ungar, 1985.

Survey of 27 private eyes, from Dashiell Hammett's Continental Op to Lawrence Block's Matt Scudder.

Geherin, David. *Sons of Sam Spade: The Private-Eye Novel in the 70s: Robert B. Parker, Roger L. Simon, Andrew Bergman*. Ungar, 1980.

Gilbert, Michael, ed. *Crime in Good Company: Essays on Criminals and Crime-Writing*. London: Constable, 1959.
This excellent collection "on behalf of the Crime Writers' Association" both defines and criticizes. Among the contributors: Josephine Bell, Michael Underwood, Maurice Procter, Cyril Hare, Raymond Chandler ("The Simple Art of Murder"), Michael Gilbert, Julian Symons, Jacques Barzun, Stanley Ellin, Eric Ambler.

Haycraft, Howard, ed. *The Art of the Mystery Story: A Collection of Critical Essays*. Simon & Schuster, 1946. Rereleased by Carroll & Graf in 1983.
The best all-round anthology of the classic essays by both authors and fans of the genre. Includes "The Detection Club Oath"; "Who Cares Who Killed Roger Ackroyd?" by Edmund Wilson; "The Locked-Room Lecture," by John Dickson Carr; "Watson Was a Woman," by Rex Stout and a treasure of others.

Jakubowski, Maxim, ed. *100 Great Detectives, or, The Detective Directory*. Carroll & Graf, 1991.
One hundred essays on fictional detectives written by the authors who selected them as favorites, each handily including listings of works featuring the detectives. In addition to the essays, Jakubowski has included (in a very condensed format) listings of the contributors' sleuths as well as a list of several beloved detectives who weren't included. This is a delightful browsing book as well as a useful reference.

Keating, H. R. F. *Whodunit? A Guide to Crime, Suspense and Spy Fiction*. London: Windward, 1982.
Mainly an alphabetical guide to writers, graded for characterization, plot, readability, and tension. Also has introductions on the nature of the genre. Many illustrations.

Lambert, Gavin. *The Dangerous Edge*. London: Barrie, 1975.
A disturbing analysis of our obsession with conflict and fear, using evidence from the works of Wilkie Collins, Sir Arthur Conan Doyle, G. K. Chesterton, John Buchan, Eric Ambler, Graham Greene, Georges Simenon, and Raymond Chandler.

Landrum, Larry. "Detective and Mystery Novels." In Inge, M. Thomas, ed. *The Handbook of American Popular Culture*, 1978. Vol. 1, pages 103–20.

Landrum, Larry N., Pat Browne, and Ray B. Browne, eds. *Dimensions of Detective Fiction*. Popular Press, 1976.
Twenty-three essays by academics cover diverse aspects of the genre and a number of individual writers.

Larmoth, Jeanne. *Murder on the Menu*. Recipes by Charlotte Turgeon. Scribner's, 1972.
Seemingly every possible situation in the English mystery, particularly in the country house or village setting, at which food could be served is described, complete with recipes. Along with the fun is some witty criticism of the genre and appropriate quotations.

Madden, David, ed. *Tough Guy Writers of the Thirties*. Southern Illinois Press, 1958.
Includes essays on the *Black Mask* authors, Dashiell Hammett, James M. Cain, and Raymond Chandler.

Magill, Frank N., ed. *Critical Survey of Mystery and Detective Fiction*. Salem Press, 1988.
A four-volume set that provides critical surveys of several thriller subgenres, including espionage and romantic suspense. Two hundred seventy authors are covered.

Mann, Jessica. *Deadlier Than the Male: An Investigation into Feminine Crime Writing*. London: David & Charles, 1981. The American title is *Deadlier Than the Male: Why Are Respectable English Women So Good at Murder?* Macmillan, 1981.
"Why is it that respectable English women are so good at murder?" asks the author who then seeks elucidation through the lives and works of Agatha Christie, Dorothy L. Sayers, Margery Allingham, Josephine Tey, and Ngaio Marsh. Her long first part is an intriguing definition of the subgenre and its heroes and heroines. Her conclusion is that these authors reflected a stable and, to them, desirable society, that in the present society of angry chaos, authors will reflect not a background received with pleasure but a background that will terrify the readers. Jessica Mann sees the subgenre becoming not an entertainment but virtually indistinguishable from the anguishedly realistic mainstream novel.

Marguiles, Edward. *Which Way Did He Go? The Private Eye in Dashiell Hammett, Raymond Chandler, Chester Himes, and Ross Macdonald*. Holmes & Meier, 1982.

The Mystery and Detection Annual. 1972 and 1973.
Donald Adams edited and published these two exemplary volumes of essays and reviews, beautifully printed and illustrated.

Panek, LeRoy. *Watteau's Shepherds: The Detective Novel in Britain, 1914–1940*. Bowling Green University Popular Press, 1979.
With introductory materials, here are critical chapters on E. C. Bentley, Agatha Christie, A. A. Milne, Dorothy L. Sayers, Anthony Berkeley Cox, Margery Allingham, John Dickson Carr, and Ngaio Marsh. Appendix I provides an intriguing analysis of the detective story plot through the use of detailed flowcharts.

Porter, Dennis. *The Pursuit of Crime: Art and Ideology in Detective Fiction*. Yale University Press, 1981.
Analysis of the appeal of the genre and its world in relation to realism.

Pronzini, Bill. *Gun in Cheek: A Study of "Alternative" Crime Fiction*.
A charmingly amusing survey of "bad," in every literary sense, but popular mystery fiction. The liberal use of quotations relieves one of the need to read the books!

Reddy, Maureen T. *Sisters in Crime*. Crossroad/Ungar/Continuum, 1988.
A critical exploration of contemporary American women series detectives.

Sayers, Dorothy L. "Introduction" to her *Great Short Stories of Detection, Mystery and Horror*.
This classic critical history on the origins and development of the detective story is often reprinted. There is also an excellent shorter introduction to the second series and one to her other anthology, *Tales of Detection*. (See listing of anthologies.)

Symons, Julian. *Critical Observations*. Ticknor & Fields, 1981.
Includes essays on: Agatha Christie, Georges Simenon, Raymond Chandler, and Dashiell Hammett.

Watson, Colin. *Snobbery with Violence: Crime Stories and Their Audience*. London: Eyre, 1971; New York: St. Martin's Press, 1972 (American edition).
The subgenre, sociologically considered, suffers badly, but the sophisticated fan will enjoy the writing.

Winks, Robin W., ed. *Colloquium on Crime: Eleven Renowned Writers Discuss Their Work*. Scribner's, 1986.
Essays by Robert Barnard, Rex Burns, K. C. Constantine, Dorothy Salisbury Davis, Michael Gilbert, Donald Hamilton, Joseph Hansen, Tony Hillerman, Reginald Hill, James McClure, Robert B. Parker, and Anne Pender.

Winks, Robin W., ed. *Detective Fiction: A Collection of Critical Essays*. Prentice-Hall, 1980. Revised edition Countryman Press, 1988.
Among the 17 essays are several of the classics: W. H. Auden, "The Guilty Vicarage"; Dorothy L. Sayers, "Aristotle on Detective Fiction"; Edmund Wilson, "Who Cares Who Killed Roger Ackroyd?"; Joseph Wood Krutch, "Only a Detective Story"; Gavin Lambert, "The Dangerous Edge"; Sayers's "Introduction" to *The Omnibus of*

Crime; Jacques Barzun, "Detection and the Literary Art." The appendix includes a description of university courses on the detective story, a critical bibliography, and "A Personal List of 200 Favorites" that includes some spy genre titles.

Winks, Robin W., ed. *The Historian as Detective: Essays on Evidence.* Harper, 1969.
The editor admits he compiled these 26 essays for fun, and the reader with tastes for historical research will share the fun as Winks draws parallels from detective stories to preface each historian's account of sleuthing for evidence.

Winks, Robin W., ed. *Modus Operandi: An Excursion into Detective Fiction.* Godine, 1982.
Perhaps the best explanation of why one reads detection, mystery, and spy fiction.

Winn, Dilys, comp. *Murder Ink: Revised, Revised, Still Unrepentant.* Perpetrated by Dilys Winn. Workman, 1984.
An anthology of sheer delight.

Winn, Dilys. *Murder Ink: The Mystery Reader's Companion.* Perpetrated by Dilys Winn. Workman, 1977.
The founder of the New York bookstore, Murder Ink, presents a delightful and irreverent miscellany, profusely illustrated, celebrating her favorite subgenre in all its guises.

Winn, Dilys, comp. *Murderess Ink: The Better Half of the Mystery.* Workman, 1979.
This is a lighthearted potpourri on women mystery writers, women in mystery stories, and women detectives. All in fun and lots of illustrations. There is, fortunately, an index to the miscellany.

CRITICISM—PARODY

So formalized a subgenre is readily parodied. To enjoy parody, the reader must be familiar with the authors parodied. Except for the book by Gorey, the following books are detective stories in which the style of the named author is parodied. The last two listed are (perhaps discreetly) by Anonymous.

Breen, Jon L. *Hair of the Sleuthhound: Parodies of Mystery Fiction.*
Twenty-two stories, brief and amusingly pointed.

Bruce, Leo. *Case for Three Detectives.* London: Bles, 1936.
Sergeant Beef solves the murder handily while Lord Simon Plimsoll (Peter Wimsey), Monsieur Amer Picon (Hercule Poirot) and Monsignor Smith (Father Brown) conjecture deviously and vainly.

Carper, Steve, ed. *The Defective Detective: Mystery Parodies by the Great Humorists.* New York: Citadel Press, 1992.

Christie, Agatha. *Partners in Crime*. London: Collins, 1929.
Tommy and Tuppence, Christie's husband and wife detective team, solve a series of cases and, in each, approach the problem as would one of the classic detectives. They mock the detectives' eccentricities of manner and speech. All the detectives were popular before 1929 when *Partners in Crime* was first published. (It is still available in paperback reprint.) Among the detectives are Dr. Thorndyke, Bull Dog Drummond, Sherlock Holmes, Father Brown, The Old Man in the Corner, Hanaud, Inspector French, Roger Sheringham, Dr. Fortune, and Poirot.

The Floating Admiral [by] Certain Members of the Detection Club. With a new introduction by Christianna Brand. Gregg Press, 1979; Ace Charter Books, 1980.
First published in 1932. Thirteen authors successively wrote a chapter, none knowing the final solution (although each in the appendix provides one, not revealed to the other authors). Among the familiar creators of this pseudoparody are G. K. Chesterton, G. D. H. and M. Cole, Henry Wade, Agatha Christie, Dorothy L. Sayers, Ronald A. Knox, Freeman Wills Crofts, Edgar Jepson, and Anthony Berkeley ("Clearing Up the Mess").

Gorey, Edward. *The Awdrey-Gore Legacy*. Dodd, 1972.
The inimitable drawings reveal all the tricks of the subgenre.

Kaye, Marvin. *The Game Is Afoot*. Sherlock Holmes parody.

Mainwaring, Marion. *Murder in Pastiche; Or, Nine Detectives All at Sea*. Macmillan, 1954.
Seeking to solve the murder on the luxury liner are passengers Atlas Poireau, Sir Jon. Nappleby, Jerry Pason, Broderick Tourneur, Trajan Beare, Miss Fan Silver, Spike Bludgeon, Mallory King, Lord Simon Quinsey.

Six Against Scotland Yard: In Which Margery Allingham, Anthony Berkeley, Freeman Wills Crofts, Father Ronald Knox, Dorothy L. Sayers, Russell Thorndike Commit the Crime of Murder Which Ex-Superintendent Cornish, C.I.D., Is Called Upon to Solve. Doubleday, 1936.

The Smiling Corpse. Wherein G. K. Chesterton, S. S. Van Dine, Sax Rohmer, and Dashiell Hammett Are Surprised to Find Themselves at a Murder. Farrar, 1935.

Encyclopedias

Still needed is an exhaustive encyclopedia for mystery and detective stories, but the following work is a promising beginning.

Steinbrunner, Chris, and Otto Penzler. *Encyclopedia of Mystery and Detection*. McGraw-Hill, 1976.

Entries are largely under authors and fictional detectives or other important characters. There are a few encyclopedia articles: "Black Mask"; "Collecting Detective Fiction"; "Comic Art Detectives"; "Dime Novels"; "Had-I-But-Known School"; "Locked Room Mysteries"; "Organizations"; "Orientals, Sinister"; "Pulp Magazines"; "Radio Detectives"; "Scientific Detectives"; "TV Detectives." Author bibliographies include full stage, screen, radio, and television versions. The author essays are usually critical. Illustrations are from books and films; there are also many portraits.

Who's Who:
Pseudonyms and Characters

Many of the reference works provide references to pseudonyms and lists of characters, particularly the detective. Hubin (see p. 117) lists all pseudonyms, provides cross-references, and indexes the series characters. The book by Penzler and others (see entry in this list) provides little that is not in Steinbrunner (above), but the organization of the material is appealing, as is the tone.

Penzler, Otto; Chris Steinbrunner; Charles Shibuk; Marvin Lachman; and Francis M. Nevins, Jr., comps. *Detectionary: A Bibliographical Dictionary of Leading Characters in Detective and Mystery Fiction, Including Famous and Little Known Sleuths, Their Helps, Rogues Both Heroic and Sinister, and Some of Their Memorable Adventures, as Recounted in Novels, Short Stories, and Films.* Overlook Press, 1977.
There are four sections: "Detectives" lists the fictional detective with a biographical sketch. "Rogues & Helpers" gives a biographical sketch for criminals and villains as well as for all types of Dr. Watsons, including police detectives secondary to the major private or amateur detective. "Cases" gives a summary of selected mystery novels. "Movies" annotates under detective or movie title a selection of movies, particularly those in series. An author index gives detective and titles of novels. Illustrations are from motion pictures.

Writer's Manuals

While meant for the writer of mysteries, to improve both style and economy, the following manuals are informative, critical, and interesting reading for the detective/mystery fan.

Blythe, Hal, Charlie Sweet, and John Landreth. *Private Eyes: A Writer's Guide to Private Investigating.* Cincinnati: Writer's Digest Books, 1993.

Burack, A. S., ed. *Writing Suspense and Mystery Fiction*. The Writer, 1977. Some 30 genre authors comment on how to do their craft (includes remarks from a few critics, one being Ogden Nash bemoaning the had-I-but-known school).

Burack, Sylvia K., ed. *Writing Mystery and Crime Fiction*. The Writer, 1985. Twenty-six essays by authors on their craft. Eight are reprinted from the 1977 edition cited above. Both editions contain the American Bar Association's "A Layman's Guide to Law and the Courts" and "Glossary of Legal Terms."

Mystery Writers of America. *The Mystery Writer's Handbook: A Handbook on the Writing of Detective, Suspense, Mystery and Crime Stories*. Edited by Herbert Brean. Harper, 1956.

Mystery Writers of America. *The Mystery Writer's Handbook*. Newly Revised Edition. Writer's Digest, 1976.
The revised edition is edited by Lawrence Treat. Both editions are needed as only a few of the articles are carried over. The authors in both editions are practitioners in the genre.

Mystery Writers of America. *Writing Mysteries: A Handbook*. Edited by Sue Grafton. Writer's Digest Books, 1992.

Roth, Martin. *The Writer's Complete Crime Reference Book*. Writer's Digest Books, 1993.

Film

Film versions have made many detectives into folk heroes, who are often identified with the actors who characterized the detectives in a series of motion pictures or in a television series. Many of the books about the detective subgenre emphasize the relationship between fiction and film with illustrations from the films. Renewed interest in a writer usually follows the release of a motion picture or television show—examples are found in Agatha Christie and Dorothy L. Sayers. As often happens among critics of the subgenre in book form, there are radically different evaluations of the subgenre in film by the following critics.

Everson, William K. *The Detective in Film*. Citadel, 1972.
He starts with Sherlock Holmes (1903) and ends with the private eyes, with fine critical evaluations of treatments by both U.S. and British filmmakers and a few foreign producers. The illustrations are a delight.

McCarty, John. *Thrillers: Seven Decades of Classic Film Suspense*. Secaucus, N.J.: Carol, 1992.

Meyers, Richard. *TV Detectives*. A. S. Barnes, 1981.
Many illustrations. Lacks an index to the detectives.

Tuska, Jon. *The Detective in Hollywood*. Doubleday, 1978.
Tuska also begins with Sherlock Holmes but treats only U.S. films.
There is much about the actors and directors interviewed by Tuska.
Profusely illustrated.

Magazines and Fanzines

The pulp magazines that made the fame of many detective story writers are long gone. Two magazines remain important to the detective short story: the venerable *Ellery Queen's Mystery Magazine* (since 1941) and *Alfred Hitchcock's Mystery Magazine* (started in 1956). Beginning in 1985 in trade-paperback format, *The New Black Mask Quarterly* has provided excellent selections of new fiction. Wide review coverage is available in *Mystery News* (bimonthly, 1981) and in *I Love a Mystery* (monthly, 1984). *The Drood Review, Mystery Scene Magazine*, and *The Armchair Detective* all review hardcover and paperback editions. Unfortunately for those looking for reviews, but luckily for those who just read voraciously, it is estimated that the annual output of crime novels is now between 1,500 and 1,800, meaning, of course, that not all new novels can (or will) be reviewed.

Three fanzines have, fortunately, achieved a permanence and regularity to support their importance. All have interesting and varied articles, both critical and bibliographical. All carry both current and retrospective reviews, and all are enlivened by long, enthusiastic, and critical letters from subscribers. *The Armchair Detective*, a quarterly fanzine, has published an index to its first 10 volumes (invaluable as a reference for reviews) and regularly includes the *Rex Stout Newsletter* and the supplementation for Barzun and Taylor, *Catalogue of Crime*. It also provides a checklist of current fiction in the subgenre. *The Poisoned Pen* is a bimonthly in its 14th year (1991); it has a continuing feature—"Subject Guide to Mystery Fiction." *Clues: A Journal of Detection* (volume 12 in 1991) is published by the Bowling Green University Popular Press twice yearly and gives the academic mind a showcase.

Associations and Conventions

Associations of mystery and crime writers serve to further the status and publishing of the subgenre and the economic welfare of writers. The U.S. and British associations present annual prizes. The prestige of these associations is recognized by publishers, who note an author's prize-winning status in advertisements and in book jacket blurbs.

ASSOCIATIONS

Detection Club
British honorary association founded in 1928. It has a delightful oath to which new members subscribe. Has published several anthologies to benefit the club. Several novels in which members of the Club wrote successive chapters (all unknowing of the final solution to the mystery) were published in the 1930s and have been reprinted in the 1970s: *Ask a Policeman, Crime on the Coast, No Flowers by Request, Double Death, The Floating Admiral, The Scoop,* and *Behind the Screen.*

Crime Writers' Association
British group founded in 1932. The "Gold Daggers" are the annual awards. There is a memorial John Creasey First Novel award.

Mystery Writers of America
Founded in 1945. "Edgars" (Edgar Allan Poe Awards) are presented in several categories at the annual dinner. An annual anthology (first one in 1946) is published for the benefit of the association. The 33rd annual anthology, *The Edgar Winners* (Dial, 1980), has an appendix listing "Edgar and Special Awards, 1945–1978": Grand Master, Best Novel, Best First Novel, Best Short Story, Best Paperback Original, Best Juvenile, Best Fact-Crime, Best Critical/Biographical Study, Outstanding Mystery Criticism, Best Motion Picture, Special Awards.

Private Eye Writers of America
Established in 1982. The Shamus award is for outstanding paperback and hardcover novels. The Eye award is for career achievement.

Sisters in Crime
Formed in 1985 to work for gender equality in crime publishing. It is an international organization with over 2600 members in 1994.

CONVENTIONS

International Congress of Crime Writers
The first was held in London in 1975; the second, New York, 1978; the third, Stockholm, 1981. (The last brought out the statement that crime really pays in Sweden—both Swedish and translated authors sell extremely well.)

BoucherCon
The annual Anthony Boucher memorial convention. The first was in 1969 and the 22nd in 1991. Anthony Boucher, a pseudonym, wrote detective and science fiction stories and was notable as a critic and reviewer. A selection of his criticism and reviews was edited by Robert E. Briney and Francis M. Nevins, Jr.: *Multiplying Villainies: Selected Mystery Criticism, 1942–1968* (A BoucherCon Book, 1973, limited to 500 copies). In the book are found the annual lists of the best mysteries, with brief annotations, published in the "Criminals

at Large" column in *The New York Times Book Review*, which he wrote from 1951 to 1968. The neophyte reader of mysteries will benefit from the reviews and the use of the lists as a reading guide. In *Rocket to the Morgue* (1942), published under the pseudonym H. H. Holmes and reprinted in paperback under Anthony Boucher, is found the neat combination of his detection and science fiction interests—the suspects are science fiction writers, amusingly articulate about the genre, and a science fiction character seemingly come to life.

There are many fan clubs, several of which publish a journal. Among the authors cherished by fans: Dorothy L. Sayers, John D. MacDonald, Rex Stout, Edgar Wallace, Sax Rohmer, Ellery Queen, and, of course, Sir Arthur Conan Doyle.

Book Clubs

Mystery Guild (Doubleday) distributes book club editions of selected current thrillers. *Mystery Guild* also stocks for distribution some older titles and omnibus volumes (usually three titles in one volume, by a single author). The *Detective Book Club* reprints current titles by three authors at a time (three-in-one volumes). All are good buys for public libraries.

Publishers

Almost all major U.S. and British houses publish some mystery (thriller) novels, and a few have large lines or named series. As most houses now have their own paperback reprint programs, several have paperback mystery series. New mystery novels are often reprinted within the year of publication, either by the house that issued the original hardcover or by a mass-market paperback publisher. Fewer thrillers are now being issued as original paperbacks. In the last few years, there has been an increased reprinting of early thrillers, resulting in many authors, long out-of-print, coming back into popularity.

Series lines by the major publishers are long standing: Crime Club (Doubleday); Red Badge (Dodd, Mead), now with a program for reprinting older titles in paperback; Cock Robin (Macmillan); Inner Sanctum (Simon & Schuster); Harper Novels of Suspense; Midnight Novels (Houghton Mifflin); Prime Crime (Berkley); and Seagull Library of Mystery and Suspense (Norton). Other publishers with extensive lines: Mysterious Press, Morrow, St. Martin's, Walker (Walker British Mysteries), Foul Play Press, and Brown Bag Mysteries. There are several new paperback lines: Academy Mystery Novellas and Academy Crime (Academy Chicago), Carroll & Graf (also hardcover); Perennial Library (Harper), Colt Mysteries (Holt), The Library of Crime Classics (International Polygonics), Quill Mysterious Classic (Morrow), International Crime Series (Pantheon), The Fingerprint Mystery Series (St. Martin's), and Classic Mystery (Scribner's).

In Great Britain, the number of publishers issuing large numbers of thrillers is perhaps greater than in the United States. Many British titles appear promptly on U.S. lists, and several of the British houses are now also established in the United States. Among the most prolific: Collins (Crime Club), Constable, Gollancz, and Macmillan, with Bodley Head, Century, and Hamish Hamilton also issuing a goodly number. There is extensive reprinting in paperback: Dent (two series—The Classic Thriller and Master-Crime), Hogarth Crime, and reprints by the paperback houses, among which Penguin has had a regular Penguin Crime Monthly series for many years. There are two interesting newer series: Pluto Crime (Pluto), a hardcover series of mysteries with left-wing attitudes, and Black Box Thrillers (Zomba Books), omnibus volumes, both hardcover and paperback, of works that have been made into motion pictures, with four titles by an author in each volume.

Dover has been reprinting, in quality paperback, classic mystery and detective novels of the nineteenth and early twentieth centuries: Mary E. Braddon, Ernest Bramah, Wilkie Collins, Freeman W. Crofts, R. Austin Freeman, Jacques Futrelle, Emile Gaboriau, Maurice Leblanc, Gaston Leroux, Arthur Morrison, Melville Davisson Post, Sax Rohmer, T. S. Stribling, Robert Van Gulik, H. E. Wood, and others.

Fifty Classics of Crime Fiction, 1900–1950, edited by Jacques Barzun and Wendell Hertig Taylor (Garland Publishing, 1976), is an ambitious reprint set. (A second set, *1950–1975*, has been published.) Its list forms a desirable basic reading guide to the detective story (to which almost all authors belong). Many of these authors have been recently reprinted in paperback editions, although the particular title may not be currently available. (There are 49 names as the first volume of the set is an introduction and only includes short stories.) This list, of course, includes the recognized classic authors in the field. Also reprinted in the set are some little-remembered authors, and this notice has led to reprinting of other titles by several of these authors in paperback editions.

Allingham, Margery. *Dancers in Mourning*. 1937.

Bailey, H. C. *Mr. Fortune: Eight of His Adventures*.

Barton, Miles (a.k.a. John Rhode). *The Secret of Hugh Eldersham*. 1930.

Bentley, E. C. *Trent's Last Case*. 1912.

Blake, Nicholas. *Minute for Murder*. 1947.

Bramah, Ernest. *Max Carrados*. 1914.

Bullett, Gerald. *The Jury*. 1935.

Chandler, Raymond. *The Lady in the Lake*. 1943.

Chesterton, G. K. *The Innocence of Father Brown*. 1911.

Christie, Agatha. *The Murder of Roger Ackroyd*. 1926.

Cole, G. D. H., and Margaret Cole. *The Murder at Crome House*. 1927.

Crispin, Edmund. *Buried for Pleasure*. 1949.

Doyle, Sir Arthur Conan. *The Hound of the Baskervilles*. 1902.

Eustis, Helen. *The Horizontal Man*. 1946.

Fearing, Kenneth. *The Big Clock*. 1946.

Freeman, R. Austin. *The Singing Bow*. 1912.

Gardner, Erle Stanley. *The Case of the Crooked Candle*. 1944.

Garve, Andrew. *No Tears for Hilda*. 1950.

Gilbert, Michael. *Smallbone Deceased*. 1950.

Grafton, C. W. *Beyond a Reasonable Doubt*. 1940.

Green, Anna Katharine. *The Circular Study*. 1900.

Hare, Cyril. *When the Wind Blows*. 1949.

Head, Matthew. *The Congo Venus*. 1950.

Heyer, Georgette. *A Blunt Instrument*. 1938.

Hilton, James. *Was It Murder?* 1935.

Huxley, Elspeth. *The African Poison Murders*. 1939.

Innes, Michael. *The Daffodil Affair*. 1942.

Kindon, Thomas. *Murder in the Moor*. 1929.

Lewis, Lange. *The Birthday Murder*. 1945.

Macdonald, Ross. *The Drowning Pool*. 1950.

Marsh, Ngaio. *A Wreath for Rivera*. 1949.

McCarr, Pat. *Pick Your Victim*. 1946.

McGuire, Paul. *A Funeral in Eden*. 1938.

Milne, A. A. *The Red House Mystery*. 1922.

Morrah, Dermot. *The Mummy Case*. 1933.

Onions, Oliver. *In Accordance with the Evidence*. 1915.

Page, Marco. *The Shadowy Third*. 1946.

Perdue, Virginia. *Alarum and Excursion*. 1944.

Phillpotts, Eden. *"Found Drowned."* 1931.

Sayers, Dorothy L. *Strong Poison*. 1930.

Snow, C. P. *Death Under Sail*. 1932.

Stout, Rex. *Too Many Cooks*. 1938.

Upfield, Arthur. *The Bone Is Pointed*. 1938.

Wade, Henry. *The Dying Alderman*. 1930.

Webster, Henry Kitchell. *Who Is Next?* 1931.

Wilkinson, Ellen. *The Division Bell Mystery.* 1932.

Witting, Clifford. *Measure for Murder.* 1945.

The following titles are included in the 1950–1975 set:

Arthur, Frank. *Another Mystery in Suva.* 1956.

Atkinson, Alex. *Exit Charley.* 1956.

Bonett, John, and Emery Bonett. *Not in the Script.* 1951.

Brown, Fredric. *The Deep End.* 1952.

Bruce, Leo. *Furious Old Women.* 1960.

Cannan, Joanna. *The Body in the Beck.* 1952.

Carr, A. Z. H. *Finding Maubee.* 1971.

Carr, Glynn. *Death Finds a Foothold.* 1961.

Clark, Philip. *The Dark River.* 1950.

Constantine, K. C. *The Man Who Liked to Look at Himself.* 1973.

Cross, Amanda. *In the Last Analysis.* 1964.

Daly, Elizabeth. *Death and Letters.* 1950.

Dewey, Thomas B. *A Sad Song Singing.* 1963.

Ellin, Stanley. *The Key to Nicholas Street.* 1952.

Fitzgerald, Nigel. *Suffer a Witch.* 1958.

Francis, Dick. *Dead Cert.* 1962.

Grierson, Edward. *The Second Man.* 1956.

Hamilton, Bruce. *Too Much Water.* 1958.

Heberden, M. V. *Engaged to Murder.* 1948.

Hillerman, Tony. *The Fly on the Wall.* 1971.

Hough, Stanley. *The Tender Killer* (U.S. title: *The Bronze Perseus*). 1959.

Hubbard, P. M. *High Tide.* 1970.

Innes, Michael. *One Man Show.* 1952.

James, P. D. *Cover Her Face.* 1962.

Keith, Carlton. *The Crayfish Dinner.* 1966.

Kuttner, Henry. *Murder of a Wife.* 1958.

Landon, Christopher. *Stone-Cold Dead in the Market.* 1955.

Lathen, Emma. *Murder Makes the Wheels Go 'Round*. 1966.

Longmate, Norman. *Strip Death Naked*. 1959.

MacDonald, John D. *Dead Low Tide*. 1953.

Marric, J. J. *Gideon's River*. 1968.

Miles, John. *The Night Hunters*. 1973.

Mole, William. *Small Venom*. 1956.

Nash, Simon. *Killed by Scandal*. 1962.

Peters, Ellis. *Never Pick Up Hitch Hikers*. 1976.

Priestly, J. B. *Salt Is Leaving*. 1975.

Procter, Maurice. *The Pub Crawler*. 1957.

Rendell, Ruth. *A New Lease of Death*. 1961.

Swinnerton, Frank. *On the Shady Side*. 1970.

Symons, Julian. *The Narrowing Circle*. 1954.

Tey, Josephine. *The Singing Sands*. 1953.

Troy, Simon. *Swift to Its Close*. 1969.

Tyrer, Walter. *Such Friends Are Dangerous*. 1954.

Van Gulik, Robert. *The Lacquer Screen*. 1960.

Watson, Colin. *Just What the Doctor Ordered*. 1969.

Waugh, Hillary. *The Missing Man*. 1964.

D's Crime Picks

Grafton, Sue. *"K" Is for Killer*. Henry Holt, 1994.

Hiaasen, Carl. *Double Whammy*. Putnam, 1987.

Hillerman, Tony. *Skinwalkers*. Harper & Row, 1987.

Knight, Kathryn Lasky. *Dark Swan*. St. Martin's Press, 1994.

Lupoff, Richard A. *The Bessie Blue Killer*. St. Martin's Press, 1994.

4 Adventure

The thirst for adventure is the vent which Destiny offers; a war, a crusade, a gold mine, a new country, speak to the imagination and offer swing and play to the confined powers.

—Ralph Waldo Emerson
Natural History of Intellect (1893)

There are two kinds of adventurers: those who go truly hoping to find adventure and those who go secretly hoping they won't.

—William Least Heat Moon
Blue Highways: A Journey into America (1983)

I am not an adventurer by choice but by fate.

—Vincent Van Gogh
The Complete Letters of
Vincent Van Gogh, vol. 2 (1958)

The test of an adventure is that when you're in the middle of it, you say to yourself, "Oh, now I've got myself into an awful mess; I wish I were sitting quietly at home." And the sign that something's wrong with you is when you sit quietly at home wishing you were out having lots of adventure.

—Thornton Wilder
The Matchmaker (1955)

If we didn't live venturously, plucking the wild goat by the beard, and trembling over precipices, we should never be depressed, I've no doubt; but already should be faded, fatalistic and aged.

—Virginia Woolf
A Writer's Diary (1924)

THEMES AND TYPES

The novel of adventure can take many different directions—it can be a story of survival, exploration, intrigue, or battle. For several decades, the leading adventure subgenre was that of spy or espionage, but the end of the cold war has contributed to a decline in its popularity. In the 1990s, the technothriller is a leading adventure genre. Writers are making big money in this adventure genre. It was reported in *Publishers Weekly* that, in 1994, Clive Cussler was paid a $14 million advance for his next two Dirk Pitt novels. Tom Clancy's 1993 best-seller *Without Remorse* reportedly sold over 2 million copies. The adventure and its subgenres are alive and well!

Sometimes even in genre fiction it is difficult to place titles or authors into subgenres. For example, Clive Cussler's novels typify adventure, with a little bit of just about every thriller genre thrown in somewhere: in the various adventures of Dirk Pitt, one finds struggles for survival, exploration of the sea and exotic locales, intrigue, daring rescues, treasure hunting, exploits of a soldier-for-hire, and male romance.

Spy/Espionage

The spy or secret agent has never been a respectable figure. He seldom appears in literature before the twentieth century as a major figure. The pattern for this genre was set in the following early classics.

Buchan, John. *The Thirty-Nine Steps* (1915).
  This introduces Richard Hannay, spy-catcher and spy who appears in several novels. *The Thirty-Nine Steps* has one of the great and long chase scenes in the genre. It became a classic motion picture.

Chesterton, G. K. *The Man Who Was Thursday: A Nightmare* (1908).
  The surreal world of anarchists and double agents.

Childers, Erskine. *The Riddle of the Sands* (1903).
  Introduces the theme of the German plot to invade England, complete with British traitor and amateur hero.

Conrad, Joseph. *The Secret Agent* (1907). *Under Western Eyes* (1911).
  The Secret Agent brings in the world of revolutionaries and anarchists. *Under Western Eyes* introduces the double agent.

Kipling, Rudyard. *Kim* (1901).
  "The Great Game" as Kim calls his spying for British intelligence in India, introduces the exotic background, an aspect that adds greatly to the appeal of the genre. How Kim, as a boy, is trained for his work is marvelously described.

Maugham, W. Somerset. *Ashenden: Or, The British Agent* (1928).
Maugham was an agent during World War I, probably the first of the agents to turn his experience into a novel. He introduces the antihero as agent. His tone is realistic and sardonic, and the outrageous or sensational is toned down to the ordinary.

Oppenheim, E. Phillips. *The Great Impersonation* (1920).
This is the only one of Oppenheim's many spy novels to survive. His first published novel of international intrigue was issued in 1898 and several more appeared during World War I. He introduced the spy world of elegant high society and exotic European cities; Monte Carlo with its gambling setting was often used.

Orczy, Baroness. *The Scarlet Pimpernel* (1905).
The aristocratic fop as a disguise for the highly intelligent agent is here at its most romantic. The theme is introduced of daring rescues from enemy countries, in this case aristocrats saved from the guillotine during the French Revolution.

The early classic authors have successors in a small group of writers who have set the tone for the spy/espionage novel. They have been imitated, but rarely excelled. Among the successors are:

Ambler, Eric
The antihero and the amateur, unwittingly caught up in the spy network, are featured. His portrayal of agents and spymasters is sardonic and unromantic; there is a general atmosphere of disillusionment in an unpleasant game. Backgrounds are exotic, especially the Balkans and the Middle East.

Fleming, Ian
James Bond, 007, the British Secret Service agent is, of course, among the immortals. Fleming had experience in naval intelligence during World War I. The first Bond adventure, *Casino Royale*, 1953, established his flamboyant characteristics. Sex and sadism in an international setting were ingredients for some outrageous adventures with Cold War spies. Linked to him is the tag "Licensed to Kill." The Bond legend has continued beyond the death of its creator. The most recent 007 title is *Brokenclaw*, written by John E. Gardner.

Greene, Graham. *Our Man in Havana* (1958).
Greene is not considered a genre fiction author but has written three spy novels important to the genre, his first being *The Confidential Agent* (1939). During World War II he was in intelligence and undoubtedly drew from his experience for *the* classic parody of the genre, *Our Man in Havana*, which reduces everything to the ridiculous. *The Quiet American* (1955) is a somber spy novel.

Household, Geoffrey. *Rogue Male* (1938).
This is the prototype story of the private individual who undertakes his own spy mission, encountering extreme danger and exciting chases.

Innes, Michael
Best known for his detective stories, Innes wrote several spy novels notable for sometimes outrageously fantastical plots and characters: *The Secret Vanguard* (1940); *Appleby on Ararat* (1941); *The Journeying Boy* (1949); *Operation Pax* (1951); *The Man from the Sea* (1955).

Le Carré, John
The Spy Who Came in from the Cold (1963) set the classic pattern for the unheroic spy, the pattern of double agents, and the anatomization of the bureaucracy of intelligence headquarters operations. Le Carré's experience was in the British Foreign Office. In *Tinker, Tailor, Soldier, Spy* (1975) and *Smiley's People* (1979), the main character is George Smiley, the antithesis of James Bond.

Marquand, John P.
Mr. Moto, the Japanese super-spy, first appeared in *No Hero* (1935). He is the complete professional spy. Marquand uses the plot device of a young American man and woman involved in intrigue by chance and, during many thrilling adventures, falling in love. The locale is usually the exotic Orient, with one story set in Hawaii. The use of the romantic amateur pair became a standard device in the genre.

Simmel, Johannes Mario. *It Can't Always Be Caviar: The Fabulously Daring Adventures and Exquisite Cooking Recipes of the Involuntary Secret Agent Thomas Lieven* (1965).
The amoral rogue amateur as reluctant spy in this novel, translated from the German, brings to the genre the picaresque antihero. Read it to know why the menus and recipes are as vital to his espionage career as, successively, a German, British, French, American, and Russian spy.

Sulzberger, C. L. *The Tooth Merchant* (1973).
While Michael Innes used the wildest fancifulness in his spy novels, Sulzberger has gone one better and spoofed the genre by blandly making mythology real in this picaresque novel of irreverent political commentary.

The host of authors writing spy novels follow the patterns set by the early authors and imitate the patterns of the successful later authors. Commonly used are the international scene, the more exotic the better; intelligence departments, the more corruptible the more realistic; exotic characters with an atmosphere of sexuality and sadism; political commentary, frequently jaundiced; the hazardous chase; the competent professional who may have a conscience. There are several spy/espionage series that trace the exploits of particular spies. The following list is selective, as the number of authors who wrote spy novels is large. Many of these authors also write in other subgenres of the thriller. The authors are grouped by the spy's country of allegiance (though, occasionally, any spy's allegiance may seem confused).

The greater number of spies belong to the United States and Great Britain; spies of both nationalities are usually in conflict, using wits *and* physical force, with Russia's spies. The protagonist is usually an intelligence agency employee but may be a freelance. Frequently, reading this subgenre is an exercise in recognizing acronyms for the intelligence agencies of the world's countries: AEC, AFF, ARVN, CIA, DGSE, DIA, GRU, ISA, KEMT, KGB, KVR, MACV, MATS, MOSSAD, NKVD, NSA, NSC, NTS, PCP, and SIS.

United States

Albrand, Martha. *A Door Fell Shut.*

Breton, Thierry, and Denis Beneich. *Softwar.*
Computer espionage.

Buckley, William F., Jr. *High Jinx. See You Later, Alligator. The Story of Henri Tod. Marco Polo, If You Can. Stained Glass. Saving the Queen. Mongoose R.I.P.*
Blackford Oates is from *Saving the Queen.*

Chacko, David. *The Black Chamber.*

Condon, Richard. *The Manchurian Candidate.*

Crosby, John. *Men in Arms.* (Horatio Cassidy)

DeAndrea, William L. *Snark. Cronus.* (Jeffrey Bellman)

Garfield, Brian. *Hopscotch.*

Gifford, Thomas. *The Glendower Legacy.*

Granger, Bill. *The November Man. The British Cross. The Shattered Eye. The Zurich Numbers. The Last Good German. Burning the Apostle.* (Deveraux, code name November Man)

Guild, Nicholas. *Old Acquaintance.* (Ray Guinnes, freelance assassin)

Hallahan, William H. *The Trade. Catch Me: Kill Me.*

Hamilton, Donald. Matt Helm in paperback series.

Hood, William. *Spy Wednesday. Mole.*

Hoyt, Richard. *Trotsky's Run.*

Hughes, Dorothy B. *The Davidian Report.*

Hyde, Anthony. *The Red Fox.*

Hynd, Noel. *Flowers from Berlin. The Sandler Inquiry. False Flags.* (Bill Mason)

Ignatius, David. *Agents of Innocence.*

Kennedy, William P. *The Masakado Lesson.*

Lambert, Derek. *The Man Who Was Saturday. The Red Dove.*

Lee, Stan. *Dunn's Conundrum.*

Littell, Robert. *The Amateur. The October Circle. The Debriefing. The Defection of A. J. Lewinter.*

Ludlum, Robert. *The Bourne Identity. The Bourne Supremacy. The Bourne Ultimatum.* (Jason Bourne)
"Ludlum deals in male fantasies, and there are few two-fisted scribes with seven-figure advances who do it better."—*Time*, March 10, 1986.

Lustbader, Eric Van. *Jian.*

Mason, F. Van Wyck. (Hugh North)

Pollock, J. C. *Payback.*

Thomas, Ross. *Missionary Stew. The Eighth Dwarf. The Cold War Swap. Twilight at Mac's Place.* (Mac McCorkle and Mike Padillo)

Trevanian. *The Eiger Sanction. Loo Sanction.*

Warga, Wayne. *Hardcover.*

Woods, Stuart. *Deep Lie.*

Great Britain
Allbeury, Ted. *Moscow Quadrille. The Judas Factor.*

Armstrong, Campbell. *White Light.*

Bagley, Desmond. *Running Blind. The Enemy.*

Canning, Victor. *Birds of a Feather. Memory Boy.*

Coles, Manning. *Drink to Yesterday.*

Cosgrave, Patrick. *Adventures of State. Cheyney's Law. The Three Colonels.* (Allen Cheyney)

Creasey, John
A number of series characters under his several pseudonyms, all grouped here: Peter Ross, Gordon Craigie, Bruce Murdoch, Mary Dell, Dr. Palfrey, Patrick Dawlish.

Deighton, Len. *The Ipcress File. Funeral in Berlin. Spy Story. Catch a Falling Spy.* (*Twinkle, Twinkle, Little Spy.*) Trilogy: *Berlin Game, Mexico Set, London Match.* Trilogy: *Spy Hook, Spy Line, Spy Sinker.*
Bernard Samson is the spy of the second trilogy.

Denham, Bertie. *Two Thyrdes. The Man Who Lost His Shadow.*

Dickinson, Peter. *Walking Dead.*

Eagleton, Clive. *Skirmish. Missing from the Record.*

Follett, Ken. *Lie Down with Lions. Eye of the Needle. The Man from St. Petersburg. Key to Rebecca.*

Forbes, Bryan. *The Endless Game.*

Forrest, Anthony. *A Balance of Dangers.* (Captain John Justice, Napoleonic Wars)

Forsyth, Frederick. *The Fourth Protocol. The Devil's Alternative. The Day of the Jackal. The Odessa File. The Dogs of War.*

Freemantle, Brian. *Charlie Muffin. Goodby to an Old Friend. Betrayals.* (Charlie Muffin)

Gardner, John. *The Nostradamus Traitor. The Garden of Weapons. The Secret Generations.* Continuation of Ian Fleming's James Bond series: *License Renewed. For Special Services. Icebreaker. Role of Honor. Win, Lose, or Die. Brokenclaw.*
Herbie Kruger is the spy of *The Garden of Weapons;* the Railton family are the spies of *The Secret Generations.*

Garner, William. *A Big Enough Wreath.* (Michael Jagger)

Gethin, David. *Point of Honor.* (Halloran)

Gilbert, Michael. *Mr. Calder and Mr. Behrens. The Empty House.*

Haggard, William. *Hard Sell. The Money Man.* (Charles Russell)

Hale, John. *The Whistle Blower.*

Hall, Adam. *Quiller. The Quiller Memorandum. The Sinkiang Executive. Quiller Meridian.* (Quiller)

Harcourt, Palma. *A Matter of Conscience. Shadows of Doubt. Climate for Conspiracy.*

Harvester, Simon. *Siberian Road.* (Dorian Silk)

Higgins, Jack. *Confessional. Exocet. Touch the Devil. The Eagle Has Landed. Eye of the Storm.* (Liam Devlin)

Hill, Reginald. *The Spy's Wife. Traitor's Blood.*

Hone, Joseph. *The Oxford Gambit.* (Peter Marlow)

Hunter, Stephen. *The Spanish Gambit.*

Luard, Nicholas. *The Robespierre Serial.*

Lyall, Gavin. *The Secret Servant. The Conduct of Major Maxim. The Crocus List.* (Major Harry Maxim)

Masters, John. *The Himalayan Concerto.*

Mather, Berkely. *With Extreme Prejudice.*

Mitchell, James. *Smear Job.* (Callan)

Moss, Robert. *Carnival of Spies.*

Perry, Ritchie. *Fools' Mate.* (Phillis)

Price, Anthony. *Our Man in Camelot. The Labyrinth Makers. Gunner Kelly. Sion Crossing.* (Dr. David Audley)

Ross, Angus. (Marcus Farrow and Charlie McGowan)

Royce, Kenneth. *The Mosley Receipt. The XYZ Man.* (Spider Scott)

Russell, Charles. *The Spy Is Dead.*

Savarin, Julian Jay. *The Hammerhead.*

Seaman, Donald. *The Wilderness of Mirrors.*

Sela, Owen. *The Kiriov Tapes.*

Thomas, Craig. *Foxfire. Wolfsbane. Wild Cat.*

Wheatley, Dennis. (Gregory Sallus)

York, Andrew. (Jonas Wilde)

U.S.S.R.

Burke, Martyn. *The Commissar's Report.*

Eagleton, Clive. *Troika.*

Giovannetti, Alberto. *Requiem for a Spy.*

Hastings, Michael. *A Spy in Winter.*

Lourie, Richard. *First Loyalty.*

Marlowe, Derek. *A Dandy in Aspic.*

McQuinn, Donald E. *Shadow of Lies.*

Pape, Gordon, and Tony Aspler. *The Music Wars.*

Prescott, Casey. *Asset in Black.*

Sela, Owen. *The Kremlin Control.*

Trenhaile, John. *A View from the Square. The Man Called Kyril. Nocturne for a General. The Gates of Exquisite View. The Mahjongg Spies.*

Van Rjndt, Philippe. *Blueprint.*

Volkoff, Vladimir. *The Set-Up.*

Israel

Haddad, C. A. *The Academic Factor. Bloody September. Operation Apricot.* (David Haham)

Karlin, Wayne. *Crossover.*

France

Brierley, David. *Cold War. Blood Group O.*

Lescroart, John T. *Son of Holmes.*
Combined spy and detection with August Lupin and a very young Nero Wolfe.

Volkoff, Vladimir. *The Turn-around.*

Bulgaria
Furst, Alan. *Night Soldiers.*

Pearson, Ridley. *Never Look Back.*

West Germany
Herlin, Hans. *Solo Run.*

COMIC

Spy stories tend to be quite grim. There are, however, a few inept and comic spies:

Benchley, Nathaniel. *Catch a Falling Spy.*

Butterworth, Michael. *Remains to Be Seen.*

Dowling, Gregory. *Double-Take.*

Gardner, John. *Air Apparent.* (Boysie Oakes)

Greene, Graham. *Our Man in Havana.*

Gwynne, P. N. *Pushkin Shove.*

Lovell, Mark. *The Only Good Apple in a Barrel of Spies.* (Appleton Porter)

Marks, Ted. *The Man from ORGY.*
Pornographic as well as comic.

Mikes, George. *The Spy Who Died of Boredom.*

Porter, Joyce. *Only with a Bargepole.* (Eddie Brown)

WOMEN

Women as spies appear frequently as secondary characters. In each of the following books, a woman is the main character; four of the women are series characters.

Aaron, David. *Crossing By Night.* (Elizabeth Pack)

Anthony, Evelyn. *Albatross. The Avenue of the Dead. The Company of Saints. The Defector. The Janus Imperative.* (Davina Graham)

Bosse, Malcolm. *The Man Who Loved Zoos.*
The woman involved in chasing a spy is a librarian.

Gilman, Dorothy (Mrs. Pollifax). *The Unexpected Mrs. Pollifax. Mrs. Pollifax and the Hong Kong Buddha.*
The first book appeared in 1966 and the ninth in 1990, all with exotic locales.

MacInnes, Helen
With *Above Suspicion* (1941) MacInnes began a best-selling line of novels of romantic international intrigue. Her female spy is usually an amateur and often paired romantically with another amateur— all in the most exotic spots in Europe. Her final novel, *Ride a Pale Horse* (1985), was her 21st.

O'Donnell, Peter (Modesty Blaise)
Modesty Blaise began in the comic strips in 1962 and appeared first in book form in 1965. She is the female James Bond.

Truman, Margaret. *Murder in the CIA.* (Colette Cahill)

The following two spy novels defy simple categorization.

Batchelor, John Calvin. *American Falls.*
A historical novel of the U.S. Civil War about the origin of the Union Secret Service and the Confederate Secret Service.

Gollin, James. *The Philomel Foundation.*
A group of young American musicians, The Antiqua Players, get involved with a spy from East Germany. Later titles about the groups belong in the amateur detective category.

Technothriller

Technothrillers emerged in the 1980s as one of the most popular types of adventure tale. Tom Clancy's *The Hunt for Red October* generated an interest in books that used technology to the point where the gadget became as important as a character. Until the enormous changes in eastern Europe at the end of the decade, the enemy was usually the Soviets and a common theme was that of the "good Russian" who in some way conveyed superior Soviet technology to the United States. More recent technothrillers use the Middle East and South America for settings. The war on drugs is also finding an important place in the plots of technothrillers.

Ballard, Robert and Tony Chiu. *Bright Shark.*

Berent, Mark. *Rolling Thunder.*

Bond, Larry. *Red Phoenix. Vortex.*

Brown, Dale. *Silver Tower. Flight of the Old Dog. Day of the Cheetah. Night of the Hawk.*

Butler, Jimmie. *The Iskra Incident.*

Carpenter, Scott. *The Steel Albatross.*

Clancy, Tom. *Clear and Present Danger. Cardinal of the Kremlin. Red Storm Rising. Patriot Games. Sum of All Fears. Without Remorse. Debt of Honor.*

Cook, Nick. *Aggressor.*

Coonts, Stephen. *Under Siege. Final Flight. Flight of the Intruder. Minotaur.*

Coyle, Harold. *Sword Point.*

Deyterman, P. T. *Scorpion in the Sea.*

Durham, Guy. *Stealth.*

Friedman, Gary. *Gun Men.*

Garn, Jake, and Stephen Paul Cohen. *Night Launch.*

Harrison, Payne. *Storming Intrepid.*

Herman, Richard, Jr. *The Warbirds.*

Ing, Dean. *The Ransom of Black Stealth One.*

Kunetka, James W. *Parting Shot.*

Leib, Franklin Allen. *Fire Arrow.*

Mason, Robert. *Weapon.*

Mayer, Bob. *Eyes of the Hammer. Dragon Sim 13.*

Merek, Jack. *Target Stealth.*

Peters, Ralph. *Red Army.*

Pollock, J. C. *Payback.*

Poyer, David. *The Med.*

Weber, Joe. *Shadow Flight. DEFCON One.*

White, Robin A. *The Flight from Winter's Shadow. Afterburn. Sword of Orion.*

Financial Intrigue/Espionage

Paul Erdman probably set this subgenre going in 1973 with *The Billion Dollar Sure Thing,* and authors have gleefully taken on the world of international banking, oil cartels, and multinational corporations as well as lesser businesses. Political chicanery is often involved, along with crooked doings among the rich and powerful. The following novels show wide variation in their plots, but money is always the prime factor.

Aaron, David. *Agent of Influence.*

Ambler, Eric. *Send No More Roses.*

Black, Gavin. *The Golden Cockatrice.* (Paul Harris)

Blankenship, William. *The Programmed Man.*

Brady, James. *Paris One.*

Browne, Gerald. *Hot Siberian.*

Cudlip, David. *Comprador.*

Duncan, Robert L. *Temple Dogs.*

Durand, Loup. *Daddy.*

Erdman, Paul E. *The Billion Dollar Sure Thing. The Palace.*

Fowlkes, Frank. *The Peruvian Contracts.*

Haig, Alec. *Sign on for Tokyo.*

Keagan, William. *A Real Killing.*

Lehman, Ernest. *The French Atlantic Affair.*

Lustbader, Eric Van. *The Miko.*

Maling, Arthur. *Schroeder's Game.*

Rhodes, Russell L. *The Styx Complex.*

Sanders, Lawrence. *The Tangent Objective.*

Stewart, Edward. *Launch.*

Sulitzer, Paul-Loup. *Money. Fortune.*

Thomas, Ross. *The Money Harvest.*

Political Intrigue and Terrorism

Common to this subgenre are many of the characteristics of the spy/espionage subgenre and the disaster subgenre, with frequent overtones of science fiction. The intent of the author is usually to make angry comments about the international political scene. Some of the books are national in background, usually with international political implications. Agencies such as the CIA are often featured. The threat of terrorism is pervasive. Betty Rosenberg picked Robert Littell's *The Amateur* and Ross Thomas's *The Mordida Man* as the prototypes. The following books show how involved the plots of these stories are with current political problems and situations. It will be interesting to observe how political changes affect survival of interest in some of these novels.

Aellen, Richard. *The Cain Conversion.*

Alexander, Patrick. *Show Me a Hero.*

Allbeury, Ted. *The Twentieth Day of January.*

Archer, Jeffrey. *Shall We Tell the President?*

Armstrong, Campbell. *Jig.*

Bagley, Desmond. *Juggernaut.*

Borchgrave, Arnaud de. *The Spike.*

Brierley, David. *Skorpion's Death.*

Buchanan, William J. *Present Danger.*

Cohen, William S., and Gary Hart. *The Double Man.*

Cole, Burt. *Blood Note.*

Collins, Larry, and Dominique Lapierre. *The Fifth Horseman.*

Coonts, Stephen. *The Red Horseman.*

Coppel, Alfred. *The Hastings Conspiracy.*

Crosby, John. *An Affair of Strangers.*

Cussler, Clive. *Deep Six.*

Drury, Allen. *Pentagon.*

Duncan, Robert L. *In the Enemy Camp.*

Easterman, Daniel. *The Last Assassin.*

Fitzgerald, Gregory, and John Dillon. *The Druze Document.*

Forsyth, Frederick. *The Devil's Conspiracy. The Negotiator.*

Garve, Andrew. *Counterstroke.*

Griffin, W. E. B. *The New Breed.*

Henissart, Paul. *Margin of Error.*

Hoyt, Richard. *Head of State.*

Hunter, Stephen. *Point of Impact.*

Leib, Franklin Allen. *Fire Arrow.*

Littell, Robert. *The Amateur.*

Ludlum, Robert. *The Bourne Identity. The Bourne Supremacy. The Bourne Ultimatum. The Icarus Agenda.*

Malashenko, Alexei. *The Last Red August.*

Morrell, David. *The League of Night and Fog.*

Moss, Robert. *Moscow Rules.*

Moss, Robert, and Arnaud de Borchgrave. *Monimbo.*

Order, Lewis, and Bill Michaels. *The Night They Stole Manhattan.*

Paul, Barbara. *Liars and Tyrants and People Who Turn Blue.*

Quinell, A. J. *In the Name of the Father.*

Salinger, Pierre, and Leonard Gross. *The Dossier.*

Seymour, Gerald. *The Harrison Affair.*

Sharp, Marilyn. *Falseface.*

Thayer, James Stuart. *Pursuit. Ringer.*

Thomas, Craig. *The Last Raven.*

Thomas, Ross. *The Mordida Man. Out on the Rim.*

Washburn, Mark. *The Armageddon Game.*

West, Morris. *Proteus.*

Wiltse, David. *Prayer for the Dead. Close to the Bone.*

Survival

Survival is a strong motive for adventure thrillers. The survival can involve escape from a burning high-rise, or from the steppes of Mongolia. The main theme that the following books have in common is this: Through wit and dogged determination, the heroes of the tale survive.

THE LONE SURVIVOR

One or a few individuals, for some reason cut off from civilization (as we know it!), resourcefully make their way out of danger.

L'Amour, Louis. *The Last of the Breed.*
A Native American pilot crashes over Siberia.

Woods, Stuart. *White Cargo.*
An entrepreneur goes after the drug cartel that had his yacht pirated.

DISASTER

Reviewers have labeled several types of novels as "disaster" thrillers. The catastrophe may be natural (i.e., nature's fury or an act of God) or manmade. Natural disasters include earthquakes, volcanic eruptions, tidal waves, meteor strikes, a new ice age, floods, plagues, aberrational behavior of bird or animal life—the only limit is the author's imagination. (However, not within that imaginative limit is the matter of the supernatural.) Manmade disasters include nuclear explosions, accidents caused by experimenting with bacteria or with humanity's biological heritage, accidents involving aircraft or ocean vessels, or accidents caused by tampering with nature's equilibrium (e.g., destroying the ozone layer)—again, the range is determined by the author's imagination. Frequently, the disaster has a political link, relating this type of book to the spy/espionage subgenre. There is also a science fiction aspect in the themes of apocalypse, doomsday, and colliding worlds. Only a few authors are now specializing in disaster novels.

The rise of this subgenre is paralleled by the popularity of the disaster motion pictures of the 1960s and 1970s, such as *The Towering Inferno, Earthquake, Airport, The Last Wave,* and *The Poseidon Adventure.* Of the last named, its producer commented: "In the first six minutes, 1,400 people are killed and only the stars survive." Why is the subgenre so popular? This writer refuses to conjecture in a world tottering on the brink of disaster! In any case, the following books offer the reader a wide choice of ways to contemplate catastrophe.

Bagley, Michael. *The Plutonium Factor.*

Bell, Madison Smartt. *Waiting for the End of the World.*

Block, Thomas H. *Mayday. Airship. Nine. Orbit.*

Buchanan, William J. *Present Danger.*

Byrne, Robert. *The Dam. Skyscraper. The Tunnel.*

Canning, Victor. *The Doomsday Carrier.*

Corley, Edwin. *The Genesis Rock.*

Cravens, Gwyneth. *The Black Death.*

Crichton, Michael. *The Andromeda Strain. Jurassic Park.*

Cussler, Clive. *Raise the Titanic.*

De Lillo, Don. *White Noise.*

Godey, John. *The Snake.*

Hailey, Arthur. *Airport.*

Herbert, James. *The Rats.*

Herzog, Arthur. *IQ 83. The Swarm. Earthsound. Heat.*

Hoyt, Richard. *Cool Runnings.*

Hyde, Christopher. *The Wave.*

Johnson, Stanley. *The Doomsday Deposit.*

MacLean, Alistair. *Goodbye California.*

McCullough, Colleen. *A Creed for the Third Millennium.*

Moan, Terrance. *The Deadly Frost.*

Moran, Richard. *Cold Sea Rising.*

North, Edmund H., and Franklin Coen. *Meteor.*

Orgill, Douglas, and John Gribbin. *The Sixth Winter.*

Page, Thomas. *Sigmet Active.*

Pearson, Ridley. *The Seizing of Yankee Green Mall.*

Racine, Thomas. *The Great Los Angeles Blizzard.*

Robinson, Logan. *Evil Star.*

Rubens, Howard, and Jack Wasserman. *Hambro's Itch.*

Scortia, Thomas N., and Frank M. Robinson. *The Nightmare Factor. The Prometheus Crisis. The Glass Inferno. Blowout.*

Slater, Ian. *Firespell.*

Slattery, Jesse. *The Juliet Effect.*

Smith, Martin Cruz. *Nightwing.*

Stern, Richard Martin. *Flood. Snowbound. The Tower. Wildfire.*

Stone, George. *Blizzard.*

Strieber, Whitley, and James Kunetka. *War Day.*

Warner, Douglas. *Death on a Warm Wind.*

Wiltse, David. *The Fifth Angel. Six Days in November.*

Male Romance

Actually, all thrillers can be labeled adventures, as can the western and much of science fiction. But in this specific subgenre, the adventurer is one who seeks adventure on land, sea, or in the air, following the old tradition of the hero who matches strength against the powers of natural elements and enjoys the danger. Not included here are war stories as such, although war is often involved. The exception is series involving naval warfare, largely derivative from the prototype Hornblower series by C. S. Forester.

Many of these books are set in wild and primitive areas of the world. Often, they feature treasure hunts or lost mines; some involve piracy; most are full of combat with villains of all sorts. They may or may not eschew romance—there may be, as for Ulysses, a patiently weaving Penelope waiting to welcome the hero home after his dalliances with Circe and others. (Paul Zweig, in *The Adventurer* [Basic Books, 1972], analyzes the lure of adventure and the character of the adventurer, tracing the literature about Ulysses, the medieval romances, Robinson Crusoe, and others. He notes "the most unrelenting masculinity of adventure literature—from the *Iliad* to James Bond," and considers the adventurer as being "in flight from women.") The adventure is considered the subgenre of male interest just as the romance is identified for women (the sweet-and-savage romance provides women with their adventure element).

The hero dominates the adventure story, although he may at times be an antihero, a type equally popular. *The Encyclopedia of Superheroes* by Jeff Rovin describes more than 1,000 heroes, including the comic book heroes (surely the prototypes for many of the paperback adventure heroes), as well as those from literature, mythology, motion pictures, and television.

There is a political angle to adventures, as many concern revolutionary action in non-European countries, gun-running, or mercenary activities. The story may concern the search for a friend or relative lost in strange circumstances, a ship or plane wreck, hijacking, hunting wild animals, pioneering treks, exploration expeditions, the overcoming of natural disasters, an escape and the ensuing chase—the possibilities are varied.

A few classic authors, both those described as genre writers and those considered to be writers of "literature," are listed first. The adventure story is the oldest of the genres in literature and is not always simple to label. The subsequent groupings of adventure authors note the more popular types of backgrounds and characters.

CLASSIC AUTHORS

Buchan, John

Burroughs, Edgar Rice. Tarzan series.

Conrad, Joseph

Curwood, James Oliver

Falkner, J. M. *Moonfleet.*

Haggard, H. Rider. *She. The Return of She. King Solomon's Mines.*

Hughes, Richard. *A High Wind in Jamaica.*

Kipling, Rudyard. *Kim.*

London, Jack

Macaulay, Rose. *The Towers of Trebizond.*
A young Englishwoman traveling through Turkey and other parts of the Middle East, on a white camel.

Sabatini, Rafael. *Captain Blood. The Sea Hawk.*

Verne, Jules

White, Stewart Edward

Wren, P. C. *Beau Geste.*

WILD FRONTIERS AND EXOTIC LANDS

> We shall not cease from exploration
> And the end of all our exploring
> Will be to arrive where we started
> And know the place for the first time.
> —T. S. Eliot, from
> "Little Gidding" (1942)

Both the often unexplored frontiers of Africa and the exotic realms of the Orient appeal to writers of adventure. (India's frontiers also provide often used background, as illustrated in "Military and Naval Adventure," p. 155.) The following grouping lists titles with plots that take place in Asia and Africa. Many of these authors, of course, also write adventure of other types.

Bagley, Desmond. *Flyaway*.

Becker, Stephen. *The Chinese Bandit. The Last Mandarin. The Blue-Eyed Shan*.

Bosse, Malcolm. *The War Lord*.

Clavell, James. *Whirlwind*.

Cleary, Jon. *High Road to China*.

Crichton, Michael. *Congo*.

Davidson, Lionel. *The Rose of Tibet*.

Easterman, Daniel. *The Ninth Buddha*.

Forester, C. S. *The African Queen*.

Grant, Maxwell. *Blood Red Rose*.

Haggard, H. Rider. *King Solomon's Mines*. The She series. *Alan Quartermain*.

Halkin, John. *Kenya*.

Innes, Hammond. *The Big Footprints*.

Lustbader, Eric Van. *French Kiss*.

Mather, Berkely. Stafford trilogy: *Pagoda Tree, The Midnight Gun, Hour of the Dog*.

Moore, William. *Bush War!*

Smith, Wilbur. *The Leopard Hunts in Darkness. The Eye of the Tiger. The Burning Shore. The Sunbird.* Ballantyne family saga: *A Falcon Flies. Men of Men. The Angels Weep.*

SOLDIER-OF-FORTUNE

The adventure hero as picaresque soldier-of-fortune appears in many adventure novels. He is frequently an antihero. These following titles exemplify the type.

Aylward, Marcus. *Harper's Folly. Harper's Luck.*

Pollock, J. C. *Mission M.I.A. Centrifuge.*

Scott, Douglas. *Eagle's Blood.*

Sela, Owen. *The Portuguese Fragment.*

WOMEN

Although women usually appear in adventure novels as a secondary love interest, they are beginning to play the role of the adventurer. The following titles are about women as adventurers.

Haggard, H. Rider
See Haggard's She series under "Classic Authors" (p. 152).

Llywelyn, Morgan. *Grania: She-King of the Irish Seas.*

O'Donnell, Peter. Modesty Blaise series.
Noted among the spy/espionage titles, but Modesty Blaise is a true adventurer.

Robertson, E. A. *Four Frightened People.*

Stevenson, Janet. *Departure.*
A nineteenth-century sea adventure.

PARODY

The adventure subgenre is very susceptible to parody, for it takes very little exaggeration in action or character to make the heroic seem ridiculous. The following novels are examples of parodies.

Bonfiglioli, Kyril. *All the Tea in China.*

Fraser, George MacDonald. The Flashman series.
The ninth in the series about this rogue antihero appeared in 1990.

Fraser, George MacDonald. *The Pyrates.*
A bawdy reworking of the romantic adventure tradition of Rafael Sabatini and Jeffery Farnol.

Gundy, Elizabeth. *The Disappearance of Gregory Pluckrose.*

MILITARY AND NAVAL ADVENTURE

The following books belong in the adventure genre rather than with serious portrayals of warfare, although many have excellent scenes of battle. The war novel, as a mainstream novel, is not included.

Beach, Edward L. *Cold Is the Sea. Run Silent, Run Deep.*
　　Submarines, United States, post-World War II.

Clancy, Tom. *The Hunt for Red October.*
　　Submarines, United States–Russian political adventure.

Cleary, Jon. *A Very Private War.*
　　Australia, World War II.

Collerette, Eric J. *Ninety Feet to the Sun.*
　　Submarines, Great Britain, World War II.

Griffin, W. E. B. The Brotherhood of War series. The Corps series.

Heath, Layne. *CW2.*

Hennessey, Max. Commander Kelly Maguire trilogy (British navy): *The Lion at Sea, The Dangerous Years, Back to Battle.* British air force trilogy: *The Bright Blue Sky, The Challenging Heights, Once More the Hawks.* Cavalry trilogy: *Soldier of the Queen, Blunted Lance, The Iron Stallions.*

Heyer, Georgette. *An Infamous Army. The Spanish Bride.*
　　The first title is an excellent story of the Battle of Waterloo; the second is about the Peninsular Campaign in the Napoleonic Wars. By the author of Regency romances.

Higgins, Jack. *Luciano's Luck. The Eagle Has Landed. The Eagle Has Flown. Storm Warning.*
　　World War II, U.S. forces.

Homewood, Harry. *Final Harbor. Torpedo! Silent Sea.*
　　Submarines, United States, World War II.

Hough, Richard. Buller trilogy: *Buller's Guns, Buller's Dreadnought, Buller's Victory.*
　　British navy, World War I.

MacLean, Alistair. *H.M.S. Ulysses. San Andreas. The Guns of Navarone. South by Java Head. Force Ten from Navarone. Where Eagles Dare.*
　　British army and navy, World War II. The first title is the author's first, the second is his 27th.

Masters, John. *Nightrunners of Bengal. Bhowani Junction.*
　　India, World Wars I and II.

Monsarrat, Nicholas. *The Cruel Sea.*
British navy, World War II.

Reeman, Douglas. *Torpedo Run. Rendezvous—South Atlantic. A Ship Must Die. Strike from the Sea. The Deep Silence.*
British navy, World War II; the last title is about submarines.

Rosenbaum, Ray. *Falcons.*

Scott, Leonard B. *The Iron Men.*

Stanley, William. *Bomber Patrol. Cloud Nineteen.*
British air force. World War I

Thomas, Craig. *Foxfire. Foxfire Down.*
Aircraft espionage, United States–Russia.

Westheimer, David. *Rider in the Wind. Von Ryan's Express. Von Ryan's Return.*
U.S. air force and army, World War II.

Wouk, Herman. *The Caine Mutiny.*
U.S. navy.

ADVENTURE BOOKS IN SERIES

Most books of the naval warfare series concern the Napoleonic wars. The imitated prototype is C. S. Forester's Hornblower series, which follows his career from midshipman to admiral. The life of Hornblower is the subject of a "biography" of C. Northcote Parkinson, *The Life and Times of Horatio Hornblower*, which is so authentic as to persuade the unwary that he really existed. Parkinson so regretted the end of the series that he started a series of his own (see entry in the following list). A few of the series deal with the naval warfare of World Wars I and II. First is the list of series on the British navy in the Napoleonic wars, plus one on the army (Cornwell), with the name of the series hero indicated.

Cornwell, Bernard. (Richard Sharp)
12th title in 1990.

Forester, C. S. (Hornblower)

Kent, Alexander. (Richard Bolitho)

Maynard, Kenneth. (Matthew Lamb)

O'Brian, Patrick. (Captain Jack Aubrey and Stephen Maturin, physician)
In the second title in the series, there is a meeting with Hornblower.

Parkinson, C. Northcote. (Richard Delancey)

Pope, Dudley. (Captain Lord Nicholas Ramage)

Woodman, Richard. (Nathaniel Drinkwater)

Other series cover the background of the British navy in the nineteenth century and in World War II, including two on the submarine service and one on the air force. There is one historical series on the army in India and one on the American Civil War.

Cornwell, Bernard. (Nathanial Starbuck)
   U.S. Civil War.

Fullerton, Alexander. (Nick Everard)

Gray, Edwyn. (Nicholas Hamilton)
   Submarines.

Jackson, Robert. (Wing Commander George Yoeman)

Lambdin, Dewey. (Alan Lewrie, Royal Navy)

MacNeill, Duncan. Captain James Ogilvie series.
   Frontier of India.

McCutchan, Philip. (Donald Cameron; St. Vincent Halfhyde, both Royal Navy and merchant marine; Commodore Kemp)

Pope, Dudley. (Yorke family)

Reeman, Douglas. Royal Marines series. (Blackwood family)

Southren, Victor H. (Edward Mainwaring)
   Eighteenth century.

Wingate, John. *Frigate. Carrier. Submarine. Red Mutiny. Go Deep.*
   Submarines, World War II.

There are also two series with a French naval background:

Logan, Mark
   Nicholas Minette.

Suthren, Victor H. (Captain Paul Gallant)
   Eighteenth century.

Paperback Male-Action/Adventure Series

The western has always been considered an action/adventure genre as have many of the examples of detective and spy/espionage stories, all of which often appear with a series hero. The following series are all original titles issued by paperback publishers and noted in trade parlance as being action/adventure. They are specifically aimed at a male audience. The prototypes for plots and characters may be found in the pulp magazines that flourished before the paperbacks took over as purveyors of action/adventure in the 1940s. In these series are found men (and sometimes women) who function as vengeance squads, martial arts experts, mercenaries, soldiers-of-fortune, detectives, and adventurers of almost any type. The western action/adventure series and "adult" westerns are listed with this genre. Such series, when successful, are highly lucrative, and publishers continually experiment with them. It would be futile to list all the evanescent series, of which only perhaps two dozen may be current at any time. The following, however, are a few of the enduring ones.

Kenneth Robeson's Doc Savage series. (Bantam)
> Currently being released in omnibus editions containing up to five previously published titles.

Don Pendleton's Mack Bolan, The Executioner series, 145th title in 1991. (Gold Eagle Books)

Warren Murphy and Richard Sapir's Destroyer series, 92nd title in 1995. (Signet)

A Miscellany

The types within the adventure novel are diverse and frequently share characteristics with other genres. The following sampling suggests the difficulty in labeling—as adventure novels—those novels of suspense (which often involve a chase theme) that do not fall into a simple genre pattern. Most of these authors specialize in adventure.

Adler, Warren. *Trans-Siberian Express.*

Benchley, Peter. *Jaws. The Deep. The Island.*

Cleary, Jon. *The Golden Sabre. The Sundowners.*
> The second title is a western set in Australia.

Cussler, Clive. *Raise the Titanic. Deep Six. Iceberg. Cyclops. Vixen 03. Night Probe. Pacific Vortex. The Mediterranean Caper.*
> The adventures of underwater recovery mariner Dirk Pitt often have elements of the disaster subgenre and also political overtones.

Gann, Ernest K. *The Aviator. The High and the Mighty. Blaze of Noon. Fate Is the Hunter.*
> Aviation adventure.

Garfield, Brian. *Recoil.*

Hagberg, David. *Critical Mass.*

Hayden, Sterling. *The Voyage.*

Herley, Richard. The Pagans trilogy: *The Stone Arrow, The Flint Lord, The Earth Goddess.*
> Stone Age England.

Household, Geoffrey. *Rogue Male. Rough Justice.*

Ing, Dean. *Blood of Eagles.*

Innes, Hammond. *The Black Tide. The Wreck of the Mary Deare. Medusa.*

Jennings, Gary. *The Journeyer.*
Marco Polo's adventures.

Langley, Bob. *Falklands Gambit.*

Mundy, Talbot. *King of the Khyber Rifles.*

Nordhoff, Charles B. *Mutiny on the Bounty.*

Poyer, D. C. *Hatteras Blue.*

Seymour, Gerald. *In Honor Bound.*

Trew, Anthony. *Sea Fever. Death of a Supertanker.*

Wales, Robert. *Harry.*
Cattle drive in Australia, 1882.

Woodhouse, Martin, and Robert Ross. Leonardo da Vinci trilogy: *The Medici Guns, The Medicine Emerald, The Medici Hawks.*
Leonardo as adventure hero.

Yates, Dornford. *Berry and Co. Adele and Co. Blind Corner. Perishable Goods.*
Curious period pieces from the 1920s (being reprinted) about the thriller adventures of a group of wealthy friends.

TOPICS

Spy/Espionage

ANTHOLOGIES

Spy stories can also be found in anthologies of mystery and detective stories.

Ambler, Eric, ed. *To Catch a Spy: An Anthology of Favorite Spy Stories.* Antheneum, 1965.
The authors included are John Buchan, W. Somerset Maugham, Compton Mackenzie, Graham Greene, Eric Ambler, Ian Fleming, Michael Gilbert. Ambler's introduction is a historical definition of the subgenre, with its lovely comment on "The early cloak-and-dagger stereotypes—the back-velveted seductress, the British secret-service numbskull hero, the omnipotent spymaster."

Bond, Raymond T., ed. *Famous Stories of Code and Cipher.* Holt, 1947.
Only a few in this anthology are spy stories, but codes and ciphers are always identified with the genre.

Dulles, Allen, ed. *Great Spy Stories from Fiction.* Harper, 1969.
A classic anthology of 32 stories with critical introductions.

BIBLIOGRAPHIES

Because many of the authors of spy/espionage novels also write mystery and detective novels, material on spy/espionage authors can also be found in some of the bibliographies (see p. 116) listed in chapter 3, "Crime."

McCormick, Donald, and Katy Fletcher. *Spy Fiction*. Facts on File, 1990.
The biocritical annotations list the works. The introduction is historical and critical. Appendix: "List of Abbreviations, Titles and Jargon Used in Espionage in Fact and Fiction"—the definitions are often amusing.

Smith, Myron J., Jr. *Cloak and Dagger Fiction: An Annotated Guide to Spy Thrillers*. Second Edition. ABC-Clio, 1982.
Briefly annotated are 318 titles, early thrillers to 1940, and over 3,000 items for 1940 to the present. There are appendices of pseudonyms, series characters, and a guide to spy organizations.

HISTORY AND CRITICISM

Additional material on the spy/espionage novel can be found in histories (see p. 119) and criticisms (see p. 120) of the detective story.

Atkins, John. *The British Spy Novel: Styles in Treachery*. London: Calder, 1984.
A critical historical survey, with illuminating quotations.

Harper, Ralph. *The World of the Thriller*. Johns Hopkins University Press, 1974 [1969].
Through an analysis of the hero and the situations of the spy subgenre, the author seeks to understand why readers become so engrossed in the books. He concludes that the subgenre, despite its sensationalism, exposes our nature to ourselves.

Merry, Bruce. *Anatomy of the Spy Thriller*. London: Gill, 1977.
The analysis of the books is idiosyncratic; to be critical, the reader should be a fan of the subgenre. The book contains a wealth of quotation.

Palmer, Jerry. *Thrillers: Genesis and Structure of a Popular Genre*. London: Edward Arnold, 1978.
An eccentric book—the author's reading seems largely of Mickey Spillane and Ian Fleming. Included here as an object lesson in distrusting titles.

Panek, LeRoy L. *The Special Branch: The British Spy Novel, 1890–1980*. Popular Press, 1981.
Contains critical essays on: William Le Queux, E. Phillips Oppenheim, Erskine Childers, John Buchan, Sapper, Francis Beeding, Sidney Horler, Graham Greene, Eric Ambler, Geoffrey Household, Peter Cheyney, Manning Coles, Ian Fleming, Len Deighton, John Le Carré, Adam Hall, Frederick Forsyth.

BACKGROUND

Beckett, Henry F. *The Dictionary of Espionage: Spookspeak in English*. Stein & Day, 1985.
International in coverage.

Buranelli, Vincent, and Nan Buranelli. *Spy/Counterspy*. McGraw-Hill, 1982.
An encyclopedia of about 400 articles on espionage, its nature and history, from Elizabethan times to the present.

Dobson, Christopher, and Ronald Payne. *Who's Who in Espionage*. St. Martin's, 1985.
Over 300 sketches of real people in spy/espionage work. Also describes the intelligence organizations for 17 nations.

JOURNALS AND ASSOCIATIONS

Journals
The Dossier: The Official Journal of the International Spy Society. 1981. Quarterly.
Contains both fact and fiction, also reviews.

Associations
International Spy Society
Fellowships by invitation. In 1984 presented its first awards, Oppy awards, named for E. Phillips Oppenheim.

D's Adventure Picks

Crichton, Michael. *The Andromeda Strain*. Knopf, 1969.

Durand, Loup. *Daddy*. Villard Books, 1988.

Gilman, Dorothy. *Mrs. Pollifax and the Hong Kong Buddha*. Doubleday, 1985.

Ludlum, Robert. *The Bourne Identity*. R. Marek, 1980.

Woods, Stuart. *White Cargo*. Simon and Schuster, 1988.

5 Romance

I still choose to enjoy the fact that, somewhere, a warrior is being tamed by an angel.

—Kelly Kimbrough
A romance reader

It is a truth universally acknowledged, that a single man in possession of a good fortune must be in want of a wife.

—Jane Austen
Pride and Prejudice (1813)

And what's romance? Usually, a nice little tale where you have everything As You Like It, where rain never wets your jacket and gnats never bite your nose and it's always daisy-time.

—D. H. Lawrence
Studies in Classic American Literature (1924)

THE APPEAL OF ROMANCE

Critics of Literature, suitably capitalized, avert their eyes disdainfully from the popular romance novels or dismiss their authors and readers with witty contempt. Yet their devoted readers, blissfully unaware that their taste is lamentable, have ensured by their demand the steady supply of romantic fiction since Henry Richardson's *Pamela* staunchly defended her virtue and attained her heart's desire. *Pamela* and novels by authors including Jane Austen, Charlotte and Emily Brontë, and Anthony Trollope are scorned by critics of Literature. However, such romance novels get a better reception in two books by British authors:

Anderson, Rachel. *The Purple Heart Throbs: The Sub-Literature of Love.* London: Hodder, 1974.

Cecil, Mirabel. *Heroines in Love, 1750–1974.* London: Michael Joseph, 1974.

In *The Purple Heart Throbs*, Rachel Anderson analyzes plots and themes of the popular romantic fiction of the nineteenth and twentieth centuries, noting the changing attitudes of society that affected (and still affect) both. Detailed plot summaries and extensive quotations reveal the constant appeal of the genre, regardless of how women's ideas and women's position in society were (and are) being transformed. In these novels, emotional experiences might be tinged with religious spirituality or aimed at sexual fulfillment, but the desired conclusion is always marriage. No fundamental difference, except in adaptation to sexual mores, distinguishes these novels from those that are popular today. There are chapters on the soap opera romance, the desert sheik epic, the doctor-nurse liaison, and the romance plot of the newly independent working woman. Anderson discusses why women read romances and analyzes the rules governing the genre. Members of the Romantic Novelists Association are given their say (in an abundance of delightful quotations) in defense of the genre: "Although they may no longer believe in God, readers do still believe in love."

In *Heroines in Love*, Cecil Mirabel provides nine stories from magazines (the earliest was published in 1780, the most recent 1969). Each is extensively and critically prefaced to form a history of the romantic heroine in magazine fiction. Each chapter comments on the stories published in a particular period (e.g., "The Horrors, 1794–1833"; "The Pure, 1830–1870"; "The Happy-Housewife Heroine, 1950–1965"). There are many quotations and summaries of typical plots. Illustrations from magazines of each period are included.

Martin Lewin, whose reviews of popular romances in *The New York Times Book Review* were a constant delight, provides *Love Stories* (Quadrangle, 1975), an anthology not of the pulp or popular romance authors but of "serious" authors (e.g., Willa Cather, Vladimir Nabokov, Shirley Jackson, Isaac Bashevis Singer, Elizabeth Spencer). He says, simply, "Love is an idea whose time has come back."

"What does a woman want?" asked Freud, who did not read romances to find the answer. (What do *men* want? The Grand Junction, Colorado, V.A. hospital reports an ardent readership for Harlequin romances.) What women want from romance novels varies in the trappings of historical period, place, and social milieu but not in the essential emotional element—true love triumphant against all odds.

Why do women read romances so voraciously? One of Betty Rosenberg's students began her paper on popular romances thus: "I stopped reading Romances when I started having them." She probably began reading them again when the routine monotony of daily living caught up with her. Women know that the escape from reality or frustration into a romance novel is an escape into fantasy, whether innocent or erotic. Women are not deluded but delighted. They identify with a heroine and a world that is beyond their attainment but not beyond their dreams. (Similarly, men who read adventure stories identify with the competent and virile hero, Walter Mittys all.) Romances are read by women of all ages, occupations (lawyers to house-wives), and economic status. A review of one of Rosemary Rogers's sweet-and-savage romances commented: "Obviously, for a large share of the female population, equal rights and liberation are one thing, fantasies quite another." All passion spent, we know we will live happily ever after.

Within the romance genre are several quite distinctive subgenres, differentiated for appeal to disparate audiences by setting, types of characters, and handling of sexual relations (i.e., is love holy and discreet as in the womanly romance, or is replete with violence and explicitness as in the sweet-and-savage romance?) The publishers (particularly of paperbacks), aware that readers choose by type, label romance books explicitly by phrase (e.g., nurse romance, Gothic romance, Regency romance, historical romance, saga), by a series title that immediately identifies the type for the reader, by a readily recognized kind of cover illustration (most notable are those for the Gothic romances), by suggestive titles (e.g., *Wicked Loving Lies*), or by length (sweet-and-savage romances are seldom less than 400 pages and are often closer to 600 pages).

The appeal of romance is addressed by 19 popular romance authors in the delightful *Dangerous Men and Adventurous Women*, edited by Jayne Ann Krentz (University of Pennsylvania Press, 1992). These writers, who obviously read and love the genre in which they write, display great respect for their readers. In essence, women read romance because these novels are an avenue of escapist fantasy in which a heroine gentles a warrior (his battleground can be anywhere from the boardroom to the bedroom to the sites of historic wars) and the two live happily ever after.

THEMES AND TYPES

Womanly Romances

The classic encompassing type of romance is the womanly romance (dominant, for example, in the Harlequin romances), contemporary in setting, with home and marriage the goals for living happily ever after. (The period romance—notably Barbara Cartland—may be essentially a womanly romance, but the historical setting adds a glamour appealing to a readership different from those who want the everyday present romantically rendered.) The earlier contemporary womanly romance was essentially "boy meets girl," in either a small town or metropolis, often in a business office (the woman marries the boss or his son), and equally often in a plot of relationships among a group of friends or family. (Much quoted is the anecdote about William Faulkner's scriptwriting days at Warner Brothers: When he left, in his office were found an empty bottle and a sheet of yellow foolscap on which he had written, five hundred times, "Boy Meets Girl.") An exotic setting was sometimes used, as in Ethel Dell's Indian romances.

After World War II, and with the change in woman's position in the world (feminism and women's liberation movements), there were definite changes in the womanly romance: more use of foreign settings, heroines were increasingly independent women (though still desirous of love and marriage), and a relaxing of social mores (i.e., permissible sexual behavior).

However, the tried-and-true romance patterns, providing a story in which happy endings are obligatory, are pursued faithfully by a large number of women authors. (The Harlequin/Mills and Boon series consist of authors who turn them out regularly; a total of 50 or more titles by each author is not unusual.) The authors continuing the traditions of womanly romances are myriad. The following lists do not attempt to include the many authors now writing for original paperback series; this would be futile until time decides which ones will survive.

The following authors wrote the prototype womanly romance.

Ayres, Ruby M.
British author, over 140 novels, her first published in 1917.

Baldwin, Faith
In her eighties, she is "the First Lady of the Love Story": currently in hardcover and paperback, about 100 novels.

Bloom, Ursula
British, "The Queen of the romantic novel," over 500 titles.

Dell, Ethel R.
British, her first work published in 1912, and on the best-seller list in 1916, several reprinted and condensed in Barbara Cartland's "Library of Love" series. " 'Yes, I am mad,' he said, and the words came quick and passionate, the lips that uttered them close to her own. 'I am mad for you, Anne, I worship you. And swear that while I live no other man shall ever hold you in his arms again. Anne—goddess—queen woman—you are mine—you are mine—you are mine.' "

Norris, Kathleen
The American Woman's dream in best-selling novels, her first published in 1911 and on the best-seller lists in 1916.

Among the prototype authors are the following that suggest a pattern of inspirational romance.

Hill, Grace Livingston
Over 50 novels (20 million copies) reprinted by Bantam Books and written from 1882 to 1947: "Mrs. Hill's novels of romance are about wholesome people whose profound faith and generous hearts let them cope with the problems of the modern world."

Loring, Emilie
Over 50 novels, more properly belonging with the inspirational type.

Montgomery, Lucy Maude
The Anne of Green Gables (first published in 1908) and the Emily series. Now considered for the young adult audience.

Porter, Gene Stratton. *Freckles. A Girl of the Limberlost.*
A best-seller in the early twentieth century, she created a world of homely innocence and sentimental purity.

Webster, Jean. *Daddy-Long-Legs* (1912).
Now considered for a young adult audience.

The following authors continued the tradition of the womanly romance.

Cadell, Elizabeth. *The Waiting Game.*
British, about 50 novels. Light comedy and suspenseful romance. "Presents a love story bound to warm the coldest heart."

Caldwell, Taylor. *Answer as a Man.*
Thirty-eight novels before her death in 1985. Twenty-five paperback titles, 25 million copies. Often the novels have a religious aspect, and are "liberally peopled by villains and schemers, and often . . . deal with family dynasties." " 'But you can't marry me. You are—Jeremy Porter—and a rich man and a lawyer, and I am only a servant girl.' "—*Ceremony of Innocence.*

Eden, Dorothy
Over 40 novels (including Gothic and historical romances). "If you put Dorothy Eden's name on a seed catalogue it would sell."—Ace Books editor.

Stevenson, D. E.
British, over 50 novels. "Funny, entertaining and clean." Mrs. Tim series: "With her usual charm and friendly understanding, Mrs. Tim makes friends, influences people and straightens out a lot of problems, including her own." Several titles available in large print, G. K. Hall & Co.

Van Slyke, Helen
Her nine novels sold six million copies. "It's all soap opera and it's all grand."—*The Best Place to Be.* "When did you last feel you really knew the people in a book . . . that you shared their pain and pleasure, in some form, in your own life? When did you find yourself smiling at something on one page and staining the next one with nice therapeutic tears? . . . Millions of readers want the kind of reality they can interpret in terms of their own experience, or within the scope of their own imagination. They don't scoff at sentiment; it never goes out of style. They believe in good and evil, in love and loyalty, and in bitterness and betrayal. This is the stuff real life is made of." " 'Old-fashioned' and 'Up to the Minute' by Helen Van Slyke."—*The Writer*, November 1975.

The traditional womanly romance continues in the following books.

Binchy, Maeve. *Echoes.*
"Warmth, poignancy, and passion . . . compelling reading."—*Los Angeles Herald Examiner.*

Pilcher, Rosamunde. *The Carousel. Shell Seekers. September.*
"I don't know where Rosamunde Pilcher has been all my life—but now that I have found her, I'm not going to let her go. The reason being that she writes romantic novels that are nearly perfect little *bon-bons*: not too much sugar, very little artificial coloring, lots of natural ingredients, ingeniously blended."—*Sleeping Tiger.* "It is warmed with honest sentiment, lubricated with tears of happiness and souped up by an ace romanticist."—*Under Gemini.*

Siddons, Ann Rivers
"Crumbling up my last Kleenex, I couldn't help but think that here, at last, was a novel that would have made Margaret Mitchell stand up and cheer."—*Pittsburgh Press.*

The following current, contemporary womanly romances show a greater variety of characters and plots and, certainly, more relaxed social and sexual attitudes.

Brown, Sandra. *Breakfast in Bed.*

Coscarelli, Kate. *Perfect Order. Fame & Fortune. Living Color.*

Dailey, Janet. *Glory Game.*

Hylton, Sara. *The Last Reunion.*

Laker, Rosalind. *This Shining Land.*

Lange, Kelly. *Trophy Wife.*

Letts, Billie. *Where the Heart Is.*

Martin, Vicki. *Tigers of the Night.*

McCaffrey, Anne. *Stitch in Snow. The Lady.*

McCorquadale, Robin. *Dansville.*

Randall, Rona. *Curtain Call.*

Rice, Luanne. *Home Fires.*

Spencer, La Vyrle. *Family Blessings.*

Steel, Danielle. *Changes. Crossings. Family Album. Full Circle. Lightning. Remembrance. The Ring. Secrets.*

Thomas, Rosie. *Sunrise.*

Villars, Elizabeth. *Adam's Daughters.*

GLITZ AND GLAMOUR

The trend appears to be an absorption of the contemporary womanly romance into the mainstream novel tradition. At the same time, the sexy novel of the rich and famous is falling into a genre pattern, described by a reviewer as the "best-seller formula of charmed lives, repressed passion, and fantasies come true." These have the setting of the international jet set of the rich, famous, international business tycoons (both sexes), Hollywood, polo-playing, and holiday resorts. The sex, usually, is steamy. Amazingly, these novels do fall into the pattern of the womanly romance at an exaggerated extreme. Both Danielle Steel and Janet Dailey (in the type of her *Glory Game*) would fit the pattern.

Beauman, Sally. *Destiny.*

Birmingham, Stephen. *Carriage Trade. Shades of Fortune.*

Booth, Pat. *Beverly Hills.*

Bradford, Barbara Taylor. *Angel. A Woman of Substance. Dangerous to Know.*

Brayfield, Celia. *Pearls.*

Briskin, Jacqueline. *The Naked Heart. Too Much Too Soon. Everything and More. Paloverde.*

Brown, Sandra. *Where There's Smoke. French Silk.*

Collins, Jackie. *Lady Boss. Hollywood Wives. Chances. Lucky.*

Conran, Shirley. *Savages. Lace. Lace II.*

Harvey, Kathryn. *Butterfly.*

Korda, Michael. *The Fortune.*

Krantz, Judith. *Dazzle. I'll Take Manhattan.*

McNaught, Judith. *Perfect.*

Michael, Judith. *Inheritance. Private Affairs.*

Mortman, Doris. *Rightfully Mine.*

Murdoch, Anna. *Family Business.*

Plain, Belva. *Blessings.*

Rann, Sheila. *Anything for Love.*

Seidel, Kathleen Gilles. *Again.*

Sheldon, Sidney. *Windmills of the Gods. If Tomorrow Comes.*

Steel, Danielle. *Daddy.*

Thomas, Rosie. *Bad Girls, Good Women.*

Vincenzi, Penny. *Old Sins.*

Wilde, Jennifer. *The Slipper.*

Wilkins, Barbara. *Elements of Chance.*

Romantic-Suspense

The romantic-suspense subgenre frequently eludes easy labeling. Novels in this category may blend into the mystery-suspense thriller subgenre (in which the mystery dominates the romance, making the novel of equal interest to both sexes), and into the spy/espionage thriller subgenre in the hands of authors such as Helen MacInnes (whose novels have equal amounts of romance and espionage). Most clearly defined is the Gothic novel, but its publishers often label it a suspense novel rather than a Gothic, seeking to evade the negative attitude toward the Gothic and the ridicule directed at its stereotyped plot.

Romantic-suspense novels are women's novels—while full of adventure and suspense, neither is allowed to diminish the heroine's romantic involvement. Many other types of romance have elements of suspense and mystery, and authors of romantic-suspense novels usually write in several other subgenres of romance as well. (Some of the following authors are also listed for other types of romance.) Plot background may be basically domestic (girl marries, goes to family estate, and husband dies or disappears; family secret leads to murder, scandal, and so forth), have an exotic foreign background (an archeological dig), or have the trappings of the period romance. The books of Mary Stewart, the queen of this subgenre, rate so satisfactorily high in romantic appeal and so strong in suspenseful foreign adventure involving both romantic leads as to be the one author in this category of interest to men as well as women readers. Many of the following authors appear in hardcover editions as well as in paperback reprints.

Aiken, Joan
"Another top-notch confection from a first-class pastry cook."—*The Smile of the Stranger.* "Tale of dicey doings in the 19th century is an agreeable if frothy diversion."—*The Five-Minute Marriage.*

Anthony, Evelyn. *Avenue of the Dead. The Company of Saints.*
"Cleverly turned out romantic suspense, sparked with the flavor of contemporary horseracing."—*The Silver Falcon.*

Black, Laura. *Falls of Gard.*

Brent, Madeleine. *Moonraker's Bride. Stormswift. A Heritage of Shadows.*
"The Phyllis Whitney of the nineteenth century British romantic suspense."—*Kirkus Reviews.*

Butler, Gwendoline. *Sarsen Place.*

Carr, Philippa. *Midsummer's Eve.*

Chance, Lisbeth. *Cutting Edge.*

Clark, Mark Higgins. *Still Watch.*

Conway, Laura
"For those who enjoy a touch of the occult in their romances."—*Take Heed of Loving Me.*

Dreyer, Eileen. *A Man to Die For. Suspense with a Dollop of Humour.* Thirty-eight are still in print in 1995.

Eberhart, Mignon Good
Fifty-nine mysteries, first in 1929, equally romantic and mysterious. "As is to be expected, the mystery is thickly sauced with sensitivity and the love interest is more important than the solution. The story is, however, not a whit the worse for it."—*Two Little Rich Girls.*

Foley, Rae
"At least Foley tells her story without the sentimentality that so often afflicts stories of romantic suspense."—*Where Helen Lives.*

Gaskin, Catherine. *The Property of a Gentleman.*

Gilbert, Anna. *Flowers for Lillian. The Leavetaking. The Long Shadows.*

Hodge, Jane Aiken. *Secret Island.*
"Cafe expresso reading with all the attractive scenic touches."—*One Way to Venice.*

Holland, Isabelle. *Flight of the Archangel.*

Holt, Victoria. *Judas Kiss. The Time of the Hunter's Moon.*
"In Australia, where Jessica encounters a jealous rival, a missing gem, and a couple of murders before finding true love—with her husband."—*The Pride of the Peacock.*

Johnston, Velda. *Shadows Behind the Curtain. Voice in the Night.*
"Star-crossed lovers, two suspicious deaths, and a dash of period flair."—*The Silver Dolphin.*

Kaye, M. M. *Death in Berlin. Death in Cyprus. Death in Kashmir. Death in Kenya. Death in the Andamans. Death in Zanzibar.*

Krentz, Jayne Ann. *Grand Passion.*

Lofts, Norah. *Lady Living Alone.*

MacInnes, Helen. *Cloak of Darkness. Hidden Target.*

Marlowe, Ann. *The Red Rocking Bird.*

Melville, Jennie. *Axwater.*

Michaels, Barbara. *Smoke and Mirrors.*

Ogilvie, Elisabeth. *When the Music Stopped.*

O'Grady, Leslie. *The Artist's Daughter. Lady Jade. Lord Raven's Widow.*

Peters, Elizabeth. *The Copenhagen Connection. Silhouette in Scarlet.* Amelia Peabody series: *Crocodile on the Sandbank. Curse of the Pharoahs. The Mummy Case. Lion in the Valley.*

Robards, Karen. *Wild Orchids.*

Roberts, Norah. *Carnal Innocence. Private Scandals. True Betrayals.*

Sherwood, Valerie. *Lisbon.*

Shreve, Anita. *Eden Close.*

Smith, Kay Nolte. *Elegy for a Soprano.*

Stewart, Mary. *My Brother Michael.*
The queen of the genre to whom others are compared.

Whitney, Phyllis A. *A Dream of Orchids. Emerald. Flaming Tree. Rainsong. Vermillion. Rainbow in the Mist.*

GOTHIC

Once the most enduring of romance subgenres, the Gothic has been eclipsed by other types. See earlier editions of *Genreflecting* for discussions of the Gothic and lists of authors who (though no longer writing—the majority no longer living) are still quite popular in libraries.

SUPERNATURAL ROMANCE

An emerging subgenre, related to romantic suspense and the Gothic but going a step further, is the supernatural romance. The heroine falls in love with a creature that would usually be consigned to the horror section, such as a vampire or werewolf. The possibilities for conflicts are myriad. Dating outside of humankind or the challenge of dealing with an immortal partner are just two of the conflicts that can arise in this type of romance. Currently, most supernatural romance is published in paperback. Tanya Huff, like many authors writing in this vein, mixes romance with horror and detection.

Carleen, Sally. *Shaded Leaves of Destiny.*

Clare, Cathryn. *Sun and Shadow.*

Faith, Barbara. *A Silence of Dreams.*

Harrison, Allie. *Dead Reckoning. Dream a Deadly Dream.*

Huff, Tanya. *Blood Lines. Blood Pact. Sing the Four Quarters.*

Karr, Lee. *Footsteps in the Night.*

Kenyon, Sherrilyn. *Daemon's Angel.*

Krinard, Susan. *Prince of Wolves.*

Lee, Rachel. *Thunder Mountain.*

Longford, Lindsay. *Lover in the Shadows.*

Miller, Linda Lael. *Forever and the Night.*

Myers, Helen R. *Night Mist. Watching for Willa. Whispers in the Woods.*

Pozzessere, Heather. *The Last Cavalier.*

Rose, Jeanne. *Heart of Dreams.*

Shayne, Maggie. *Kiss of the Shadow. Twilight Illusions. Twilight Memories.*

Stevens, Amanda. *Dark Obsession. The Seventh Night.*

Toombs, Jane. *Return to Bloodstone. The Woman in White.*

Tracy, Marilyn. *Something Beautiful.*

Historical Romance

The historical romance can be divided into two groupings. The first presents authentic historical background, characters, and events, although fictitious characters and events are often, perhaps usually, introduced either as conjecture or to make a full and lively tale. The degree to which fictionalization is used and the seriousness of the author's historical attitude may provide the criteria differentiating the historical *novel* from the historical *romance*, although this writer's criteria are derived from the intelligence shown by the author in interpreting history and the quality of the writing. Many novels hover uneasily between the two types. Therefore, the serious reader devoted to the historical novel may find some historical romances of interest and the reader of historical romances may enjoy some historical novels, the latter dependent on readability in a popular sense.

The second group is more properly labeled "period" romance. Although these romances may introduce historical characters as part of the background, their intent is the creation of a dream of romance set safely in another time far distant from the mundane present (the romance is then more believable in a society detached from the reader's). The reader escapes into a past world of glamour, recreated skillfully in all details of life—speech, clothing, food, furnishings, and the like—so that a time and place are evoked in which the reader can live vicariously.

The characteristics of the types of historical romance can be contrasted in essentials. All re-create a historical period and atmosphere, usually with great detail—in the historical romance/novel, the period is essential to that particular novel; in the period romance, the atmosphere is merely the romantic aura of another time within which lovers may play out their story. The historical characters and events—kings, queens, wars—in the historical novel/romance are the plot essentials; in the period romance they merely add to the background.

The reader with a strong interest in history will welcome extensive description of background, the way of life and incidents of the time, while the romance reader may find such description excessive. One reader's insistence on being given the "real" story of authentic characters and events contrasts with another reader's desire for a "romantic" plot, even if it means sacrificing the facts of history. The most successful writers of historical romance know the exact mixture of fact and fiction to satisfy the genre fans. (In the sweet-and-savage and plantation romance subgenres, the only necessity is sex in an exotic setting.) Present in all types of romance fiction is adventure, given fuller scope the less the plot is restricted by historical authenticity.

(Similar comparisons may be made for the western and some thriller subgenres. The reader of westerns may be interested in the authentic history of the American West as well as in a story of adventure. The reader of spy/espionage and the political-terrorist thrillers may be drawn to the depiction of international affairs and political intrigue as well as the more sensational story lines.)

Historical romance in all its variations, from serious history through period background to simple costume romance, is probably the most published type of romance. A scanning of the best-seller lists, from the turn of the century on, will show a persistent interest. The following early prototypes are still available in reprint.

Haggard, H. Rider. *She* (1887).

Hope, Anthony. *The Prisoner of Zenda* (1894).

McCutcheon, George Barr. *Graustark* (1901).

Orczy, Baroness. *The Scarlet Pimpernel* (1905).

The following lists of authors come under three main groups. First, the historical novel, which (perhaps a trifle arbitrarily) can be separated from the historical romance. Following this, between the historical novel and the historical romance, is an intriguing type—the "Royals" romance. Then comes the period romance, including period and costume types, excepting the Regency period romance, which is in a separate subsection. A brief annotation is provided for many titles that indicates the period or historical characters.

HISTORICAL NOVEL

The following authors display a serious respect for history. Many will appeal to costume romance readers as they often supply adequate dollops of romance. Indeed, some, like Sabatini, allow the costume romance characteristics to dominate the history.

Dumas, Alexandre
The *Three Musketeers* includes a spy/espionage plot.

Scott, Sir Walter

Some selective modern examples are:

Barnes, Margaret Campbell

Bell, Pamela. *Treason's Gift. Wintercombe.*

Bryher

Druon, Maurice

Duggan, Alfred

Fast, Howard

Forester, C. S. Hornblower series.

Graves, Robert

Hackett, Francis

Heyer, Georgette. *The Spanish Bride. An Infamous Army. Lord John.*

Odenbourg, Zoe

Renault, Mary
"The historical novel recognizes man's need to transmit his tradition of the past and feels a responsibility for doing so with a respect for factual truth. This attitude distinguishes the historical novelist from the costume romanticist."—Renault.

Sabatini, Rafael. *Scaramouche.*

Sutcliffe, Rosemary

Tranter, Nigel. *The River Realm. James, By the Grace of God.*
About James IV and James V of Scotland.

Treece, Henry

Undset, Sigrid. *Kristin Lavransdatter.*

Yourcenar, Marguerite. *The Memoirs of Hadrian.*

THE "ROYALS"

Biography of royal personages has long been a popular type of publication. Many historical novels, treating history in terms of a country's rulers, have been, at least partially, biographies of kings. Recently, there have been several romances about queens and princesses, perhaps a continuing type. The following list contains only books about the women royals.

Hill, Pamela. *Tsar's Woman.*
Catherine I, Russia.

Kay, Susan. *Legacy.*
Elizabeth I, England. Winner of both the Georgette Heyer and Betty Trask prizes, 1985.

Lambton, Anthony. *Elizabeth & Alexandra*.
Queen Victoria's granddaughters: Alix, married to Czar Nicholas II; Ella, married to Grand Duke Serge.

Meyerson, Evelyn Wilde. *Princess in Amber*.
Queen Victoria's daughter, Princess Beatrice.

Plaidy, Jean. Georgia Saga: *Queen in Waiting. The Princess of Celle* (Sophia Dorothea, divorced wife of George I, England). *Caroline the Queen* (and others). Victorian Saga: *The Captive of Kensington Palace. Victoria in the Wings. The Queen and Lord M. The Queen's Husband. The Widow of Windsor. Victoria Victorious.* See also her earlier novels on Isabella of Spain, Katharine of Aragon, Mary of Scotland.

PERIOD ROMANCE

The period romance, or costume romance, places the love story within the romantic aura of another time, the dream given credibility by its remoteness from the reader's own experience, and enhanced, for women readers, by great detail on dress, food, and mannered social activity. (Harlequin Books, in publicity for its Masqueraders series, notes that five out of ten women read romances and four out of the ten read historical romances, undoubtedly of the costume variety.) The most popular period romance, and the one commonly labeled by publishers, is the Regency romance. However, all periods are used—the medieval, eighteenth century, and Victorian England being among the dominant periods—and publishers tend to use labels such as "a delightful Georgian" (Playboy Press) or "Victorian romance" as well as Regency. The Edwardian period (turn of the century to World War I) has become popular following the television series *Upstairs, Downstairs*. The background of social history is often colorfully and extensively developed, particularly by those writers who use one period almost exclusively. The following books attest to the popularity of the period romance, which is almost infinite in its variety.

Adler, Elizabeth. *Leonie*.
Turn-of-the-century France.

Aiken, Joan
Many of her novels use period background.

Alexander, Kate. *Fields of Battle. Friends and Enemies.*

Allen, Hervey. *Anthony Adverse* (eighteenth to nineteenth centuries).

Arlen, Leslie. Borodin family series (early-twentieth-century Russia).

Ashfield, Helen. *Emerald. Pearl. Ruby. Sapphire. The Michaelmas Tree* (Victorian).

Black, Laura. *Albany* (Georgian).

Blake, Jennifer. *Fierce Eden* (U.S. West, nineteenth century).

Bristol, Leigh. *Legacy* (post-reconstruction Charleston).

Brooks, Betty. *Viking Mistress* (thirteenth-century North America).

Brown, Mary. *Playing the Jack* (Georgian).

Burns, Patricia. *Stacey's Flyer* (Victorian). *Kezzy* (nineteenth century).

Caldwell, Taylor. *Glory and the Lightning.*

Carr, Robyn. *The Braeswood Tapestry* (seventeenth century). *By Right of Arms* (fourteenth century). *The Troubadour's Romance* (twelfth century).

Cartland, Barbara.
  "The world's all-time best-selling romantic novelist." About 300 novels to date, at the rate of 14 to 20 a year. A biography: Henry Cloud, *Barbara Cartland: Crusader in Pink* (London: Weidenfeld, 1979).
  "The Cartland formula is costume romance, fairy tales with passive heroines, men who are never less than perfection, and love that is spiritual. Although Cartland always finds a way to titillate her readers by maneuvering the lovers into bed, sex is never consummated without marriage."
  There are some happy endings (all ". . ." in the quotations are Barbara Cartland's—this is her distinctive style, as are the one-sentence paragraphs).

> With his mouth holding her captive, he carried her away into a glorious secret kingdom of their own where there was no pride . . . only a fiery, uncontrolled ecstatic love—*The Proud Princess.*

> Then there were only the mountain peaks and the "knife-edge" of ultimate joy—*The Magnificent Marriage.*

> "I love . . . you . . . too," she whispered against the Marquis's lips and there was no need for words—*The Bored Bridegroom.*

> On the sea of reflection the light from the rising moon touched softly moving waves with silver as if they caressed the body of the goddess of love—*Kiss the Moonlight.*

> They were one and he carried her towards the burning glory of the sun—*The Devil in Love.*

> Our lives will be so beautiful that we will attain a perfection that is known only to the gods—*The Perfection of Love.*

>> The Earl looked at Baptista, thinking it would be impossible for any woman to look more lovely or so pure and untouched.
>> Then as if he could not help himself, his arms tightened and slowly, as if it was a moment he would savor and remember, his lips came down on hers.

He could feel the ecstasy she was experiencing vibrate from her lips to his, and awaken in him sensations he had never known before.

It was so perfect that for a moment he was dazzled by it, as if they were enveloped by a light divine— *Signpost of Love.*

"I want you . . . as a man wants a woman . . . I can no longer protect you from myself."

"How stupid you are, dear Guardie! . . . I want to feel your arms around me . . . your lips against mine . . . I want to be yours, yes, really and truly."—*The Innocent Heiress.*

Chadwick, Elizabeth. *The Wild Hunt. The Running Vixen. The Leopard Unleashed* (twelfth-century Wales).

Cleeve, Brian
"Lively characters of all classes, combined with love, torture, heroism, and a blend of social satire and social uplift, make this—like Cleeve's others—several hundred cuts above the usual historical flimflam."—*Judith.* "Her youthful man-hating is dissolved into healthy sexuality through the offices of a young male librarian whom she loves and nearly loses during her subsequent trial for high treason."—*Kate.*

Coffman, Elaine. *When Love Comes Along.* McKinnon series.

Coleman, Bob. *The Later Adventures of Tom Jones* (Georgian).

Cookson, Catherine. *The Bannaman Legacy. The Black Velvet Gown. The Whip. Tilly Trotter. Tilly Trotter Wed. Tilly Trotter Widowed* (Victorian).

Costain, Thomas. *The Black Rose* (Medieval). *The Silver Chalice.*

Dailey, Janet. *The Pride of Hannah Wade* (U.S. West, nineteenth century).

Darrell, Elizabeth. *At the Going Down of the Sun.*

DeBlasis, Celeste. *The Proud Breed. The Tiger's Woman* (U.S. West). *Wild Swan. Swan's Chance* (U.S. Civil War period). *A Season of Swans.*

Drummond, Emma. *Beyond the Frontier. Forget the Glory* (Victorian).

Dunnett, Dorothy. *The Game of Kings. Queen's Play. The Disorderly Knights. Pawn in Frankincense. The Ringed Castle. Checkmate.*
"The intricate plotting and counter-plotting make it as much a game of detection as an exercise in historical fiction."—*The Disorderly Knights.* Part of a six-volume series with a sixteenth-century Scottish adventurer hero.

Esler, Anthony
Purple prose and passion and touches of sweet-and-savage romance. "Spirited and unashamed costume romantic."—*Blade of Castlemayne.*

Eulo, Elena Yates. *A Southern Woman* (Civil War, Tennessee).

Faulkner, Colleen. *Captive* (eighteenth-century Native American).

Fisher, Alan. *The Three Passions of Countess Natalya* (Russian revolution).

Fitzgerald, Valerie. *Zeminda* (India, nineteenth century).

Fowler, Robert H. *The Spoils of Eden* (Barbados, seventeenth century).
Some sweet-and-savage aspects.

Freyer, Gayle. *The Prince of Cups* (Italy, fifteenth century).

Garlock, Dorothy. *Sins of Summer* (Idaho, nineteenth century).

Gear, Kathleen O'Neal. *Thin Moon and Cold Mist* (Civil War).

Gellis, Roberta. Roselynde Chronicles: *Roselynde. Alinor. Joanna. Gillian. Rhiannon. Sybelle* (Medieval).
Original paperback series, reprinted in hardcover by Gregg Press, 1984.

Gibbs, Mary Ann
Author of many Victorian romances.

Gilbert, Anna
"A decorous, agreeable tale about love and loss in England of the 1880's."—*The Look of Innocence* (Winner of Britain's Romantic Novel of the Year Award).

Gluyas, Constance
For "those who like their historical romances more romantic than historical."—*Born to Be King*.

Golon, Sergeanne.
"Filled with adventure, coincidence, narrow escape, mystery, period background—all the things that make up a nicely old-fashioned historical novel." "Plunging once more into the turbulent adventure of gorgeous, sensuous, heroic, psychic crackshot Angelique."—*Angelique and the Ghosts*. Ninth in the Angelique series.

Gould, John. *No Other Place. The Wines of Pentagoet* (American colonies, seventeenth century).

Gower, Iris. *Proud Mary. Spinner's Wharf* (Edwardian).

Grant, Maxwell. *Blood Red Rose* (China, 1920s).

Hannah, Kristin. *If You Believe* (Washington State, nineteenth century). *The Enchantment* (New Mexico, nineteenth century).

Hardwick, Mollie. *The Crystal Dove* (Victorian). *The Merry Maid* (Elizabethan).

Heaven, Constance. *Castle of Doves* (Spain, 1830s). *The House of Kuragin. Heir to Kuragin* (Tsarist Russia). *The Queen and the Gypsy* (Elizabethan). *The Wind from the Sea* (England, 1793–1803).

Heyer, Georgette
"Simon rises from page to lord and advisor to King Henry by dint of hard work and real ability. His single-minded quest for advancement leaves no room in his life for women—until he meets the Lady Margaret."—*Simon the Coldheart.*

" 'Leonie, you will do well to consider. You are not the first woman in my life.' "
She smiled through her tears.
" 'Monseigneur, I would so much rather be the last woman than the first,' she said."—*These Old Shades*

Hinger, Charlotte. *Come Spring* (Kansas, 1881).

Hodge, Jane Aiken
"By day the governess to [Lord] Hawth's bastards, Kate roves the countryside on horseback at night, masquerading as Kit, a male. . . . The book is a virtual spoof of historical romances."—*Red Sky at Night, Lovers' Delight.*

Holland, Cecelia. *Belt of Gold* (ninth century). *Pillar of the Sky* (England, prehistoric).

Holt, Victoria. *Demon Lover* (France, nineteenth century).
"An accurate portrayal of the intrigue of the Elizabethan court."
"For those addicted to ruffles and flourishes and gossipy travails."—*My Enemy the Queen.* "A young British schoolmistress becomes involved with an arrogant French count and is caught up in the terror of the opening days of the revolution."—*The Devil on Horseback.*

Ibbotson, Eva. *Magic Flutes* (England, France, nineteenth century). *A Company of Swans* (early twentieth century).

Irwin, Margaret. *The Bride. Royal Flush* (England, France, seventeenth century). *The Stranger Prince* (Prince Rupert, seventeenth century).

Jagger, Brenda. *A Song Twice Over* (Victorian).

Jarman, Rosemary Hawley
"Manages to convey the lush, devious bawdy ambiance of her chosen century, makes lively a time, place and society that once were and still seem passing strange."—*The King's Grey Mare.*

Jekel, Pamela. *Natchez* (Louisiana, eighteenth and nineteenth centuries).

Johansen, Iris. *The Beloved Scoundrel* (England, nineteenth century). *The Magnificent Rogue* (Scotland, sixteenth century).

Kaufman, Pamela. *Shield of Three Lions* (Medieval). *Banners of Gold.*

Kaye, M. M.
"Leisurely, panoramic . . . rich in adventure, heroism, cruelty and love, rich in India." "An Indian *Gone with the Wind*."—*The Far Pavilions*.

Kells, Susannah. *A Crowning Mercy* (seventeenth century).

Kelly, Carla. *Daughter of Fortune* (American West, seventeenth century).

Kent, Katherine. *Tawney Rose* (Georgian).

Knight, Alanna. *The Black Duchess* (Elizabethan).

Koen, Karleen. *Through a Glass Darkly* (eighteenth century).

Laker, Rosalind. *Jewelled Path. What the Heart Keeps* (Edwardian). *To Dance with Kings* (five generations of women and kings). *The Silver Touch* (eighteenth century).

Llywelyn, Morgan. *Grania* (Elizabethan).

Lofts, Norah. *Day of the Butterfly* (Victorian). *The Pargeters* (England, seventeenth century). *A Wayside Tavern* (England, from sixteenth century on).
"Our knight's adventures in the land of the Moors, his lady's struggle at home during his long absence make delightfully dramatic reading and provide a superficial but intriguing portrait of one way of English life as it was lived 500 years ago."—*Knight's Acre*. "I do not want to be a lady. I want to be a wool merchant." "A gentle fifteenth-century tale of Women's Liberation."—*The Maud Reed Table*.

MacCoun, Catherine. *The Age of Miracles* (Medieval).

Macdonald, Malcolm. *For They Shall Inherit. An Innocent Woman. A Notorious Woman.*

Marshall, Edison. *Benjamin Blake. Yankee Pasha.*

Martin, Kat. *Bold Angel* (Medieval). *Natchez Flame* (United States, nineteenth century). *Dangerous Angel* (England, eighteenth century).

Martin, Rhona. *Gallows Wedding* (fifteenth century).

Michaels, Barbara. *Wait for What Will Come. Wings of the Falcon.*

Miller, Linda Lael. Orphan Train trilogy (United States, nineteenth century).

Mitchell, Margaret. *Gone with the Wind.*

Montague, Jeanne. *Midnight Moon* (Georgian).

Montupet, Janine. *The Lacemaker* (seventeenth-century France).

Moore, Susan. *Paths of Fortune* (Victorian).

Murray, Frances. *The Belchamber Scandal* (Victorian).

Nickson, Jeanne. *Shadow of the Condor* (South America).

Ogilvie, Elisabeth. *Jennie About to Be. The World of Jennie G* (Scotland / Maine, early nineteenth century).

Pearson, Diane. *Czardas. The Summer of the Barshinskeys.*

Penman, Sharon Kay. *Here Be Dragons* (King John of England). *The Sunne in Splendour* (King Richard III of England).

Plaidy, Jean. "Queen of popular historical novels." Several series: Georgian Saga (10 titles); Victorian Saga (6 titles); Norman trilogy (*The Bastard King, The Lion of Justice, The Passionate Enemies*); Plantagenet Saga (14 titles). Also a trilogy on Lucrezia Borgia and quartets on each of the following: Catherine de' Medici, Charles II, Isabella and Ferdinand, Catherine of Aragon, and the Stuarts.

Plain, Belva. *Crescent City* (U.S. South, nineteenth century).

Ripley, Alexandra. *Charleston. On Leaving Charleston* (antebellum South). *The Time Returns* (Lorenzo de' Medici, Florence). *From Fields of Gold* (antebellum South).

Roberts, Ann Victoria. *Louisa Elliott* (Victorian).

Robinson, Margaret A. *Courting Emma Howe* (early-twentieth-century Washington State).

Rofheart, Martha
"The author moves easily through castles, festivals, and trysts."— *Fortune Made His Sword.*

Sabatini, Rafael
"He was born with a gift of laughter and a sense that the world was mad." [Opening sentence of *Scaramouche*.] "Delightfully courtly, flowery, old-fashioned but not dated. . . . Nobody writes historical romances like this anymore—more's the pity."—*Scaramouche*. "Why is a book by Sabatini almost impossible to stop reading?"—*Time*, March 9, 1976. "From the neck down [his heroines] might as well be buried in moth balls."—*Time*, March 9, 1976.

Seton, Anya. *My Theodosia* (Theodosia Burr). *Katherine* (wife of John of Gaunt). *The Winthrop Woman* (niece of first governor of Massachusetts).

Shannon, Dell. *The Dispossessed* (seventeenth century). *The Scalpel and the Sword* (Napoleonic).

Shannon, Doris. *Family Money* (United States, early twentieth century).

Shellabarger, Samuel. *Captain from Castille. Prince of Foxes. The King's Cavalier.*

Stirling, Jessica. *The Good Provider* (nineteenth-century Scotland).

Summerson, Rachel. *Dishonourable Intentions* (Victorian).

Suyin, Han. *The Enchantress* (China, eighteenth century).

Thornton, Elizabeth. *Dangerous to Love* (Georgian England).

Tremaine, Jennie. *Maggie* (Edwardian). Georgian series.

Trollope, Joanna. *Leaves from the Valley* (Victorian).

Veryan, Patricia. The Golden Chronicles: *Practice to Deceive. Journey to Enchantment* (Georgian). *Love Alters Not. Dedicated Villain.* Tales of the Jewelled Men: *Time's Fool. Had We Never Loved. Ask Me No Questions. A Shadow's Bliss.*

Villars, Elizabeth. *One Night in Newport. The Normandy Affair.*

Winsor, Kathleen. *Forever Amber* (England, seventeenth century).

Wolf, Joan. *Born of the Sun* (Saxon).

Woodhouse, Sarah. *A Season of Mists* (Georgian).

Yerby, Frank
"It swashes where it ought to swash. . . . And there's this beautiful Greek slave girl Zenobia."—*The Saracen Blade.*

Zaroulis, Nancy. *The Last Waltz* (Boston, nineteenth century).

Regency

The most popular period romance features the Regency period (England in the first third of the nineteenth century) and is, for many readers, epitomized by the novels of Georgette Heyer. She is, in the diction of the Regency, "The Nonpareil," and all other authors using the period are "poor drab" imitators (for example, publishers notes on jackets or paperback covers: "In the grand tradition of Georgette Heyer" or "The best since Georgette Heyer." A reviewer denigrated Barbara Cartland as the "poor woman's Georgette Heyer"). The Friends of the English Regency, a California association of devotees of Georgette Heyer and the Regency romance, holds an annual assemblée (at which there is period dancing in costume), publishes a newsletter, and presents a "Georgette" award for the best new Regency romance.

The Regency world is one of high society, the London Season of the wealthy and titled enjoying the assemblies at Almack's, the dandies in their fashionable garb. The country estate is also featured, as are the fashionable doings at Bath. Frequently, the heroine is impoverished, the daughter of a poor country parson, or an orphan, but always she is a lady. Manner and dress are of utmost importance. The moral tone is licentious, but love reforms all rakes. (*The Dandy: Brummell to Beerbohm* by Ellen Moers devotes the first hundred pages to the Regency period.)

The following prototypes differ in style, but all reflect a mode of life immediately recognizable as characterizing the Regency. Fanny Burney's *Evelina*, published prior to the Regency, foreshadows the Regency tone.

Austen, Jane
"It is a truth universally acknowledged, that a single man in possession of a good fortune must be in want of a wife."—*Pride and Prejudice* (1813).

Several authors have written novels about Austen's characters, of more interest to Janeites than to the usual Regency fan, with the exception of the one by John Coates.

Aiken, Joan. *Mansfield Revisited.*

Coates, John. *The Watsons.*
Continuation of an unfinished novel.

Gillespie, Jane. *Ladysmead. Teverton Hall.*

Karr, Phyllis Ann. *Lady Susan.*
Reworking of an unfinished novel.

Royde-Smith, Naomi. *Jane Fairfax.*

White, T. H. *Darkness at Pemberly.*
A detective story about the present-day Darcys, with a nice romance as well.

Wilson, Barbara Ker. *Antipodes Jane* (originally titled *Jane Austen in Australia*).
An 1803 fictional trip to Australia, not really Regency in tone.

Bulwer-Lytton, Edward
"The season was unusually dull, and my mother, after having looked over her list of engagements, and ascertaining that she had none worth staying for, agreed to elope with her new lover."— *Pelham; or, The Adventures of a Gentleman.* First published in 1828 but revised in 1840 as the libertine Regency tone offended Victorian taste.

Burney, Fanny
"We have been a-shopping, as Mrs. Mirvan calls it, all this morning, to buy silks, caps, gauzes, and so forth."—*Evelina; or, The History of a Young Lady's Entrance into the World* (1778).

Farnol, Jeffery
"He took the standard ingredients [of the Regency]—bucks, duellists, pugilists, smugglers and haughty ladies—and fitted them into variations of the standard nineteenth-century plot based on usurped or disputed birthrights. . . . [A novelist] wearing his heart on his sleeve but writing with his tongue in his cheek." Many have as a solver of mysteries Jasper Shrig, the Bow Street Runner. His first novel was published in 1910.

The following authors capitalize on the surefire plot in which a spirited heroine captures a rakish hero in an aristocratic setting.

Aiken, Joan. *The Smile of the Stranger.*

Angers, Helen. *A Lady of Independence.*

Ashfield, Helen. *The Marquis & Miss Jones.*

Balogh, Mary. *A Masked Deception. Beyond the Sunrise. Dancing with Clara. The First Snowdrop. Kate & the Soldier. Lady Liza's Luck.*

Bell, Anthea. *A London Season.*

Beverley, Jo. *Deirdre and Don Juan. An Arranged Marriage.*

Blythe, Juliet. *The Parfait Knight* (blind heroine).

Brown, Diana. *Come Be My Love.*

Cartland, Barbara
"Spunky young orphan heiress Petrina Lyndon climbs over the wall of her school to run away to London and become a lady-bird."— *Loves, Lords, and Lady-Birds.*

Cheshire, Chloe. *A Gypsie at Almack's.*

Chesney, Marion. The Six Sisters series, A House for the Season series, The Traveling Matchmaker series. The Poor Relation series.

Clare, Cathleen. *Letitia.*

Clark, Gail. *The Baroness of Bow Street.*
"There is added delight in the thoroughness with which the author presents a full picture of the Regency period—dress, manners, mores, even slang."—*Dulcie Bligh.* Both novels involve detection and Bow Street Runners.

Courtney, Caroline. *Libertine in Love.*

Cummings, Monette. *The Beauty's Daughter. Lady Sheila's Groom. See No Evil.*

Darcy, Clare
Her 14 Regencies all have a name as title and have been called "the best since Georgette Heyer."

"The heroine masquerading as a boy, is befriended by the elegant, proud Redmayne. She is running away, he thinks he is in search of another beauty."—*Elyza.*

" 'The neighborhood is *very* thin of eligible men. . . . Obviously I have raised three daughters with more hair than wit.' "— *Gwendolyn.*

Delmore, Diana. *Leonie.*

Diamond, Jacqueline. *Forgetful Lady. A Lady of Letters.*

Drummond, June. *The Bluestocking. The Unsuitable Miss Pelham. The Imposter.*

Dunn, Carola. *Lavender Lady. Lord Iverbrook's Heir. Lady and the Rake. His Lordship's Reward.*

Ellingson, Marnie. *Dolly Blanchard's Fortune. The Wicked Marquis.*

Ewing, Jean R. *Rogue's Reward. Scandal's Reward.*

Fellows, Catherine. *The Marriage Masque.*

Freeman, Joy. *The Last Frost Fair. A Suitable Match.*

Gordon, Susan. *Match of the Season.*

Hewitt, Elizabeth. *True Colors.*

Heyer, Georgette

To her 29 Regency romances should be added *These Old Shades, Devil's Cub,* and *The Talisman Ring.* Not only do they have the tone of the Regency, but the characters in the first two titles are found, along with descendants, in *An Infamous Army,* as are also those from *Regency Buck. The Talisman Ring* is one of the great examples of her inimitable dialogue: one rereads the novels for the sheer amusement in the dialogue and delight in the use of period language. Her gift, or talent, in this respect has been imitated but never equaled.

The biography by Jane Aiken Hodge, *The Private World of Georgette Heyer* (London: Bodley Head, 1984), is lavishly illustrated and of particular interest for the details on Heyer's collection of information on historical background.

The following passages are from *The Quiet Gentleman,* selected to suggest the amusement to be derived from her style.

> "Providence has decreed that he should succeed to his dear father's honours," pronounced the Dowager, thinking poorly of Providence.

> "Well, now you come to ask me," said Mr. Warboys, with the air of one making a discovery, "I don't know what I mean! Spoke without thinking! Often do! Runs in the family: uncle of mine was just the same. Found himself married to a female with a squint all through speaking without thinking."

> "Parrot-faced is she?" said the viscount, interested. "Lay you a monkey she don't peck me! Dear boy, did you ever *see* my aunts? Three of 'em, all parrot-faced, and all hot at hand! Father's frightened of 'em—m'mother's frightened of 'em! Freddy won't face 'em. Only person who can handle 'em's me! No bamming—true as I stand here! Ask Anyone!"

"Phantom! Let me assure you that we have nothing of that sort at Stanyon! I should not countenance it; I do not approve of the supernatural."

"My father was a great reader, though not, of course, during the hunting season."

"You would become disgusted with my odious common sense. Try as I will, I *cannot* be romantic!" said Miss Morville.

His eyes danced. "Oh, I forbid you to try! Your practical observations, my absurd robin, are the delight of my life!"

Miss Morville looked at him. Then, with a deep sigh, she laid her hand in his. But what she said was: "You must mean a sparrow!"

"I will not allow you to dictate to me, now or ever, Miss Morville! I mean a robin!" said the Earl firmly, lifting her hand to his lips.

Hill, Fiona
"A Georgette Heyerish bit of flummery—with considerably more wit and pizzazz than the legendary Georgette herself."—*The Autumn Rose*. (The type of review that leads the Heyer fan astray: alas, *not* true!) "Three nubile lasses . . . on the chessboard of marriage-making that is a full-time activity for the titled class."—*The Stanbroke Girls*.

Hodge, Jane Aiken
"A willful miss who objects so strongly to being married, sight unseen, to an arrogant lord, friend of her dead brothers, that she runs away from her dreadfully mercenary uncle."—*Runaway Bride*.

Kelly, Carla. *Miss Billings Treads the Boards*.

Kidd, Elizabeth. *A Hero for Antonia*.

Laine, Annabel. *The Reluctant Heiress. The Melancholy Virgin.*
The second title is also a detective story, with Bow Street Runners.

Lee, Elsie. *The Nabob's Widow*.
"A spirited beauty. . . . The problem is . . . to find her a husband."—*A Prior Betrothal*.

Ley, Alice Chetwynd. *A Reputation Dies*.

Lovelace, Jane. *Eccentric Lady*.

Manley, Edna A. *Agatha*.

Matthews, Laura. *Alicia. The Lady Next Door. The Nomad Harp.*

Metzger, Barbara. *My Lady Innkeeper. Lady Whilton's Wedding. Angel for the Earl.*

Orwig, Sara. *Spy for Love.*

Rabe, Sheila. *The Accidental Bride.*

Ramsey, Eileen Ainsworth. *The Mysterious Marquis.*

Randolph, Ellen. *The Rusden Legacy.*

Reeves, Barbara. *Georgina's Campaign. The Dangerous Marquis.*

Rigg, Jennifer. *The Slipper Down Chant.*

Simonson, Sheila. *Bar Sinister. A Cousinly Connexion. Lady Elizabeth's Comet.*

Smith, Joan. *Imprudent Lady. Lover's Vows. No Place for a Lady. Old Lover's Ghost. The Savage Lord Griffin.*

Veryan, Patricia. *Feathered Castle. Married Past Redemption. The Noblest Frailty. Sanguinet's Crown. Some Brief Folly.*

Vivian, Daisy. *Fair Game. The Forrester Inheritance. Rose White, Rose Red. A Lady of Quality. A Marriage of Convenience. Return to Cheyne Spa.*

Walsh, Sheila. *A Highly Respectable Marriage.*

Westhaven, Margaret. *The Willful Wife.*

Wolf, Joan. *Fool's Masquerade. Margarita. The Rebellious Ward.*

Zumwalt, Eva. *Love's Sweet Charity.*

Inspirational Historical Romance

The inspirational historical romance is being issued by several denominational publishers, including Bethany House, Harvest House, Nelson, Tyndale, and Zondervan. Though in the past these books have not received wide distribution, some of the trade paperback series are now frequently found on chain bookstore shelves, supermarket racks, and in prebound editions. The settings differ from series to series; the North American frontier is popular, but other settings abound, including Eastern Europe during World War II, and Ireland during the "troubles."

Popular series include:

Bacher, June Masters. *Love Follows the Heart. Love's Enduring Hope.*

Oke, Janette. Canadian West series, Seasons of the Heart series, and Love Comes Softly series.

Phillips, Michael R. Stonewyke trilogy.

Phillips, Michael R., and Judith Pella. The Highland Collection.

Thoene, Bodie, and Brock Thoene.

Prehistoric Epic

The prehistoric epic has become very popular since the publication of Jean Auel's *Clan of the Cave Bear* in 1980, the first in her Earth's Children series. It is in many ways a period romance, as the settings, drawn from archaeological and anthropological research, provide a distant and romantic arena for the action. Often, even though the settings, costumes, and tools are scientifically correct, the heroine exhibits traits and follows social mores belonging more in the late twentieth century than in prehistoric times.

Allan, Margaret. *The Mammoth Stone.*

Auel, Jean. *Clan of the Cave Bear. The Mammoth Hunters. The Valley of Horses. The Plains of Passage.*
An Ayla, a contemporary-style woman born in the Upper Paleolithic era, domesticates horses and discovers romance.

Gear, W. Michael, and Kathleen O'Neal Gear. *People of the Wolf. People of the Fire.*

Harrison, Sue. *Mother Earth, Father Sky. My Sister the Moon.*
In *Mother Earth, Father Sky*, a young Native American woman comes of age at the end of the last Ice Age.

Kurten, Bjorn. *Singletusk.*
A male protagonist goes on a quest to bring back a healer.

Mackey, Mary. *The Year the Horses Came.*
Matriarchal European society in 4372 B.C.

Sarabande, William. The First Americans series.
Series about prehistoric humans crossing a land bridge to the Americas.

Shuler, Linda Lay. *She Who Remembers.*
An Anasazi woman becomes special after traveling with the god Kokopelli.

Thomas, Elizabeth Marshall. *Reindeer Moon. The Animal Wife.*
Realistic tales of young Siberian woman in a hunting-gathering society about 20,000 years ago.

Wolf, Joan. *Daughter of the Red Deer.*

Saga

The family saga romance has ties to both the historical and period romances, although there are popular examples with contemporary settings. Most of these romances span several volumes. The saga, or generational history, covers the interrelations of succeeding generations within a family, usually with emphasis on a patriarchal or matriarchal figure. Those series in which the family relationships provide the basic plot elements are firmly in the romance tradition. Those with an embracing historical sweep (notably the series devised by Engel, such as The Kent Family Chronicles and Wagons West) have men as the pivotal characters. Women are not ignored in these historical series (for Engel is cannily aware that 70 percent of the fiction readers are women), but they provide romantic background rather than the dominant romantic story line.

Because the genre proved so popular in the 1970s, the saga label appears in publishers' advertising and on paperback covers for single-volume novels that barely fit the definition. Some novels, such as the Poldark series, achieve the saga label through sheer number of volumes and an extensive cast of characters. Others among historical and period romances have a sequel, or sequels, without real similarity to the saga pattern.

Several patterns are dominant in current sagas. In the United States, the pattern might be: an immigrant family rising to wealth and power over several generations; plantation life in the Deep South with an emphasis on master-slave relations; history from colonial times and the movement westward. In Britain, the pattern might be: landed family history and relations between aristocrats and their servants; a family of any class or period or periods, changing through the generations.

Several of the series current in the United States are designed and "produced" by Book Creations, Inc., the brainchild of the late Lyle Kenyon Engel. Engel's successor originates the series idea, makes contracts with the authors, does the editorial work, and arranges for publication with major paperback publishers.

The following prototype books show that one or two dominant characters may ensure an enduring readership for a saga.

De La Roche, Mazo. Jalna series (16 novels).
    First novel of series published in 1927.

Galsworthy, John. *The Forsyte Saga* (3 vols.), followed by *A Modern Comedy* (3 vols.) and *End of the Chapter* (3 vols.).
    First volume of *The Forsyte Saga* published in 1922.

Walpole, Hugh. The Herries Chronicle (4 vols.)
    First volume published in 1930.

Many generational series or sagas are now appearing. The matriarchy-dominated saga seems of increasing importance, as does the saga centered on a business empire, sometimes run by a woman. Only time will tell which of the following several types of generational sagas will survive for continued readership. The historical adventure series tends to intermingle with the saga. In some of the following instances, the number of volumes is noted (though the series may be ongoing).

Anand, Valerie. *The Proud Villeins. The Ruthless Yeomen.*
    Thirteenth century.

Argo, Ellen. *The Crystal Star. The Yankee Girl.*
    Projected to be a trilogy.

Birmingham, Stephen. *The Auerbach Will. The LeBaron Secret.*

Bissell, Elaine. *Women Who Wait. As Time Goes By. Family Fortunes.*

Bosse, Malcolm. *The Warlord. Fire in Heaven.*
Chinese background.

Bradford, Barbara Taylor. *Woman of Substance. Hold the Dream. To Be the Best. Act of Will. The Women in His Life.*

Briskin, Jacqueline. *Paloverde. The Naked Heart.*

Carr, Philippa. *Knave of Hearts. Voices in a Haunted Room. The Return of the Gypsy.*

Cleary, Jon. *The Beauford Sisters.*
Australian background.

Coffman, Virginia. *The Gaynor Women. Dinah Faire. Veronique. Marsanne.*

Coleman, Lonnie. Beulah Land series (3 vols.).
Plantation South (United States).

Cookson, Catherine. *Tilly. Tilly Wed. Tilly Alone.* (British titles: *Tilly Trotter. Tilly Trotter Wed. Tilly Trotter Widowed*). *The Rag Nymph.*

Corris, Peter. *The Gulliver Fortune* (Australian family).

Cradock, Fanny. Lorme family (Britain, 5 vols.).

Dailey, Janet. Calder saga: *This Calder Sky. This Calder Range. Stands a Calder Man. Calder Born, Calder Bred.*

Danielson, Peter. Children of the Lion series.

Delderfield, R. F. Swann family (Britain, 3 vols.). Craddock family (Britain, 2 vols.).

Dennis, Adair, and Janet Rosenstock. The Story of Canada series.

Doig, Ivan. *Dancing at the Rascal Fair. English Creek. Ride with Me, Mariah Montana.*

Elegant, Robert. *Dynasty. Mandarin.*

Ellis, Julie. *The Hampton Heritage. The Hampton Women* (The South). *Commitment. Lasting Treasures.*

Fast, Howard. Lavette family (United States, 5 vols.).

Gaan, Margaret. *Red Barbarian. White Poppy. Blue Mountain.*
Chinese background.

Gaskin, Catherine. *The Ambassador's Women.*

Gavin, Catherine. *The Sunset Dream.*

Gellis, Roberta. Roselynde Chronicles. Heiress series. Royal Dynasty series.
Engel creation. Respectively, Medieval England, the French Revolution, and history of England.

Gilchrist, Rupert. Dragonard series (Caribbean plantation, 5 vols.).

Giles, Janice Holt. Cooper and Fowler families (U.S. West, 4 vols.).

Goldreich, Gloria. *Leah's Journey. Leah's Children.*

Graham, Winston. Poldark series (Cornwall, 10 vols.).

Haines, Pamela. *The Diamond Waterfall.*

Harris, Marilyn. Eden family (7 vols.).
Takes the Eden family from eighteenth century England to twentieth century America.

Harrison, Sara. Tennent family: *The Flowers of the Field. A Flower That's Free.*

Highland, Monica. *Lotus Land.*

Hill, Deborah. Merrick family (New England, 2 vols.).

Hill, Pamela. *The House of Cary.*

Howard, Elizabeth Jane. Cazalet Chronicle series.

Howatch, Susan. *The Rich Are Different. Sins of the Fathers. The Wheel of Fortune.* The Church of England Series: *Glittering Images. Glamorous Powers. Ultimate Prizes. Scandalous Risks. Mystical Paths.*

Jakes, John. *North and South. Love and War. Heaven and Hell.* Kent Family Chronicles: *The Bastard, The Rebels, The Seekers, The Furies, The Titans, The Warriors, The Lawless,* and *The Americans.*
Engel creation. United States.

Johansen, Iris. Wind Dancer trilogy.

Johnson, Walter Reed. Oakhurst saga (United States, 4 vols.).
Engel creation; sweet-and-savage.

Jourlet, Marie de. Windhaven series (Bouchard family, U.S. South and West, 14 vols.).
Sweet-and-savage.

Laker, Rosalind. Easthampton trilogy (England).

L'Amour, Louis. Sackett clan (England and U.S. West, 14 vols.).

Lavender, William. Hargrave Journal trilogy (United States).

Long, William Stewart. The Australians series.
Engel creation. 13 volumes.

Longstreet, Stephen. *All or Nothing. Our Father's House.*

Lord, Shirley. *Golden Hill.*

Lustbader, Eric Van. Asian series: *The Ninja. Black Heart. The Miko. Jian.*

Macdonald, Malcolm. Stevenson family: *The World from Rough Stones. The Rich Are with You Always. Abigail.*

Mackey, Mary. *McCarthy's List. A Grand Passion.*

Masters, John. Rowlands family.

McCullough, Colleen. *The Thorn Birds* (Australia).

Melville, Ann. *The Lorimer Line. Alexa.*

Park, Ruth. *The Harp in the South. Missus. Poor Man's Orange.*

Phillips, Michael, and Judith Pella. The Russians series.

Porter, Donald Clayton. Colonization of America series.
Engel creation.

Price, Eugenia. *Savannah. To See Your Face Again. Stranger in Savannah.*

Rayner, Claire. Performers series (England, 10 vols.).

Rofheart, Martha. *The Savage Brood.*

Ross, Dana Fuller. Wagons West series.
Engel creation.

Scott, Michael William. Rakehell Dynasty (United States, 3 vols.).

Engel creation.

Skelton, C. L. The Regiment quartet.

Smith, George. The American Freedom series (Glencannon family, 2 vols.).

Smith, Wilbur. Ballantyne family (Africa).

Spellman, Cathy Cash. *So Many Partings. An Excess of Love.*

Stine, Whitney. The Oklahomans series.

Stirling, Jessica. Beckman trilogy.

Stubbs, Jean. Brief Chronicles Saga/Howarths of Garth: *Kit's Hill. The Ironmaster. The Vivian Inheritance. The Northern Correspondent.* Victorian.

Thane, Elswyth. Williamsburg series. (United States, 7 vols.).

Wall, Robert E. The Canadians series.

Winston, Daoma. *The Fall River Line.*

Zollinger, Norman. *Chapultapec* (Mexico, nineteenth century).

Sweet-and-Savage Romance

"Hot Historicals," as the publishers gloatingly label them within the trade, also known as sweet-and-savage romances, have evoked a host of epithets: "erotic histories" (more erotic than history), "rape sagas," "bodice rippers," "hysterical Romance," "tit-and-bum epics," "sand-and-tit epics." They are too "hot" for the genteel reader of historical romances, who, fortunately, can recognize them—and avoid them—by their length (400 to 600 pages) and by their titles: infinite combinations of the words *love, desire, passion, captive, madness, fire, savage, fury, torment*, and so on.

Rosemary Rogers launched this subgenre in 1974 with a novel that provided its label—*Sweet, Savage Love*. A reviewer succinctly epitomized the subgenre's plot in *Sweet, Savage Love* in one sentence: "The heroine is seduced, raped, prostituted, married, mistressed." Another reviewer just as tersely summed up the subgenre's characteristics: "The prose is purple, the plot thin, and the characters thinner" (regarding *The Wolf and the Dove* by Kathleen E. Woodiwiss). Exotic historical settings are used lavishly, particularly those allowing for pirates, sultans, and harems. A variation of the sweet-and-savage romance is the plantation romance, with basic ingredients of miscegenation, incest, Cain versus Abel, slave uprisings, insanity, and murder. Usually they are set in the post–Civil War South but may be set in the West Indies or in any locale in which the basic plot ingredients can seethe. Both types are loaded with sex scenes, explicit to the extent of justifying the label "soft porn." Women readers may not want their sexual fantasies to be realistic, but they do want them to be explicit. (For the male reader, there are the sexual fantasies provided by Ian Fleming's James Bond and Mickey Spillane's Mike Hammer.)

These sultry romances had their heydey in the 1970s, mainly as paperback originals. They have become part of the standard historical romance pattern, usually in a more subdued form. There has also been a trend in paperback series toward much more sensuous and erotically explicit plots. Sweet-and-savage characteristics have been subsumed within the saga or historical romance rather than becoming dominating aspects.

Over 30 authors specialized in this type, among them Jennifer Blake, Shirley Busbee ("My idea of the most perfect book I could write would be a sexy, lurid Georgette Heyer story"), Anthony Esler, Gimone Hall, Susanna Leigh, Fern Michaels, Marilyn Ross, Jennifer Wilde, and Donna Comeaux Zide. Some of the authors of this type of romance who appear in *Twentieth Century Romance and Gothic Writers* are in the following list as examples. Their works range from the blatantly sexual to the overtly suggestive.

Blake, Stephanie. *Wicked Is My Flesh. Scarlet Kisses. Unholy Desires.*

Dailey, Janet
> "America's best-selling romance novelist." A contemporary rather than historical background. (Author of about 50 Harlequins without the "slightly risqué love scenes" of the sweet-and-savage romances.) Her 1991 best-seller was *Aspen Gold*. "Until Dailey adds a final unexpected twist, the plot adheres closely to the captive-in-love-with-captor formula."—*Touch the Wind*.

Kells, Susannah. *The Fallen Angels.*

Matthews, Patricia

"Sarah is sexually abused at every turn—not that she minds. Still, as a lady should be, she's ever faithful in spirit to her true love, the first man who raped her."—*Love's Wildest Promise.*

She had consecutive best-sellers on the *New York Times* list:

> *Love's Avenging Heart; Love's Dying Dream; Love, Forever More; Love's Golden Destiny; Love's Magic Moment; Love's Many Faces; Love's Pagan Heart; Love's Raging Tide; Love's Sweet Agony; Love's Wildest Promise.*

McBain, Laurie

"The beautiful orphan Elysia Demarice ran away from her evil aunt and stopped at an inn for the night. She awoke in the morning to find herself in the bed of Alex Trevigne, the handsome Marquis they called 'The Devil.' She didn't know how she had gotten there and he was not about to let her go." "He seemed propelled by demons as he loved into the night and morning—becoming more of her body and soul than she herself." "A totally plotless 428-page novel."—*Devil's Desire.*

Peters, Natasha. *Savage Surrender.*

Radcliffe, Janette

(This is one of the pseudonyms used by Janet Louise Roberts, whose heroines, in the novels under her name, were usually raped by the hero.) "Predictably, he proceeds to rape Barbara, whom he takes as his concubine until his ship is captured by pirates."—*Stormy Surrender.*

Rogers, Rosemary

"Most women do have a rape fantasy. But there is a difference between actual rape, which is horrifying, and fantasy. In the rape fantasy, you pick the man and the circumstances. It's not at all scary." Interview with Rosemary Rogers.

"Overpowered by her lover-turned-husband and repeatedly raped by bandits and sex-starved soldiers, she bounces back each time as fresh and beautiful and feisty as ever."—*Dark Fires.* "She writhed, gasping, as his fingers touched her intimately, exploringly, and for a moment, as his body poised over her, she thought he would let her go. Her lips parted . . . there was a stabbing shaft of agony between her thighs that seemed to tear all the way into her belly, causing her body to arch up against his with shocked surprise." "Flickering torchlights and wine forced between her lips. . . . With a feeling of shock she found her thighs nudged apart. . . . There was a stabbing shaft of agony. Her last thought as she slipped into unconsciousness was, 'And I don't even know his name. I'm tired of being raped. Don't I count as a person?' "—*Wicked Loving Lies,* with the last plaintive query being on page 654.

Small, Beatrice. *This Heart of Mine.*
The 600-page sequel to *Skye O'Malley.*

Winsor, Kathleen. *Robert and Arabella.*
"Fantasy of epic lust."

Woodiwiss, Kathleen E.
"I'm insulted when my books are called erotic. I believe I write love stories with a little spice."—Woodiwiss. "Aislinn, a Saxon maid, is raped by Ragnor, one of the Norman conquerors, who also kills her father and degrades her mother."—*The Wolf and the Dove.* "She makes a desperate deal with a condemned man who is to be executed the next day. If he marries her, she will spend the night with him." "Each touch was fire, each word was bliss, each movement in their union a rhapsody of passion that rose and built until it seemed that every instrument in all the world combined to bring the music of their souls into a consuming crescendo that left them still and quiet, warm like the softly glowing aftercoals of a universal holocaust."—*Shanna.*

Plantation Romance
The plantation romance, a subspecies of sweet-and-savage, has as its basic ingredients interracial sex, incest, Cain versus Abel, slave uprisings, insanity, and murder. *Mandingo* by Kyle Onstott (1957) set the pattern and is continually used as a comparative reference. Almost all were paperback originals, usually in series. Lance Horner continues the *Mandingo* story in the Falconhurst series (seven novels) about the Maxwell family, and has also written several similar, separate books, (e.g., *Golden Stud*). Marie de Jourlet's Windhaven series is now in its 14th volume. In hardcover is the 32nd novel by Frank Yerby, *McKenzie's Hundred*, a plantation type, as were several of his earlier books.

Spicy
The spicy romance has grown out of the sweet-and-savage type. It features erotic scenes but without the kidnappings and rapes so often found in its predecessor. Generally, the characters are monogamous or serially monogamous. Marriage plays an important role.

Jude Deveraux's many novels involving different, far-flung members of the Montgomery family throughout history have evolved from sweet-and-savage to spicy romance. Even though her early works in the Velvet series and James River trilogy featured rapes and kidnappings, the characters were not promiscuous. The women are proactive rather than reactive, as in the sweet-and-savage type.

Other popular authors writing in this vein include:

Quick, Amanda. *Dangerous. Deception. Desire. Mistress. Mystique. Ravished. Reckless. Rendezvous. Scandal. Seduction. White.*
These all have a Regency setting that is merely a vague backdrop.

Spencer, LaVyrle. *Bittersweet. Morning Glory.*

Taylor, Janelle. *Follow the Wind.*

Time Travel Fantasy-Romance

The books that fall into this category use time travel as a backdrop for the romance. The obstacle facing the lovers is not merely one of having different backgrounds or one of living in different time zones but the difficulty of living in different centuries. This is a very popular type in paperback but is also published in hardcover. Unlike most romances, male authors frequently appear.

Alexander, Karl. *Time After Time.*
H. G. Wells in late-twentieth-century San Francisco.

Bonds, Parris Afton. *For All Time.*
Stacie finds herself suddenly in 1872 and falls for her own grandfather.

Bretton, Barbara. *Tomorrow and Always.*

Danvers, Dennis. *Time and Time Again.*
Reincarnation separates and reunites lovers through the centuries.

Deveraux, Jude. *Knight in Shining Armour.*
Tears at a crypt bring a medieval knight into the present.

Gabaldon, Diana. *Outlander. Dragonfly in Amber. Voyager.*
Following World War II, a former army nurse vacationing in Scotland is cast back into the eighteenth century.

Hannah, Kristin. *When Lightning Strikes.*

Mallory, Tess. *Jewels of Time.*

Matheson, Richard. *Somewhere in Time* (originally titled *Bid Time Return*).
Using self-hypnosis, a playwright goes back in time to find a woman he fell in love with from an old portrait.

Moon, Modean. *Evermore.*
Civil War–era lovers are reunited through incarnation.

TOPICS

Bibliographies and Biographies

Biographical sketches of the authors currently writing romantic novels for both hardcover and paperback publishers appear in the journals listed in "Review Journals" (see pp. 202-203). Recognizing the great popularity of the romance, many women's magazines have, in recent years, featured articles on best-selling authors of romantic novels. The following six biographical works are a beginning in this area, but much more is needed.

Falk, Kathryn, Melinda Helfer, and Kathe Robin, comps. *Romance Reader's Handbook*. Romantic Times, 1989.

This work devotes half of its pages to an alphabetical list of more than 2,000 pseudonyms of romance writers. Easily understood distinctions between pseudonym, legal name not used for authorship purposes, and legal name used for authorship purposes are provided. There is no indication of criteria for inclusion; entries appear to be personal selections of the compilers. Broader coverage can be found in Eileen Fallon's *Words of Love* (see next entry) and Mary Jane Kay's *The Romantic Spirit* (see below). Criteria for inclusion in the reading lists found in the "Recommended Reads" section is also not clearly stated; again selections appear to be favorites of the compilers or have favorable reviews in *Romantic Times*. The lists are intended to serve as guides for the avid reader of "Bookstores That Care," addresses of authors, and "Source Section," which includes advice on getting published, lists of agents and publishers, and advertisements for book search services.

Fallon, Eileen. *Words of Love: A Complete Guide to Romance Fiction*. Garland, 1984.

Two bibliographies form the bulk of this work: "Historically Important Writers," covering 66 authors, and "Current Romance Authors," covering 162 authors. Information for the second part was obtained by questionnaire and includes some comment of critical interest in addition to bibliographical information. This cannot be considered a definitive listing of genre authors for either period. Prefatory chapters include a brief history of romance from classical times through the eighteenth century, and a chapter on the Regency novel.

Kay, Mary Jane. *The Romantic Spirit: A Romance Bibliography of Authors and Titles*. MJK Enterprises, 1983.

Alphabetical list of authors, with titles and note of those in numbered paperback series, but does not give publisher or date. Category is noted when pertinent. Pseudonyms are listed. The appendix lists 23 paperback series (some no longer published), including the numbered ones in sequence. Two supplementary volumes have been issued covering 1982–1984 and 1985–1986.

Radcliffe, Elsa J. *Gothic Novels of the Twentieth Century: An Annotated Bibliography*. Scarecrow Press, 1979.

This bibliography is omnivorous and eccentrically uncritical in scope, defining the Gothic very broadly to include many novels of detection, mystery, romantic suspense, historical romance, and some simple sentimental romances. The compiler also lists works noted "not Gothic" simply because the author is being listed for other works. About half of the 1973 listings are annotated in a very personal and idiosyncratic manner—some are helpful and amusing, particularly when critical, others are of questionable judgment. However, one instance will indicate the caution necessary in using the bibliography. Under Mary Stewart, noting that her works are often published as Gothics but that the compiler does not consider them Gothic, she lists 13 titles, six with annotation, but does *not* annotate the one title that is pure Gothic, *Nine Coaches Waiting*.

Ramsdell, Kristin. *Happily Ever After: A Guide to Reading Interests in Romance Fiction*. Libraries Unlimited, 1987.
This bibliography groups romances under the areas of contemporary, historical, saga, gay, inspirational, young adult, and historical romance. Each section defines the subgenre, discusses its appeal, and gives hints on advising the reader. It has a name/title index and a subject index.

Twentieth-Century Romance and Historical Writers. 3d ed. Edited by Aruna Vasudevan. St. James Press, 1994.
The total number of authors (more than 300) is greatly increased (to more than 400) when the many pseudonyms are added, such as Victoria Holt with listing of books published under six pseudonyms. There are brief biographical data, a list of all published works, a statement by the author (if supplied), and a critical summation, this last of unequal quality. (An added cross-reference for this work, inexplicably missed: Elizabeth Peters, see Barbara Michaels.)

History and Criticism

Romance as a genre has been woefully neglected by historians, bibliographers, and critics. (Literary historians have treated the eighteenth- and nineteenth-century Gothic novel, however, with only tangential significance for the modern genre romance.) What is available is largely found in periodicals; newspapers and popular and trade magazines have had a joyous time celebrating the blooming of romance in recent years with articles on best-selling authors, publishers, series, and the phenomenon of romance as a genre. Little of this publicity is critically definitive, nor have these ephemera been gathered into a bibliography. The genre has not (as have westerns, detective fiction, science fiction, and fantasy) been systematized into a recognized course of study at the college level, and so has not amassed the resultant paraphernalia of bibliographies, guides, histories, scholarly journals, and the like. There is an indication of increasing interest by academics in this area as more articles on genre romance appear in the *Journal of Popular Culture* and in a few papers presented at the joint annual conventions of the Popular Culture Association and the American Culture Association. (The 1981 convention program evidenced a strong feminist tone in several presentations on other genres—western, detective, science fiction, horror, fantasy—and a few talks on aspects of the romance: "Reading the Romance: Popular Literature and the Fantasies of Compensation"; "The Love of Rape: Women as Victim in the Bodice-Ripper"; "True Confessions: Sin, Suffering and Reformation"; "The Feminine Mistake: The Covert Functions of Popular Romance.") The following two books are examples of historical criticism. Much work remains to be done in this genre.

Anderson, Rachel. *The Purple Heart Throbs: The Sub-Literature of Love.* London: Hodder, 1974.
This unique and hard-to-obtain book is discussed at the beginning of this chapter. The authors described are largely British, but many were also read in the United States.

Mussell, Kay. *Women's Gothic and Romantic Fiction: A Reference Guide.* Greenwood Press, 1981.
This is the first attempt to systematize the material—bibliography, history, criticism—on the romance genre. The emphasis is on the romance in American culture, although, necessarily, there is much reference to British prototypes. Coverage is from colonial times, with much material on nineteenth-century romance writers. The chapters are critical, with bibliographical essays that generally have bibliographies and notes appended. The chapter titles give the scope: "History of Women's Gothic and Romantic Fiction"; "Bibliographies, Reference Works, and Sources for the Study of Major Authors of Gothic and Romantic Fiction"; "Related Genres: Mystery Stories, Governess Stories, Melodrama, and Film Adaptations"; "Literary and Social History Approaches to Gothic and Romantic Fiction"; "Sociological and Psychological Approaches to Gothic and Romantic Fiction: Studies of Reading and Audience"; "Popular Commentary on Gothic and Romantic Fiction: Journalism, Reviews, and How-to Advice." There are two appendices: "Collection and Research Facilities"; "Selected Chronology." (The book does not include any reference to Radcliffe's *Gothic Novels of the Twentieth Century*.)

The best survey of the romance in the United States is in Russel Nye's *The Unembarrassed Muse: Popular Arts in America* (Dial, 1970) in the chapters "Stories for the People" and "Novels in the Marketplace," both of which cover writings from colonial times.

The following critical works, with the exception of Guiley, concern themselves with women as readers of romance and as they are portrayed in romance. Romance novels considered to be sociological and psychological statements on the nature and status of women, and about why women read romances, are critical approaches that often overshadow the fact that a multitude of women read them for pleasure.

Frenier, Miriam Darce. *Good-Bye Heathcliff: Changing Heroes, Heroines, Roles, and Values in Women's Category Romances.* Greenwood Press, 1988.
Analysis of the appeal of category romances in relation to women's roles and feminist goals in the 1970s and early 1980s. The subtitle really is descriptive of the contents!

Guiley, Rosemary. *LoveLines: A Romance Reader's Guide to Printed Pleasures.* Designed by J. C. Saures. Facts on File, 1983.
This lavishly illustrated potpourri on the genre romance novel celebrates the modern paperback series in all aspects: history, publishing,

cover art, authors, categories of the genre, and how to write them. There are many lists of types, including the 23 titles that "belong in every romance library."

Jensen, Margaret Ann. *Love's $weet Return: The Harlequin Story*. Popular Press, 1984.
Not only the Harlequin story but the Harlequin stories are the burden of this gracefully written text. Why have they been such good sellers? Their quality is well known to romance readers who approve of the authors and characteristics of plots and characters. Why the novels appeal is analyzed here, down to the addition of sex when the time is right.

Krentz, Jayne Ann, ed. *Dangerous Men & Adventurous Women: Romance Writers on the Appeal of the Romance*. University of Pennsylvania Press, 1992.
Nineteen authors, beloved of romance readers, contributed essays on the appeal of their genre, the aspects of fantasy and character in the books they write, and descriptions of their readers. Many of the essays rebut feminist criticism of the genre.

Mussell, Kay. *Fantasy and Reconciliation: Contemporary Formulas of Women's Romance Fiction*. Greenwood Press, 1984.
She breaks romance formulas down into six types, series, erotic, gothic, romantic suspense, romantic biographies, and historical.

Radway, Janice. *Reading the Romance: Women, Patriarchy, and Popular Literature*. University of North Carolina Press, 1984.
The current definitive statement on why women read genre romances and what this readership implies for social attitudes of women and toward women. Using discussion with readers, the author analyzes the types of romance read and, in one chapter, describes the ideal romance.

Thurston, Carol. *The Romance Revolution: Erotic Novels for Women and the Quest for a New Sexual Identity*. University of Illinois Press, 1987.

CRITICISM—PARODY

Atwood, Margaret. *Lady Oracle*.
The heroine of this mainstream novel writes costume romances, and long passages from the romances enliven the text.

Cartwheel, Rosemary. *Love's Reckless Rash*. St. Martin's, 1984. (A Charlatan Romance).
A wicked parody of the sweet-and-savage romance. "She knew instinctively that she was either close to falling in love or she was developing a tendency toward pyromania."

Green, Jonathan. *Sweet Nothings: Love Quotes for Lovers & Other Fools*. Quill, 1984.

The 3,000-odd quotations range from classical times to the present and are arranged in 25 categories. The attitudes are, lamentably for the romantic at heart, decidedly sardonic: "Hell's afloat in lover's tears" (Dorothy Parker). The last section, "In Dreams," quotes at more extended length than in the previous sections from the romance, including some of the prototype authors and a passage from the Silhouette romances style sheet.

Oates, Joyce Carol. *A Bloodsmoor Romance.*
A mainstream novel and a parody throughout of the period romance.

Simmonds, Posy. *True Love.* London: Cape, 1981.
The author does a cartoon strip, for sophisticated adults, in the *Guardian*. This is a devastating series on a secretary's fantasy love dreams that are in sad conflict with reality.

Weldon, Fay. *The Hearts and Lives of Men.* A parody of soap-opera romance.

Writer's Manuals

The market for paperback romances took off in the 1970s, and there was a need for authors to produce the seemingly unlimited number of titles issued monthly in the several serials. In certain years, it has been estimated, upwards of 200 new authors appeared. Now available for these authors are several manuals providing instruction in the very formalized patterns demanded by the different types of romances. Readers of romance should find the manuals illuminating and amusing.

The organization of each of the following manuals differs, but basically each provides information on the types of romance, plots, characters (particularly hero and heroine), publishers and their requirements, and tips on how to write effectively (dialogue, descriptions, etc.).

Biederman, Jerry, and Tom Silberkleit. *Your First Romance.* . . . With an introduction by Kathryn Falk. St. Martin's, 1984.
The initial and final paragraphs for 20 romances are provided by 20 established writers (Jennifer Blake, Patricia Matthews, Jude Deveraux, et al.) and the neophyte is invited to fill in the story. All types of romances are suggested. There is a biographical and critical introduction for each author. Sample tip sheets are provided for Candlelight Ecstasy Romance, Worldwide Library Superromance, and Signet Scarlet Ribbons Historical Romance.

Burack, Sylvia K., ed. *Writing and Selling the Romance Novel.* The Writer, 1983.
An anthology of essays by successful romance authors. Several discuss types of romances: category (Barbara Delinsky); Regency (Donna Meyer, Joan Aiken); romantic-suspense (Barbara Mertz, Phyllis A. Whitney); historical (Rosalind Laker). Tip sheet information is provided for 25 series.

Falk, Kathryn. *How to Write a Romance and Get It Published: With Intimate Advice from the World's Most Popular Romantic Writers.* Illustrations by Ignatius Sahula. Crown, 1983.

The publisher of *Romantic Times* has organized, with extended commentary, essays by 53 authors of romance and 11 editors of paperback romance series (including Lyle Engel, Book Creations) to explain in detail everything a neophyte author might want to know, and many things that might not be anticipated.

Kent, Jean, and Candace Shelton. *The Romance Writers' Phrase Book.* Perigee Books, 1984.

Although this is designed as a serious handbook for romance authors, the reader of romance (and others) might find it a source of hilarity. The phrases are grouped and subheaded: "Physical Characteristics—Female, Male, Body Movement"; "Facial Expressions"; "Humor"; "Eyes"; "Voices"; "Emotions"; "Sex" (subdivided into "Desire, Attraction: Touching"; "Embracing: Kisses"; "Lovemaking"); "Miscellaneous"; "Colors." Example of "Emotions": "She was shocked when his eyes suddenly filled with fierce sparkling." One could write a book!

Paludan, Eve. *Romance Writer's Pink Pages: The Insider's Guide to Getting Your Romance Novel Published.* Prima, 1993.

Authorship and marketing of love stories from an insider's perspective. Includes an index.

Wibberley, Mary. *To Writers with Love: On Writing Romantic Novels.* London: Buchan & Enright, 1985.

The author is a prolific Mills & Boon romance writer. This is a personal and delightful description of how to write, drawn from her own experience. It is full of common sense, surprises, and exceptionally good advice. For example: "(Note: readers do not like huge chunks of descriptive matter. They skip them. Then they have to go back, because they've missed some small but vital piece of information in the bits they've skipped, and they get annoyed and probably won't buy your next book, and serve you right.)"

Review Journals

The following journals are for the devoted readership of the genre and are much more than review journals, as the annotations indicate. Their emergence parallels the genre's recent and amazing publishing activity and growth in reading audience.

Affaire de Coeur: For the Romantic at Heart. 1981– . Monthly, published by Barbara N. Keenan, Fremont, California.

Provides star-rated reviews, news, and brief articles. Sponsors the annual Rom-Con conference.

Romantic Times. 1981– .

This publication contains reviews, annotations, excerpts from new romances, publishing and author news, biographies of romance authors, interviews, and advertisements. The romance reader who is as enthralled as the publisher with every tidbit about romance will have a feast. The publisher and editor, Kathryn Falk, is an active apologist and publicist for romance. *Romantic Times* and Long Island University's Institute for Continuing Education, with Kathryn Falk as a conference director, announced the first Romantic Book Lovers Conference in New York City for April 17, 1982. In 1986 this publication became a monthly, incorporating with *Rave Reviews*.

Authors Associations

Romance writers do not feel comfortable within the standard authors associations and so have formed their own groups. Though the association in the United States is some 20 years behind its British counterpart, it has gotten off to a very lively and enthusiastic start.

Romance Writers of America

The founding convention was held in Houston, Texas, in June 1981 and drew an unexpectedly large attendance of writers and fans. An award, the Golden Heart, was established as the association's prize. The 14th annual convention was held in Hawaii in July 1995.

Romantic Novelists Association

This British group was founded in 1960. It presents an annual award for the best romance, often having runner-up awards and a histori-cal romance award. Its members are highly articulate apologists for the genre. (Although not given by this association, there is another romance award in England, "Historical Novel Prize in Memory of Georgette Heyer," honoring her not only for her Regency romances but for her historical romances in which she took pride. Another prize was announced in 1984, the Betty Trask Prize [£12,500] for authors under 35 publishing a first novel "of romantic or traditional, rather than experimental nature.")

Conferences

In addition to the annual conference of the Romance Writers of America (10th in 1991), there have been many regional conferences. The annual West Coast Rom-Con is sponsored by *Affaire de Coeur* (14th in 1995). The most elaborate—the Romantic Times Book Lovers Conference—is sponsored by *Romantic Times* (14th in 1995 in Ft. Worth, Texas). See past issues of *Romantic Times* for the extensive programs and the post-conference photographs—it's a romantic ball!

Publishers

Along with the continuing predominant publication of romance in the paperback lines, there has been an increase in the amount of hardcover romance publication. Three publishers issue the greatest number: Doubleday, St. Martin's, and Walker. Also, almost all hardcover publishers now have their own paperback lines. There has also been an increase in the number of trade paperback genre titles.

The library market benefits from the increase in hardcover and trade paperback romances available. Whether the pattern of reprinting paperback series in library editions will continue is not definite; Gregg Press (Chivers Press, London) has reprinted Silhouette titles in hardcover, and some Harlequin titles have been reprinted in large-print format by Thorndyke Press. Brandywyne Books is issuing Heirloom editions in hardcover, but they are priced out of the library market at $35 to $50 for authors such as Jennifer Wilde, Janet Dailey, and Jude Deveraux. Severn House is issuing reasonably priced reprints in hardcover, some of authors who did not receive the recognition due them in paperback, others of early works by popular authors that were originally issued in paperback only. That romances are appearing regularly on the best-seller lists in both hardcover and paperback editions should make for a steady publishing program in the genre.

Though the feminist movement is not sympathetic to the romance genre, one notable feminist publisher should be familiar to both librarians and romance readers—Virago Press. (A virago is defined as both a manlike or heroic woman and a bold, impudent, wicked woman.) This British house, whose books are now distributed in the United States, issues elegant trade paperbacks, reprinting works by women (and a few by men on women) of the nineteenth and twentieth centuries. Although most would not be classified as genre fiction, they are all novels about women, and many are romances, some bittersweet. Following is a selection of the house's authors (a few especially recommended titles are noted), with some key nineteenth-century authors listed first.

> Braddon, Mary E.; Broughton, Rhoda; Eden, Emily (*The Semi-Attached Couple, The Semi-Detached House*); Oliphant, Mrs.; Ward, Mrs. Humphrey.

> Atwood, Margaret; Cather, Willa; Comyns, Barbara (*Our Spoons Came from Woolworths*); Delafield, E. M.; Farrell, M. J. (Molly Keane); Franklin, Miles (*My Brilliant Career*); Glasgow, Ellen; Jameson, Storm; Jesse, I. Tennyson; Kaye-Smith, Sheila; Kennedy, Margaret (*The Constant Nymph*); Lehmann, Rosamond; Leverson, Ada (*The Little Attleys*); Macaulay, Rose (*Told By an Idiot*); O'Brien, Kate; Renault, Mary; Robertson, E. Arnot (*Four Frightened People, Ordinary Families*); Sackville-West, Vita; Smith, Stevie; Stead, Christina; Taylor, Elizabeth; West, Rebecca; Wharton, Edith.

It is notable that in hardcover the following types of romance are the most prominent: historical and period romances with a great many Regencies;

Gothic and romantic suspense; and sagas, both period historical and contemporary. In England, the period and historical romances are dominant, with many sagas present. The following British publishers have strong hardcover lines: Bodley Head, Century, Collins, Gollancz, Robert Hale, Hodder, Michael Joseph, and Macdonald. Many of their titles are released in the United States, with the strongest romance programs from Doubleday (with a labeled line—Starlight Romances), St. Martin's, and Walker (heavy importation of British titles). Other publishers in the United States with regular romance publication: Arbor House, Delacorte, Dodd, Dutton, Harper, Macmillan, Morrow, Putnam, and Simon & Schuster.

PAPERBACK PUBLISHERS

While great numbers of romances still appear regularly, the number of issuing publishers has recently decreased drastically. Several publishers have series lines, noted in the following list, in addition to issuing both original titles and reprints. There has been an increase in the number of trade paperback romances, despite some price resistance, and these are in a satisfactory format for libraries. (Avon, Ballantine/Fawcett, and Jove have issued many; this may relate to the fact that several paperback publishers are now also publishing in hardcover, such as Ballantine, Bantam, and Pocket Books/Poseidon.)

The following U.S. paperback publishers issue romances regularly: Ace/Charter, Avon Ballantine/Fawcett, Bantam, Berkley, Dell, Harlequin/Worldwide, Jove, Leisure, NAL/Signet, Pocket Books, Popular Library/Warner, and Zebra. Strong lines for all these houses are in the historical romance and Regency romance. Romance in the American West appears in many of the period romances. There has been a trend noted toward "futuristic" romance (romance combined with the genres of fantasy and science fiction). The Timeswept imprint from Love Spell features time travel fantasy-romances.

For years, Harlequin led sales in category romances. Silhouette was started up as competition but now both houses are owned by the Canadian company Torstar. They have numerous imprint titles.

The "inspirational" romance is being issued by several denominational publishers (and also in the Silhouette Inspiration series). Guideposts started up a book club in 1993 called "Forever" Romances. They are reprints of paperbacks that are sold only through mailorder.

Tip sheets (guidelines) are available for most of the series romance lines. These guidelines spell out the characters (and age limits) of the hero and heroine, their economic situation, clothes, setting, and the type of love story permissible. Tip sheets require constant revision as the limits of sensuality are steadily extended. Whereas once a series might have been labeled "sweet," meaning no explicit sex, it may now be labeled "spicy," "sensual," or "steamy" (stopping just short of soft-core pornography). The tip sheets are available on request from the publishers, and both libraries and readers of romance might find them useful. Several of the writer's manuals for the romance novel reprint tip sheets.

D's Romance Picks

Chesney, Marion. *Miss Tonks Turns to Crime.* St. Martin's Press, 1993.

Deveraux, Jude. *Highland Velvet.* Pocket Books, 1982.

Doig, Ivan. *Dancing at the Rascal Fair.* Atheneum, 1987.

Gabaldon, Diana. *Outlander.* Delacorte, 1991.

Spencer, LaVyrle. *The Gamble.* Jove, 1987.

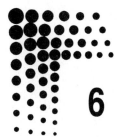

6 Science Fiction

The last man on Earth sat in a room. There was a knock on the door.

—Anonymous

"I love you sons of bitches. You're the only ones with guts enough to *really* care about the future, who *really* notice what machines do to us, what wars do to us, what cities do to us, what tremendous misunderstandings, mistakes, accidents and catastrophes do to us. You're the only ones zany enough to agonize over time and distances without limit, over mysteries that will never die, over the fact that we are right now determining whether the space voyage for the next billion years or so is going to be Heaven or Hell."

—Kurt Vonnegut, Jr.
God Bless You, Mr. Rosewater (1965)

At the core of hard sf [science fiction] lies the experience of science.

—Gregory Benford
The Ascent of Wonder (1994)

Sf [science fiction] allows us to understand and experience our past, present, and future in terms of an imagined future.

—Kathryn Cramer
The Ascent of Wonder (1994)

THEMES AND TYPES

The reader trying to comprehend and understand science fiction is faced with the obstacle of the lack of an encompassing definition for all aspects and types of science fiction. Science fiction, fantasy, and horror are all very closely linked. It is not at all uncommon for writers to cross the lines between these genres from book to book, and, indeed, sometimes even within the same book.

Science fiction could be described as the literature of "what if?" What if there were life on other planets? What if someone were to travel faster than light? What if there were people that lived inside a world rather than on its surface? What if all the men on a planet were to die off? What if one could go into a world created by a computer program? What if . . . ? the possibilities of science fiction are as endless as the imagination. The areas covered in science fiction are as diverse as are the readers of the genre. Some stories are set in a near future with scenarios that are probable. Others are set so far in the future, or in the past, that they seem nigh on impossible, let alone improbable. A science fiction reader has both a willing suspension of disbelief and a questioning mind.

Many science fiction readers like to communicate with other readers. Fans are responsible for a multitude of fanzines as well as frequent conventions. (For a look at science fiction fandom from a mystery point of view, try Sharyn McCrumb's *Bimbos of the Death Sun* [TSR, 1988] and *Zombies of the Gene Pool* [Simon & Schuster, 1992].) Science fiction readers, editors, and writers "talk" over the Internet on several different newsgroups. To keep up with what fans are reading, one can subscribe to rec.arts.sf.written and read reviews and criticism firsthand.

How to differentiate between fantasy and science fiction is a frequently debated question. Because the readers, writers, and publishers of science fiction (SF is the accepted nickname in the genre) and fantasy all tend to have strong opinions about where a particular work fits into the genre categories, there is never going to be any one good way of making the distinction. Even querying the authors themselves sometimes brings surprising opinions. One might think that dragons, being mythical creatures, fall into the fantasy realm. Anne McCaffrey, best-selling author of the Pern series, emphatically claims that her dragons, and the unique characteristics of the planet Pern, have a scientific basis, and so her works dealing with the dragons of Pern are science fiction rather than fantasy. Many of her fans disagree. Orson Scott Card, Nebula and Hugo award-winning author, claims that his knowledge of science is not extensive, that his stories come from his imagination so they are fantasy. Also, Card has stated that one can tell the genre by the cover illustration: rivets denote science fiction, while foliage denotes fantasy. Some consider science fiction to be a subgenre of fantasy and others consider fantasy to be a subgenre of science fiction.

For this guide, I used my personal opinion as the criterion when deciding where each book fit. As no two people ever seem to have agreed on exactly where the demarcation is, this seemed to be the most expedient way. Science fiction readers should check chapter 7, "Fantasy" (as Fantasy readers should check this chapter). IMHO (Internetese for "in my humble opinion"), science fiction novels are those that deal with scientific topics, space travel, aliens, and recognizably Earth-variant worlds or life-forms that have not been touched by magic. Time travel, not occasioned by magic, is here, as are stories of distant civilizations (whether present-day or set many years in the future or in the past) that show some relationship to Earth or Earth life-forms.

However, the late Betty Rosenberg wrote:

Science fiction *is* speculative—speculative about the potential uses of science and speculative about the potential future of mankind on this world and within the universe. The two themes may combine within the same novel, usually with one being subordinate. Although authors in the field tend to specialize in an aspect or aspects of science fiction, most do wander through the universe of science fiction themes. Unlike other genres, the best examples of the work and ideas of science fiction authors are often found in the short story.

That it is short on characterization and long on gimmicks and ideas is a frequent criticism of science fiction. (Space opera is said to have only adventure and neither characterization nor ideas.) Much science fiction is thesis fiction, bearing a statement about science fact, human nature, man in relation to nature or the universe, man in conflict with the universe, man speculating on his future in the universe. Greater emphasis, therefore, is often placed on situations or solutions than on the creatures (not necessarily human) who are the protagonists.

The critical works pose science fiction as the most philosophical, poetical, intellectual, and religious of the genre fictions. It is concerned with the mystery of the universe, man's place in it, and man's ultimate destiny: the continuation of humankind in its basic nature and humanity. Science fiction expresses faith in human ingenuity, human intelligence, and the human spirit. Technology is considered in terms of service to mankind and the natural world. The biological sciences are considered as they might heighten or increase the capacity and quality of the human mind. Religion is viewed as a means of salvation. The end is to augment the quality of life. Science fiction has been labeled a fiction of questions: What if . . . ? If only . . . ? If this goes on . . . ?

Mention must be made of the great variations of length in published science fiction. Short stories are vitally alive and well, as are short shorts, novelettes, novellas, novels, and multivolume tomes. More so than in any other genre, readers are willing to read science fiction of any length.

The following analysis of science fiction themes shows their diversity. Each theme defines an aspect of the genre. That a title is listed under a certain theme does not necessarily mean that this is the only theme present in the novel. Some titles are listed under several themes.

Hard Science

The term *scientific extrapolation* is often used concerning stories of hard science—not necessarily predictions of what will come with scientific experimentation and increased knowledge but imaginative projections of possibility, if not probability. (The folklore of science fiction abounds in instances of scientific discoveries first predicted in a science fiction tale.) The pride of authors in this field *is* that their scientific information is authentic; though what they do with it may not, as yet, be known to science.

Some of the hard sciences played with in science fiction are:

Mathematics (the fourth dimension, spatial or in time)

Cybernetics (the mind of the machine, artificial intelligence)

Meteorology (characters *do* something about or to affect the weather)

Archaeology (carbon-14 dating)

Exobiology ("The study of life-forms beyond the earth—has been defined as a science without a subject. Despite this, its nonexistent material has fascinated mankind for at least 2000 years" [from *Time Probe: The Sciences in Science Fiction*, edited by Arthur C. Clarke].)

Physics (gravity, relativity—traveling faster than the speed of light, atoms and neutrons, antimatter)

Medicine (extraterrestrial medicine, brain surgery, plague)

Astronomy (space flight, black holes)

Physiology (effect of change of atmosphere on human body in space travel)

Chemistry (drugs)

Biology (mutations, genetic future, immortality)

Other topics: computers, cosmology, cryonics, cyborgs, rockets, technology, and inventions.

Many examples of the use of hard science will be found in the short story as well as in the novel. The following list is only a brief sampling of authors.

Anderson, Poul. *Brain Wave. Tau Zero.*

Asimov, Isaac. *I, Robot. The Rest of the Robots.*

Baxter, Stephen. *Anti-Ice.*

Benford, Gregory. *Artifact.*

Bear, Greg

Caidin, Martin. *Cyborg.*

Campbell, John W., Jr.

Campbell, John W., Jr.

Clarke, Arthur C. *The Fountains of Paradise. Rendezvous with Rama.*

Clement, Hal. *Mission of Gravity.*

Forward, Robert L. *Dragon's Egg.*

Niven, Larry. *Neutron Star.*

Pohl, Frederik. *Beyond the Blue Event Horizon. Mining the Oort.*

Reeves-Stevens, Garfield. *Dark Matter.*

Robinson, Kim Stanley. *Red Mars. Green Mars.*

Sheffield, Charles. *Godspeed.*

Simak, Clifford D.

Wells, H. G.

White, James. *Hospital Station.*

Williamson, Jack. *Beachhead.*

New Wave

Human nature realistically treated, however exotic the context, takes precedence over hard science and gadgetry, still liberally used, in these novels deriving from the soft sciences (psychology, sociology, religion, and the like). Sex, drugs, oriental religions, art, morality, ecology, overpopulation, politics—the topics encompassed within the subgenre seemingly have no limit. The amorphousness of definition for new wave as a distinctive type of science fiction simply indicates that new wave aspects were always present in the works of some science fiction writers. There was, however, a movement toward liberalizing the scope for themes acceptable for science fiction and expanding the imaginative vision for writers and readers. So much current science fiction, apart from the strictly adventure types, is imbued with new wave aspects that the new wave label is now used to indicate the prototype novels of the 1960s and 1970s. The following list is of authors that were influential in making new wave ideas standard in science fiction

Aldiss, Brian. *Barefoot in the Head.*

Ballard, J. G. *The Crystal World. Love and Napalm.*

Brunner, John. *The Sheep Look Up. Stand on Zanzibar.*

Budrys, Algis. *Rogue Moon.*

Burgess, Anthony. *A Clockwork Orange.*

Delany, Samuel R. *Driftglass.*

Dick, Philip K. *Martian Time-Slip. The Three Stigmata of Palmer Eldritch.*

Disch, Thomas M. *334. Camp Concentration.*

Ellison, Harlan. *Alone Against Tomorrow. Dangerous Visions.*

Farmer, Philip José

Harrison, Harry. *Make Room! Make Room!*

Malzberg, Barry. *Beyond Apollo.*

Moorcock, Michael. *The Final Programme.*

Russ, Joanna

Sheckley, Robert. *Journey Beyond Tomorrow.*

Sladek, John

Spinrad, Norman

Sturgeon, Theodore

Tiptree, James, Jr.

Watson, Ian. *The Embedding.*

Wolfe, Gene. *The Fifth Head of Cerberus.*

Zelazny, Roger

Ecology

Three themes emerge in novels on humanity and its natural environment: manipulation and control of the environment; corruption of the environment by man and the destruction of some or all forms of life on Earth; and alien environments with distinctive characteristics, flora, and fauna. Catastrophe is often linked to overpopulation and pollution as well as to planned changes in environmental patterns. The following authors use themes suggested by the discouraging kinds of ecological problems facing the world.

Aldiss, Brian. *Helliconia Spring. Helliconia Summer. Helliconia Winter.*

Anthony, Piers. *Omnivore.*

Ballard, J. G. *The Wind from Nowhere. The Crystal World.*

Blish, James, and Norman L. Night. *A Torrent of Faces.*

Brunner, John. *Stand on Zanzibar. The Sheep Look Up.*

Clement, Hal. *Cycle of Fire. Close to Critical.*

Harrison, Harry. *Make Room! Make Room!*

Niven, Larry, and Jerry Pournelle. *The Mote in God's Eye.*

Silverberg, Robert. *The World Inside.*

Thomas, Theodore L., and Kate Wilhelm. *The Year of the Cloud.*

Yarbro, Chelsea Quinn. *Time of the Fourth Horseman.*

Messianic/Religious

In a science fiction world created for this theme, disillusionment has sullied the euphoric promise for the future offered by science and technology. Human needs and emotions somehow remained unsated in the millennium of technology. A savior, messiah, or superman brings redemption and salvation. Questions of theology and metaphysics regarding the expanding universe imagined by science fiction have uneasily juxtaposed science and faith and introduced speculation on future religions. The following authors base their books on religions currently in practice, or else they invent their own theologies.

Blish, James. *A Case of Conscience.*

Butler, Octavia. *The Parable of the Sower.*

Clarke, Arthur C. *Rendezvous with Rama. Childhood's End.*

Dick, Philip K. *Galactic Pot-Healer.*

Farmer, Philip José. *The Lovers.*

Gunn, James E. *This Fortress World.*

Heinlein, Robert A. *Stranger in a Strange Land.*

Henderson, Zenna. *The People: No Different Flesh. Pilgrimage.*

Herbert, Frank. *Dune. Dune Messiah. Children of Dune. The God Makers. Heretics of Dune. Chapterhouse: Dune.*

La Plante, Richard. *Tegné.*

Lackey, Mercedes. *Sacred Ground.*

Lewis, C. S. *Out of the Silent Planet. That Hideous Strength.*

Miller, Walter M., Jr. *A Canticle for Leibowitz.*

Moorcock, Michael. *Behold the Man!*

Simak, Clifford D. *Time and Again.*

Smith, Cordwainer. *Norstrilia.*

Stewart, Sean. *Passion Play.*

Tepper, Sheri S. *Raising the Stones.*

Vidal, Gore. *Messiah. Kalki.*

Vonnegut, Kurt, Jr. *The Sirens of Titan. Cat's Cradle.*

Zelazny, Roger. *Lord of Light. Isle of the Dead.*

Dystopia/Utopia

Opposed to the ideal society, utopia, is the dystopia, a horrid society, frequently the subject of science fiction. Dystopia comes into existence through many causes. Frequently it derives from the failure or corruption of rule by a scientific elite. Technology and human nature prove incompatible; psychology is used to manipulate, not improve, human nature; biological tinkering evolves monsters; and so on. The pessimism of dystopian science fiction is political and sociological as well as antiscience and antitechnology. Dystopian novels are hortatory and polemical: only by avoiding their mistakes can we achieve a future better than they depict. (There is, however, little positive utopian vision beyond a return to a simpler, more idyllic society or a religious salvation. See "Messianic/Religious," p. 213.) As this theme has a long literary history, it has been the topic of novels not usually considered as science fiction. Among the following authors are several whose writings are outside the realm of this genre (Bellamy, Huxley, Orwell, and Skinner).

Asimov, Isaac. *Pebble in the Sky. The Caves of Steel.* Foundation Trilogy.

Bellamy, Edward. *Looking Backward: 2000–1887.*

Bradbury, Ray. *Fahrenheit 451.*

Brin, David. *Glory Season.*

Brunner, John. *Shockwave Rider.*

Burroughs, William S. *Nova Express.*

Gunn, James E. *The Joy Makers.*

Harrison, Harry. *Make Room! Make Room!*

Heinlein, Robert A. *Starship Troopers. To Sail Beyond the Sunset.*

Hoyle, Fred. *Ossian's Ride.*

Huxley, Aldous. *Brave New World. Island.*

Le Guin, Ursula K. *Always Coming Home.*

Leiber, Fritz. *Gather, Darkness!*

Orwell, George. *1984.*

Pohl, Frederik, and Cyril Kornbluth. *The Space Merchants.*

Reynolds, Mack. *Looking Backward, from the Year 2000.*

Robinson, Kim Stanley. *Pacific Edge. Wild Shore. The Gold Coast.*

Skinner, B. F. *Walden Two.*

Tepper, Sheri S. *The Gate to Women's Country.*

Vonnegut, Kurt, Jr. *Player Piano.*

Apocalypse

Survival after the almost total destruction of Earth—the nature of the disaster, its effect on the nature of man, and the shape of society thereafter—is a common theme. The disaster may be natural (e.g., plague, planet colliding with Earth) or man-caused (e.g., nuclear war). This theme pervades the works of many science fiction writers besides those in the following list.

Ballard, J. G. *The Drowned World. The Burning World. The Crystal World.*

Balmer, Edwin, and Philip Wylie. *When Worlds Collide.*

Brin, David. *The Postman.*

Brunner, John. *The Sheep Look Up.*

Card, Orson Scott. *Folk of the Fringe.*

Christopher, John. *The Death of Grass.*

Crowley, John. *Engine Summer.*

Dick, Philip K. *Dr. Bloodmoney.*

Dickson, Gordon R. *Wolf & Iron.*

Frank, Pat. *Alas, Babylon.*

Hoban, Russell. *Riddley Walker.*

Hoyle, Fred, and Geoffrey Hoyle. *The Inferno.*

Lewitt, Shariann. *Memento Mori.*

Miller, Walter M., Jr. *A Canticle for Leibowitz.*

Murphy, Pat. *The City, Not Long After.*

Roessner, Michaela. *Vanishing Point.*

Sheffield, Charles. *The Ganymede Club.*

Stewart, George R. *Earth Abides.*

Tepper, Sheri S. *The Gate to Women's Country.*

Turner, George. *Drowning Towers.*

Vonnegut, Kurt, Jr. *Cat's Cradle.*

Whitmore, Charles. *Winter's Daughter.*

Wilhelm, Kate. *Juniper Time.*

Wyndham, John. *The Day of the Triffids.*

Yarbro, Chelsea Quinn. *Time of the Fourth Horseman.*

Alternate and Parallel Worlds

History as it might have been: What if there had been a significant change in a historical event? What, then, would have been the pattern of history? What would the present be and why? This theoretical analysis of historical cause and effect is often conjoined to the parallel world theme: parallel Earths and parallel universes exist simultaneously with our Earth, conceived, perhaps, along a spatial fourth dimension. (In some worlds of fantasy, characters can be transported out of one parallel universe and into another.) This theme has been used by many science fiction authors in addition to those in the following list, as well as by authors of the mainstream novel (e.g., Vladimir Nabokov).

In the early 1990s, some of the cyberpunk authors started writing in the alternative history vein, which was promptly christened "steam punk."

Anthony, Piers. *Out of Phaze. Robot Adept. Phaze Doubt.*

Asimov, Isaac. *The End of Eternity.*

Blaylock, James. *Lord Kelvin's Machine. The Paper Grail.*

Bova, Ben. *Triumph.*

Card, Orson Scott. The Chronicles of Alvin Maker. *Seventh Son. Red Prophet. Prentice Alvin. Alvin Journeyman.*

de Camp, L. Sprague. *Lest Darkness Fall.*

Dick, Philip K. *The Man in the High Castle. Now Wait for Last Year. Flow My Tears, the Policeman Said. Eye in the Sky.*

Farmer, Philip José. *The Gate of Time. Sail On, Sail On.*

Gibson, William, and Bruce Sterling. *The Difference Engine* (steam punk).

Harrison, Harry. *Tunnel Through the Deeps. West of Eden. Winter in Eden. Return to Eden.*

Hogan, James P. *The Proteus Operation.*

Laumer, Keith. *Worlds of the Imperium.*

Leiber, Fritz. *Destiny Times Three.*

Lupoff, Richard A. *Countersolar! Circumpolar!*

O'Leary, Patrick. *Door Number Three.*

Rucker, Rudy. *The Hollow Earth* (steam punk).

Roberts, Keith. *Pavane.*

Sawyer, Robert J. The Quintaglio trilogy.

Sheckley, Robert. *Mindswap.*

Simak, Clifford D. *Ring Around the Sun.*

Somtow, S. P. *The Aquiliad: Aquila in the New World.*

Turtledove, Harry. *A Different Flesh. Agent of Byzantium.* Videssos series. Tale of Krispos series. *The Guns of the South. World War: In the Balance.*

Vance, Jack. *Alastor.*

Wilson, Robert Charles. *Gypsies. Mysterium.*

Wingrove, David. *Chung Kuo.*

Time Travel, Time Warp

Travel into either the past or the future is a dream in all literature and not restricted to science fiction. Whether limited to the body or mind, the experience is both desirable and frightening. Science fiction uses great ingenuity in the methods of travel and equal imagination in depicting the experiences of the travelers. This is a favorite ploy in space opera and fantasy. Playing with time has intrigued many science fiction and fantasy writers, and the following list merely suggests the number of books on the theme. Many examples can be found in children's books as well.

Aldiss, Brian. *Cryptozoic! Frankenstein Unbound.*

Anderson, Poul. *Tau Zero. The Corridors of Time.*

Appel, Allen. *Twice upon a Time. Till the End of Time. Time After Time.*

Asimov, Isaac. *Pebble in the Sky. The End of Eternity.*

Ballard, J. G. *The Crystal World.*

Barnes, John. *Kaleidescope Century.*

Benford, Gregory. *Timescape.*

Bester, Alfred. *The Stars My Destination.*

Bishop, Michael. *No Enemy But Time.*

Blish, James. *Midsummer Century.*

Brunner, John. *The Productions of Time. Quicksand.*

Dalton, Sean. *Turncoat.*

David, James F. *Footprints of Thunder.*

Dick, Philip K. *Counter-Clock World.*

Dickson, Gordon R. *Time Storm.*

Fenn, Lionel. *Time: The Semi-Final Frontier.*

Haldeman, Joe. *The Forever War.*

Harrison, Harry. *The Technicolor Time Machine.*

Heinlein, Robert A. *The Door Into Summer. Farnham's Freehold.*

Laumer, Keith. *The Great Time Machine Hoax. Back to the Time Warp.*

Mason, Lisa. *Summer of Love. The Golden Nineties.*

May, Julian. *The Many-Colored Land.*

Moorcock, Michael. The Dancers at the End of Time: *An Alien Heat. The Hollow Lands. The End of All Songs.*

Niven, Larry. *A World out of Time. World of Ptavvs.*

O'Leary, Patrick. *Door Number Three.*

Pohl, Frederik. *The Age of the Pussyfoot.*

Powers, Tim. *The Anubis Gates.*

Sawyer, Robert J. *End of an Era.*

Silverberg, Robert. *The Masks of Time. The Time Hoppers.*

Varley, John. *Millennium.*

Vinge, Vernor. *Marooned in Real Time.*

Wells, H. G. *The Time Machine. When the Sleeper Wakes.*

Willis, Connie. *The Doomsday Book.*

Wright, S. Fowler. *The World Below.*

Lost Worlds

These are the matter of romantic science fiction, now largely displaced as a subject by the interplanetary universe. There are large elements of fantasy and adventure in the many examples still popular—prehistoric animals, strange races of men, and background in archaeology and anthropology. The prehistoric epic in the romance section (see p. 188) is very closely related, with substantial overlap. Some are serious novels about primitive man and vanished types. The following books are some of the prototypes.

Bishop, Michael. *Ancient of Days.*

Burroughs, Edgar Rice. *At the Earth's Core.*

Doyle, Sir Arthur Conan. *The Lost World.*

Golding, William. *The Inheritors.*

Haggard, H. Rider. *She. King Solomon's Mines.*

Verne, Jules. *Journey to the Centre of the Earth.*

More recent books in this vein include Robert T. Bakker's *Raptor Red* and Edward Myers's Mountain Made of Light series.

Immortality

Whether science can ultimately confer immortality upon mankind is considered in science fiction, but whether such immortality would be a blessing or a curse is the real question. There are many immortal beings to be found in science fiction stories. (One such immortal in *Venus on the Half-Shell*, by Kilgore Trout, says bluntly, "Immortality is a pain in the ass." For more on this book, see "Parody," p. 237.) The following books treat this theme seriously.

Aldiss, Brian. *Moment of Eclipse.*

Banks, Iain M. *Feersum Endjinn.*

Barnes, John. *Kaleidescope Century.*

Grimwood, Ken. *Replay.*

Gunn, James E. *The Immortals.*

Haldeman, Joe. *Buying Time.*

Heinlein, Robert A. *Time Enough for Love.*

Shaw, Bob. *One Million Tomorrows.*

Silverberg, Robert. *Born with the Dead.*

Spinrad, Norman. *The Iron Dream. No Direction Home.*

Vance, Jack. *To Live Forever.*

van Vogt, A. E. *The Weapon Makers.*

Zelazny, Roger. *This Immortal.*

Psionic Powers

The powers of precognition, telepathy, clairvoyance, telekinesis, and teleportation displayed by characters in science fiction make current research in parapsychology seem naïve. Science fiction invented the term *psionics* (psychic electronics) to describe these powers of the mind. Such powers are often inherent in the superman theme and are often manifest among alien beings. The variations on this theme have fascinated many science fiction authors, not just those in the following list.

Ashwell, Pauline. *Project Far Cry.*

Bester, Alfred. *The Stars My Destination. The Demolished Man.*

Blish, James. *Jack of Eagles.*

Bradley, Marion Zimmer. Darkover series.

Brunner, John. *The Whole Man.*

Clement, Hal. *Needle.*

Dickson, Gordon R. *Dorsai!*

Gould, Steven C. *Jumper.*

Harrison, Harry. *Death Word.*

Henderson, Zenna. *Pilgrimage.*

Herbert, Frank. *Dune.*

Ingrid, Charles. The Patterns of Chaos series.

King, Stephen. *Firestarter.*

Le Guin, Ursula K. *The Lathe of Heaven.*

McAuley, Paul J. *Eternal Light.*

McCaffrey, Anne. *To Ride Pegasus. The Rowan. Pegasus in Flight. Damia. Damia's Children. Lyon's Pride.*

Murphy, Pat. *Falling Woman.*

Pohl, Frederik. *Drunkard's Walk.*

Roberts, Keith. *The Inner Wheel.*

Russ, Joanna. *And Chaos Died.*

Silverberg, Robert. *Dying Inside.*

Simak, Clifford D. *Time Is the Simplest Thing.*

Stewart, Sean. *Resurrection Man.*

Sturgeon, Theodore. *The Dreaming Jewels. More Than Human.*

van Vogt, A. E. *Slan.*

Vinge, Joan D. *Catspaw. Psion.*

Wilson, Robert Charles. *Gypsies.*

Zelazny, Roger. *The Dream Master.*

Space Opera

These novels may be called westerns in space suits. Naïve space-adventure stories of extravagant and fantastic dimensions, they usually involve galactic empires and their space battles. The serious science fiction author and fan complain that space opera gives science fiction a bad name, though a few books take the form of good, straightforward adventure stories, and a few are realistic space adventure. Some are written with humor or as comedy or parody. (See also "Galactic Empires," p. 222.) Some are serious science fiction or science fantasy in the frame of space opera adventure. The following list could be extended almost infinitely!

Although much maligned, space operas are, in truth, a great deal of fun. They feature almost everything one could want in a story—action, adventure, intrigue, and romance. The *Star Wars* movies from George Lucas are excellent examples of space opera. There is excellent writing turning up in space opera and, though many space operas are formulaic dreck, there are well-written novels in this subgenre that have received (most deservedly) respected awards.

Anthony, Piers. *Total Recall.*

Bujold, Lois McMaster. *Barrayar. The Vor Game. Warrior's Apprentice. Brothers in Arms. Mirror Dance.* The continuing saga of the militaristic Vorkosigan family.

Burroughs, Edgar Rice. Barsoom (Mars) series.

Cherryh, C. J. *Downbelow Station.* Award-winning science fiction set on a politically warring space station.

Delany, Samuel R. *Nova.*

King, Stephen. The Dark Tower series: *The Gunfighter. The Drawing of the Three. The Wastelands.* A very dark space opera from the king of horror fiction.

Laumer, Keith. *Galactic Odyssey.*

McCaffrey, Anne, and Elizabeth Moon. *Sassinak.*

McCaffrey, Anne, and Elizabeth Ann Scarborough. *Powers That Be. Power Lines. Power Play.*
Retired due to lung damage incurred in the line of duty, Major Yanaba Maddock is asked to spy on her new friends and neighbors on a planet hiding many secrets.

Moon, Elizabeth. *Hunting Season. Sporting Chance.*

Smith, Edward E. "Doc." *The Skylark of Space.* Lensman series.

van Vogt, A. E. *The Voyage of the Space Beagle.*

Vance, Jack. *The Five Gold Bands.*

Weis, Margaret. The Star of the Guardians trilogy. *The Lost King.*

Williamson, Jack. *The Legion of Space.*

Zahn, Timothy. *Dark Force Rising. Heir to the Empire.* A trilogy of books set a short time after the Star Wars films.

Galactic Empires

While galactic empires are the setting for space opera adventures, they are also the subject of serious views of communities and worlds of humans and aliens in a variety of political and sociological relationships. Although adventure enters into the following books, their authors are more interested in sociological and political comment.

Anderson, Poul. *Mirkheim. Trader to the Stars. Harvest of Stars. Harvest the Fire. The Stars Are Also Fire.*

Asimov, Isaac. Foundation series.

Bova, Ben. *Privateers.* The Exiles trilogy.

Bradley, Marion Zimmer. Darkover series.

Brin, David. *Startide Rising. Brightness Reef.*

Brunner, John. *Endless Shadow.*

Card, Orson Scott. *The Memory of Earth. The Call of Earth. The Ships of Earth.*

Heinlein, Robert A. *A Citizen of the Galaxy.*

Le Guin, Ursula K. *The Left Hand of Darkness.*

McCaffrey, Anne. Dragonriders of Pern series.

Morris, Janet, and Chris Morris. *Threshold.*

Niven, Larry, and Jerry Pournelle. *The Mote in God's Eye.*

Shaw, Bob. *Orbitsville. The Palace of Eternity.*

Simak, Clifford D. *Way Station.*

Stapledon, Olaf. *Star Maker.*

Stirling, Bruce. *Schmismatrix.*

van Vogt, A. E. *The Weapon Shops of Isher. The Weapon Makers.*

Williams, Walter Jon. *Rock of Ages.*

Williamson, Jack, and James E. Gunn. *Star Bridge.*

Wolfe, Gene. *Nightside the Long Sun.*

Militaristic

Themes portraying all varieties of military connection are present in science fiction, from mercenaries and war to antimilitary and parody. Often, a militaristic theme is present in space opera (see p. 220) and stories of galactic empires (see above).

Bujold, Lois McMaster. *The Vor Saga. Barrayar. The Vor Game. Warrior's Apprentice. Brothers in Arms. Mirror Dance.*

Cherryh, C. J. *Rimrunners.*

Dickson, Gordon R. Dorsai series.

Feintuch, David. *Midshipman's Hope.*

Harrison, Harry. *Bill, the Galactic Hero* (parody).

Heinlein, Robert A. *Starship Troopers.*

Hubbard, L. Ron. Mission Earth series (10 vols.).

Rosenberg, Joel. *Not for Glory. Hero.*

Turtledove, Harry. Videssos series.

Willis, Connie, and Cynthia Felice. *Light Raid.*

Space Travel

Although space flight has actually been achieved, its reality only adds to science fiction's obsession with spaceships, starships, interstellar travel, and galactic empires. Flight in space is still *the* dominating romantic theme in science fiction. Not to be caught short when colonizing follows exploration, science fiction has a guide (covering eight extrasolar planets Earth has colonized) at hand:

Wolfe, L. Stephen, and Roy L. Wysack. *Handbook for Space Pioneers: A Manual of the Galactic Association (Earth Branch).*

This theme, as used by the following authors, ranges from space travel as science to space travel as fantasy.

Aldiss, Brian W. *Non-Stop.*

Anderson, Poul. *Tau Zero.*

Bear, Greg. *Anvil of Stars.*

Benford, Gregory, and David Brin. *Heart of the Comet.*

Brin, David. *Startide Rising.*

Cherryh, C. J. *Downbelow Station.*

Clarke, Arthur C. *2001: A Space Odyssey. Prelude to Space. Rendezvous with Rama. 2061: Odyssey Three.*

Heinlein, Robert A. *Citizen of the Galaxy. Have Space Suit—Will Travel.*

Pohl, Frederik. *Gateway.*

Sheffield, Charles. *The Ganymede Club.*

Simak, Clifford D. *Shakespeare's Planet.*

Stableford, Brian. *Man in a Cage.*

van Vogt, A. E. *Rogue Ship.*

Verne, Jules. *From the Earth to the Moon.*

Alien Beings

The possible and ingenious forms taken by alien beings are seemingly limitless, and authors' imaginations truly run wild. They may be monsters (perhaps plant-like or reptilian), humanoid (a freak of Darwinian evolution, perhaps), godlike, or even disembodied intelligences (as in Fred Hoyle's *The Black Cloud*). They may be invaders of Earth or encountered on other planets. The relationships of human and alien, friendly or antagonistic, offer the writers ingenious possibilities. Space opera (see p. 220) and fantasy (see chapter 7, "Fantasy," p. 258) have a field day in the creation of alien beings, especially BEM (Bug-Eyed Monsters), whose portrayal on the magazine cover *made* science fiction art an abiding joy. (Monsters of another type appear in chapter 8, "Horror," p. 287.) Color paintings of the aliens found in the works of several novelists (e.g., Larry Niven's "Thrints," van Vogt's "Ixtl," Jack Chalker's "Czill," James Blish's "Lithians") are found in Wayne Douglas Barlowe and Ian Summers's *Barlowe's Guide to Extra-Terrestrials*. The following list is only a brief sampling, and many examples are found in the short story. (Several anthologies on alien beings are listed in "Theme Anthologies," p. 240.)

Aldiss, Brian. *The Dark Light Years.*

Arneson, Eleanor. *Ring of Swords.*

Asimov, Isaac. *The Gods Themselves.*

Bear, Greg. *The Forge of God. Anvil of Stars.*

Bova, Ben. *Voyagers. Voyagers II.*

Brin, David. *The Uplift War.*

Brunner, John. *The Atlantic Abomination. The Crucible of Time.*

Butler, Octavia. *Imago.*

Card, Orson Scott. *Ender's Game. Speaker for the Dead. Xenocide.*

Cherryh, C. J. *Cuckoo's Egg. Foreigner. Invaders.*

Clarke, Arthur C. *Imperial Earth.*

Clement, Hal. *Mission of Gravity. Needle.*

de Camp, L. Sprague. *Rogue Queen.*

Douglas, Carole Nelson. *Probe. Counterprobe.*

Forward, Robert L. *The Dragon's Egg. Starquake.*

Foster, Alan Dean. *A Call to Arms. The False Mirror. The Spoils of War.*

Gentle, Mary. *Ancient Light. Golden Witchbreed.*

Gunn, James E. *The Listeners.*

Haldeman, Joe. *The Forever War.*

Heinlein, Robert A. *The Puppet Masters.*

Hoyle, Fred. *The Black Cloud.*

Le Guin, Ursula K. *The Left Hand of Darkness.*

Leiber, Fritz. *The Wanderer.*

Lindholm, Megan. *Alien Earth.*

McAuley, Paul J. *Of the Fall.*

Niven, Larry. *The Smoke Ring. The Integral Trees.*

Niven, Larry, and Jerry Pournelle. *Footfall. The Mote in God's Eye.*

Niven, Larry, Jerry Pournelle, and Steven Barnes. *The Legacy of Heorot. Beowulf's Children.*

Pohl, Frederik. *The Day the Martians Came.*

Reeves-Stevens, Garfield. *Nighteyes.*

Robinson, Spider, and Jeanne Robinson. *Stardance.*

Saberhagen, Fred. *The Berserker Throne.*

Silverberg, Robert. *Downward to the Earth. Invaders from Earth.*

Stapledon, Olaf. *Star Maker.*

Tepper, Sheri S. *Grass. Raising the Stones.*

Turtledove, Harry. *A World of Difference.*

van Vogt, A. E. *Voyage of the Space Beagle.*

Wells, H. G. *The War of the Worlds.*

Computers, Automation

The computer is capable of an amazing number of ingenious functions under human programming, but the science fiction authors see the computer as a thinking machine. So well does it think and plan and even reproduce itself in some stories that it makes humanity unnecessary and precipitates a future in which the machines hum contentedly and people are obsolete. Whether man and computer will live in cooperative harmony or in a master-slave relationship provides a controversial theme for science fiction authors.

The worry that the machine—computer or robot—may end up running human society is a recurrent theme in science fiction: Is science, in all its aspects, a blessing or curse for humanity? The idea of a completely automated society is often analyzed in a similar manner. The following books present some aspects, both intriguing and disturbing, of our coexistence with the computer.

Bear, Greg. *Blood Music*.

Blish, James. *Midsummer Century*.

Brunner, John. *The Shockwave Rider*.

Budrys, Algis. *Michaelmas*.

Compton, D. G. *The Steel Crocodile*.

Dick, Philip K. *Vulcan's Hammer*.

Frayn, Michael. *The Tin Men*.

Harrison, Harry, and Marvin Minsky. *The Turing Option*.

Heinlein, Robert A. *The Moon Is a Harsh Mistress*.

Herbert, Frank. *Destination: Void*.

Johannesson, Olaf. *The Tale of the Big Computer*.

Lafferty, R. A. *Arrive at Easterwine*.

Ouellette, Pierre. *The Deus Machine*.

Pohl, Frederik. *Man Plus*.

Stableford, Brian. *The Walking Shadow*.

Cyberpunk

All-pervasive technology and the perversion of it by a rebellious underground subculture is a major element of this type. *Do Androids Dream of Electric Sheep?*, a 1968 title by Philip K. Dick from which the film *Blade Runner* was adapted, is a forerunner of modern cyberpunk.

For a quick introduction to cyberpunk, try some of the stories in *Mirrorshades*, edited by Bruce Sterling. It has been called "the definitive collection of cyberpunk short fiction."

Baird, Wilhelmina. *Clipjoint*.

Cadigan, Pat. *Fools*.

Gibson, William. *Neuromancer. Count Zero. Mona Lisa Overdrive. Virtual Light*.

Kadrey, Richard. *Metrophage*.

Mason, Lisa. *Arachne.*

Rucker, Rudy. *Wetware.*

Scott, Melissa. *Burning Bright.*

Stephenson, Neal. *Snow Crash.*

Stanwick, Michael. *Vacuum Flowers.*

Sterling, Bruce. *Islands in the Net.*

Williams, Walter John. *Voice of the Whirlwind.*

Robots, Androids, Cyborgs

The robot is a machine, usually with a human form but purely mechanical. An android is an artificial human, organic in composition. A cyborg is a human altered with artificial parts to perform certain functions or modified to exist in outer space. The computer is essential to all three forms. Pervading all stories or robots, androids, and cyborgs is the often tricky problem of the interrelationship of human and machine. One bit of science fiction folklore exists for the robot—Asimov's three laws of robotics: 1) A robot may not injure a human being or, through inaction, allow a human being to come to harm; 2) A robot must obey the orders given by human beings, except where such orders would conflict with the first law; 3) A robot must protect its own existence as long as such protection does not conflict with the first or second law. The robots in the following works are more sophisticated than those now available and give intriguing hints of possible futures.

Allen, Roger MacBride. *Caliban.*

Asimov, Isaac. *I, Robot. Caves of Steel.*

Bayley, Barrington J. *The Garments of Caean.*

Benford, Greg. *Great Sky River.*

Bester, Alfred. *Golem 100.*

Dick, Philip K. *Do Androids Dream of Electric Sheep? We Can Build You.*

Harrison, Harry. *War with the Robots.*

Laumer, Keith. *A Plague of Demons.*

Leiber, Fritz. *The Silver Eggheads.*

Lem, Stanislaw. *The Cyberiad.*

McCaffrey, Anne. *The Ship Who Sang.*

Pohl, Frederik. *Man Plus.*

Shelley, Mary. *Frankenstein.*

Silverberg, Robert. *Tower of Glass.*

Simak, Clifford D. *City. Time and Again. A Choice of Gods.*

Sladek, John. *Roderick. Roderick at Random. Tik Tok.*

van Vogt, A. E. *Mission to the Stars.*

Watson, Ian. *The Cyborg and the Sorcerer. The Wizard and the War Machine.*

Zindell, David. *Neverness.*

Social Criticism

The sociological bases of human society are an insistent theme in science fiction, notably in the projection of dystopias and utopias (see p. 214). The science fiction authors also study the phenomena of social change to anticipate direction and project consequences. The following authors forecast possibilities, however strange the new societies may seem.

Aldiss, Brian W. *The Dark Light Years.*

Asimov, Isaac. *The Gods Themselves.*

Ballard, J. G. *High-Rise.*

Brackett, Leigh. *The Long Tomorrow.*

Brunner, John. *Stand on Zanzibar.*

Clarke, Arthur C. *The City and the Stars.*

de Camp, L. Sprague. *Rogue Queen.*

Delany, Samuel R. *Triton.*

Dick, Philip K. *Time out of Joint. Radio Free Albemuth.*

Disch, Thomas M. *On Wings of Song.*

Farmer, Philip José. *The Lovers.*

Godwin, Parke. *The Snake Oil Wars. Waiting for the Galactic Bus.*

Gunn, James E. *The Joy Makers.*

Keyes, Daniel. *Flowers for Algernon.*

Kingsbury, Donald. *Courtship Rite.*

Le Guin, Ursula K. *The Left Hand of Darkness.*

Lem, Stanislaw. *One Human Minute. A Perfect Vacuum.*

McDonald, Ian. *Demolition Road.*

Niven, Larry, and Jerry Pournelle. *Oath of Fealty.*

Panshin, Alexei. *Rite of Passage.*

Pohl, Frederik, and Cyril M. Kornbluth. *The Space Merchants.*

Roberts, Keith. *Pavane.*

Robinson, Spider. *Mind Killer.*

Simak, Clifford D. *City.*

Tepper, Sheri S. *Grass.*

Varley, John. *The Ophiuchi Hotline.*

Wells, H. G. *The First Men in the Moon.*

Wylie, Philip. *The Disappearance.*

The Superman

The superman in science fiction is *not* the comic-strip figure. Whether an evolutionary projection of man, an alien, or an immortal god, the superman is endowed with capacities of extraordinary, supersensory or supernatural mental power and may also possess superhuman physical powers. The relationship between humanity and the superman is uneasy, and many stories show mutual antagonism or a humanity that fears (sometimes for good reason!) supermen. The superman as messiah is also used. As in the following books, this theme is usually accompanied by disturbing philosophical insights.

Anderson, Poul. *Brain Wave.*

Bester, Alfred. *The Computer Connection.*

Clarke, Arthur C. *Childhood's End.*

Henderson, Zenna. *Pilgrimage. The People: No Different Flesh.*

Kress, Nancy. *Beggars in Spain. Beggars and Choosers.*

La Plante, Richard. *Tegné.*

Stapledon, Olaf. *Odd John.*

Sturgeon, Theodore. *More Than Human.*

van Vogt, A. E. *Slan.*

Watson, Ian. *Alien Embassy. Converts.*

Williamson, Jack. *Darker Than You Think.*

Women in Science Fiction

The independent woman has long been a science fiction tradition. Young adult novels were an early arena for strong, independent female characters. Examples of those are *Podkayne of Mars* by Robert A. Heinlein (1963) and the Telzey series by James H. Schmitz (started in 1964). Along the same lines is the recent *Unwillingly to Earth* by Pauline Ashwell. Strong women assuming the responsibility for rebuilding civilization after an apocalypse has been a common theme in recent science fiction, evidenced in the following titles.

Butler, Octavia. *The Parable of the Sower.*

Sargent, Pamela. *The Shore of Women.*

Tepper, Sheri S. *Gate to Women's Country.*

Wren, M. K. *A Gift upon the Shore.*

Love and Sex

The two themes of love and sex were late bloomers for science fiction and are often still of secondary or minor interest. They assumed importance and the concern of many science fiction authors with the emergence of the new wave—the soft sciences, particularly psychology and sociology. A shift in emphasis from a scientific thesis toward the story of human relations, however bizarre the context, increased the scope for the love story and sexual relationships and, incidentally, often gave some much-needed depth to characterizations. (Sex often introduces some welcome humor: "On Saturn the sexes are three" begins a limerick by B. T. Xerxes found in Tom Boardman's anthology *An ABC of Science Fiction*.) The following works are quite specific on the topics of love and sex.

Single-sex societies can bring up a number of issues and interesting situations for science fiction. In Lois McMaster Bujold's *Ethan of Athos*, an obstetrician from an all-male planet is sent out into what he perceives as the perverted heterosexual world to secure new ova needed for survival of the species on his planet. In David Brin's *Glory Season*, the featured planet was settled by women who did not want to live with men and thus created clone clans. In both books, some of the conflict derives from the necessity for heterosexual contact of some sort.

Anderson, Poul. *Virgin Planet.*

Atwood, Margaret. *The Handmaid's Tale.*

Charnas, Suzy McKee. *Motherlines. Furies.*

Delany, Samuel R. *Dhalgren. Stars in My Pocket Like Grains of Sand.*

Heinlein, Robert A. *Time Enough for Love.*

Le Guin, Ursula K. *The Left Hand of Darkness. The Dispossessed.*

Pohl, Frederik, and Cyril Kornbluth. *Search the Sky.*

Russ, Joanna. *The Female Man. We Who Are About To . . .*

Scott, Melissa. *Shadow Man.*

Slonczewski, Joan. *A Door into Ocean.*

Sturgeon, Theodore. *Venus Plus X.*

Vinge, Joan D. *The Snow Queen. World's End.*

Detectives in Science Fiction

A neat combining of these two genres produces galactic policemen and private eyes—human, alien, and mechanical. For a good historical survey, see the chapter "Crime: From Sherlock to Spaceships" in Sam Moskowitz's *Strange Horizons*. Anthologies collect some of the short stories, and readers may be interested in the following.

Asimov, Isaac, Martin H. Greenberg, and Charles G. Waugh, eds. *Sherlock Holmes Through Time and Space*. Bluejay, 1985.

Asimov, Isaac, Martin H. Greenberg, and Charles G. Waugh, eds. *The 13 Crimes of Science Fiction*. Doubleday, 1979.
Each of the stories is labeled: Hard-Boiled Detective; Psychic Detective; Spy Story; Analytical Detective; Whodunit; Why-Done-It; Inverted; Locked Room; Cipher; Police Procedural; Trial; Punishment.

DeFord, Miriam Allen, ed. *Space, Time & Crime*. Paperback Library, 1964.

Santesson, Hans Stefan, ed. *Crime Prevention in the 30th Century*. Walker, 1969.

As in the standard detective story, there is the use of a series detective in several of the following examples.

Adams, Douglas. *Dirk Gently's Holistic Detective Agency. The Long Dark Tea-time of the Soul.*

Anderson, Kevin J. *Blindfold.*

Asimov, Isaac. *The Caves of Steel. The Naked Sun. Robots and Empire. The Robots of Dawn.*
Features detective Lige Baley and robot R. Daneel Olivaw.

Banks, Iain. *Feersum Endjinn.*

Bear, David. *Keeping Time.*
"Last of the private eyes" in the twenty-first century.

Bester, Alfred. *The Demolished Man.*
Lincoln Powell, telepathic cop, 2301 A.D.

Biggle, Lloyd, Jr. *Watchers of the Dark.*
Jan Darzek, private eye.

Blake, William Dorsey. *My Time Is Yours.*
Reggie Moon, private eye.

Chandler, A. Bertram. *Bring Back Yesterday.*
John Peterson, private eye.

Clement, Hal. *Needle.*

Dick, Philip K. *Do Androids Dream of Electric Sheep?*
Rick Deckard, Blade Runner private eye.

Dozois, Gardner, and George Effinger. *Nightmare Blue.*
Karl Jaeger, last private eye on Earth.

Foster, Alan Dean. *Cyber Way.*
A Navajo tribal police officer in the next century.

Garrett, Randall. *Murder and Magic. Too Many Magicians. Lord Darcy Investigates.*

Goulart, Ron. *Dr. Scofflaw. Hail Hibbler. The Big Bang. Upside, Downside.*
Jake and Hildy Pace, private eyes, twenty-first century. Zack Tourney, Federal Police Agency.

Haiblum, Isidore. *Nightmare Express. Outerworld.*

Jones, Gwyneth. *Flower Dust.*

Karling, Marvin, and Lewis M. Andrews. *Gomorrah.*
Victor Slaughter.

Killough, Lee. *Deadly Silents. The Doppelgänger Gambit.*

Lem, Stanislaw. *Tales of Pirx the Pilot.*
"Technological detective stories."

Lieberman, Herbert. *Sandman.*

MacLean, Katherine. *Missing Man.*
George Sanford, telepathic private eye.

McQuay, Mike. Mathew Swain series.
Private eye, twenty-first century.

Niven, Larry. *The Patchwork Girl.*
Gil "The Arm" Hamilton. Amalgamated Regional Militia.

Nolan, William F. *Space for Hire.*
Sam Space, private eye.

Panshin, Alexei. *Star Well.*

Reaves, J. Michael. *Darkworld Detective.*
Kamus of Kadizar, private eye.

Sawyer, Robert J. *Golden Fleece.*

Shatner, William. *Tekwar.*

Spruill, Steven G. *The Psychopath Plague. The Imperator Plot.*
Detective team: Human and alien.

Tucker, Wilson. "To the Tombaugh Station." "Time Exposure."

Vance, Jack. *Miro Hetzel.*

Wallace, Ian. *The Purloined Prince. Deathstar Voyage. The Sign of the Mute Medusa.*
Claudine St. Eyre, detective.

Zahn, Timothy. *A Coming of Age.*

Science Fantasy

This term is not susceptible to simple definition. While science fiction basically subscribes to the laws of nature as we know them, science fantasy invents new laws, new nature, a new cosmology. There was a close relationship between science fiction and fantasy in the early development of the genre (magazine titles such as *The Magazine of Fantasy and Science Fiction, Fantastic Science Fiction,* and *Science Fantasy* indicate the merging), and the current writers of science fiction may intermingle science fiction and fantasy. Some authors write both. (There is an arbitrary separation of some types of works into the later chapters on fantasy [chapter 7] and on horror [chapter 8], while alternate and parallel worlds, time travel, and other fantasy themes are included in this chapter.) The following few authors illustrate an approach to science fiction now used by many authors.

Bradbury, Ray

Bradley, Marion Zimmer. Darkover series.

Brown, Fredric

Butler, Octavia E. *Wild Seed.*

Delany, Samuel R. *Neverÿona: Or, The Tale of Signs and Cities.*

Jones, Diana Wynne. *A Sudden Wild Magic.*

Kennealy-Morrison, Patricia. The Keltiad series.

McCaffrey, Anne. *Crystal Singer. Killashandra.* Dragonriders of Pern series.

Silverberg, Robert. *Lord Valentine's Castle. Majipoor Chronicles. Valentine Pontifex.*

Smith, Cordwainer

Spinrad, Norman. *Child of Fortune. The Void Captain's Tale.*

Wolfe, Gene. The Book of the New Sun series: *The Shadow of the Torturer. The Claw of the Conciliator. The Sword of the Lictor. The Citadel of the Autarch.*

TOPICS

"Best" Authors and Their Best

A list of "best" authors and their best works is impossible to compile except on an eccentric basis. Included here are most of the winners of Hugo and Nebula awards, and their award-winning titles. Many of these authors are listed as examples earlier in this chapter. Not included are classic authors (e.g., Edgar Rice Burroughs, Jules Verne, and H. G. Wells) and those no longer writing (whose works may still be available in paperback). Most of the following authors are currently writing or appear regularly on lists of the "best." Many more titles could be listed for most of these authors. The ones listed are those most often cited. A few authors are listed without title, indicating that critics consider important the influence of the author's work as a whole.

Aldiss, Brian. *The Long Afternoon of Earth. Greybeard. The Dark Light Years. Barefoot in the Head.* Helliconia trilogy.

Anderson, Poul. *Brain Wave. Tau Zero. The Star Fox. Three Hearts and Three Lions.*

Anthony, Piers. *Chthon. Omnivore.*

Asimov, Isaac. *The Gods Themselves.* The Foundation Trilogy. *Opus 100. Opus 100* contains 99 works tied together with autobiographical notes.

Ballard, J. G. *The Wind from Nowhere. The Crystal World. Vermilion Sands.*

Barnes, John. *Mother of Storms* (D's pick for the 1995 Nebula Award).

Bass, T. J. *Half Past Human.*

Bear, Greg. *Moving Mars.*

Bester, Alfred. *The Demolished Man. The Stars My Destination.*

Bishop, Michael. *No Enemy But Time.*

Blish, James. *Cities in Flight. A Case of Conscience.*

Boucher, Anthony

Bradbury, Ray. *I Sing the Body Electric. The Martian Chronicles. The October Country. The Illustrated Man.*

Brin, David. *Startide Rising.*

Brown, Fredric. *Martians Go Home.*

Brunner, John. *Squares of the City. Stand on Zanzibar.*

Budrys, A. J. *Rogue Moon. Who?*

Bujold, Lois McMaster. *The Vor Game. Barrayar.*

Bulchev, Kirill. *Half a Life and Other Stories.*

Burgess, Anthony. *A Clockwork Orange. The Wanting Seed.*

Burroughs, William S. *Nova Express.*

Card, Orson Scott. *Ender's Game.*

Cherryh, C. J. *Downbelow Station.*

Clarke, Arthur C. *Rendezvous with Rama. Childhood's End.*

Clement, Hal. *Close to Critical. Needle. Mission of Gravity.*

Compton, D. G. *Synthajoy.*

Davidson, Avram. *Or All the Seas with Oysters.*

Delany, Samuel R. *Nova. Babel 17. Dhalgren. The Einstein Intersection.*

Del Rey, Lester. *Nerves.*

Dick, Philip K. *The Man Who Japed. The Man in the High Castle.*

Dickson, Gordon R. *Soldier Ask Not. Dorsai!*

Disch, Thomas M. *334.*

Ellison, Harlan. *I Have No Mouth and I Must Scream. The Beast Who Shouted Love at the Heart of the World. Ellison Wonderland.*

Farmer, Philip José. *To Your Scattered Bodies Go.*

Finney, Jack. *The Body Snatchers.*

Galouye, Daniel G. *Dark Universe.*

Gibson, William. *Neuromancer.*

Haldeman, Joe. *The Forever War.*

Harrison, Harry. *Bill, the Galactic Hero. Make Room! Make Room!*

Heinlein, Robert A. *Time for the Stars. Double Star. Glory Road. Starship Troopers. Stranger in a Strange Land. The Moon Is a Harsh Mistress.*

Herbert, Frank. *Dragon in the Sea. Dune.*

Keyes, Daniel. *Flowers for Algernon.*

Knight, Damon. *Hell's Pavement.*

Kornbluth, Cyril. *The Syndic.*

Kuttner, Henry. *Mutant. The Dark World. Earth's Last Citadel. Fury.*

Lafferty, R. A. *The Reefs of Earth. Past Master.*

Le Guin, Ursula K. *The Left Hand of Darkness. The Dispossessed.*

Leiber, Fritz. *The Wanderer. A Spectre Is Haunting Texas.*

Leinster, Murray

Lem, Stanislaw. *Mortal Engines. Solaris.*

Malzberg, Barry N. *Beyond Apollo.*

Matheson, Richard. *I Am Legend. The Shrinking Man.*

May, Julian. *The Many-Colored Land.*

McCaffrey, Anne. *Dragonflight. Restoree. The Ship Who Sang.*

McIntyre, Vonda N. *Dreamsnake.*

Miller, Walter M., Jr. *A Canticle for Leibowitz.*

Moorcock, Michael. *Behold the Man. The Cornelius Chronicles.*

Niven, Larry. *A Gift from Earth. Neutron Star. Ringworld. The Integral Trees.*

Pangborn, Edgar. *A Mirror for Observers.*

Panshin, Alexei. *Rite of Passage.* Anthony Villiers series.

Pohl, Frederik. *Man Plus. Gateway.*

Reynolds, Mack

Roberts, Keith. *Pavane.*

Robinson, Kim Stanley. *Red Mars. Green Mars.*

Russ, Joanna. *And Chaos Died.*

Shute, Nevil. *On the Beach.*

Silverberg, Robert. *A Time of Changes. The Masks of Time.*

Simak, Clifford D. *Way Station. City. Here Gather the Stars.*

Sladek, John. *Mechasm.*

Smith, Cordwainer. *You Will Never Be the Same. Space Lords.*

Smith, George O. *Highways in Hiding.*

Spinrad, Norman. *The Iron Dream.*

Stapledon, Olaf. *The Star Maker.*

Strugatsky, Arkady, and Boris Strugatsky. *Prisoners of Power. Roadside Picnic. Monday Begins on Saturday.*

Sturgeon, Theodore. *More Than Human. The Dreaming Jewels.*

Taine, John

Tenn, William. *Of Men and Monsters.*

Tiptree, James, Jr.

Vance, Jack. *The Dying Earth. Eyes of the Overworld.*

van Vogt, A. E. *The World of Null-A. Voyage of the Space Beagle.*

Vonnegut, Kurt, Jr. *Sirens of Titan. Slaughterhouse Five. Cat's Cradle.*

Wallace, Ian. *Deathstar Voyage.*

Weinbaum, Stanley G. *The Black Flame.*

Wilhelm, Kate. *Let the Fire Fall. Where Late the Sweet Birds Sang.*

Williamson, Jack. *The Humanoids.*

Willis, Connie. *Doomsday Book.*

Wolfe, Gene. *The Claw of the Conciliator. The Citadel of the Autarch.*

Wyndham, John. *The Midwich Cuckoos. Day of the Triffids. Rebirth.*

Zelazny, Roger. *Lord of Light. Isle of the Dead. And Call Me Conrad.*

Parody

Despite the serious tenor of most science fiction, there is a persistent stream of comedy and parody. Parody is the delight of the sophisticated reader, who will come across instances naturally. The reader should be familiar with common science fiction themes before reading parody.

Adams, Douglas. *The Hitchhiker's Guide to the Galaxy. The Restaurant at the End of the Universe. Life, the Universe and Everything. So Long, and Thanks for All the Fish.*

Aldiss, Brian. *The Eighty-Minute Hour: A Space Opera.*

Greenberg, Martin H., ed. *Foundations Friends.*

Harrison, Harry. *Planet Story*, illustrated by Jim Burns. *Bill, the Galactic Hero.*

Pratchett, Terry. *Strata.*

Pronzini, Bill, and Barry N. Malzberg. *Prose Bowl.*

Robinson, Spider. *Callahan's Crosstime Saloon.*

Sladek, John. *The Lunatics of Terra.*

Trout, Kilgore. *Venus on the Half-Shell.*
　　The author is Philip José Farmer. Kilgore Trout is a character invented by Kurt Vonnegut, Jr. Trout is a writer of science fiction and his works are discussed, with much delightful quotation, in Vonnegut's *God Bless You, Mr. Rosewater.* (Among the many organizations and fan groups involved in science fiction is to be found the "Friends of Kilgore Trout.")

Weiner, Ellis. *National Lampoon's Doon.*

Poetry

Verse is not ordinarily associated with science fiction (though it is readily associated with fantasy). The following books suggest that there ought to be more verse in this genre. (See David Brin's *Startide Rising*, in which the dolphins speak in haiku form.)

Kenin, Millea, ed. *Aliens & Lovers: An Anthology of Erotic Poetry with Fantasy and Science Fiction Themes.* Unique Graphics, 1983.

Lucie-Smith, Edward, ed. *Holding Your Eight Hands: An Anthology of Science Fiction Verse.* Doubleday, 1969.
By science fiction authors and others.

Anthologies

The best way to become acquainted with the characteristics of authors in the science fiction genre, and particularly with the work of new authors, is through anthologies. Both the theme anthologies and the critical and historical collections may have stories from all periods and often suffer from repetition of much-anthologized pieces. The short story is a very popular form in both science fiction and fantasy. Though the following listing of anthologies is long, it is by no means exhaustive.

Bear, Greg, ed. *New Legends.* Tor, 1995.

Best Science Fiction. Omni Books, 1992– .

Boucher, Anthony, ed. *A Treasury of Great Science Fiction.* Doubleday, 1959. 2 vols.

Boucher, Anthony, and J. Francis McComas, eds. *The Best from Fantasy and Science Fiction.* Little, Brown, 1952.

Bova, Ben, ed. *Forward in Time: A Science Fiction Story Collection.* Walker, 1973.

Bova, Ben, et al. *Future Quartet: Earth in the Year 2042, a Four-Part Invention.* Avon Books, 1994.

Bradbury, Ray, ed. *Timeless Stories for Today and Tomorrow.* Bantam, 1952.

Brown, Fredric, ed. *Science Fiction Carnival: Fun in Science Fiction.* Bantam, 1957.

Clareson, Thomas D., ed. *A Spectrum of Worlds.* Doubleday, 1972.

Datlow, Ellen. *Alien Sex: 19 Tales by Masters of Science Fiction and Dark Fantasy.* Dutton, 1990.

Datlow, Ellen, ed. *Omni Visions.* Omni Books, 1993.

de Camp, L. Sprague, and Catherine Cook de Camp, eds. *3000 Years of Fantasy and Science Fiction*. Foreword by Isaac Asimov. Lothrop, 1972.

Dozois, Gardner, ed. *Modern Classics of Science Fiction*. St. Martin's Press, 1992.

Ellison, Harlan, ed. *Again, Dangerous Visions*. Doubleday, 1972.

Ellison, Harlan, ed. *Dangerous Visions*. Doubleday, 1967.

Garnett, David, ed. *New Worlds 3*. Gallancz, 1993.
New Worlds 1 and *New Worlds 2* are also available.

Greeley, Andrew M., and Michael Cassuth, eds. *Sacred Visions*. Tor, 1991.

Harrison, Harry, ed. *The Year 2000*. Doubleday, 1970. *Galactic Dreams*. Tor. 1994. (Humor).

Hartwell, David G., ed. *Christmas Stars*. Tor, 1992.

Hartwell, David G., and Kathryn Cramer, eds. *The Ascent of Wonder: The Evolution of Hard SF*. Tor, 1994.

Hotel Andromeda. Ace Books, 1994.

Le Guin, Ursula K., and Brian Attebery, eds. *The Norton Book of Science Fiction: North American Science Fiction, 1960–1990*. W. W. Norton, 1993.

Manson, Cynthia, and Charles Ardai, eds. *Aliens and UFOs: Extraterrestrial Tales from Asimov's Science Fiction and Fact*. Smithmark, 1993.

Pohl, Frederik, ed. *Galaxy: Thirty Years of Innovative Science Fiction*. Playboy, 1980.

Pohl, Frederik, ed. *Yesterday's Tomorrows: Favorite Stories from Forty Years as a Science Fiction Editor*. Berkley Books, 1982.

Pohl, Frederik, Martin Harry Greenberg, and Joseph Olander, eds. *The Great Science Fiction Series*. Harper, 1980.
Twenty-one stories, each introduced by the author. Series following a character or theme are among the most popular types of science fiction.

Preiss, Byron, and Robert Silverberg, eds. *The Ultimate Dinosaur: Past, Present, Future*. Bantam Books, 1992.

Robinson, Kim Stanley, ed. *Future Primitive: The New Ecotopias*. Tor, 1994.

Rucker, Rudy, ed. *Mathanauts*. Arbor House, 1987. (Mathematics).

Rusch, Kristine Kathryn, ed. *The Best of Pulphouse: The Hardback Magazine*. St. Martin's Press, 1991.

Rusch, Kristine Kathryn, and Edward L. Ferman, eds. *The Best from Fantasy & Science Fiction: A 45th Anniversary Anthology*. St. Martin's Press, 1994.

Schmidt, Stanley, ed. *Analog: Writers' Choice* (vol. 5). Dial, 1983.

The Science Fiction Hall of Fame. Doubleday, 1970–73. 3 vols.
Selections chosen by the Science Fiction Writers of America as the best in the genre.

Shippey, Tom, ed. *The Oxford Book of Science Fiction Stories.* Oxford University Press, 1992.

Smith, David Alexander, ed. *Future Boston: The History of a City, 1990–2100.* T. Doherty, 1994.

Spinrad, Norman, ed. *Modern Science Fiction.* Anchor, 1974.
The 21 stories—grouped as "The Golden Age," "The Postwar Awakening," and "The Full Flowering"—are preceded by an introduction, and 10 briefer critical essays are interspersed among the stories. An author in the genre and a critic who says baldly, "Please understand, this first-generation science fiction was godawful stuff," commands one's respect. The anthology and the criticism are highly recommended as an introduction to the genre.

Wynorski, Jim, ed. *They Came from Outer Space: 12 Classic Science Fiction Tales That Became Major Motion Pictures.* With a special introduction by Ray Bradbury. Doubleday, 1980.

THEME ANTHOLOGIES

These anthologies provide an intriguing introduction to the imaginative variety of attitudes on most of the themes explored and to the authors in the genre. Themes are noted in the following list, unless the title is self-explanatory.

Aldiss, Brian, ed. *Galactic Empires.* St. Martin's, 1977. 2 vols.

Aldiss, Brian, ed. *Perilous Planets: An Anthology of Way-Back-When Futures.* London: Weidenfeld, 1978. (Space voyage).

Aldiss, Brian, ed. *Space Opera: An Anthology of Way-Back-When Futures.* London: Weidenfeld, 1974.

Anderson, Susan Janice, and Vonda N. McIntyre, eds. *Aurora: Beyond Equality.* Fawcett, 1976. (Women).

Asimov, Isaac, ed. *Tomorrow's Children.* Doubleday, 1966.

Asimov, Isaac, et al., eds. *Election Day 2084: A Science Fiction Anthology on the Politics of the Future.* Prometheus, 1984.

Asimov, Isaac, et al., eds. *Machines That Think: The Best Science Fiction Stories About Robots and Computers.* Holt, 1983. Republished as *War with the Robots.* Wings, 1992.

Asimov, Isaac, et al., eds. *The Science Fiction Weight-Loss Book.* Crown, 1983. (Overeating, overweight, dieting).

Asimov, Isaac, et al., eds. *The Seven Deadly Sins of Science Fiction*. Crest, 1980.

Asimov, Isaac, et al., eds. *Starships*. Fawcett/Crest, 1983.

Bryant, Edward, ed. *Among the Dead, and Other Events Leading Up to the Apocalypse*. Macmillan, 1973.

Carr, Terry, ed. *Dream's Edge: Science Fiction Stories About the Future of Planet Earth*. Sierra Club, 1980.

Carr, Terry, ed. *The Fellowship of the Stars*. Simon & Schuster, 1975. (Alien beings).

Clarke, Arthur C., ed. *Time Probe: The Science of Science Fiction*. Delacorte, 1966.

Conklin, Groff, ed. *Invaders of Earth*. Grossett, 1962. (Alien beings).

Conklin, Groff, ed. *Science Fiction Thinking Machines*. Vanguard, 1954.

Dann, Jack, ed. *Wandering Stars: An Anthology of Jewish Fantasy and Science Fiction*. Harper, 1974. (Religion).

Derleth, August, ed. *Beachheads in Space*. Pellagrini, 1952. (War).

Disch, Thomas M., ed. *Bad Moon Rising*. Harper, 1973. (Politics).

Disch, Thomas M., ed. *The Ruins of Earth: An Anthology of Stories of the Immediate Future*. Putnam, 1971. (Ecological disaster).

Dozois, Gardner, ed. *A Day in the Life: A Science Fiction Anthology*. Harper, 1972. (Future life).

Elliot, Jeffrey, ed. *Kindred Spirits: An Anthology of Gay and Lesbian Science Fiction Stories*. Alyson, 1984.

Elwood, Roger, ed. *And Walk Now Gently Through the Fire and Other Science Fiction Stories*. Chilton, 1972. (Biology and religion).

Elwood, Roger, ed. *Chronicles of a Comer and Other Religious Science Fiction Stories*. John Knox, 1974.

Elwood, Roger, ed. *Future City*. Trident, 1973.

Elwood, Roger, ed. *Saving Worlds*. Doubleday, 1973. (Ecology).

Elwood, Roger, ed. *Signs and Wonders*. Revell, 1972. (Religion).

Ferman, Edward L., and Barry N. Malzberg, eds. *Arena: Sports SF*. Doubleday, 1976.

FitzGerald, Gregory, ed. *Neutron Stars*. Fawcett, 1977. (Decay of our supernovaed culture).

Goldin, Stephen, ed. *The Alien Condition*. Ballantine, 1973. (Alien beings).

Ghidelia, Vic, ed. *The Devil's Generation*. Lancer, 1973. (Child's mind).

Greenberg, Martin Harry, and Joseph D. Olander, eds. *Tomorrow, Inc.: Science Fiction Stories About Big Business*. Taplinger, 1976.

Greenberg, Martin Harry, and Patricia S. Warrick, eds. *Political Science Fiction: An Introductory Reader*. Prentice-Hall, 1974.

Haldeman, Joe, ed. *Cosmic Laughter: Science Fiction for the Fun of It*. Holt, 1974.

Haldeman, Joe, ed. *Study War No More: A Selection of Alternatives*. St. Martin's, 1977.

Hill, Douglas, ed. *The Shape of Sex to Come*. London: Pan, 1978.

Margulies, Leo, and Oscar J. Friend, eds. *From Off This World*. Merlin, 1949. (Alien beings).

Mason, Carol, Martin H. Greenberg, and Patricia Warrick, eds. *Anthropology Through Science Fiction*. St. Martin's, 1974.

McCarthy, Shawna, ed. *Isaac Asimov's Space of Her Own*. Dial, 1983. (Stories by women).

Miller, Walter M., and Martin H. Greenberg, eds. *Beyond Armageddon: Twenty-One Sermons to the Dead*. Fine, 1985.

Mohs, Mayo, ed. *Other Worlds, Other Gods*. Doubleday, 1971. (Religion).

Monteleone, Thomas F., ed. *The Arts and Beyond: Visions of Man's Aesthetic Future*. Doubleday, 1977.

Moskowitz, Sam, ed. *The Coming of the Robots*. Collier, 1963.

Moskowitz, Sam, ed. *When Women Rule*. Walker, 1972.

Pohl, Frederik, and Carol Pohl, eds. *Jupiter*. Ballantine, 1973.

Polsby, Nelson W., ed. *What If—? A Selection of Social Science Fiction*. Lewis Publishing, 1982.

Preiss, Byron, ed. *The Planets*. Bantam, 1985.

Pronzini, Bill, and Barry N. Malzberg, eds. *Bug-Eyed Monsters*. Harvest/ Harcourt Brace Jovanovich, 1980.

Ryan, Alan, ed. *Perpetual Light*. Warner Books, 1982. (Religion).

Sargent, Pamela, ed. *Bio-Futures: Science Fiction Stories About Biological Metamorphosis*. Vintage, 1975.

Sauer, Bob, ed. *Voyages: Scenarios for a Ship Called Earth*. Ballantine, 1971.

Schmidt, Stanley, ed. *Aliens from Analog*. Dial, 1983.

Schmidt, Stanley, ed. *Analog's Children of the Future*. Dial, 1982.

Schmidt, Stanley, ed. *Analog's Lighter Side*. Dial, 1983.

Schmidt, Stanley, ed. *War and Peace: Possible Futures from Analog*. Dial, 1983.

Scortia, Thomas, ed. *Strange Bedfellows: Sex and Science Fiction*. Random, 1973.

Scortia, Thomas, and George Zebrowski, eds. *Human Machines: An Anthology of Stories About Cyborgs*. Vintage, 1975.

Silverberg, Robert, ed. *Deep Space*. Nelson, 1973. (Space travel).

Silverberg, Robert, ed. *Galactic Dreamers: Science Fiction as Visionary Literature*. Random, 1977.

Silverberg, Robert, ed. *The Infinite Web*. Dial, 1977. (Ecology).

Silverberg, Robert, ed. *Mind to Mind*. Dell, 1974. (Telepathy).

Silverberg, Robert, ed. *The Science Fiction Bestiary*. Dell, 1974.

Silverberg, Robert, ed. *Trips in Time*. Nelson, 1977.

Stone, Idella, ed. *14 Great Tales of ESP*. Fawcett, 1969.

Stover, Leon E., and Harry Harrison, eds. *Apeman, Spaceman*. Doubleday, 1968. (Anthropology).

Warrick, Patricia, Martin Harry Greenberg, and Joseph Olander, eds. *Science Fiction: Contemporary Mythology*. The SFWA-SFRA Anthology. Harper, 1978.
Ten sections, each with an introductory essay and a critical bibliography: technology and progress; journeys into the unknown; dimensions of time and space; alien; machine and robot; androids, cyborgs; the city; utopias and dystopias; apocalypse.

Wollheim, Donald, ed. *The End of the World*. Ace, 1956.

Another access to reading by theme may be found through the "Checklist of Themes" in *The Science Fiction Encyclopedia*, edited by Peter Nicholls (see "Encyclopedias," p. 247, for a fuller description). For each theme, the encyclopedia article provides definition, history, and criticism of the treatment of the theme in general literature as well as in science fiction, including the key works (both short stories and novels). Most of the themes analyzed in this chapter are listed, and the following is a short selection to indicate the diverse approaches available to the reader: black holes, clones, communications, cosmology, cryonics, discovery and invention, genetic engineering, mathematics, metaphysics, mutants, politics, psychology, reincarnation, terraforming, time paradoxes, war, weather control.

The Visual Encyclopedia of Science Fiction, edited by Brian Ash (see "Encyclopedias"), is arranged under themes and has a similar access to both novels and short stories. There are 19 major themes, with further subdivision under each theme (e.g., under "Warfare and Weaponry" is a division on "War with the Aliens"): spacecraft and star drives; exploration and colonies; biologies and environments; warfare and weaponry; galactic empires; future and alternative histories; utopias and nightmares; cataclysms and dooms; lost and parallel worlds; time and nth dimensions; technologies and artifacts; cities and cultures; robots and androids; computers and cybernetics; mutants and symbiotes; telepathy, psionics, and ESP; sex and taboos; religion and myths; inner space.

ANTHOLOGY SERIES

Several works among the annual and numbered series anthologies present only original short stories; the others reprint from the magazines for the genre. Some of the following series have ceased publication, but their cumulated numbers form an important anthology. "Best" is not to be taken literally—merely a selection from the year's output.

Andromeda. 1976– .

The Astounding Analog Reader. 1972–73. 2 vols.

The Best from Fantasy and Science Fiction (24th series, 1982).

The Best from Galaxy. 1972–1974. 2 vols.

The Best Science Fiction of the Year. 1967– (vol. 16, 1987).
   Has also been published under the titles *The Best Science Fiction and Fantasy of the Year* and *Terry Carr's Best Science Fiction and Fantasy of the Year.*

The Best SF 1–7, edited by Edmund Crispin. 1955–1977.

Chrysalis. (#10, 1983).

Full Spectrum (#4 in 1993) edited by Lou Aronica, Amy Stout, and Betsy Mitchell.

The Hugo Winners. 1962– (vol. 5, 1986).

Infinity. #1–5, 1970–1972.

Isaac Asimov Presents the Great SF Stories.

Nebula Award Stories. 1965– (#24, 1989).

New Dimensions. 1971– (#10, 1980).

New Writing in Science Fiction. 1964– .

Nova. (#3, 1973).

Omni Best Science Fiction

Orbit. 1965– (#21, 1980).

Quark. #1–4, 1970–1971.

Spectrum. #1–5, 1962–1967.

Star Science Fiction Stories, edited by Frederik Pohl. #1–6, 1953–1959.

Terra SF: The Year's Best European SF. 1981– .

Universe, edited by Terry Carr. #1–17, 1971–1987.

Universe, edited by Robert Silverberg and Karen Haber. (#1, 1990).

The Year's Best Science Fiction.

The Year's Best SF, edited by Judith Merril. #1–12, 1956–1968.

Bibliographies

Most of the following books include authors who write both science fiction and fantasy. Good bio-bibliographical listings are to be found in *The Science Fiction Encyclopedia* (see "Encyclopedias"). The following annotations indicate whether the books include any considerable historical and critical material as well.

Ash, Brian. *Who's Who in Science Fiction*. Taplinger, 1976.
Brief bio-bibliographical listings with critical evaluations of characteristics of a science fiction writer. Prefaced with a "Chronological Guide: 100 Leading Writers and Editors in Their Main Periods of Production," from 1800 to the 1970s.

Barron, Neil, ed. *Anatomy of Wonder: A Critical Guide to Science Fiction*. Third Edition. Bowker, 1987.
Critically annotated author listings are grouped by period or type with introductory essays: "The Emergence of Science Fiction: The Beginnings to the 1920s," by Thomas Clareson; "Science Fiction between the Wars: 1918–1938," by Brian Stableford; "The Modern Period: 1938–1980," by Joe De Bolt and John R. Pfeiffer; "Children's Science Fiction," by Francis J. Molson; "Foreign Language Science Fiction," by several authors, covering German, French, Russian, Italian, Japanese and Chinese. "Research Aids" includes chapters on indexes, bibliographies, history and criticism, author studies, film and television, illustration, classroom aids, magazines, library collections, and a core collection checklist.

Bleiler, Everett Franklin. *The Checklist of Fantastic Literature: A Bibliography of Fantasy, Weird and Science Fiction Books Published in the English Language*. Shasta, 1948.

Burgess, Michael. *Reference Guide to Science Fiction, Fantasy, and Horror*. Libraries Unlimited, 1992.

Clarke, Ignatius Frederick, comp. *The Tale of the Future from the Beginning to the Present Day: An Annotated Bibliography*. Second Edition. London: Library Association, 1972.

Currey, L. W. *Science Fiction and Fantasy Authors: A Bibliography of First Printings of Their Fiction and Selected Non-Fiction*. G. K. Hall, 1980.
Two hundred fifteen authors.

Fletcher, Marilyn P., comp. and ed. *Reader's Guide to Twentieth-Century Science Fiction*. American Library Association, 1989.
Includes biographical sketches and plot summaries.

Justice, Keith L. *Science Fiction, Fantasy and Horror Reference: An Annotated Bibliography of Works About Literature and Film*. McFarland, 1989.

Newman, John, and Michael Unsworth, comps. *Future War Novels: An Annotated Bibliography of Works in English Published Since 1945*. Oryx Press, 1985.
Plot summary and criticism of 191 novels.

Pringle, David. *Science Fiction: The 100 Best Novels: An English-Language Selection*, 1949–1984. London: Xanadu, 1985.
The titles are presented chronologically, each with full, and very readable, story analysis and critical evaluation. Michael Moorcock's foreword suggests that while anyone might quarrel with some of the selections, most readers would agree on at least 50, "an excellent percentage."

Pringle, David. *The Ultimate Guide to Science Fiction*. Pharos Books/St. Martin's Press, 1990.
Science fiction enthusiasts will enjoy paging through Pringle's work. It provides brief synopses of all the major (and some of the minor) science fiction novels and short stories written in English since the term *science fiction* was coined (approximately 1929). In the introduction, Pringle pokes fun at science fiction clichés and outlines the beginnings of science fiction writing. Pringle explains the structure of every entry and evaluates each work. Where appropriate, he includes the names of sequels, related works, film versions, and author pen names. Occasionally he also inserts quotations from other science fiction critics. The A-to-Z list contains nearly 3,000 entries. Works are arranged alphabetically by title. To enable readers to quickly find an entry, Pringle uses two types of cross-references: variant titles for the same book and parent novels of series or related works.

A Reader's Guide to Science Fiction. By Baird Searles, Martin Last, Beth Meacham, and Michael Franklin. With a foreword by Samuel R. Delany. Avon, 1979.
The authors run the Science Fiction Shop, New York City. Lists 200 authors with biocritical annotation. Has a guide to major science fiction series. Useful listing of a suggested basic library of 50 volumes.

Reginald, R. *Science Fiction and Fantasy Literature: A Checklist, 1700–1974*. Gale, 1979.

Reginald, Robert. *Science Fiction and Fantasy Literature, 1975–1991: A Bibliography of Science Fiction, Fantasy, and Horror Fiction Books and Nonfiction Monographs*. Gale, 1993.
Cites approximately 22,000 monographs. Lists series titles, awards and other topics of interest to readers.

Smith, Curtis C., ed. *Twentieth-Century Science Fiction Writers*. London: Macmillan, 1981.

This volume contains bibliographies of 532 British and American writers. An appendix lists 35 foreign language writers and five major fantasy writers. For each author there are brief biographical identification, a signed and critical essay, and the bibliography, including nonscience fiction works separately grouped. A personal statement was solicited by the editor and is present for some authors. There are an extensive prefatory reading list and a bibliography of studies of individual authors.

Watson, Noelle, and Paul E. Schellinger, eds. *Twentieth-Century Science Fiction Writers*. 3d ed. St. James Press, 1991.

Encyclopedias

The following encyclopedias contain considerable bibliographical, historical, and critical material.

Ash, Brian, ed. *The Visual Encyclopedia of Science Fiction*. London: Coppleston; New York: Harmony Books, 1977.

Arranged in 19 "Thematics," each section written by a science fiction author known for works in the theme, e.g., Isaac Asimov on robots and androids. Each theme is further subdivided by topics. In addition to works internally discussed, each section has a bibliography. Prefaced by a chronology (1805–1976) of important events and publications. Sections on fandom, science fiction art, cinema and television, magazines, anthologies, and the like. Lavishly illustrated in color and black-and-white.

Gunn, James, ed. *The New Encyclopedia of Science Fiction*. Viking-Penguin, 1988.

Summaries, criticism, bibliographical, and historical information on people, books, topics, trends, and films in science fiction.

Holdstock, Robert, ed. *Encyclopedia of Science Fiction*. London: Octopus Books, 1978.

Jakubowski, Maxim, and Malcolm Edwards. *The SF Book of Lists*. Berkley, 1983.

Idiosyncratic in arrangement and content and, sadly, without index, but amusing, eccentric, and amazingly informative for the interested browser.

Nicholls, Peter, ed. *The Science Fiction Encyclopedia*. Dolphin Books, Doubleday, 1979.

Alphabetical arrangement of themes, biography, and other topics, with many cross-references. Historical and critical with extensive bibliographical material. Biographical listings for many little-known authors. Many of the articles are extended critical essays. Black-and-white illustrations.

Tuck, Donald Henry. *The Encyclopedia of Science Fiction and Fantasy Through 1968*. Advent, 1974.
First two volumes are bio-bibliographical and international in scope. The third is a miscellany.

Tymn, Marshall B., ed. *The Science Fiction Reference Book*. Starmont House, 1981.

Dictionaries

Rogow, Roberta. *FutureSpeak: A Fan's Guide to the Language of Science Fiction*. Paragon House, 1991.
An overall survey of the world of science fiction from books to movies to fandom.

History

Science fiction history may start either in classical literature or in the nineteenth century, depending on an author's definition of the genre. Many of the following books are critical to the point of being controversial. They are written by authors of the genre and by fans, both lay and academic. In addition to the following books, the reader will find considerable historical material in encyclopedias (see p. 247) and in critical works (see p. 249).

Aldiss, Brian W. *Billion Year Spree: The True History of Science Fiction*. Doubleday, 1973.
Begins with Mary Shelley's *Frankenstein*. Bibliography of works consulted.

Appel, Benjamin. *The Fantastic Mirror: Science Fiction across the Ages*. Pantheon, 1969.
From early man's wonder stories and fantastic voyages to the present, with the twentieth century dismissed briefly in the last two chapters. More lyrical than factual.

Del Rey, Lester. *The World of Science Fiction, 1926–1976: The History of a Sub-Culture*. Garland, 1979.
In terms of the magazines that published genre.

Gerber, Richard. *Utopian Fantasy: A Study of English Utopian Fiction Since the End of the Nineteenth Century*. Second Edition. McGraw-Hill, 1973.
Unchanged from 1955 edition except that "Appendix: An Annotated List of English Utopian Fantasies" now covers 1901–1971.

Green, Roger Lancelyn. *Into Other Worlds: Space-Flight in Fiction from Lucian to Lewis*. Abelard-Schumann, 1958.

Gunn, James. *Alternate Worlds: The Illustrated History of Science Fiction*. Prentice-Hall, 1975.
Covers Greek times to the present, lavishly illustrated in color and black-and-white.

Kyle, David. *A Pictorial History of Science Fiction*. London: Hamlyn, 1976.
Covers Greek times to the present, lavishly illustrated in color and black-and-white.

Nicholson, Marjorie Hope. *Voyages to the Moon*. Macmillan, 1948.
Fictional voyages through the eighteenth century, with an "Epilogue" on the nineteenth and twentieth centuries. Delightful text and illustrations.

Rottensteiner, Franz. *The Science Fiction Book: An Illustrated History*. London: Thames and Hudson, 1975.
Topically organized (e.g., "Why there is no sex in science fiction") and imaginatively illustrated in color and black-and-white. Important for the survey of science fiction in European countries: Soviet Union, France, Japan, Italy, Spain, Rumania, Germany. Appended chronology: c.160 (Lucian) to 1974.

Scholes, Robert, and Eric S. Rabkin. *Science Fiction: History, Science, Vision*. Oxford, 1977.
The first one-third of the book is history, the latter parts are criticism.

Criticism

The quantity of critical exposition on science fiction is daunting but dated. The quality varies from the fandom popular to the academic obscurant, with, fortunately, some lively and imaginative discussion in between, both by authors of the genre and fans in the academic world. The following is merely a sampling to show the wealth of commentary available.

Aldiss, Brian W., ed. *Hell's Cartographers: Some Personal Histories of Science Fiction Writers*. London: Weidenfeld, 1975.
Essays by Robert Silverberg, Alfred Bester, Harry Harrison, Damon Knight, Frederik Pohl, Brian Aldiss.

Allen, L. David. *Science Fiction: An Introduction*. Cliff Notes, 1973.
The teaching of science fiction, junior high school through college, is flourishing. The two guides define the genre and, together, present criticism of an anthology and 23 major works of fiction.

Amis, Kingsley. *New Maps of Hell: A Survey of Science Fiction*. Harcourt, 1960.
Distinguishes science fiction as social criticism from science fiction as adventure.

Ash, Brian. *Faces of the Future: The Lessons of Science Fiction*. Taplinger, 1975.

Asimov, Isaac. *Asimov on Science Fiction*. Doubleday, 1981.
Essays from Asimov's prolific publications grouped by topics, such as the writing of science fiction, history, writers, fans, predictions and reviews. Forms an appealing introduction to the genre.

Bleiler, Everett F., ed. *Science Fiction Writers: Critical Studies of the Major Authors from the Early Nineteenth Century to the Present Day*. Scribner's, 1982.
Seventy-six authors analyzed in essays by various hands.

Bloom, Harold, ed. *Classic Science Fiction Writers*. Chelsea House, 1995.
History, criticism, biography, bibliography.

Bretnor, Reginald, ed. *Science Fiction Today and Tomorrow: A Discussive Symposium*. Harper, 1974.
Fifteen essays by authors in the genre defining and criticizing the genre.

Carter, Paul A. *The Creation of Tomorrow: Fifty Years of Magazine Science Fiction*. Kent State University Press, 1977.

Clareson, Thomas D., ed. *Many Futures, Many Worlds: Theme and Form in Science Fiction*. Kent State University Press, 1977.

Clareson, Thomas D., ed. *SF: The Other Side of Realism*. Popular Press, 1971.

Clareson, Thomas D., ed. *Voices for the Future: Essays on Major Science Fiction Writers*. Popular Press, 1976– .
All three collections above contain essays on diverse topics by genre authors and academic fans. *Voices for the Future* (a continuing series) expanded in volume 3 (1981) to include essays on fantasy authors.

Delany, Samuel R. *The Jewel-Hinged Jaw: Notes on the Language of Science Fiction*. Dragon Press, 1977.

Fredericks, Casey. *The Future of Eternity: Mythologies of Science Fiction and Fantasy*. Indiana University Press, 1982.
Explication of the use of the world's great myths.

Kitterer, David. *New Worlds for Old: The Apocalyptic Imagination, Science Fiction, and American Literature*. Archon Press/Doubleday, 1974.
Critical and historical survey from Poe to Vonnegut, emphasizing the American nature of science fiction.

Knight, Damon, ed. *Turning Points: Essays in the Art of Science Fiction*. Harper, 1977.
Twenty-three essays by authors in the genre.

Lefanu, Sarah. *Feminism and Science Fiction*. Indiana University Press, 1988.

Lundwell, Sam J. *Science Fiction: What It's All About*. Ace, 1971.
Translated from the Swedish.

Moskowitz, Sam. *Strange Horizons: The Spectrum of Science Fiction*. Scribner's, 1976.
Includes chapters on religion, anti-Semitism, civil rights, women's liberation, birth control, psychiatry, crime, teenagers, war, unexplained phenomena, and art.

Nicholls, Peter, ed. *Science Fiction at Large: A Collection of Essays by Various Hands About the Interface Between Science Fiction and Reality*. London: Gollancz, 1976.
Eleven lectures presented at an institute held in London.

Parrinder, Patrick. *Science Fiction: Its Criticism and Teaching*. London: Methuen, 1980.
This British textbook is a work of critical definition, introducing and analyzing the genre.

Riley, Dick, ed. *Critical Encounters: Writers and Themes in Science Fiction*. Ungar, 1978.
Nine essays.

Rose, Mark, ed. *Science Fiction: A Collection of Critical Essays*. Prentice-Hall, 1976.
Eleven essays defining the genre.

Staicar, Tom, ed. *The Feminine Eye: Science Fiction and the Women Who Write It*. Ungar, 1982.

Suvin, Darko. *Metamorphoses of Science Fiction: On the Poetics and History of a Literary Genre*. Yale University Press, 1979.

Williamson, Jack, ed. *Teaching Science Fiction: Education for Tomorrow*. London: Chiswick Press, 1980.
Anthology of essays by science fiction authors and teachers at several school levels.

Wolfe, Gary K. *The Known and the Unknown: The Iconography of Science Fiction*. Kent State University Press, 1979.
The themes of science fiction and the images relating to them.

Wolfe, Gary K., ed. *Science Fiction Dialogues*. Introduction by James Gunn. Academy Chicago, 1983.
Seventeen essays.

Wollheim, Donald A. *The Universe Makers: Science Fiction Today*. Harper, 1971.
Idiosyncratic, imaginative, and amusing: by a science fiction editor and a fervent fan.

Writer's Manuals

The following are meant to instruct writers in their craft but are also illuminating for the reader of the science fiction genre.

Bretnor, Reginald, ed. *The Craft of Science Fiction: A Symposium on Writing Science Fiction and Science Fantasy.* Harper, 1976.
Essays by 15 preeminent authors of the genre.

Card, Orson Scott. *How to Write Science Fiction and Fantasy.* Writer's Digest Books, 1990.

Grant, C. L., ed. *Writing and Selling Science Fiction.* By the Science Fiction Writers of America. Writer's Digest, 1976.
Ten essays by members of SFWA.

Intersections: The Elements of Fiction in Science Fiction. By Thomas L. Wymer, Alice Calderonello, Lowell P. Leland, Sara Jayne Steen, and R. Michael Evers. Popular Press, 1978.
Includes chapters on plot, character, setting, point of view, language, tone, theme and value, and symbol and myth.

Ochoa, George, and Jeffrey Osier. *The Writer's Guide to Creating a Science Fiction Universe.* Writer's Digest Books, 1993.

Spinrad, Norman. *Staying Alive: A Writer's Guide.* Donning, 1983.

Writing Science Fiction and Fantasy. By the editors of *Analog* and *Isaac Asimov's Science Fiction Magazine.* St. Martin's Press, 1991.

Poetry—Bibliographies

Green, Scott E. *Contemporary Science Fiction, Fantasy, and Horror Poetry.* Greenwood, 1989.
Lists magazines and presses publishing poetry in these genres. Provides biographical directory of poets.

Magazines

Of the hundreds of science fiction and fantasy magazines started since the 1920s, few have survived. The multitude of original paperback anthologies possibly contributed to their demise. However, a few magazines are still successful, being an important showcase for new authors. Most contain reviews, critical articles, and scientific explication. (For a full history of the magazines, see "Encyclopedias," p. 247.) The following magazines usually include fantasy; they also provide reviews and, often, columns or articles on science.

Amazing Stories. 1926– .

Analog. (*Astounding Science Fiction*). 1930– .

Argosy Science Fiction. 1977– .

Galileo. 1977– .

Isaac Asimov's Science Fiction Magazine. 1977– .

Magazine of Fantasy and Science Fiction. 1949– .

Omni. 1978– .

Critical Journals

There are a multitude of fanzines of varying quality—and uncertain continuance—containing news, articles, and reviews. The following are for general readership.

Locus. 1968– .

Riverside Quarterly. 1964– .

Science Fiction Review. 1978– .

Starship: The Magazine About SF (formerly *Algol*). 1963– .

Two journals resulting from the increasing interest of academics in science fiction are strong in articles on history and criticism:

Extrapolation: Journal of the MLA Seminar on Science Fiction. 1959– . Modern Language Association, U.S.

Foundation: The Review of Science Fiction. 1972– . British.

Reviews

Most of the magazines and fanzines of science fiction contain reviews. There are, however, two outstanding sources of reviews:

Locus. 1968.

Science Fiction Chronicle. 1979.

In addition to extensive reviews of varying length, they list just about everything published in science fiction and fantasy. They are also good sources for up-to-date information on awards.

Associations and Conventions

ASSOCIATIONS

Science Fiction Writers of America
The association was founded in 1965. It sponsors the annual "Nebula" awards for several categories of science fiction writing. It has a motto: The Future Isn't What It Used to Be.

Science Fiction Research Association
Academic and research orientation but open to all.

CONVENTIONS

Fans and writers form many associations and hold innumerable conventions, usually combining science fiction and fantasy, and often adding horror and the supernatural. *The International Science Fiction Yearbook 1979* provides a long list of both types. "Con" is usually part of the conference name.

World Science Fiction Convention ("WorldCon").
The first, 1939; the fifty-third was held in Glasgo, Scotland in 1995.

World Science Fiction Writers' Conference.
The first, 1976; held annually.

(William Marshall writes a series of detective novels featuring Detective Chief Inspector Harry Feiffer and the police of the Yellowthread Street station in Hong Kong. In *Sci Fi: A Yellowthread Street Mystery* [London: Hamish Hamilton, 1981], the city has been taken over by the All-Asia Science Fiction and Horror Movie Congress: The streets and jails are full of fans in costume and The Spaceman is on a murder spree. Richard Purtill's mystery novel *Murdercon* presents a very critical and lively picture of a science fiction convention in San Diego, California.)

Awards

Awards are generally reported in the various science fiction magazines as soon as possible after the results are announced. For a comprehensive listing of awards, consult *Reginald's Science Fiction and Fantasy Awards: A Comprehensive Guide to the Awards and Their Winners* by Daryl F. Mallett and Robert Reginald (Borgo, 1991).
The following are the best-known major awards for science fiction:

Hugo
Awarded at World Science Fiction Conventions. Named after Hugo Gernsback, it is voted on by members of the annual WorldCon; in other words, the winner is selected by readers of science fiction.

Nebula
> Awarded by the Science Fiction Writers of America, the winners are selected by a vote of the members of the organization. A prerequisite of membership is the publication of a work of science fiction, fantasy, or horror by the candidate. This prestigious award is a writer's award.

Locus
> Resulting from a poll by the fanzine *Locus*.

Lists of award-winning titles can be found in several of the previously listed bibliographies (see p. 245), encyclopedias (see p. 247), and histories (see p. 248).

Science Fiction Book Clubs

There are two major clubs, one in the United States and one in Britain. The British club reprints or distributes the publisher's hardcover edition. The U.S. club, owned by Doubleday, publishes hardcover club editions of both hardcover and paperback originals and also original omnibus editions. The clubs issue an extensive number of titles and are an important source of hardcover editions for libraries. For other book clubs in the United States, England, and Europe, see *The International Science Fiction Yearbook 1979*.

Publishers

Isaac Asimov, at the Science Fiction Writers of America annual banquet in 1973, said that science fiction is "the only thriving form of fiction in America today." The international list of publishers in *The International Science Fiction Yearbook 1979* is extensive. For years, science fiction was published most extensively in paperback, with a few of the "big" authors and major anthologies coming out in hardcover. As the acceptance (and commercial success) of science fiction has grown, hardcover publication has increased. The advantage to publishing in hardcover is that the books have a better chance of being reviewed and a better chance of reaching a mainstream audience. Science fiction fans really do seem to like the paperback versions better. It is not uncommon on the Internet to read correspondence from a reader asking if a specific title is so essential to read immediately that it should be purchased in hardcover; the reader will usually wait for the paperback edition. Science fiction readers have also been know to donate hardcover copies of a title when the paperback is released because they can then purchase the size that keeps their collection consistent!

Anthologies appear widely in both forms. Critical works, which used to be issued largely in hardcover, are now appearing regularly in both formats. Illustrated science fiction novels (as well as fantasy) are published in both formats but, notably, in greater numbers in paperback originals. Some originally unillustrated hardcover novels are illustrated for their paperback reprintings.

The following publishers issue science fiction, most issuing both originals and reprints. Special series are noted. The list is selective, as many publishers issue an occasional science fiction title.

Arbor House

Arkham House

AvoNova (Morrow)

Baen Books

Bantam/Doubleday/Dell

Bluejay Books
Now defunct, they did, however, issue some great titles that have retained popularity with fans.

DAW

Del Rey/Ballantine

Donald M. Grant

Dover
Excellent quality trade paperback for both science fiction and fantasy, specializes in reprinting the classics.

Gollancz (London)

Harcourt Brace

HarperCollins (UK)

Incunabula Press

New American Library

Old Earths Press

Penguin USA

Popular Library/Questar

Pulphouse

Putnam/Berkley/Ace

ROC

Signet Fantasy and Science Fiction

Simon and Schuster/Pocket

Spectra (Bantam)

St. Martin's

Tor Books
 The publisher most often selected by readers of *Locus* as the best.

Underwood-Miller

Walker

Warner/Questar

Zebra Pinnacle

D's Science Fiction Picks

Bujold, Lois McMaster. *Barrayar*. Baen, 1991.

Herbert, Frank. *Dune*. Chilton Books, 1965 (reprinted by Berkley in 1983 and by Putnam in 1984).

Stephenson, Neal. *Snow Crash*. Bantam, 1992.

Tepper, Sheri S. *Raising the Stones*. Doubleday, 1990.

Willis, Connie. *Doomsday Book*. Bantam, 1992.

7 Fantasy

> [D]ifficult truths can sometimes only be told through the medium of fantasy.
>
> —Lisa Goldstein

> A fiction evoking wonder and containing a substantial and irreducible element of supernatural or impossible worlds, beings or objects with which the reader or the characters within the story become on at least partly familiar terms.
>
> —C. N. Manlove
> *Modern Fantasy* (1975)

> "So knights are mythical!" said the younger and less experienced dragons. "We always thought so."
>
> —J. R. R. Tolkien
> *Farmer Giles of Ham* (1976)

Modern fantasy is inextricably entangled with science fiction because of its publishing history; most of the pulp magazines and anthologies feature both. Also, many of the authors write in both fields or use elements of both in one or the other forms. A very simple distinction can be made: science fiction deals with the possible (though not necessarily probable), being based, however tenuously, on scientific (hard or soft) knowledge; fantasy deals with the impossible, being based on magic or the supernatural. To put it another way, science fiction follows and obeys the laws of nature in the universe as we know it, however fantastic some of its devices may seem; fantasy strictly follows a set of laws formulated by each author for an imaginary world, rules that need not be congruent with the laws of nature but only with their author's logic. What fantasy and science fiction share is a preoccupation with "other" worlds—science fiction with a universe that predictably follows laws of nature (though still full of mystery); fantasy with a universe boundlessly extended by the author's imagination. Fantasy is the world of magic, of inexplicable occurrences that don't have a foundation in the reality of the world as we know it. It is the realm of faerie, of heroes, of dragons, unicorns, and sorcerers.

There is a distinction made between "high" and "low" fantasy. Low fantasy is set in the world as we know it to be governed by nature's laws. Nonrational happenings occur but are not explained, rationally or irrationally—by natural law they just shouldn't happen! Magic and supernatural beings are present. High fantasy is set in imaginary, secondary worlds, their "natural" order or laws set by supernatural beings (e.g., gods, fairies). Magical powers abound amongst wizards and magicians, and a fantasy flora and fauna provide dragons, unicorns, or whatever. "Dark" fantasy is used to describe the horror, ghost, and supernatural tales of chapter 8, "Horror." "Weird" fantasy, centering on horror, the occult, and supernatural creatures, makes an appearance in science fiction and in the categories of fantasy discussed in this chapter. Weird fantasy is also considered in chapter 8.

This analysis could go on ingeniously to the amazement of any reader with firm convictions about the similar or dissimilar natures of science fiction and fantasy. Argument is rendered futile by the characteristics of the works themselves. The authors may rationalize the fantastic elements of the story, doing without the devices of magic or sorcery, so that the irrational may seem possible. This book evades distinguishing the two fields by definition, and arbitrarily (through this author's fantastic logic) places certain categories within the science fiction themes: science fantasy, alternate/parallel worlds, psionic powers, time travel. In addition, of course, many of the novels cited under science fiction contain elements of fantasy. The reader must consider the chapters on science fiction (chapter 6) and fantasy as being symbiotic.

Further confusing the definition of fantasy is the reader's prior association of fantasy with literature for children. The world of faerie, myth, and an unnatural bestiary (e.g., dragons, unicorns) is the accepted realm of childhood's imaginings. That adults continue to love fairy tales, folklore, mythology, and odd little people and monsters is attested by the popularity of adult fantasy. (Many adults also continue to enjoy fantasy written for children.) We stubbornly believe in and welcome magic, whatever our chronological age.

THEMES AND TYPES

Sword-and-Sorcery

The world of adventure, in which magic works, in which heroes and heroines wage epic combat with forces of evil, is the matter of one of fantasy's (currently) most popular types of publication—the heroic fantasy, or fantastic romance. These tales feature sorcerers and magicians, large elements of the supernatural, much romance, and often a quest with daunting hazards. Some use magic only sparingly, concentrate on adventure, and are often noted as being in the tradition of Edgar Rice Burroughs's Barsoom series. Usual backgrounds are galactic or akin to medieval European kingdoms. Multivolume series are common. Many of the following authors also appear on science fiction lists. The heroes, and sometimes heroines, of the sword-and-sorcery, magic-filled adventures usually inhabit a world created for them, and typically appear in trilogies or in open-ended series.

Anderson, Poul. *Three Hearts and Three Lions.*

Brackett, Leigh. Stark series.

Brooks, Terry. The Landover series: *Magic Kingdom for Sale . . . Sold! The Black Unicorn. Wizard at Large. The Tangle Box.*

Brust, Steven. *Jherg. Taltos. The Phoenix Guards.*

Burroughs, Edgar Rice. Barsoom series.

Carter, Lin. Thongor of Lemuria series.

Cherryh, C. J. *Gate of Ivrel. Well of Shiuan. Fires of Azeroth.*

Clayton, Jo. Dancer trilogy.

Cooper, Louise. Time Master trilogy. *Star Ascendant.*

de Camp, L. Sprague. Pusedian series. Novaria series. The Reluctant King series: *The Goblin Tower. The Clocks of Iraz. The Unbeheaded King.*

Delany, Samuel R. *Tales of Nevèrÿon. Nevèrÿon. Flight from Nevèrÿon.*

Eddings, David. Belgariad series. Mallorean series. Ellenium series. Tamuli series.

Feist, Raymond E. Riftwar series: *Magician. Silverthorn. A Darkness at Sethanon. Prince of the Blood. Magician* is most frequently available in two volumes as *Magician: Apprentice* and *Magician: Master.*

Goodkind, Terry. Sword of Truth series.

Heinlein, Robert A. *Glory Road.*
His only sword-and-sorcery novel.

Howard, Robert E. Conan series.
Wrote other series, but this is the memorable one. Continued by L. Sprague de Camp, Lin Carter, Poul Anderson, Robert Jordan, and others.

Jordan, Robert. The Wheel of Time series. *The Eye of the World. The Great Hunt. The Dragon Reborn. The Shadow Rising. The Fires of Heaven. Lord of Chaos.* The Conan chronicles.

Lackey, Mercedes. Last Herald Mage series (homosexual protagonist). Heralds of Valdemar trilogy. Bardic Voices series.

Le Guin, Ursula K. The Earthsea trilogy: *A Wizard of Earthsea, The Tombs of Atuan, The Farthest Shore.*

Lee, Tanith. *The Birthgrave. East of Midnight.*
Swordswoman.

Leiber, Fritz. Fafhrd and the Gray Mouser series.

Lustbader, Eric Van. Sunset Warrior trilogy.

McKillip, Patricia A. The Hed trilogy: *The Riddle-Master of Hed, Heir of Sea and Fire, Harpist in the Wind.*
For children but read by adults.

Moorcock, Michael. The Chronicle of Prince Corum and the Silver Hand. Elric of Melniboné series. Hawkmoon series.

Moore, C. L. Jirel of Joiry series.

Norman, John. Gor series.
Could almost be classed as a sexist parody.

Norton, André. Witch World series.
The Gregg Press reprint, seven volumes, contains a chronology of the series and a map.

Rosenberg, Joel. Guardians of the Flame series.

Russ, Joanna. Alyx series.
Swordswoman.

Saberhagen, Fred. Lost Swords series. Swords series.

Silverberg, Robert. Lord Valentine series: *The Desert of Stolen Dreams. Lord Valentine's Castle. Majipoor Chronicles. Valentine Pontifex.*

Vance, Jack. The Dying Earth series.

Watt-Evans, Lawrence. The Lords of Dûs series: *The Lure of the Basilisk. The Seven Altars of Dûsarra. The Sword of Bheleu. The Book of Silence.*

Weis, Margaret, and Tracy Hickman. Death Gate: *Dragon Wing. Elven Star. Fire Sea. Serpent Mage. The End of Chaos. Into the Labyrinth. Seventh Gate.*

Williams, Tad. *The Dragonbone Chair. Stone of Farewell. To Green Angel Tower.*

Zelazny, Roger. Amber series: *Nine Princes in Amber. The Guns of Avalon. Sign of the Unicorn. The Hands of Oberon. The Courts of Chaos. Trumps of Doom.*

And, of course, there are the parodies of sword-and-sorcery.

Chalker, Jack L. Dancing Gods series: *The River of Dancing Gods. Demons of the Dancing Gods. Vengeance of the Dancing Gods.*

Pratchett, Terry. *The Color of Magic. The Light Fantastic.*

Dungeons and Dragons

The game of Dungeons and Dragons (role playing in a sword-and-sorcery setting) has fostered a considerable body of original paperback publications too various for listing. TSR has had great success marketing books based on their various fantasy role-playing games. The most popular authors are the duo of Margaret Weis and Tracy Hickman. Also extremely popular, in hardcover with users of public libraries, is R. A. Salvatore. Many of these fantasy novels, based on the game, verge on horror, with vampires, werewolves, and other types of shapeshifters playing important roles. Popular authors writing these novels include:

Weis, Margaret, and Tracy Hickman

Golden, Christie

Salvatore, R. A.

Bergstrom, Elaine

Lowder, James

King, J. Robert

Elrod, P. N.

Parkinson, Dan

Thurston, Robert

Some of the names of series that fall into this area are:

Ravenloft

Forgotten Realms

Dragonlance

Shadowrun

GreyHawk

Al-Qadim

Dark Sun

Battletech

The following prototype authors have written books that have a fantasy role-playing setting.

Cushman, Carolyn. *Witch and Wombat*. (Parody)

Rosenberg, Joel. Guardians of the Flame: The Warriors (*The Sleeping Dragon. The Sword and the Chain. The Silver Crown*).

Saga, Myth, and Legend

In the following books, distinctive type of sword-and-sorcery (or magic-and-adventure) places the story in the worlds of myth, saga, and legend (Eddic, Celtic, Welsh, etc.).

Alexander, Lloyd. The Prydain Chronicles: *The Book of Three. The Black Cauldron. The Castle of Llyr. Taran Wanderer. The High King.*
Although for the young, also read by adults. Welsh legend.

Bell, Clare. *The Jaguar Princess.*

Bradley, Marion Zimmer. *The Firebrand.*

Chant, Joy. Vandarei series: *Red Moon and Black Mountain. The Grey Mane of Morning. The High Kings. When Voiha Wakes.*
Celtic, pre-Arthurian.

Cherryh, C. J. *Rusalka. Chernevog. Yvgenie.* (Russian).

de Lint, Charles. *Svaha.*

Flint, Kenneth C. *The Dark Druid. Cromm.* (Celtic).

King, Bernard. *Vagr-Moon.*

Llywelyn, Morgan. *Red Branch. Finn McCool.*

McAvoy, R. A. *Grey Horse. Book of Kells.*

Milan, Victor, and Melinda Snodgrass. *Runespear.*

Norton, André, and Susan Shwartz. *Imperial Lady.* (Han China).

Paxson, Diana L., and Adrienne Martine-Barnes. *Master of Earth and Water.*
Third-century Irish outlaw/poet Fionn MacCumhal.

Tarr, Judith. *Lord of Two Lands.*
Alexander.

Vance, Jack. Lyonesse series: *Suldrun's Garden. The Green Pearl.* (Celtic, pre-Arthurian).

Walton, Evangeline. The Mabinogion series: *The Prince of Annwn. The Children of Llyr. The Song of Rhiannon. The Virgin and the Swine.*

Weis, Margaret, and Tracy Hickman. Rose of the Prophet series. (Middle East).

ARTHURIAN LEGEND

The most enchanting of the legendary backgrounds is the Arthurian, with Merlin often the dominating figure.

Berger, Thomas. *Arthur Rex: A Legendary Novel.*

Bradley, Marion Zimmer. *The Mists of Avalon.*

Bradshaw, Gillian. *Hawk of May. Kingdom of Summer. In Winter's Shadow.*

Charrette, Robert N. *A Prince Among Men.*

Chopra, Deepak. *The Return of Merlin.*

Godwin, Parke. *Firelord. Beloved Exile.*

James, Cary. *King and Raven.*

Jones, Courtway. *Witch of the North. In the Shadow of the Oak King.*

Kane, Gil, and John Jakes. *Excalibur!*

Kennealy-Morrison, Patricia. The Keltiad series.

Lawhead, Steve. *Taliesin. Merlin. Arthur.*

Monaco, Richard. *Parsival; or, A Knight's Tale. The Grail War. The Final Quest.*

Munn, H. Warner. *King of the World's Edge. Merlin's Godson. Merlin's Ring.*

Newman, Sharan. *Guinevere. The Chessboard Queen. Guinevere Evermore.*

Norton, Andrew. *Merlin's Mirror.*

Nye, Robert. *Merlin.*

Rice, Robert. *The Last Pendragon.*

Stewart, Mary. *The Crystal Cave. The Hollow Hills. The Last Enchantment. The Wicked Day.*

Tolstoy, Nikolai. *The Coming of the King: The First Book of Merlin.*

White, T. H. *The Once and Future King* (collective title for: *The Sword in the Stone, The Witch in the Wood* [*The Queen of Air and Darkness*], *The Ill-Made Knight, The Candle in the Wind*). *The Book of Merlyn* (concludes the series).

Woolley, Persia. *Child of the Northern Spring. Queen of the Summer Stars. Guinevere: The Legend in Autumn.*

The following are some of the background books available to identify characters and illuminate the legends used in novels of this genre.

The Arthurian Encyclopedia.

Thompson, Raymond H. *The Return from Avalon: A Study of the Arthurian Legend in Modern Fiction.* (Contributions to the Study of Science Fiction and Fantasy, No. 14).

Tolstoy, Nikolai. *The Quest for Merlin.*

ROBIN HOOD AND SHERWOOD FOREST

McKinley, Robin. *Outlaws of Sherwood.*
A feminist version of Robin Hood.

Roberson, Jennifer. *Lady of the Forest.*
A prequel, this story tells of the assemblage of the well-known characters of the Robin Hood legend.

Fairy Tales

The publication of retellings of fairy tales and old folktales is a growing trend. Some of the stories told in the following novels will be familiar; others will seem to be new, but with an underlying feeling that they have been told before. Tor Books' Fairy Tale Series, created by Terri Windling, was written for adults. About the books in this series, Lisa Goldstein wrote that "difficult truths can sometimes only be told through the medium of fantasy."

Cherryh, C. J. *Rusalka.*
Based on Eastern European stories.

Napoli, Donna Jo. *The Magic Circle.*
This retelling of "Hansel and Gretel" from a different viewpoint is an example of a dark fairy tale told in a way that changes one's views of villain and hero.

McKinley, Robin. *Deerskin.*
This tale unveils the horrors of incest in a tale of a beautiful princess and her dog.

Tepper, Sheri S. *Beauty.*
Beauty pricks her finger on her 16th birthday and instead of sleeping for 100 years she travels to the twenty-first century.

Weis, Margaret, and Tracy Hickman. Rose of the Prophet series, based on Middle Eastern tales, complete with djinns.

Wrede, Patricia C. *Snow White and Rose Red.*

Yolen, Jane. *Briar Rose*.
> Jane Yolen combines the tale of sleeping beauty with the horrors of the holocaust.

Humorous Fantasy

Not all fantasy based in fairy and folk tales is dark; some is light and humorous. In fact, many of the following stories have a foundation in the old stories. Frequently, humorous fantasy includes elements of familiar fairy and folktales. Often full of topical jokes, such books present more humor to the well-read.

Anthony, Piers. Xanth series.
> Books in this series are full of puns and plays on words. *Question Quest* (the 14th book in the series) actually recaps many of the events found in earlier books.

Asprin, Robert. The M.Y.T.H. series.
> Humorous tales with humorous titles—*Hit or MYTH, Little MYTH Marker, MYTHing Link*.

Friesner, Esther. Majyk series.

Gaiman, Neil, and Terry Pratchett. *Good Omens: The Nice and Accurate Prophecies of Agnes Nutter, Witch*.
> A demon and an angel try to stop the apocalypse because they are having too good a time in this world to see it all end.

Turtledove, Harry. *The Case of the Toxic Spell Dump*.
> Even on magic carpets, accidents can happen, and a wild series of events turns an inspector for the Environmental Perfection Agency into a detective.

Watt-Evans, Lawrence, and Esther Friesner. *Split Heirs*.
> Triplets are split up at birth, the girl to be raised as a prince and the two princes to be raised as a magician's apprentice and a shepherd.

Parallel Worlds

Another type of magic-and-adventure fantasy is usually placed in the kingdoms of medieval or Renaissance times. Authors sometimes use a recognizable country, sometimes invent a fantasy land.

Aiken, Joan. *The Stolen Lake*.

Anderson, Poul. *A Midsummer Tempest*.
> The world of Shakespeare.

Anthony, Piers, and Robert Kornwise. *Through the Ice*.

Bradley, Marion Zimmer. Darkover series.

Card, Orson Scott. *Seventh Son. Red Prophet. Prentice Alvin* (alternate nineteenth-century United States).

Coney, Michael Greatrex. *Fang, the Gnome. King of the Scepter'd Isle.*

Cullen, Seamas. *Astra and Flondrix.*
Although all sword-and-sorcery is full of romance, few share this one's erotic label. A medieval world, with Tolkien tradition echoes.

Donaldson, Stephen R. *The Chronicles of Thomas Covenant, the Unbeliever.* First Chronicle: *Lord Foul's Bane. The Illearth War. The Power That Preserves.* Second Chronicle: *The Wounded Land. The One Tree. White Gold Wielder.* Mordant's Need series: *The Mirror of Her Dreams. A Man Rides Through.*

Eddison, E. R. *The Worm Ouroboros.* The Zimiamvian trilogy: *Mezentian Gate, A Fish Dinner in Memison, Mistress of Mistresses.*
Strong elements of myth and legend in this challenging read from early in the century.

Foster, Alan Dean. The Spellsinger series: *The Day of the Dissonance. The Hour of the Gate. The Moment of the Magician. The Paths of the Perambulator.*
A land of intelligent, talking animals and wizards.

Haggard, H. Rider. The She series: *Wisdom's Daughter. She. Ayesha. She and Allen.*

King, Stephen, and Peter Straub. *The Talisman.*

Kurtz, Katherine. Deryni saga, which includes The Legends of Camber of Culdi series, The Heirs of Saint Camber series, and The Histories of King Kelson series.
Medieval England, Scotland, and Wales.

L'Engle, Madeleine. The Unicorn trilogy: *A Wrinkle in Time, A Wind in the Door, A Swiftly Tilting Planet.*
Time travel. For the young but read by all ages.

MacAvoy, R. A. *The Book of Kells.*

MacAvoy, R. A. Damiano series: *Damiano. Damiano's Lute. Raphael.*
Medieval Italy.

Moorcock, Michael. *Gloriana; or, The Unfulfill'd Queen.*
Elizabeth in Albion, a faerie world.

Peake, Mervyn. The Gormenghast trilogy: *Titus Groan, Gormenghast, Titus Alone.*
The world of the Gothic imagination.

Simmons, Dan. *Endymion.*

Tarr, Judith. The Hound and the Falcon trilogy: *The Isle of Glass, The Golden Horn, The Hounds of God*.
Medieval Italy.

Wilson, Robert Anton. The Schrodinger's Cat series. Illuminatus trilogy.

Tolkien Tradition

The works of Tolkien have strongly influenced fantasy writers of sword-and-sorcery and magic-and-adventure. His Middle Earth of elves, complete with language and laws, is often imitated, as is his version of the heroic quest and the conflict of good and evil.

Brooks, Terry. *The Sword of Shannara. The Elfstones of Shannara. The Wishsong of Shannara. The Talismans of Shannara. The Druid of Shannara. The Elf Queen of Shannara.*

Douglas, Carole Nelson. Taliswoman series. *Cup of Clay. Seed Upon the Wind.*
A young woman accidentally stumbles into another world and finds many traveling companions in this first of a Tolkien type series.

Tolkien, J. R. R. *The Hobbit.* The Lord of the Rings: *The Fellowship of the Ring. The Two Towers. The Return of the Ring. The Silmarillion.*

The following is a selection from the considerable body of secondary material on Tolkien.

Beard, Henry N., and Douglas C. Kenney. *Bored of the Rings: A Parody of J. R. R. Tolkien's The Lord of the Rings.* NAL, 1969.
Product of the *Harvard Lampoon.*

Collins, David R. *J. R. R. Tolkien: Master of Fantasy.* Lerner, 1992.

Day, David. *A Tolkien Bestiary.* Random, 1979.

Day, David. *Tolkien: The Illustrated Encyclopedia.* Macmillan, 1991.

Foster, Robert. *The Complete Guide to Middle-Earth: From the Hobbit to The Silmarillion.* Del Rey, 1978.

Helms, Randal. *Tolkien's World.* Houghton, 1974.

Kocher, Paul Harold. *Master of Middle Earth: The Fiction of J. R. R. Tolkien.* Houghton, 1972.

Shippey, T. A. *The Road to Middle-Earth.* Houghton, 1983.

Tyler, J. E. A. *The New Tolkien Companion.* St. Martin's, 1980.

C. S. Lewis

This author belongs in a category of his own, as unique as the universes he created. His books are read by both adults and children.

The Chronicles of Narnia: *The Lion, the Witch and the Wardrobe. Prince Caspian. The Voyage of the "Dawn Treader." The Silver Chair. The Horse and His Boy. The Magician's Nephew. The Last Battle.*
Delight adults as well as children for whom the series was written. Witches and magic along with the religious message.

The Space trilogy: *Out of the Silent Planet, Perelandra, That Hideous Strength.*
Interplanetary romances, pervaded by the conflict of good and evil, with a strongly religious tone. Contain elements of Arthurian legend and feature the magician Merlin.

Secondary works on C. S. Lewis include:

Ford, Paul. *Companion to Narnia.* Harper, 1980.

Manlove, C. N. *The Chronicles of Narnia: The Patterning of a Fantastic World.* Twayne, 1993.

Schakel, Peter J. *Reading with the Heart: The Way into Narnia.* Eerdmans, 1980.

World of Faerie

The world of faerie is not the same as the world of fairy tales. It is a place of elven-type people with powers that, to humans, seem magical. Often, the interaction of humans and residents of faerie sets up the conflict. Time moves at a different pace in this world that coexists side by side with ours. Sometimes, a rift between the worlds allows someone of faerie descent into our world, or vice versa. There also seems to be a great proclivity for humans and those of faerie blood to fall in love with each other. There are some notable adult treatments. Lord Dunsany and MacDonald have been influential on modern writers of fantasy. As the following books show, adults often retain a love of the faerie world.

Dean, Pamela. *Tam Lin.*
A young woman rescues her love from the Queen of Faerie.

de Lint, Charles. *Greenmantle. Jack the Giant Killer. The Wild Wood.*

Dietz, Tom. *Fireshaper's Doom.*

Dunsany, Lord. *The King of Elfland's Daughter* (1924).

Goldstein, Lisa. *Strange Devices of the Sun and Moon*.
An Elizabethan stationer believes that her son may be the changeling prince of Faerie.

Holdstock, Robert. *Mythago Wood* (1985).

Kushner, Ellen. *Thomas the Rhymer*.
Told from varying points of view, Thomas' disappearance into the faerie realm.

King, Stephen. *The Eyes of the Dragon*.

MacDonald, George. *Phantastes: A Faerie Romance for Men and Women* (1858).
A nineteenth-century author of children's books.

McKillip, Patricia A. *Something Rich and Strange*.

Sherman, Josepha. *A Strange and Ancient Name*.
A prince of Faerie, trying to defeat a curse, must sojourn in our world to find out his family history.

Warner, Sylvia Townsend. *Kingdom of Elfin* (1977).
Sophisticated series of stories, first published in *The New Yorker*.

Urban Fantasy

In this cyberpunk version of the fantasy world, magic and technology share a place in gritty, dangerous cities. Drugs, racism, gangs, and other scourges of modern life are evident. This is the world where our contemporary cities, or maybe even the cyberpunk cities of the future, are the site of a rift between our world and the world of faerie. Such works are not pastoral, as most fantasy tends to be.

Brust, Steven. *The Gypsy*.

Bull, Emma. *War for the Oaks. Finder*.

de Lint, Charles. *Dreams Underfoot. Memory and Dream. Moonheart*.

Lackey, Mercedes, et al. The Serrated Edge series.

Shetterly, Will. *Elsewhere. Nevernever*.

A Bestiary

UNICORNS

Often portrayed as one-horned horses, unicorns in the following books are viewed in different ways. They are generally good creatures that possess magic.

Anthony, Piers. *Unicorn Point.*

Beagle, Peter. *The Last Unicorn.*

Bishop, Michael. *Unicorn Mountain.*

Lee, John. *The Unicorn War.*

Pierce, Meredith Anne. *Birth of the Firebringer. Dark Moon.*
A young unicorn saves his clan by bringing them fire.

DRAGONS

Dragons are often portrayed as telepathic creatures. Dragons have been portrayed in many different ways throughout history (e.g., Western and Eastern art portray dragons differently).

Dickson, Gordon R. *The Dragon and the George. The Dragon at War.*

Frankos, Steven. *Beyond Lich Gate.*

Hambly, Barbara. *Dragonsbane.*

Kellogg, Marjorie B. *The Dragon Quartet.*

Norton, André, and Mercedes Lackey. *The Elvenbane.*

Rowley, Christopher. *A Sword for a Dragon. Dragons of War.*

UNCOMMON COMMON ANIMALS

The animals in the following fantasy stories interact in cultures much as humans do. They have speech, emotions, and conflicts.

Adams, Richard. *Watership Down.* (Rabbits).

Bell, Clare. *Ratha's Creature. Clan Ground. Ratha and Thistle Chaser.* (Cats).

Hawdon, Robin. *A Rustle in the Grass.* (Ants).

Horwood, William. *Duncton Wood.*

Jacques, Brian. The Redwall series, where mice battle evil. *Redwall. Mattimeo. Mariel of Redwall. Salamandastron. Martin the Warrior.*

Wangerin, Walter. *The Book of the Dun Cow.*

Williams, Tad. *Tailchaser's Song.* (Cats).

Literary and Fictional Characters Live!

The characters of fiction and other forms of literature take on historical reality in a fantasy world rich in literary allusion. Some of their creators join their characters. The following books make the reader draw on whatever allusions his or her lifetime's worth of reading has provided.

Anderson, Poul. *A Midsummer Tempest*.

Bova, Ben. *Triumph*.
   Joseph Stalin and Franklin Delano Roosevelt.

Davidson, Avram. *The Phoenix and the Mirror*.
   Virgil as a wizard.

de Camp, L. Sprague, and Fletcher Pratt. *The Compleat Enchanter: The Magical Misadventures of Harold Shea* (collective title for: *The Incomplete Enchanter, The Castle of Iron: A Science Fantasy Adventure, The Wall of Serpents*).

Farmer, Philip José. Riverworld series. *To Your Scattered Bodies Go. The Fabulous Riverboat. The Dark Design. The Magic Labyrinth. Gods of Riverworld*.
   The author joins with the characters.

Myers, John Myers. *Silverlock*.
   An ignored and woefully neglected classic. The picaresque hero's adventures are in the worlds of great Western literature. The reader's delightful challenge is to identify stories, characters, and allusions.

Powers, Tim. *The Anubis Gates*.

Rucker, Rudy. *The Hollow Earth*.

Human Comedy

Fantasy written strictly for adults is merely a variation of mainstream fiction. Most of the titles previously listed are considered adult fantasy, but many are enjoyed equally by children and adults. However, most of the following books are not intended for children. A few are from standard fantasy (and science fantasy) in which the authors are discussing philosophical ideas.

Anthony, Piers. Incarnations of Immortality series: *On a Pale Horse. Bearing an Hourglass. With a Tangled Skein. Wielding a Red Sword. Being a Green Mother. For Love of Evil. And Eternity*.
   The characters are embodied abstractions: death, time, fate, war, life, evil, and good.

Ballard, J. G. *The Unlimited Dream Company*.
Science fiction or fantasy; the comment is clear.

Beagle, Peter. *A Fine and Private Place*.
A modern classic of love and death in a New York cemetery with a sardonic talking raven.

Bisson, Terry. *Talking Man*.

Blish, James. After Such Knowledge tetralogy: *Doctor Mirabilis*. *Black Easter or Faust Aleph-Null*. *The Day After Judgment*. *A Case of Conscience*.
An intriguing combination of adult fantasy, complete with magic and science fiction.

Cabell, James Branch. *Jurgen*.
That this was once banned in the United States as pornographic is now incomprehensible. Ironic romantic fantasy.

Carroll, Jonathan. *The Land of Laughter*.
Present-day United States, with a strong overtone of horror.

Chalker, Jack L. Soul Rider series.
A science fantasy interface of magic and dystopia.

de Camp, L. Sprague, and Fletcher Pratt. *Tales from Gavagan's Bar*.
Modern comedy.

Ende, Michael. *The Neverending Story*. *Momo*.
Published in Germany for children. Examples of fantasy of ideas taken over by adult readers.

Findley, Timothy. *Not Wanted on the Voyage*.
Not the traditional Noah's ark legend. (A seemingly irresistible theme. Completely adult and irreverent is Jeanette Winterson's 1985 novel, *Boating for Beginners*.)

Finney, Charles. *The Circus of Dr. Lao*.
Contains one of this writer's favorite passages in modern literature: "I am a calm, intelligent girl," Miss Agnes reassured herself. "I am a calm, intelligent girl, and I have not seen Pan on Main Street. Nevertheless, I will go to the circus and make sure."

Gray, Alasdair. *Lanark*. *Janine*. *Unlikely Stories*.
Unique.

Hales, E. E. Y. *Chariot of Fire*.
Dante's and Milton's Hell through modern eyes.

Harrison, M. John. City of Viriconium series: *The Pastel City*. *A Storm of Wings*. *The Floating Gods*. *Viriconium Nights*.
Science fantasy of a doomed world.

Heinlein, Robert A. *Job: A Comedy of Justice*.

Helprin, Mark. *Winter's Tale.*
   Present-day New York and a magic horse.

Hoban, Russell. *The Lion of Boaz-Jachin and Jachin-Boaz. Kleinzeit.*
   Modern fables of identity and death.

MacAvoy, R. A. *Tea with the Black Dragon.*
   Dragons and computers!

McDonald, Ian. *Desolation Road.*

Scarborough, Elizabeth Ann. *Healer's War.*
   A nurse in Vietnam receives a magical healing talisman.

Sullivan, Faith. *Mrs. Demming and the Mythical Beast.*
   Pan stranded in Minnesota.

Tepper, Sheri S. *North Shore. South Shore.*
   Interesting science fantasy treatment of death and religion.

Wellman, Manly Wade. Silver John series: *The Old Gods Waken. After Dark. The Lost and the Lurking. The Hanging Stones. The Voice of the Mountain.* John Thurstone series: *What Dreams May Come.*
   Silver John series is about a minstrel-guitarist in Appalachia who battles evil with faith. John Thurstone series is concerned with ancient customs and psychic research.

Williams, Charles. *War in Heaven. Descent into Hell. Many Dimensions. Place of the Lion. Shadows of Ecstasy. The Greater Trumps. All Hallow's Eve.*
   Theological fantasy of the cosmic war between good and evil.

Wolfe, Gene. The Book of the New Sun series: *The Shadow of the Torturer. The Claw of the Conciliator. The Sword of the Lictor. The Citadel of the Autarch.*
   Science fantasy of philosophical questions.

There are even fantasy detective stories, such as:

Goulart, Ron. *The Prisoner of Blackwood Castle.*
   A detective of the Challenge International Detective Agency in a land of magic.

Wolfe, Gene. *Free Live Free.*
   A private detective in a modern setting of fantasy and science fiction.

Shared Worlds and Franchise Universes

The introduction of shared-world stories, in which an imaginary world is created by an editor or author and is then used as a background by several authors, has resulted in the publication of several series. As in any set of works created by committee, there is bound to be some variation in quality, but the following series have been popular ("relentlessly popular," noted one review). The stories belong in the category of magic-and-adventure.

In a franchise universe, sometimes called a sharecropper universe, books written by relatively unknown authors are published with a famous author's name prominently splashed across the cover (the true author's name appears in small print). Avon's Arthur C. Clarke's Venus Prime series were all written by Paul Preuss, and some of Harry Turtledove's books appear under an "Isaac Asimov Presents" banner.

Bradley, Marion Zimmer, Julian May, and André Norton. *Black Trillium.* Three grand dames of fantasy writing, three princesses, three quests, three magical talismans; one single tale, cowritten by the three was not enough so André Norton followed up with *Golden Trillium* and Julian May with *Blood Trillium.*

THIEVES' WORLD-SANCTUARY SERIES

The creation of Robert Lynn Asprin and Lynn Abbey in 1978. Among the contributing authors: Lynn Abbey, Poul Anderson, Robert Lynn Asprin, Robin W. Bailey, Marion Zimmer Bradley, John Brunner, C. J. Cherryh, Christine DeWeese, David Drake, Diane Duane, Philip José Farmer, Joe Haldeman, Vonda McIntyre, Chris Morris, Janet Morris (who has done separate novels on Thieves' World: *Beyond Sanctuary, Beyond Wizard-Wall, Beyond the Veil*), Andrew Offutt, Diana L. Paxson, A. E. van Vogt. The first six volumes (original paperbacks) were gathered into two volumes by the Science Fiction Book Club (with endpaper maps):

Volume I brings together books 1–3: *Sanctuary: Thieves' World, Tales from the Vulgar Unicorn, Shadows of Sanctuary.*

Volume II brings together books 4–6: *Cross Currents: Storm Season, The Face of Chaos, Wing of Omen.*

Book 7: *The Dead of Winter.*

Book 8: *Soul of the City.* (Contains a "badly needed dramatis personae of the world of Sanctuary.")

Book 9: *Heroes in Hell.*

MAGIC SERIES

A universe of magic created by Larry Niven in his *The Magic Goes Away.* Niven then edited two illustrated volumes:

The Magic May Return.
Stories by Fred Saberhagen, Dean Ing, Steven Barnes, Poul Anderson, and Mildred Downey Boxon.

More Magic.
Stories by Larry Niven, Bob Shaw, Dian Girard, and Roger Zelazny.

FAIR AT ITHKAR SERIES

Magic in Ithkar, volumes 1 and 2. Edited by André Norton and Robert Adams.
Stories by Lin Carter, George Alec Effinger, Linda Haldeman, R. A. Lafferty, and others.

SEAPORT OF LIAVEK

Liavek. Edited by Will Shetterly and Emma Bull. (1985).
Stories by Gene Wolfe, Patricia Wrede, Steven Brust, Patricia Dean, and others.

SWORD OF KNOWLEDGE SERIES

Created by C. J. Cherryh, each novel has a different coauthor (listed after the titles).

A Dirge for Sabis. (Leslie Fish).

Wizard Spawn. (Nancy Asire).

Reap the Whirlwind. (Mercedes Lackey).

BOLOS SERIES

Created by Keith Laumer.

Honor of the Regiment.

The Unconquerable.

TOPICS

Anthologies

There is often a combining of fantasy and ghost or horror stories in anthologies. Several of the following anthologies have considerable critical material, as well as stories.

Adams, Robert, et al., eds. *Barbarians*. NAL/Signet, 1986.
Sword-and-sorcery.

Asimov, Isaac, Charles G. Waugh, and Martin Harry Greenberg, eds. *Isaac Asimov Presents the Best Fantasy of the 19th Century*. Beaufort, 1982.

Asimov, Isaac, et al., eds. *100 Great Fantasy Short Stories*. Doubleday, 1984.

Boyer, Robert H., and Kenneth Zahorski, eds. *The Fantastic Imagination: An Anthology of High Fantasy*. Avon, 1977–78. 2 vols.

Bradley, Marion Zimmer. *The Best of Marion Zimmer Bradley's Fantasy Magazine*. Warner Books, 1994.

Bradley, Marion Zimmer, ed. *Sword and Sorceress: An Anthology of Heroic Fantasy*. Volume 10. DAW, 1993.

Carr, Terry, ed. *Kingdoms of Sorcery*. Doubleday, 1976.

Carr, Terry, ed. *Realms of Wizardry*. Doubleday, 1976.

Carr, Terry, and Martin Harry Greenberg, eds. *A Treasury of Modern Fantasy*. Avon, 1981.

Dann, Jack, and Gardner Dozois, eds. *Bestiary*. Ace, 1985.

Dann, Jack, and Gardner Dozois, eds. *Magicats*. Ace, 1984.

Dann, Jack, and Gardner Dozois, eds. *Unicorns!* Ace, 1982.

Davidson, Avram, ed. *Magic for Sale*. Ace, 1983.

de Camp, L. Sprague, ed. *Warlocks and Warriors*. Putnam, 1970.

Del Rey, Lester, and Risa Kessler, eds. *Once upon a Time: A Treasury of Modern Fairy Tales*. Illustrated by Michael Pangrazio. Ballantine Books, 1991.
Ten original fairy tales.

Donaldson, Stephen R., comp. *Strange Dreams: Unforgettable Fantasy Stories*. Bantam Spectra, 1993.

Foster, Alan Dean, and Martin H. Greenberg, eds. *Smart Dragons, Foolish Elves*. Ace, 1991.

Greenberg, Martin H., ed. *After the King: Stories in Honor of J. R. R. Tolkien*. Introduction by Jane Yolen. Tor, 1992.

Hartwell, David G., comp. *Masterpieces of Fantasy and Wonder*. Guild-American Books, 1989.

Manguel, Alberto, ed. *Black Water: The Book of Fantastic Literature*. Potter, 1984.
An eclectic and extensive anthology (976 pages), including many foreign authors and many not usually considered genre authors. A classic collection.

McKinley, Robin, ed. *Imaginary Lands*. Berkley/Ace, 1985.

Mobley, Jane, ed. *Phantasmagoria: Tales of Fantasy and the Supernatural*. Anchor, 1977.
Two sections: "The Wondrous Fair: Magical Fantasy"; "The Passing Strange: Supernatural Fiction."

Neugroschel, Joachim, comp. & ed. *Yenne Velt: The Great Works of Jewish Fantasy and Occult*. Stonehill, 1976; Pocket Books, 1978. Wings Books, 1991.

Nolan, William F., and Martin H. Greenberg. *The Bradbury Chronicles: Stories in Honor of Ray Bradbury*. ROC, 1991.

Parry, Michel, ed. *Savage Heroes: Tales of Magical Fantasy*. Taplinger, 1980.

Rabkin, Eric S., ed. *Fantastic Worlds: Myths, Tales, and Stories*. Oxford University Press, 1979.
This is a critical analysis of fantasy as well as an anthology, for the essay commentary is extensive. The scope is eclectic, covering fantasy as a literature in both mainstream and genre examples. Divisions are: Myth; Folktale; Fairy Tale; Fantasy; Horror Fiction; Ghost Stories; Heroic Fantasy; Science Fiction; Modern Fantasy. There is an annotated bibliography.

Rottensteiner, Franz. *The Slaying of the Dragon: Modern Tales of the Playful Imagination*. Harcourt, 1985.
Eleven tales—seven are translations.

Shippey, T. A., comp. *Oxford Book of Fantasy Stories*. Oxford University Press, 1994.
A good sampling of classic stories.

Shwartz, Susan, ed. *Moonsinger's Friends: An Anthology in Honor of André Norton*. Bluejay Books, 1985.
A role model for women writers of fantasy.

Silverberg, Robert, and Martin Harry Greenberg, eds. *The Fantasy Hall of Fame*. Arbor House, 1983.
Members at the World Fantasy Convention selected their favorite 22 stories for inclusion in this first Hall of Fame anthology.

Whispers: An Anthology of Fantasy and Horror. Doubleday, 1977– .
The third volume appeared in 1983. Stories from the magazine *Whispers*.

The Year's Best Fantasy Annual began in 1988. Name changed to *Year's Best Fantasy and Horror* in 1990. St. Martin's. Edited by Ellen Datlow and Terri Windling.

The Year's Best Fantasy Stories. #13, DAW, 1987.

Yolen, Jane. *Xanadu 2*. Tor, 1994.

Bibliographies, Biographies, Guides

Many of the works listed under science fiction contain material on fantasy. The following works illustrate that fantasy, as a genre, relates to both children's and adults' interests.

Ashley, Mike. *Who's Who in Horror and Fantasy Fiction*. Elm Tree Books, 1977.
Annotations and critical bio-bibliography for 400 authors. Additional sections: "Chronology," c.2000 B.C.–1977; "An index to key stories and books"; "Selected weird fiction anthologies," annotated; "Weird and horror fiction magazines," annotated; "Awards," August Derleth Fantasy Award and World Fantasy Award.

Barron, Neil. *Fantasy Literature*. Garland, 1990.

Bloom, H. *Modern Fantasy Writers*. Chelsea House, 1995.

Bloom, Harold, ed. *Classic Fantasy Writers*. Chelsea House, 1994.

Burgess, Michael. *Reference Guide to Science Fiction, Fantasy, and Horror*. Libraries Unlimited, 1992.

Hall, Hal W., ed. *Science Fiction and Fantasy Reference Index, 1985–1991: An International Author and Subject Index to History and Criticism*. Libraries Unlimited, 1993.

Rovin, Jeff. *The Fantasy Almanac*. Dutton, 1979.
Alphabetical definitions of authors, characters, mythological and supernatural beings and beasts, places, and the like in mythology, folklore, fairy tale, literature, comic strip, motion picture, and television. Illustrated.

Searles, Baird, Beth Meacham, and Michael Franklin. *A Reader's Guide to Fantasy*. Facts on File, 1982.
Bibliography and criticism for over 160 authors. Introduction for neophytes.

Tymn, Marshall B., Kenneth J. Zahorski, and Robert H. Boyer. *Fantasy Literature: A Core Collection and Reference Guide*. Bowker, 1979.
The core collection, more than 240 works, is an alphabetical and critically annotated selection of adult fantasy, although much of the material is suitable for all ages. There is an extensive introductory essay. The listings of "Fantasy Scholarship," periodicals, societies, and organizations are briefly annotated.

Waggoner, Diana. *The Hills of Faraway: A Guide to Fantasy*. Atheneum, 1978.
An eclectic selection of 996 titles, critically annotated, of interest to adults. There is an extensive and critical introductory essay. An appendix, "Subgenres of Fantasy," lists titles (numbered as in the annotated list) by type: magic, mythic fantasy, faerie, ghost fantasy, horror fantasy, sentimental fantasy, magic time travel, travels from one universe to another, science fantasy, fairy-story fantasy, toy tales, animal fantasy, worlds of enchantment, new histories, new universes.

Gazetteers and Atlases

These three delightful books will enchant all fans of fantasy, and many of science fiction, for they describe and map the lands that readers' imaginations have made real.

Holdstock, Robert, and Malcolm Edwards. *Lost Realms*. Illustrations by John Avon, Bill Donohoe, Godfrey Dowson, Dick French, Mark Harrison, Michael Johnson, Pauline Martin, David O'Connor, Colleen Payne, Scitex 350, Carolyn Scrace. Limpsfield, England: Dragon's World, 1984.
Describes with reference to history, legend, and use in fiction, places familiar to readers of fantasy: islands, continents, cities, undersea, and underworld. Examples of the diversity: Avalon, Middle Earth, Lemuria, Mu, Troy, Shambhala, Eldorado, Atlantis, Plutonia, Pellucidar, Tuonela, Yggdrasil, Faerie (Land of Youth). The color illustrations are vivid fantasy. The bibliography includes some fiction.

Manguel, Alberto, and Gianni Guadalupi. *The Dictionary of Imaginary Places*. Illustrated by Graham Greenfield. Maps and charts by James Cook. Macmillan, 1980.
Clearly this is a labor of love. Imaginary places (countries, castles, islands, whatever) from all types of literature and films are described in straight-faced gazetteer style, complete with information on the inhabitants, flora and fauna, and social customs. The source work is cited. There are 150 maps and 100 illustrations. The scope is international and, of course, encompasses much more than genre fiction. There is an index of authors and titles. This is not simply a reference book but may be read with delight for its own sake: "Should a traveller lose his way in Wonderland, information can be obtained from a knowledgeable caterpillar smoking a hookah. . . . Several places in Wonderland are worth a visit: the White Rabbit's dainty cottage; the Duchess' house with its spicy though somewhat neglected kitchen; and the Mad Hatter's outdoor tearoom, open all hours." This writer notes, with regret, the absence of Commonwealth (John Myers Myers, *Silverlock*) and Abalone, Arizona (Charles G. Finney, *The Circus of Dr. Lao*). The authors invite additional citations for a supplement or revised edition.

Post, J. B., comp. *An Atlas of Fantasy*. Revised Edition. Ballantine, 1979. This is much improved in map reproduction from the first edition (Mirage Press, 1973), with some changes. The following is a selection from the contents; many are for works cited in this guide. The listing is in order of sequence in the atlas.

Baum, L. Frank. "Oz and Environs."

Burroughs, Edgar Rice. "The Worlds of . . ." Barsoom [Mars]; Pal-Ul-Don (Tarzan series); Land of the Ant Men (Tarzan series); Onthar and Thenar (Tarzan series); The Lost Empire (Tarzan series); Amtor (Venus series); Pellucidar (Hollow Earth-Pellucidar series); The Moon (*The Moon Maid*); Poloda and Umos (*Beyond the Furthest Star*); Caspak and Caprona (*The Land That Time Forgot*); Wild Island.

Cabell, James Branch. "Poictesme."

Howard, Robert E. "Hyperborian Age." (Conan series).

Tolkien, J. R. R. "The Worlds . . ." Middle Earth (*Lord of the Rings*); Gondor and Mordor (*Lord of the Rings*); Thror's Map (*The Hobbit*); Wilderland (*The Hobbit*); Beleriand (*The Silmarillion*).

Eddison, E. R. "The Three Kingdoms and Ouroboros Country": Ouroboros Country (*The Worm Ouroboros*); The Three Kingdoms (*Mistress of Mistresses*); The Campaign in North Rerek and the Meszrian Border (*Mistress of Mistresses*).

Sleigh, Bernard. "Fairyland." (*Ancient Mappe of Fairyland*).

Lewis, C. S. "Narnia."

Myers, John Myers. "Commonwealth." (*Silverlock*).

Hamilton, Edmond. "The Worlds of Captain Future." (*Captain Future*, a pulp magazine, 13 maps).

Brackett, Leigh. "Leigh Brackett's Mars."

Smith, Clark Ashton. "Hyperborea." (*Hyperborea*); Zothique (*Hyperborea*).

Norton, André. "The Witch World."

Le Guin, Ursula K. "Earthsea." (*A Wizard of Earthsea*).

Zelazny, Roger. "Dilfar and Environs." (*Warlocks and Warriors*).

Moorcock, Michael. "The Young Kingdoms." (Elric series).

Vance, Jack. "*The Dying Earth*."

Leiber, Fritz. "Lankhmar in the Land of Nehwon." (Fafhrd and the Grey Mouse series).

Alexander, Lloyd. "Prydain." (three maps).

Carter, Lin. "Lemuria."

Bradbury, Ray. "Mars." ("The Million Year Picnic").

Campbell, J. Ramsey. "The Severn Valley at Brichester." (*The Inhabitant of the Lake*).

Herbert, Frank. *Dune.*

Kuttner, Henry. "Atlantis." (Elek series).

Jakes, John. "Tyros." (Brak series).

Dain, Alex. "Kanthos, Sulmannon, and Anzor." (*Banc of Kanthos*).

Kurtz, Katherine. "Gwynedd and Its Neighbors." (Deryni series).

McCaffrey, Anne. "Pern." (The Dragonriders of Pern series).

Fraser, George MacDonald. "The Duchy of Strackanz." (*Royal Flash*).

Lovecraft, H. P. "The Worlds of H. P. Lovecraft"; Dreamworld; Arkham.

Adams, Richard. "The Beklan Empire." (*Shardik*).

Brackett, Leigh. "The Worlds of Eric John Stark." (*The Ginger Star. The Hounds of Skaith. The Reavers of Skaith*).

Brooks, Terry. "The Four Lands." (*The Sword of Shannara*).

Donaldson, Stephen R. "The Land." (*The Chronicles of Thomas Covenant the Unbeliever*).

History and Criticism

In addition to the following works, material on fantasy will be found among some histories (see p. 248) and criticisms (see p. 249) of science fiction.

Attebery, Brian. *Strategies of Fantasy.* Indiana University Press, 1992.

Boyer, Robert H., and Kenneth J. Zahorski, eds. *Fantasists on Fantasy: A Collection of Critical Reflections.* Avon, 1984.
Essays by George MacDonald, G. K. Chesterton, H. P. Lovecraft, Sir Herbert Reed, James Thurber, J. R. R. Tolkien, August Derleth, C. S. Lewis, Felix Martí-Ibáñez, Peter S. Beagle, Lloyd Alexander, André Norton, Jane Langton, Ursula K. Le Guin, Mollie Hunter, Katherine Kurtz, Michael Moorcock, and Susan Cooper.

Brook-Rose, Christine. *A Rhetoric of the Unreal: Studies in Narrative and Structure, Especially of the Fantastic.* Cambridge University Press, 1981.
Includes reference to science fiction and horror as well as fantasy.

Carter, Lin. *Imaginary Worlds: The Art of Fantasy*. Ballantine, 1973.
On sword-and-sorcery.

de Camp, L. Sprague. *Literary Swordsmen and Sorcerers: The Makers of Heroic Fantasy*. Arkham House, 1976.
The key authors discussed are William Morris, Lord Dunsany, H. P. Lovecraft, E. R. Eddison, Robert E. Howard, Fletcher Pratt, Clark Ashton Smith, J. R. R. Tolkien, and T. H. White.

Filmer, Kath, ed. *Twentieth Century Fantasist's Essays on Culture, Society and Belief in Twentieth-century Myghopoeic Literature*. St. Martin's Press, 1992.

Hillegas, Mark R., ed. *Shadows of Imagination: The Fantasies of C. S. Lewis, J. R. R. Tolkien, and Charles Williams*. Southern Illinois University Press, 1969.
Twelve essays.

Irwin, W. R. *The Game of the Impossible: A Rhetoric of Fantasy*. University of Illinois Press, 1976.
An essay in definition of fantasy and the fantastic in English literature from 1880.

Le Guin, Ursula K. *The Language of the Night: Essays on Fantasy and Science Fiction*. HarperCollins, 1992.
On the writing and reading of fantasy and science fiction—an eloquent statement.

Magill, Frank N., ed. *Survey of Modern Fantasy Literature*. Salem Press, 1983. 5 vols.
Covers high and low fantasy, fairy tales, folklore, Arthurian legend, horror. Discusses 341 authors.

Manlove, C. N. *Modern Fantasy: Five Studies*. Cambridge University Press, 1975.
The authors discussed are Charles Kingsley, George MacDonald, C. S. Lewis, J. R. R. Tolkien, and Mervyn Peake.

Rabkin, Eric S. *The Fantastic in Literature*. Princeton University Press, 1976.
Discusses the fantastic in many types of literature, including fairy tale, detective fiction, horror fiction, and science fiction.

Rottensteiner, Franz. *The Fantasy Book: An Illustrated History from Dracula to Tolkien*. Collier Books, 1978.
There are 202 illustrations, 40 in color, from books of fantasy, the pulps, and motion pictures. A good part relates to the following chapter on ghosts and horror. There is a section on "The International Contribution." The bibliography is excellent, with many foreign citations.

Schlobin, Roger C., ed. *The Aesthetics of Fantasy, Literature and Art*. London: Harvester Press, 1982.
   Essays by Gary K. Wolfe, C. N. Manlove, W. R. Irwin, Kenneth J. Zahorski, Robert H. Boyer, and others.

Timmerman, John H. *Other Worlds: The Fantasy Genre*. Popular Press, 1983.
   The author defines fantasy in terms of story, characters, another world, magic and the supernatural, and the quest.

Journals

Some science fiction journals (see p. 253) also include fantasy.

Fantasy Review. 1979– .
   Essential monthly, incorporates *Science Fiction and Fantasy Book Review* and *Fantasy Newsletter*.

Marion Zimmer Bradley's Fantasy Magazine. 1988– .

Whispers. 1973– .
   Contains fiction (both fantasy and horror) as well as general news.

Associations and Conventions

The following listings are specifically for fantasy, but many of the science fiction associations and conventions (see p. 254) also involve fantasy.

ASSOCIATIONS

American Tolkien Society

British Fantasy Society
   Founded in 1971. Publication *Dark Horizons*, 1971– .

The Fantasy Association
   Founded 1973. Publication: *Fantasies*.

The International Wizard of Oz Club
   Founded 1957.

CONVENTIONS

Fantasy Faire Science Fiction Convention
   Eleventh, 1981, Los Angeles.

World Fantasy Convention
   Sixteenth, 1991, Tucson, AZ

Other specialized groups and fanzines are listed in Tymn's *Fantasy Literature* and in *The International Science Fiction Yearbook 1979*.

Awards

In addition to the following fantasy awards, special recognition for fantasy is often found among science fiction awards (see p. 254).

August Derleth Fantasy Award
The British Fantasy Society, 1972– .

Grand Master of Fantasy Award: "Gandalf"
World Science Fiction Convention, 1974– . Also called the Tolkien Award; named for Tolkien character.

World Fantasy Award: "Howard"
World Fantasy Convention, 1975– . Award named for Howard Phillips Lovecraft and Robert E. Howard.

Other awards are cited in *The International Science Fiction Yearbook 1979*.

Publishers

While the worlds of fantasy and science fiction are incredibly intertwined, it is no surprise that, for the most part, publishers will publish in both genres. The following lists the houses that have been most active in publishing fantasy in the last few years.

Ace/Putnam

Baen

DAW

Del Rey

Gollancz

Headline

HarperCollins (UK)

Knopf

Morrow

ROC

Spectra (Bantam)

Tor

TSR

Viking

Writer's Manuals

Some science fiction writer's manuals (see p. 252) also include fantasy.

Card, Orson Scott. *How to Write Science Fiction and Fantasy.* Writer's Digest Books, 1990.

Writing Science Fiction and Fantasy. By the editors of *Analog* and *Isaac Asimov's Science Fiction Magazine.* St. Martin's Press, 1991.

D's Fantasy Picks

Heinlein, Robert A. *Glory Road.* Putnam, 1963.

Napoli, Donna Jo. *The Magic Circle.* Dutton, 1993.

Norton, André, and Mercedes Lackey. *The Elvenbane.* Tor, 1991.

Weis, Margaret, and Tracy Hickman. *Dragon Wing.* Bantam, 1998.

White, T. H. *The Once and Future King.* Ace, 1987, c1958.

8 Horror

"Where there is no imagination there is no horror."

—Sir Arthur Conan Doyle
Sherlock Holmes
in *A Study in Scarlet* (1887)

you want to know
whether i believe in ghosts
of course i do not believe in them
if you had known
as many of them as i have
you would not
believe in them either

—Don Marquis
Ghost in *Archy and Mehitabel* (1927)

THEMES AND TYPES

Terror of the unknown haunts us all. Some readers avoid the horror genre; others delight in being frightened. The emotional and spiritual response to reading horror stories—true fright—must be evoked for the tale to be successful. This reaction may be labeled an "affective fallacy" in academic jargon, but it is, nevertheless, a truly visceral reaction. The appeal of horror is not to the intellect, however staunchly the reader thinks he can distinguish between reality and fantasy.

The matter of horror stories derives from the supernatural and the occult: ghosts, ghouls, apparitions, poltergeists, witches, and warlocks; vampires and werewolves; monsters and mummies; demonology and black magic; voodoo and witch doctors; nightmares and hallucinations; reincarnation and mind- or soul-stealing; extrasensory perception, as in precognition, telepathy, and telekinesis. In a more embracing sense, we fear the inimical, dark forces of nature that are beyond both our comprehension and our control. There *is* something arising from that primordial slime when the moon is full!

The label "weird" fantasy is common. The magazine *Weird Tales* (1923–1954) supplied stories for many anthologies. Two can still be found in libraries, *Weird Tales: The Magazine That Never Dies* edited by Marvin Kaye (Doubleday, 1988) and *Weird Tales: A Selection in Facsimile of the Best From the World's Most Famous Fantasy Magazine* edited by Peter Haining (Carroll & Graf, 1990). Horror tales have always appeared and still appear in the science fiction and fantasy magazines and anthologies. Many authors write in all three of these genres—however, the Bug-Eyed Monster, once popular in science fiction, loses some quality of horror by not being of this world.

Horror fiction has a literary source in the Gothic novel of the eighteenth and nineteenth centuries that reveled in the supernatural with a gloss of romance. The twentieth-century Gothic novel is determinedly romantic while it uses scary occult and supernatural plot devices. Thrillers—the mystery-suspense, detective, and disaster subgenres—also use elements of horror.

The mingling of genres through the use of horror's more obvious themes leads to inconsistent labeling of novels by publishers and reviewers, and to confusion on the part of the reader as to which genre a book belongs. Faced with a novel labeled "medical-horror," the reader of "doctor-nurse" romances is unlikely to be tempted, but other instances are not as obvious. Also, there is the labeling of novels of psychological suspense, which, admittedly, are filled with the terror of horror stories, but they lack elements of the occult or supernatural.

As in all the genres, there is imitation, especially in original paperbacks, of a successful novel: the endless variations of *Rosemary's Baby*, vampires, haunted houses, demonic possessions, evil children, monstrous animals, and so on. The following listings are very selective, illustrating a variety of horror themes rather than myriad authors. Some of the titles cited are collections of short stories (many authors write almost entirely in this form). As in fantasy, a number of the following authors are not usually categorized as genre authors.

Short Story Collections: Individual Authors

The horror tale is probably best known in the form of the short story. Most of the classic and modern authors are available in published collections. They and others are readily found in the many anthologies (see p. 301) listed later in this chapter. Most of the following collections contain a variety of the types of horror tale.

Aickman, Robert. *Cold Hand in Mine. Night Voices: Strange Stories. The Wine Dark Sea.*

Barker, Clive. *The Books of Blood. Cabal.*

Bierce, Ambrose. *Ghost and Horror Stories.*

Blackwood, Algernon. *Tales of the Mysterious and the Macabre. Tales of the Uncanny and Supernatural.*

Bloch, Robert. *Out of the Mouths of Graves. Chills.*

Bowen, Elizabeth. *The Cat Jumps and Other Stories.*

Collier, John. *Fancies and Goodnights.*

Collins, Wilkie. *Tales of Terror and the Supernatural.*

Copper, Basil. *Here Be Daemons: Tales of Horror and the Uneasy. Voices of Doom: Tales of Terror and the Uncanny.*

Derleth, August. *Dwellers in Darkness.*

Dinesen, Isak. *Seven Gothic Tales. Winter's Tales.*

Doyle, Sir Arthur Conan. *The Best Supernatural Tales*, edited by E. F. Bleiler.

Du Maurier, Daphne. *Echoes from the Macabre: Selected Stories.*

Etchison, Dennis. *The Dark Country. The Blood Kiss.*

Hartley, L. P. *The Traveling Grave, and Other Stories.*

Harvey, W. F. *Midnight Tales.*

Leiber, Fritz. *Heroes and Horrors.*

Long, Frank Belknap. *The Hounds of Tindalos.*

Lumley, Brian. *Fruiting Bodies and Other Fungi.*

Oates, Joyce Carol. *Night-Side.*

Poe, Edgar Allan

Ryan, Alan. *The Bones Wizard.*

Wellman, Manly Wade. *Who Fears the Devil. Worse Things Waiting.*

Ghost Stories

The following collections contain ghost (short) stories by a particular author. Other collections by these authors may be available. For some of the classic authors, the title given is of a recent collection; others are available.

Blackwood, Algernon. *Best Ghost Stories.*

Bowen, Elizabeth. *The Demon Lover and Other Stories.*

Coppard, A. E. *Fearful Pleasures.*

Cox, Michael, and R. A. Gilbert, eds. *Victorian Ghost Stories: An Oxford Anthology.*

Dalby, Richard, ed. *The Mammoth Book of Ghost Stories.*

Dalby, Richard, ed. *Modern Ghost Stories by Eminent Women Writers.*

Davies, Robertson. *High Spirits*.

De La Mare, Walter. *The Wind Blows Over*.

Dickens, Charles

Dunsany, Lord. *God, Men and Ghosts*.

Greenberg, Martin H., ed. *Civil War Ghosts*.

James, M. R. *Ghost Stories of an Antiquary*.

LeFanu, J. S. *Ghost Stories and Mysteries*.

McSherry, Frank D. *Great American Ghost Stories*.

Munby, A. N. L. *The Alabaster Hand and Other Ghost Stories*.

Onions, Oliver. *The First Book of Ghost Stories: Widdershins*. Includes "The Beckoning Fair One," *the* classic ghost story.

Wakefield, H. Russell. *The Best Ghost Stories of H. Russell Wakefield*.
The author required that a ghost story should "bring upon you the odd, insinuating little sensation that a number of small creatures are simultaneously camping on your scalp and sprinkling ice-water down your back-bone."

Walter, Elizabeth. *Dead Woman and Other Haunting Experiences. In the Mist and Other Uncanny Encounters. The Sin-Eater and Other Scientific Impossibilities*.

Young, Richard Alan, and Judy Dockrey Young, eds. *Ghost Stories from the American Southwest*.

The Occult and Supernatural

Here are stories of the unseen and malevolent, the macabre and ghostly: poltergeists, girls transformed by night into bats, cats, monkeys, snakes; souls being stolen or sold to the Devil; minds being read or invaded. The possibilities for inexplicable acts are limited only by the author's dark imagination. Many of the horror stories currently being published center on psychological horror, the terrors often having an explicable cause, however deranged the mind from which the horror emanates. For the much-imitated Lovecraft school of horror, see "Cosmic Paranoia" (p. 293). The older writers on these themes often wrote short stories, and many of the following books are collections of such stories. Recently, there have been many full-length novels written by authors who typically pen short stories.

The occult embraces all mysterious things beyond human understanding. The term is also used to describe those sciences, often appearing in horror literature, that involve knowledge and use of the supernatural. The supernatural encompasses all things existing or occurring outside humanity's normal experience. A supernatural event cannot be explained by any known force of nature. Following a belief in supernatural forces is the belief that these forces intervene to control nature and the universe and that these forces are above ordinary nature. Naturally, then, it follows that supernatural beings and powers exist, which are active in the ordinary world. A person sensitive to such forces beyond the physical world is called a psychic or medium. The term *psychic* refers to happenings beyond natural (or known) physical processes; that is, a psychic phenomena supersedes the physical laws of nature, and, therefore, must be caused by spiritual or supernatural agencies.

The following list includes a miscellany of themes and presents authors important in the genre.

Aiken, Joan. *The Windcreep Weepers. The Green Flash.*

Anderson, Michael Falconer. *The Covenant.*

Andrews, V. C. *Flowers in the Attic. Petals in the Wind. Seeds of Yesterday.*
All are macabre, gothic soap operas.

Anthony, Piers. *Shade of the Tree.*
Supernatural.

Bloch, Robert. *Psycho.*

Block, Lawrence. *Ariel.*
Evil child.

Bradbury, Ray. *The October Country. Something Wicked This Way Comes.*

Bradley, Marion Zimmer. *The Inheritor.*
Poltergeist.

Campbell, Ramsey. *Incarnate. Hungry Moon. Midnight Sun.*

Coyne, John. *Hobgoblin.*
A fantasy role-playing game akin to Dungeons and Dragons.

Farris, John. *Fiends.*

Feist, Raymond E. *Faerie Tale.*

Gannett, Lewis. *The Living One.*

Grant, Charles L. *The Sound of Midnight. In a Dark Dream.*
Children with supernatural powers.

Hawthorne, Nathaniel

Herbert, James. *The Dark. The Spear.*

Hinkemeyer, Michael T. *The Harbinger.*
"Tales that go straight through you like rats' fangs."

Hodgson, William Hope

Irving, Washington

King, Francis. *Voices in an Empty Room.*
Paranormal communication.

Kipling, Rudyard. *Phantoms and Fantasies.*

Koontz, Dean R. *Darkfall.*
Voodoo.

Laski, Marghanita. *The Victorian Chaise Lounge.*
Nightmare.

Leiber, Fritz. *Our Lady of Darkness.*

Machen, Arthur

McCammon, Robert R. *Usher's Passing.*
Descendants of Poe's Usher family.

Masterton, Graham. *The Manitou. Revenge of the Manitou. Burial.*

Merritt, Abraham

Mills, James. *The Power.*

O'Brien, Fitz-James

Poe, Edgar Allan

Raucher, Herman. *Maynard's House.*

Saul, John. *Shadows.*

Saki

Sherman, Nick. *The Surrogate.*

Slade, Michael. *Ghoul.*

Slater, Philip. *How I Saved the World.*
Psychic.

Straub, Peter. *Floating Dragon.*

Strieber, Whitley. *Black Magic.*
Telepathy.

Wells, H. G.

Wilde, Oscar. *The Picture of Dorian Gray.*

Woods, Stuart. *Under the Lake.*

Ghosts

The ghost, often haunting a house or a person, is the most pervasive presence in the horror genre. Most ghosts are malevolent, but some are sad or plaintive. The crux of these tales may be the answer to the question, Why can't the dead rest?

Ashe, Rosalind. *Moths.*

Brody, Jean. *A Coven of Women.*

Disch, Thomas M. *The Businessman: A Tale of Terror.*

Fraser, Anthea. *Whistler's Lane.*

Herbert, James. *Haunted.*

Hynd, Noel. *A Room for the Dead.*

Jackson, Shirley. *The Haunting of Hill House.*

James, Henry. *The Turn of the Screw.*

James, Peter. *Possession.*

Lofts, Norah. *Gad's Hall. The Haunting of Gad's Hall.*

Michaels, Barbara. *Here I Stay. The Walker in the Shadows. Ammie Come Home.* The ghost haunts these novels of romantic suspense.

Saul, John. *The Unloved.*

Cosmic Paranoia

The mythology created by H. P. Lovecraft, with its malevolent life-force, nightmares, monsters, and "The Great Old Ones," has had an important influence on horror literature. (See his *Supernatural Horror and Literature* in "History and Criticism," p. 306.) Following are his works and some of his followers.

Berglund, Edward P., ed. *The Disciples of Cthulhu.* DAW, 1976.
An anthology of stories by followers of Lovecraft. The editor describes the Cthulhu Mythos as "a malign pantheon, including the octopoid Cthulhu, that lurk practically everywhere, and that any mortal mixing with them is going to end up dead, mad or worse."

Bloch, Robert. *Strange Eons.*

Koontz, Dean R. *Phantoms.*

Lovecraft, H. P. *At the Mountains of Madness. The Dunwich Horror. The Lurking Fear. The Shuttered Room. The Tomb.*
"All my tales are based on the fundamental premise that common human laws and emotions have no validity or significance in the cosmos-at-large." Lovecraft created an entire mythology, the Cthulhu Mythos, and defined it as "the fundamental lore or legend that this world was inhabited at one time by another race who, in practicing black magic, lost their foothold and were expelled, yet live on outside, ever ready to take possession of this earth again." The publisher Arkham House is named for Lovecraft's fantasy land (for a map, see Post's *An Atlas of Fantasy* [see p. 281]).

Schreffler, Philip A. *The H. P. Lovecraft Companion*. Greenwood, 1977.
   Summaries of stories and an "Encyclopedia of Characters and Monsters" of the Cthulhu Mythos.

Weinberg, Robert E., and Martin H. Greenberg, eds. *Lovecraft's Legacy*. Tor, 1990.
   Original horror tales in honor of Lovecraft's centennial.

Stephen King

Stephen King's first novel was published in 1973, and he quickly became the modern name defining the horror genre. Books he wrote under the name Richard Bachman are now published under his own name. His horror novels are best-sellers and generate long reserve lists in libraries. They have been made into movies and television mini-series, and many of them are also available in audio format on cassette tapes. Other authors liked by readers of King include Dean R. Koontz and Robert McCammon.

Demonic Possession and Exorcism

The taking over of an innocent mind by a demon or ghost, sometimes through domination by a psychotic living person, is one of the most terrifying themes in folklore. Belief in possession is so widespread that many religions have accepted rituals for exorcising the evil spirits. The following listing is selective, as several very popular modern prototypes have led to seemingly endless imitations. (See also "Mind Control," p. 298).

Blatty, William. *The Exorcist*.

Bloch, Robert. *Lori*.

Campbell, Ramsey. *The Parasite*.

Coyne, John. *The Piercing. The Searing*.

De Felitta, Frank. *Golgatha Falls*.

Farris, John. *Son of the Endless Night*.

Household, Geoffrey. *The Sending*.

Levin, Ira. *Rosemary's Baby*.

Ross, Clarissa. *Satan Whispers*.

Strieber, Whitley. *Unholy Fire*.

Thompson, Gene. *Lupe*.

Walton, Evangeline. *Witch House*.

Haunted Houses

A house possessed is only a tiny bit less terrifying than a mind possessed. Haunted houses have long been a staple in the horror genre. What town does not feature a haunted house as a Halloween fund-raising project? The following tales tell of dealings with homes or lodgings that display malevolence.

Brite, Poppy Z. *Drawing Blood.*

King, Stephen. *The Shining.*

Satanism, Demonology, and Black Magic

Worshipping the devil, pacts with the devil, raising the devil, hauntings by demons, transmigration of souls, magicians and black magic—the diversity of topics is frightening.

Bester, Alfred. *Golem 100.*

Blish, James. *Black Easter.*

Bontly, Thomas. *Celestial Chess.*

Campbell, Ramsey. *Obsession.*

Collier, John. *Of Demons and Darkness.*

Garton, Roy. *Crucifax Autumn.*

Spellman, Cathy Cash. *Bless the Child.*

Stewart, Fred Mustard. *The Mephisto Waltz.*

Straczynski, J. Michael. *Demon Light.*

Straub, Peter. *Shadowland.*

Talbot, Michael. *The Bog.*

Thompson, Gene. *Lupe.*

Wellman, Manly Wade. *The School of Darkness. The Old Gods Waken.*

Wheatley, Dennis. *The Devil Rides Out. The Satanist. Strange Conflict. To the Devil a Daughter. Gateway to Hell.*

Witches and Warlocks

Witches often appear in the historical romance, but as secondary characters. In the following books, the witch and the warlock are persons of reality, in the present as well as in the past, and they may be practitioners of either white or black witchcraft.

Buchan, John. *Witch Wood*.

Copper, Basil. *Not After Nightfall*.

Curtis, Peter. *The Devil's Own*.
Pseudonym of Norah Lofts.

Gunn, David. *The Magicians*.
A private eye, Casey, takes on a case involving black magicians, witches, and warlocks.

Hamilton, Jessica. *Elizabeth*.

Harris, Marilyn. *The Conjurers*.

Heidish, Marcy. *The Torching*.

Leiber, Fritz. *Conjure Wife*.

Levin, Ira. *Rosemary's Baby*.

Rice, Anne. *The Witching Hour*.

Updike, John. *The Witches of Eastwick*.

Warner, Sylvia Townsend. *Lolly Willowes*.
A genteel classic. Witchcraft without horror; a witch's coven in an English village in this century.

Monsters

Monstrous creations by a freakish nature—taking unnatural form from any of the elements of water, earth, air, or plant or animal—abound in horror fiction. The following four books offer manmade monsters or automata whose history goes back to the legendary golem created by Jewish cabalistic rites.

Koontz, Dean R. *Watchers*.

Shelley, Mary. *Frankenstein; or, The Modern Prometheus*.
First published in 1818. May be considered as part of science fiction, e.g., androids, mad scientist. Many imitations and film versions.

Stevenson, Robert Louis. *The Strange Case of Dr. Jekyll and Mr. Hyde*.
First published in 1886. The drug and psychological aspects are influential for science fiction also.

Wiesel, Elie. *The Golem: The Story of a Legend*.

Vampires

Those restless undead who escape their graves at night to drink the blood of innocent sleepers are stock folklore figures, now largely identified with Bram Stoker's Count Dracula. Although there has been a recent trend toward making the vampire legend humorous, most examples are macabre if not horrifying. Some vampires, instead of going after the blood of their victims, covet their minds or souls. Lichtenberg's vampires come from another planet.

Daniels, Lee. *The Black Castle. The Silver Skull.*

Geare, Michael, and Michael Corby. *Dracula's Diary.*
   Tongue-in-cheek.

Greenburg, Dan. *The Nanny.*

Guigonnat, Henri. *Daemon in Lithuania.*

Hambly, Barbara. *Those Who Hunt the Night.*

Huff, Tanya. *Blood Lines. Blood Pact. Blood Price. Blood Trail.*

King, Stephen. *Salem's Lot.*

Lee, Tanith. *Sabella; or, The Blood Stone.*

Lichtenberg, Jacqueline. *Those of My Blood.*

Linssen, John. *Tabitha fffoulkes: A Love Story About a Reformed Vampire and His Favorite Lady.*

Martin, George R. R. *Fevre Dream.*

Newman, Kim. *Anno-Dracula.*

Raven, Simon. *Doctors Wear Scarlet.*

Rice, Anne. *Interview with the Vampire. The Vampire Lestat. Queen of the Damned.*

Saberhagen, Fred. *The Dracula Tapes. A Matter of Taste.*

Simmons, Dan. *Carrion Comfort.*

Stoker, Bram. *Dracula.*
   First published in 1897, the novel, like its hero, has never died and has produced blood-thirsty progeny in novel, stage play, and motion picture. The Count Dracula Society, founded in 1962, publishes *The Count Dracula Quarterly,* and presents annual awards for films, literature, and television, the Mrs. Ann Radcliffe Awards. *The Illustrated Dracula* (Drake, 1975) contains stills from the 1931 Bela Lugosi film. *The Dracula Book,* by Donald F. Glut (Scarecrow, 1975) is illustrated from films and comic strips.

Strieber, Whitley. *The Hunger.*

Sturgeon, Theodore. *Some of Your Blood.*

Tremayne, Peter. *Bloodright: A Memoir of Mircea, Son of Vlad Tepes, Prince of Wallachia, Also Known as Dracula . . . Born on This Earth in the Year of Christ 1431, Who Died in 1476 but Remained Undead. . . . The Revenge of Dracula. The Palace: A Historical Horror Novel.*

Yarbro, Chelsea Quinn. *Hotel Transylvania. The Palace. Blood Games. Path of the Eclipse. Tempting Fate. A Flame in Byzantium. Crusader's Torch. Darker Jewels.*

Animals Run Rampant, Werewolves

One of man's primal fears is that of attack by monstrous types of animals, but another is that of attack by ordinary animals turned horrifying. One of the most fearsome animals in folklore is the wolf. More fearsome is the magic transformation of a man into a wolf (lycanthropy) or werewolf. (In Oriental folklore, a common motif is the dual nature of woman as fox or cat.)

Boucher, Anthony. *The Compleat Werewolf.*

Copper, Basil. *House of the Wolf.*

DiSilvestro, Roger L. *Ursula's Gift.*

Du Maurier, Daphne. *The Birds.*

Dvorkin, David. *Ursus.*

Endore, Guy. *The Werewolf of Paris.*

Gregory, Stephen. *The Cormorant.*

Koontz, Dean. *Watchers.*

Prantera, Amanda. *Strange Loop.*

Rouché, Berton. *The Cats.*

Smith, Wayne. *Thor.*

Strieber, Whitley. *The Wolfen.*

Tessier, Thomas. *The Nightwalker.*

Yarbro, Chelsea Quinn. *The Godforsaken.*

Mind Control

The domination of another's mind by the living or by the dead, by humans or by demons, is a strong theme in folklore and horror literature. It appears in several religions and is related to the rite of exorcism (see "Demonic Possession and Exorcism," p. 294).

Brookes, Owen. *Deadly Communion.*

Chesbro, George C. *Veil.*

Hallahan, William H. *The Keeper of the Children.*

Koontz, Dean R. *Strangers.*

Lumley, Brian. *The House of Doors.*

Siodmak, Curt. *Donovan's Brain.*

Medical Horror

Doctors, sometimes mad, and hospitals in which unnatural medicine is practiced, exist in a horrifying subgenre. (*Not* to be confused with the category of the same name in chapter 5, "Romance.")

Cook, Robin. *Brain. Coma. Fever. Godplayer. Harmful Intent. Vital Signs. Mutation. Mindbend.*

Katz, William. *Facemaker.*

Klein, Daniel. *Embryo. Wavelengths.*

Palmer, Michael. *Natural Causes.*

Pearson, Ridley. *The Angel Maker.*

Ravin, Neil. *Seven North.*

Saul, John. *Creature.*

Shobin, David. *The Obsession. The Seeding. The Unborn.*

Slattery, Jesse. *The Juliet Effect.*

Spruill, Steven G. *My Soul to Take.*

Zimmerman, R. D. *Mindscream.*

Psychological Horror

Many of the horror stories currently being published center on psychological horror, and the terrors often do have an explicable cause, however deranged the mind from which the horror emanates. Serial killers fall into this category.

Bloch, Robert. *Psycho.*

Coyne, John. *Fury.*

Craig, Kit. *Twice Burned.*

Harris, Thomas. *Silence of the Lambs.*

King, Stephen. *Misery.*

Klavan, Andrew. *Animal Hour.*

Krabbé, Tim. *The Vanishing.*

McCammon, Robert R. *Mine.*

Monninger, Joseph. *Incident at Potter's Ridge.*

Reeves-Stevens, Garfield. *Dark Matter.*

Stirling, Blake. *Chiller.*

Splatterpunk

Graphic violence, gore, sex, and a dismal outlook are attributes of horror's cutting edge. *Splatterpunks: Extreme Horror,* edited by Paul M. Sammon, offers a selection of stories from the best-known writers of this type. A sampling of authors who write in this subgenre are:

Barker, Clive

Brite, Poppy Z.

Lansdale, Joe R.

Schow, David

Shirley, John

Skipp, John, and Craig Spector

Detectives and Horror

A detective is sometimes engaged in cases involving the supernatural, with the detection plot often secondary to the eerie background.

Ackroyd, Peter. *Hawksmoor.*

Blatty, William Peter. *The Exorcist. Legion.*

Clements, Mark A. *Children of the End.*

Copper, Basil. *Necropolis.*

Huff, Tanya. *Blood Lines*

Koontz, Dean R. *Whispers.*

Morgan, Robert. *Things That Are Not There.*

Strieber, Whitley. *The Wolfen.*

Comic Horror

Surprisingly enough, horror—the most uncomedic of genres—can sometimes be combined with comedy.

Moore, Christopher. *Practical Demonkeeping: A Comedy of Horrors.*

TOPICS

Anthologies

The large number of horror anthologies indicates both the popularity of such collections and the significant incidence of the short story in the genre. There are several inveterate anthologists; the listings here are but a selection from their volumes. Other horror stories will be found in anthologies listed for science fiction (see p. 238) and fantasy (see p. 276), and some authors from those fields appear in the following anthologies. The anthologies have not been grouped by theme, as only a few are completely single-minded in scope.

Alfred Hitchcock's Supernatural Tales of Terror and Suspense. Random, 1974.

Asimov, Isaac, Charles G. Waugh, and Martin Harry Greenberg, eds. *Isaac Asimov Presents the Best Horror and Supernatural of the 19th Century.* Beaufort, 1983.

Beck, Robert E., ed. *Literature of the Supernatural.* Lothrop, 1974.
The illustrations from museum collections add imaginatively to the stories.

Bishop, Michael, and Ian Watson, eds. *Changes.* Ace, 1983.
Humans transformed.

Campbell, Ramsey, ed. *New Tales of the Cthulhu Mythos.* Arkham, 1980.
In the manner of Lovecraft: see his entry for definition of the Cthulhu Mythos.

Campbell, Ramsey, ed. *Superhorror.* St. Martin's, 1977.

Carr, Terry, ed. *The Ides of Tomorrow: Original Science Fiction Tales of Horror.* Little, Brown, 1976.

Child, Lincoln, ed. *Dark Banquet: A Feast of Twelve Great Ghost Stories.* St. Martin's, 1985.

Curran, Roger, ed. *The Weird Gathering and Other Tales.* Fawcett Crest, 1979.
Mostly about women.

Daniels, Lee, ed. *Dying of Fright: Masterpieces of the Macabre.* Illustrated by Lee Brown Coye. Scribner's, 1976.
An exemplary anthology. Provides prefatory essay for each author and eerie illustrations. Authors: Washington Irving; Edgar Allan Poe; Nathaniel Hawthorne; J. Sheridan Le Fanu; F. Marion Crawford; M. R. James; Ambrose Bierce; Algernon Blackwood; William Hope Hodgson; W. F. Harvey; Lord Dunsany; H. P. Lovecraft; Frank Belknap Long; Henry Kuttner; John Collier; Anthony Boucher; Robert Bloch; Ray Bradbury; Carter Dickson; Fritz Leiber; Richard Matheson; Joseph Payne Brennan.

Datlow, Ellen, ed. *Blood Is Not Enough.* W. Morrow, 1989.

Disch, Thomas M., and Charles Naylor, eds. *Strangers: A Collection of Curious Tales.* Scribner's, 1977.

Dziemianowicz, Stefan R., Robert Weinberg, and Martin H. Greenberg, eds. *Weird Tales: 32 Unearthed Terrors.* Bonanza Books, 1988.

Elwood, Roger, ed. *The Berserkers.* Trident, 1974.

Elwood, Roger, ed. *Monster Tales: Vampires, Werewolves and Things.* Rand, 1974.

Fellowell, Duncan, ed. *Drug Tales.* St. Martin's, 1980.
Alcohol, cigarettes, pills, elixirs.

Gorman, Ed, and Martin H. Greenberg, eds. *Predators.* ROC, 1993.

Grant, Charles L., ed. *The Dodd, Mead Gallery of Horror.* Everest House/Dodd, 1983.

Grant, Charles L., ed. *Fears.* Berkley, 1983.

Grant, Charles L., ed. *Night Visions.* Dark Harvest series, first title in 1984.

Grant, Charles L., ed. *Nightmares.* Playboy Press, 1979.

Green, Roger Lancelyn, ed. *Thirteen Uncanny Tales.* With color frontispiece and line drawings in the text by Ray Ogden. London: Dent, 1970.

Greenberg, Martin Harry, and Charles G. Waugh, eds. *Cults! An Anthology of Secret Societies, Sects, and the Supernatural.* Beaufort, 1983.

Haining, Peter, ed. *Deadly Nightshade.* Taplinger, 1978.

Haining, Peter, ed. *Everyman's Book of Classic Horror Stories.* London: Dent, 1976.

Haining, Peter, ed. *The Fantastic Pulps.* St. Martin's, 1975.

Haining, Peter, ed. *Gothic Tales of Terror.* Taplinger, 1972. 2 vols.

Haining, Peter, ed. *The Third Book of Unknown Tales of Horror*. London: Sidgwick, 1980.

Haining, Peter, ed. *The Witchcraft Reader*. Doubleday, 1970.

Jones, Stephen, ed. *The Mammoth Book of Terror*. Carroll & Graff, 1993.

Jones, Stephen, ed. *The Mammoth Book of Vampires*. Carroll & Graff, 1993.

Jones, Stephen, ed. *The Mammoth Book of Zombies*. Carroll & Graff, 1993.

Lamb, Hugh, ed. *Cold Fear: New Tales of Terror*. Taplinger, 1978.

Lamb, Hugh, ed. *Return from the Grave*. Taplinger, 1977.

Lamb, Hugh, ed. *Terror by Gaslight*. Taplinger, 1976.

Lamb, Hugh, ed. *The Thrill of Horror*. Taplinger, 1975.

Lamb, Hugh, ed. *Victorian Nightmares*. Taplinger, 1977.

Lamb, Hugh, ed. *A Wave of Fear: A Classic Horror Anthology*. Taplinger, 1974.

McCauley, Kirby, ed. *Dark Forces: New Stories of Suspense and Supernatural Terror*. St. Martin's, 1976.

Manguel, Alberto, ed. *Black Water*. Potter, 1984.

Manley, Seon, and Gogo Lewis, eds. *Sisters of Sorcery: Two Centuries of Sinister Stories by the Gentle Sex*. Lothrop, 1975.

Manley, Seon, and Gogo Lewis, eds. *Sisters of Sorcery: Two Centuries of Witchcraft Stories by the Gentle Sex*. Lothrop, 1976.

Masterton, Graham, ed. *Scare Care*. Tor, 1989. Severn House, 1990.

Olson, Paul F., and David B. Silva, eds. *Post Mortem*. St. Martin's Press, 1989.

Parry, Michel, ed. *Beware of the Cat: Stories of Feline Fantasy and Horror*. Taplinger, 1973.

Parry, Michel, ed. *Great Black Magic Stories*. Taplinger, 1977.

Parry, Michel, ed. *The Hounds of Hell: Stories of Canine Horror and Fantasy*. Taplinger, 1974.

Parry, Michel, ed. *The Roots of Evil: Weird Stories of Supernatural Plants*. Taplinger, 1976.

Parry, Michel, ed. *The Supernatural Solution: Chilling Tales of Spooks and Sleuths*. Taplinger, 1976.

The Playboy Book of Horror and the Supernatural. Playboy Press, 1967.

Pronzini, Bill, ed. *Creature!: A Chrestomathy of "Monstery."* Arbor House, 1981.

Pronzini, Bill, ed. *Mummy!: A Chrestomathy of Cryptology.* Arbor House, 1980.

Pronzini, Bill, ed. *Voodoo!: A Chrestomathy of Necromancy.* Arbor House, 1980.

Pronzini, Bill, ed. *Werewolf!* Arbor House, 1979.

Pronzini, Bill, Barry N. Malzberg, and Martin Harry Greenberg, eds. *The Arbor House Treasury of Horror and the Supernatural.* Arbor House, 1981.

Protter, Eric, ed. *A Harvest of Horrors: Classic Tales of the Macabre.* Vanguard, 1980.

Protter, Eric, ed. *Monster Festival.* Illustrated by Edward Gorey. Vanguard, 1965.

Sayers, Dorothy L., ed. *Great Short Stories of Detection, Mystery and Horror.* Series One to Three. London: Gollancz, 1929–34.

Shadows. Edited by Charles L. Grant. Doubleday, 1978– .

Shepard, Leslie, ed. *The Dracula Book of Great Vampire Stories.* Citadel, 1974.

Skarda, Patricia L., and Nora Crow Jaffe, eds. *The Evil Image: Two Centuries of Gothic Short Fiction and Poetry.* Meridian Book, New American Library, 1981.

Sullivan, Jack, ed. *Lost Souls: A Collection of English Ghost Stories.* Ohio University Press, 1984.

The Times Anthology of Ghost Stories. London: Cape, 1975.

Waugh, Charles G., Martin H. Greenberg, and Frank D. McSherry, Jr., eds. *Yankee Witches.* Tapley, 1988.

Winter, Douglas E., ed. *Prime Evil: New Stories by the Masters of Modern Horror.* New American Library, 1988.

Wolf, Leonard, ed. *Wolf's Complete Book of Terror.* Potter, 1979.

The Year's Best Horror Stories. DAW, Series 18, 1990.

Bibliographies

Barzun, Jacques, and Wendell Hertig Taylor. "Ghost Stories, Studies and Reports of the Supernatural, Psychical Research, and E.S.P." In *A Catalogue of Crime.* Harper, 1971, 699–722.

Barron, Neil, ed. *Horror Literature.* Garland, 1990.

Bleiler, Everett F. *The Guide to Supernatural Fiction: A Full Description of 1,775 Books from 1750 to 1960, Including Ghost Stories, Weird Fiction, Stories of Supernatural Horror, Fantasy, Gothic Novels, Occult Fiction, and Similar Literature.* (With Author, Title, and Motif Indexes). Kent State University Press, 1983.

An exemplary guide. The annotations are lengthy and critical (the author seems to have read everything), and they cover an author's short story collections as well as novels. Invaluable is the "Index of Motifs and Story Types," over 40 pages; the index terms are defined and form a critical analysis of the themes in the literature.

Kendrick, Walter M. *The Thrill of Fear: 250 Years of Scary Entertainment.* Grove/Weidenfeld, 1991.

Tymn, Marshall B. *Horror Literature: A Core Collection and Reference Guide.* Bowker, 1981.

An engrossing guide. Part I, Fiction, contains five essays, each with extensive annotated bibliography: "The Gothic Romance: 1762–1820," by Frederick S. Frank; "The Residual Gothic Impulse: 1824–1873," by Benjamin Franklin Fisher IV; "Psychological, Antiquarian, and Cosmic Horror: 1872–1919," by Jack Sullivan; "The Modern Masters: 1920–1980," by Gary William Crawford; "The Horror Pulps: 1933–1940," by Robert Weinberg. Part II: "Supernatural Verse in English," by Steve Eng. Part III, Reference Sources, is by Mike Ashley, with chapters on "Biography, Autobiography, and Bibliography"; "Criticism, Indexes, and General Reference"; "Periodicals"; "Societies and Organizations"; "Awards"; "Research Collections." There is a "Core Collection Checklist," and "A Directory of Publishers."

Encyclopedias

Spignesi, Stephen J. *The Complete Stephen King Encyclopedia: The Definitive Guide to the Works of America's Master of Horror.* Contemporary Books, 1991.

Sullivan, Jack, ed. *The Penguin Encyclopedia of Horror and the Supernatural.* With an Introduction by Jacques Barzun. Viking, 1986.

An exemplary encyclopedia of awesome text and abundant fearful illustrations which covers literature, art, film, radio, television, music, and illustration. "The main criteria for coverage are that the evocation of fear, whether supernatural or psychological, be the main or at least the major part of the artist's interest and that the work be either historically important or of enduring quality." There are 54 theme essays in alphabetical sequence with names (authors, artists, composers, actors, film directors), and film titles. All entries are signed, and the list of contributors is impressive. All of the theme essays (and, indeed, all the entries) are engrossing reading. A few of the theme essays are noted to indicate specific significance to genre fiction, although the whole work is, of course, relevant: "Definitions: Horror, Supernatural, and Science Fiction"; "Detection and Ghosts"; "The Devil, Devils, Demons"; "Frankenstein: The Myth"; "Ghosts"; "Horror and Science Fiction"; "Mad Doctors"; "Occult Fiction"; "Poltergeists"; "Possession"; "Vampires"; "Werewolves"; "Zombies." The work is invaluable for reader advisors as a critical guide to authors, their works, and types of fiction within the genre. Of particular use is the lengthy essay "Writers of Today," a critical roundup of current authors, each listed with a cross-reference within the main alphabet. Jacques Barzun's introduction, "The Art and Appeal of the Ghostly and Ghastly," undoubtedly will become a classic in the literature.

History and Criticism

The definitive history and criticism of the horror genre are yet to be written. Until they are, the following books may be used for background on various aspects of the genre.

Bleiler, E. F., ed. *Supernatural Fiction Writers: Fantasy and Horror*. Scribner's, 1985. 2 vols.
Brief biography and criticism of 148 authors.

Briggs, Julia. *Night Visitors: The Rise and Fall of the English Ghost Story*. London: Faber, 1977.

Daniels, Lee. *Living in Fear: A History of Horror in the Mass Media*. Scribner's, 1975.
The book for first reading to understand and appreciate the genre. Discusses classic and modern authors and the horror film. The illustrations are exceptional.

Haining, Peter. *Terror: A History of Horror Illustrations from the Pulp Magazines*. London: Souvenir Press, 1976.
Includes chapters on "Gothic Chapbooks and Shilling Shockers," "Penny Bloods and Penny Dreadfuls," and "Victorian Sensational Fiction," as well as on the later pulp magazines, which carried these weird tales, luridly and erotically illustrated.

Joshi, S. T. *The Weird Tale*. University of Texas, 1990.
The fantastic writings of Arthur Machen, Lord Dunsany, Algernon Blackwood, M. R. James, Ambrose Bierce, and H. P. Lovecraft are surveyed.

King, Stephen. *Danse Macabre*. Everest House, 1979.
These essays in history and criticism of the horror novel and film are personal and often anecdotal, while sharply critical and interpretative. Recommended reading for those who are *not* fans of the genre.

Lovecraft, Howard Phillips. *Supernatural Horror in Literature*. With a New Introduction by E. F. Bleiler. Dover, 1973.
Essential reading as definition, history, and criticism. "The one text of the truly weird is simply this—whether or not there be excited in the reader a profound sense of dread, and of contact with unknown spheres and powers; a subtle attitude of awed listening, as if for the beating of black wings or the scratching of outside shapes and entities on the known universe's utmost rim."

Puntner, David. *The Literature of Terror: A History of Gothic Fictions from 1765 to the Present Day*. London: Longman, 1980.
Interesting interrelation of the gothic literary tradition, fantasy, and the horror-supernatural story.

Sullivan, Jack. *Elegant Nightmares: The English Ghost Story from Le Fanu to Blackwood*. Ohio University Press, 1978.

Film

Horror films have always been a staple product of the film industry since its beginnings. But in recent years, they have become one of the most prevalent film genres, as the following histories testify.

Clarens, Carlos. *An Illustrated History of the Horror Film*. Putnam, 1967.

Everson, William K. *Classics of the Horror Film*. LSP Books, 1975.

Golden, Christopher, ed. *Cut!: Horror Writers on Horror Film*. Berkeley Books, 1992.

McCarty, John, ed. *The Fear Makers: The Screen's Directorial Masters of Suspense and Terror*. St. Martin's Press, 1994.

Nottridge, Rhoda. *Horror Films*. Crestwood House, 1992.

Pirie, David. *A Heritage of Horror: The English Gothic Cinema, 1946–1972*. Avon, 1974.

Prewer, S. S. *Caligari's Children: The Film as a Tale of Terror*. Oxford University Press, 1980.

Skal, David. *The Monster Show: A Cultural History of Horror*. Norton, 1993.

Timpone, Anthony, ed. *Fangoria's Best Horror Films*. Crescent Books, 1994.

Background

The publications of the Society of Psychical Research contain studies of occult happenings (e.g., mediumship, survival after death, precognition, and parapsychology) designed to verify their authenticity. Many studies of the occult, psychic phenomena, and the supernatural are published by folklore societies, with much mention of ghosts and poltergeists. The following books are samples from a large body of available literature.

Clarie, Thomas C. *Occult Bibliography: An Annotated List of Books Published in English, 1971 Through 1975*. Scarecrow, 1978.

Clarie, Thomas C. *Occult/Paranormal Bibliography: An Annotated List of Books Published in English, 1976 Through 1981*. Scarecrow, 1984.

Haining, Peter. *A Dictionary of Ghost Lore*. Prentice-Hall, 1984. Brief descriptions.

Conventions

World Horror Convention
The first (annual) was held in Nashville, Tennessee, in 1991.

Publishers

Arkham House was founded in 1939 to preserve the writings of H. P. Lovecraft and now publishes horror, fantasy, and science fiction. Dover Books, the reprinter of Lovecraft's *Supernatural Horror in Literature*, has a strong line of trade quality paperback reprints of the classics, listed in its catalog as the "Dover Library of Ghost Stories." Carroll & Graf have brought out several huge horror anthologies in their Mammoth line of trade paperbacks, including *The Mammoth Book of Zombies*. Severn House reprints genre titles in hardcover, often from original paperback releases. The Abyss line, from the conglomerate that includes Dell and Delacorte, is dedicated solely to publishing horror. Other houses publishing horror novels include the following:

Arkham House

Abyss (Dell and Delacorte)

Bantam

Carroll & Graf

DAW

Gollancz

HarperCollins

Headline

Knopf

Little, Brown

Putnam

St. Martin's Press

Simon and Schuster

Tor

Warner Books

Mark V. Zeisling

Awards

Bram Stoker Award

Review Journals

Horror is most often reviewed with science fiction and fantasy (see both "Critical Journals," p. 253, and "Journals," p. 284). *Necrofile*, started in 1991, is a quarterly review source devoted to reviewing horror. It attempts to list all horror currently being published in the United States and Great Britain.

D's Horror Picks

Huff, Tanya. *Blood Lines.* Daw Books, 1993.

Koontz, Dean R. *Watchers.* Putnam, 1987.

Leiber, Fritz. *Conjure Wife.* Ace, 1977.

Smith, Wayne. *Thor.* St. Martin's Press, 1992.

Spellman, Cathy Cash. *Bless the Child.* Warner Books, 1993.

Author/Title Index

Subject Index

Series Character Index